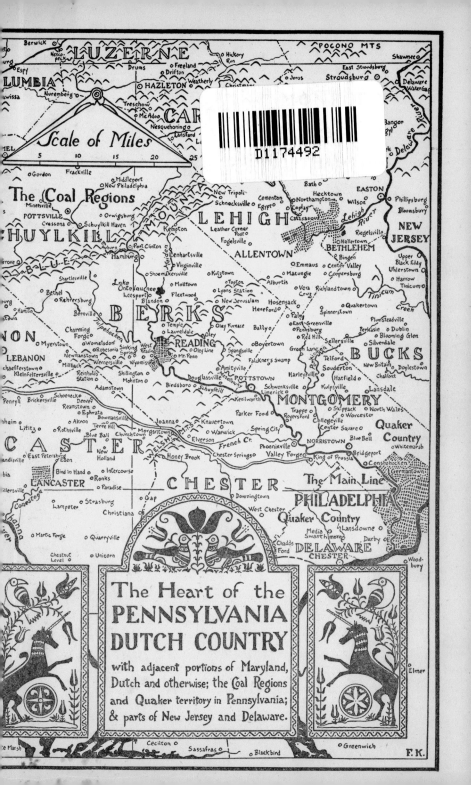

THE PENNSYLVANIA DUTCH

THE MACMILLAN COMPANY
NEW YORK · BOSTON · CHICAGO
DALLAS · ATLANTA · SAN FRANCISCO

MACMILLAN AND CO., LIMITED
LONDON · BOMBAY · CALCUTTA
MADRAS · MELBOURNE

**THE MACMILLAN COMPANY
OF CANADA, LIMITED**
TORONTO

THE
Pennsylvania Dutch

by FREDRIC KLEES

THE MACMILLAN COMPANY : NEW YORK

1950

To my sister
Eleanor Klees Seltzer

Contents

vii

Illustrations

THE PENNSYLVANIA DUTCH

A Forward Glance

The Pennsylvania Dutch is the story of a people, of their past and of their present, and of the qualities that set them off from their neighbors. To a surprisingly complete degree the Pennsylvania Dutch are unlike their fellow Americans. The language they spoke for nearly two centuries, and that some of them speak to this very day, was and is different. Their religions, for the most part, are different. Their barns and sometimes their houses, their way of farming, the way they cook their food: these are different too. Their clothing, their wagons, their horses, their guns, their pottery, their china—in the past, at least—all were different; even their proverbs, their prayers, and their lullabies were different. Theirs was a way of life that differed from that of the rest of America not in one or two but literally in scores of ways.

In the melting pot of America they retained their individuality. Their strong concentration in a relatively small area enabled this people to stay Dutch; only this prevented them from being assimilated by the English colonists as the Holland Dutch in New York and the French Huguenots both in South Carolina and in Pennsylvania had been. In half a dozen or more Pennsylvania counties it was as right and natural as rain to be Dutch. There it was the other fellow, the Quaker or the Scotch-Irishman, who was the "foreigner." There English and not Dutch was the alien tongue. The Quakers and Scotch-Irish who found themselves living in a Pennsylvania Dutch world had to learn to talk Dutch and eat sauerkraut or move to a part of America where English was spoken and cabbage was eaten boiled. Most of them chose to move.

The difference in language made communication difficult between the Dutch and their English-speaking neighbors. On the borders of the Dutch country where Dutch met Quaker, the Quakers were largely content to dwell in their silence, and the Dutch in turn were willing to keep to themselves. Hence the marked disparity between two such neighboring counties as Quaker Chester and Dutch Berks. But it was not only their language that set the Dutch apart; it was their whole way of life—in other words, their culture. Broadly speaking, the Dutch country was an island of Rhenish civilization in an English sea.

Though loyal to America from the start, the Pennsylvania Dutch were set in their ways, and these ways were not the ways of their neighbors. In preserving their own culture they succeeded in doing what no other non-English group in colonial America was able to do. They built up a way of life, useful and creative, not necessarily better than those of the Quaker, the Scotch-Irishman, the Yankee, and the Virginia planter, but different from any of them.

Yet to speak of a Dutch way of life is misleading, for there were three ways rather than one. Religion determined the three paths the Dutch were to follow. As a man worshiped in colonial Pennsylvania, so he lived. The three principal religious groups, "plain people," "church people," and Moravians, each of which formed a cultural pattern of its own, differed radically from one another.

The "plain people," so called from the plainness of their archaic dress—their bonnets and shawls and broadbrim hats—were the first of these groups to reach Pennsylvania and by far the most picturesque. They are the Mennonites, the Amish, the Dunkards (or the Brethren, to use the name they prefer), and the River Brethren. Before the Revolution the Schwenkfelders could have been numbered among the "plain people," but since then they have turned worldly and "gone gay"; today they must be counted as "church people." Whether Mennonite, Amish, Brethren, or one of the lesser sects, the "plain people" have captured the public attention by their anachronistic dress and their unworldly ways. They have been photographed and written about so much that many people assume that all Pennsylvania Dutchmen are "plain people." The Moravians and the "church people"—Lutheran, Reformed, United Brethren, Evangelical—are either ignored or forgotten; yet the Moravians gave birth to the most highly developed of the three Pennsylvania Dutch cultures, and the "church people," to whom nine out of every ten Pennsylvania Dutchmen belong, produced the dominant tradition. To know only the Mennonites, Amish, and Dunkards is to know only one of the three Pennsylvania Dutch cultures and only a small part of the whole.

Of the seven Pennsylvania Dutch churches of colonial times, all except the Dunkards are among the oldest Protestant religions. The Lutheran and Reformed churches were two of the original churches of the Reformation. If Luther's break with Rome is taken as the beginning of the Reformation, then the Lutheran Church will be regarded as the original Protestant church. If John Hus's attempt to found a church is considered a still earlier manifestation of Protestantism, then the Moravian Church is the most ancient among Protestant churches. The Reformed Church, much the same age as the Lutheran, is old too. This is the church of Zwingli, of Zurich and Geneva and Heidelberg. The church founded by Schwenkfeld, a contemporary of Luther and Zwingli, is yet another of the early Protestant churches. To these must be added the Mennonites and the Amish, descendants of the still earlier Anabaptists. Yet another connection with the dim past comes through the Waldenses, that early group of Protestant martyrs celebrated by Milton in his famous sonnet. In the first half of the sixteenth century the Waldenses joined the Mennonites and the Reformed Church in large numbers. Any claim to be the oldest Protestant church must be hedged about with so many modifications that it is difficult to state positively that this honor belongs to any one church; yet one can say that the Mennonites, Amish, Moravians, Lutherans, Reformed, and Schwenkfelders are the earliest existing Protestant groups. Furthermore, the seven Pennsylvania Dutch churches of colonial days represent the three chief movements of the Reformation: Anabaptism, Lutheranism, and Calvinism. These three, numerically speaking at least, became the leading religions of the Pennsylvania Dutch.

The "plain people" and the Moravians founded small colonies here and there in the province; the "church people," Reformed and Lutheran alike, settled all over the map of Dutch Pennsylvania. Though Lancaster County is the stronghold of the "plain people" and Bethlehem, Nazareth, and Lititz were once wholly Moravian, all these places have many Lutheran and Reformed inhabitants today. There are Lutheran and Reformed churches in all the Pennsylvania Dutch counties, but there are whole counties that hardly know the "plain people" and the Moravians. So deeply entrenched are the "church people" that in Bethlehem, Pennsylvania's chief Moravian city, there are twelve Lutheran churches and eight Reformed ones to two Moravian churches. Even the Pennsylvania Dutch who have joined other churches, be it United Brethren, Evangelical, Episcopalian, Presbyterian, or Methodist, have far more in common with the "church people" than with the "plain people" or even the Moravians. The unworldliness of the "plain people" and the emphasis of the Moravians on the suffering of Christ had little effect on the Lutherans and the Reformed; nor did the "plain people" and the Moravians have much influence one on the other.

It may be that the culture of the "church people" became the dominant one because it was better suited to America and to the modern era. Both the Reformed and Lutheran churches are vigorous middle-of-the-road churches. There is nothing fantastic, nothing fanatical about either of them. They are at the very core of the Protestant tradition.

At first sight the "church people" are much less interesting to the average American: they are so like the people he has known all his life. They pass unnoticed in any crowd. And in a sense this is true; most Pennsylvania Dutchmen are like the inhabitants of any fairly average American town. Yet there is always a difference. Nor is it merely a matter of geography, of the difference, say, between a man from Calais, Maine, and one from San Diego, California, though that does enter in. It lies deeper than that: it is the folk culture, the manners and customs formed by the life his forefathers lived for centuries along the Rhine and from eight to ten generations in Pennsylvania. This gives the Pennsylvania Dutchman a characteristic coloring, sometimes barely discernible but usually as obvious as a red barn door at high noon.

Throughout this book Berks County has received an emphasis that calls for an apology to those Pennsylvania Dutchmen living beyond its borders. I have referred to Berks County again and again because it is the part of the Dutch country I know best. The emphasis on Berks County has one advantage: it is the county par excellence of the "church people." In putting stress on the Berks County way of life I have of necessity stressed the dominant Pennsylvania Dutch culture.

But religion by itself is not enough to explain this people; to it must be added the past. No one can know or understand the Pennsylvania Dutch, or any other people, without knowing their past. The religious persecutions abroad, the weary crossing of the Atlantic, the terror of the Indian wars, the struggle for freedom: all these helped to make the Dutch what they are today. It is a past well worth cherishing. Their insistence on religious freedom, on the right to vote, and on the essential equality of man are the heartblood of American democracy. Furthermore, the skill of Pennsylvania Dutch farmers and the clever hands of Dutch workmen helped to form the basic pattern of American agriculture and industry. With six colonies to the north, six to the south, and the unknown West just beyond the Alleghenies, the Dutch were in the very center of colonial America. Spiritually this was the center as well as physically, for this was the land of the log cabin, the Kentucky rifle, and the covered wagon. And just to the south, where Quaker and Dutch hills and valleys meet, lay Valley Forge, and to the west the Dutch town of Gettysburg. But possibly of still greater significance was the fact that in Penn's province Swede and Finn met English, Welsh, and Irish Quakers, Scotch-Irish Presbyterians, and French Huguenots; and Dutch from the Low Countries met Dutch from the Rhineland and Swiss from Alpine valleys. From the start Pennsylvania was a melting pot, a United Nations in little. As Pennsylvania went, so went the nation. This is far closer to the truth than the exploded adage about Maine.

In addition to all this I celebrate the Dutch way of life: the Christmas *putz*,[1] the crazy-clean housewife with a broom, Amish wagons on Ridge Road, clocks set half an hour ahead, apple tarts and *snitz*[2] pies, fat red barns, horse chestnuts spilling their nuts on the brick pavements of village streets. In part I write because my heart is full and I must. And not only my heart but my head and my very liver and lights are so crammed with ideas and notions and miscellaneous information about the Pennsylvania Dutch that if I don't soon get them out of my system I'll be stopping people in the street, like the ancient mariner in

[1] The Moravian Christmas crib or crèche under the Christmas tree.
[2] Dried apples.

Coleridge's ballad, fixing them with a glittering eye while I tell my tale. Then, too, I have a more serious purpose. I hope to correct a few of the weird beliefs about the Dutch that the rest of the country cherishes so fondly: that the Amishman paints his gate blue to tell the world that he has a daughter ripe for marriage; that the cabalistic signs on the barns were painted there to scare away witches; that seven sweets and seven sours are an inevitable part of every meal. I hope particularly to scotch the conventional picture of the Dutch farmer as an ignorant oaf in a broadbrim hat and a bushy beard who beats his wife and daughters as mercilessly as Simon Legree did the slaves and who, to while away the time, murders a witch and casts a spell or two over his neighbor's cattle. To listen to the rest of America tell it, south-eastern Pennsylvania is a land of medievalism and melodrama.

Such fabrications most Dutch dismiss with contempt. If people elsewhere are simpletons enough to believe such rubbish, why bother to set them straight? As long as Lancaster and Reading and Bethlehem know the facts, what does it matter what the rest of the world thinks? Such gross ignorance has come about largely because the historians for a long time treated the Pennsylvania Dutch so casually. As many of the early records of Germantown and Ephrata and Bethlehem were in German script, to ignore them was easier than to read them. Nor was the culture of the Pennsylvania Dutch a literary one, and since in both England and New England culture meant literature and the Dutch had produced no *Hiawatha* nor *Scarlet Letter* it was obvious that they had no culture worthy of the name. Music at Bethlehem and printing at Germantown and Ephrata were rarely mentioned, folk art went unnoticed, and naturally anything as low as cooking was disregarded. The great bank barns were passed over in silence. The log cabin was attributed to New England, the rifle to Kentucky, and the covered wagon to the West. Even the theology of the Pennsylvania Dutch churches aroused little interest, while the origin of Santa Claus and the Christmas tree, of candles on Christmas Eve, of the Easter rabbit and dyed eggs went unstudied: such things were too trifling to merit investigation. Nor did it occur to any of these men to ask why America, unlike England, drove on the right-hand side of the road. Even the great contributions of the Dutch to medicine in the nineteenth century were overlooked. Literature was the only culture with a capital C.

Provinciality, as well as ignorance, was to blame for the historians' neglect of the culture built up by the Dutch. Until fairly recent years a large proportion of American historians were New Englanders who took it for granted that Lexington and Concord and Bunker Hill were the Revolution. Things west of the Hudson or even west of the Connecticut were of relatively minor importance. Pennsylvania historians, too, were often at fault. Many of them wrote as though the Quakers alone had settled Pennsylvania. The Pennsylvania Dutch were mentioned only to be taken to task for every way in which they differed from the Quakers. The Dutch contribution to the life of the nation was either ignored or misrepresented.

This attitude on the part of the historians engendered a deep-seated regionalism in the Dutch and heightened their provinciality; the former good, the latter bad. There is virtue in being a good Pennsylvania Dutchman just as there is virtue in being a good down-Easter or a good New Yorker. Luckily the Dutch country escaped most of the trumped-up regionalism that has become so absurd a feature of life in the Southwest and the South. The only parallel in the Dutch country to the grown men of the Southwest getting all dressed up to play cowboy and the women of the South decking themselves out in hoopskirts to drum up the tourist trade is a hoedown and apple-butter cooking held once a year in a park near Allentown. There the men wear the straw hats and overalls of the stage rube and the women the sunbonnets and calicoes of the old-fashioned country woman. Otherwise a man with a broadbrim hat, a bushy beard, and barn-door breeches is an Amishman and not a man dressed up to play the part.

Not everyone living in the Dutch country is Pennsylvania Dutch, nor are all the Dutch confined to Pennsylvania. I think of the Pennsylvania Dutch as the descendants of the Germans and Swiss who came to Pennsylvania before the Revolution. To the Germans, most of whom came from the Rhineland, I would add the handful of Moravians, whether from Bohemia or Silesia or Moravia itself, and the French Huguenots who had fled to the Rhineland and who came to Pennsylvania with the Palatines and Württembergers. I would not include among the Pennsylvania Dutch the descendants of the Hessian mercenaries, nor the later Germans who came to America after the revolutions of 1832 and 1848, nor any of the immigrants who reached these shores still later in the century. Many of these people were admirable, men and women of sterling character, but they were not what I think of as Pennsylvania Dutch.

I count as Dutch only those who have retained something of the culture—not necessarily the dialect but the Dutch pattern of life. This is partly a matter of geography and partly not. A Dutchman living in the heart of the Dutch country is inescapably Dutch. A Philadelphian of Pennsylvania Dutch blood may have kept to Dutch ways and may have stayed a Pennsylvania Dutchman though he has lived his life within sight of City Hall clock, or he may have lost all his Dutch coloring and become merely a drab Philadelphian. It is not even necessary to be a Pennsylvanian: Marylanders from Frederick County and Canadians from the neighborhood of Kitchener are as Dutch as the Dutch from Lancaster and Lebanon. Virginians from the upper half of the Valley still have many Dutch ways, and even some North Carolinians are kin to the Pennsylvania Dutch. There are plenty of Pennsylvania Dutch in the Middle West, too, though most Middle Westerners of Dutch blood have intermarried with the descendants of Yankees and Southerners and keep only a trace of Dutchness. Last there are those Pennsylvania Dutchmen who are Dutch in heart but not in blood. Whether English, Quaker, Scotch-Irish, Welsh, Negro, gypsy, or Holland Dutch, Swede, or Finn, many of them speak with an accent as broad as *snitz un knep* and are fully as Dutch in all their ways as Stolzfus, Spang, or Moyer.

Throughout this book I use the word *Dutch* instead of *German* to describe these people because this is the name by which they have been known for more than two centuries. Yet there are many, particularly those with an eye to learning, who insist on using the term *Pennsylvania German*. An uncouth name, say I; one unsanctioned by time or use on man's tongue. The champions of the name *Pennsylvania German* declare furiously that the Pennsylvania Dutch are not Dutch at all—certainly not Holland Dutch—but mainly a mixture of Palatines, Württembergers, Alsatians, and Swiss, all of these people of German blood. Of course; so much is obvious. How, then, did men come to give the name *Dutch* to the German, Swiss, and French Huguenot settlers in southeastern Pennsylvania? May it not have been because the Pennsylvania Dutch in their own speech referred to themselves as *Deitsch*? By an easy transition this became *Dutch* in English. But a more important reason for the use of the word *Dutch* is that in the late seventeenth century and the early eighteenth the Germans as a whole were commonly called Dutch, as they were back in the fifteenth and sixteenth centuries as well. *Dutch* is an older word than *German,* and for centuries it was used as the name for the inhabitants of Germany.

The people of Holland were called *low Dutch* to distinguish them from the Dutch of "high Germany." Only gradually was the sense of the word restricted to the Holland Dutch, an English usage of *Dutch* that diverged from both the Dutch use and the German. In Holland itself the word *duitsch* refers to the German language and dialects exclusive of those of Holland. Although Shakespeare in *The Merry Wives of Windsor* chose to write, "They . . . set spurres, and away; like three Germane diuels, three Doctor Faustasses," most of his countrymen went on calling the Germans Dutch. When German settlers began to appear in Germantown and along the banks of the Skippack, their English neighbors quite naturally referred to them as Dutch and have gone on doing so ever since. That they knew both words, *German* and *Dutch,* is shown by their use of one for the village of Germantown and the other for the people themselves. In Virginia the word *Dutch* acquired an even looser meaning. There it was used to describe any foreigner, for the Dutch from Pennsylvania who settled in the Valley of Virginia were the only "foreigners" the Virginians knew in colonial times.

Pennsylvania German is not a term freely used in speech; it comes unnaturally to men's lips. Though it may be more nearly exact than *Pennsylvania Dutch,* it has none of the connotations of the older term. It is a new, naked, pedantic compound. It brings with it the taint of the hyphen, since it seems to mean a German living in Pennsylvania; and most emphatically the Pennsylvania Dutch are not that. I, for one, will have none of it.

I have tried to make this book a comprehensive treatment of the Pennsylvania Dutch in which everything was touched on and nothing ignored. With such a purpose in mind I have of necessity been forced to dwell lightly on certain phases of Pennsylvania Dutch life and character. For more detailed information more authoritative books will have to be consulted. To many of them my debt is enormous. From many I have borrowed so freely that at times it seems to me that nothing is mine. From one flower after another I have stolen the honey; only the hive in which I have stowed it away is my own. With old Burton I can quote Macrobius: *"Omne meum, nihil meum,* 'tis all mine, and none mine." I owe an everlasting debt to those investigators of things Pennsylvania Dutch who have preceded me. In the bibliography I have tried to indicate those to whom I owe most.

Part One

RELIGION

The Mennonites

The sight of Mennonites coming out of their plain meetinghouse on Sunday, the glimpse of an Amish buggy on the road, or the spectacle of the "plain people" behind their stalls at Friday market have often startled travelers in southeastern Pennsylvania. Having no idea that such people existed, they feel that they have dropped back into an earlier century. The impression made by these sectarians is such a vivid one that it has given rise to one of the most widely spread misconceptions about the Pennsylvania Dutch, that one and all wear bonnets or broadbrim hats. At the very most only one out of ten Pennsylvania Dutchmen dresses "plain"; the rest, usually "church people" or Moravians, look like the great mass of Americans elsewhere.

The Mennonites, the parent church of the Amish, are one of the oldest religious groups in Pennsylvania. Their belief in adult baptism, the most important of their doctrines, attracts no particular attention today from the rest of the world. In the Mennonite baptism water is usually poured on the head, although occasionally the man or woman joining church may kneel in a running stream and be baptized by water from the hand. It is their plain dress rather than their method of baptism that calls attention to the Mennonites. Avoiding the bright colors loved by the Amish, the Mennonites usually dress in black or gray. The women wear small, neat black bonnets with house caps of fine white linen under them. Their dresses, with tight bodices and full skirts, have long tight sleeves and high necks. A kerchief of the same material as the dress comes to a point at the waist in front and in back and at both shoulders. Often aprons are worn and shawls instead of coats. The men, usually clean-shaven, wear flat broadbrim hats and coats with stand-up collars without lapels. In the speech of the more worldly of the Pennsylvania Dutch, to join the Mennonite Church is to "turn plain," a phrase aptly chosen.

The meetinghouses, with benches and whitewashed walls and a coal stove in the center, are severe and plain. The men sit on one side and the women on the other; the older people sit in the front. The broadbrim hats are hung on pegs on the wall or on racks suspended above the benches from the ceiling. As there is a church attendance of almost 100 per cent, the meetinghouses are often large. A Mennonite has to be very sick to stay home from church. Even a baby is taken to church as soon as he is five weeks old. There is no organ or instrumental music of any kind, nor is there a choir. Instead there is hearty, full-voiced singing by the whole congregation.

Except among the more liberal groups of Mennonites the ministry is not an educated one. The ministers are chosen from the congregation by lot; none of them has had special education or preparation for preaching. Even their consent to act as ministers is taken for granted. A Mennonite proposed by the congregation as a possible minister cannot easily withdraw. He may feel unworthy or he may believe that to preach a sermon is beyond his powers; but the choice is the Lord's, not his. At the service at which a minister is chosen Bibles are placed before the candidates. In one of the Bibles is a slip of paper with the verse from Proverbs 16:33, "The lot is cast into the lap; but the whole disposing thereof is of the Lord." The man who selects the Bible with this slip of paper is the one chosen. He serves as minister for life and without pay. Nor can he be dismissed by the congregation except for gross misdemeanor. In colonial days the uneducated ministry worked to the advantage of the Mennonites. Where Reformed and Lutherans by the hundred or even thousand went without clergy and often without churches, the Mennonites could always provide themselves with ministers from within their own congregations. There was not the dependence on Europe for leadership that early hampered the growth of the Reformed and Lutheran churches and later hamstrung the Moravian Church.

The Mennonites in their settlement at Germantown in 1683 planted the first German colony in America. It was the Mennonites who led the way to this new land of Goshen. An even earlier attempt to establish a Mennonite colony on this side of the Atlantic had been made in 1662, when Cornelius Plockhoy and twenty-five Dutch Mennonite families had tried to build a utopia where the Whorekill flows into the Delaware. There they set up a cooperative society where all men were free to worship as they pleased, where each man was the equal of every other man, and where poverty was to be abolished. Slavery was forbidden. A free school was established. For two years this tiny utopia went its happy way, and then the English came and "plundered what belonged to the Quaking Society of Plockhoy to a naile." Plockhoy escaped and for thirty years somehow or other he managed to keep alive in the early American wilderness. In 1694, old and blind, he turned up in Germantown, his wife leading him. There the Mennonites took up a collection for him, gave him a lot on which they built a little house, and in front of the house they planted a tree. Here Plockhoy lived quietly for the last few years of his life.

Germantown was soon followed by other settlements, along the Skippack and the Pequea, and later along the Swatara and the Tulpehocken. Most of the early Mennonites were Swiss driven to the Palatinate by persecution, though some of them came directly from Switzerland. Many of them were helped on their way by Dutch members of their faith. The Mennonites of Amsterdam set up a Committee of Foreign Needs, which by 1732 had received over three thousand requests for aid, of which a large number were granted.

The larger part of the Mennonite emigration took place in the early eighteenth century. Practically all the Mennonites who came to America at this time settled in Pennsylvania. Later in the eighteenth century a few made their way down the Great Valley to Maryland and Virginia, and in the nineteenth century to Canada and the West. In Pennsylvania the Mennonites settled in the placid valleys and the gently rolling hills south and east of the first range of mountains. After Germantown the earliest settlement was in the upper half of what was then Philadelphia County but is now Montgomery, and later in upper Bucks and Lancaster County, all Mennonite centers to this day. Except for Germantown the Mennonite country began twenty miles to the north of Philadelphia; to the west, with rare exceptions, it was fifty or more miles away. The land on which the Mennonites settled was good, and that of the Lancaster Plain more than good. Most of the early Mennonites were farmers, though in Germantown some were weavers and artisans. Even today almost all Mennonites are farmers.

It has been one of the glories of the Mennonite Church that the first American protest against slavery, made in Germantown in 1688, was in part a Mennonite document. Presented to the Quaker meeting in Germantown 175 years before the Emancipation Proclamation, it was signed by four men: Pastorius, a German pietist; Gerrit Hendricks, a Mennonite; and Derik and Abraham Op den Graff, two Mennonites turned Quaker. They found it "a terror, or fearful thing, that men should be handelled so [as slaves] in Pennsylvania." "How fearful and faint-hearted are many at sea," they wrote, "when they see a strange vessel, being afraid it should be a Turk, and they should be taken, and sold for slaves into Turkey. Now, what is *this* better done, than Turks do?" The monthly meeting, finding this protest too weighty a document for it to act upon, sent it to the quarterly meeting, which in turn passed it on to the yearly meeting, where it was quietly shelved. This evidence of a tender conscience and courage in the Mennonites when all the rest of the world took slavery for granted is greatly to their credit. None of the Mennonites ever owned slaves, not even those who in the next century moved to Virginia.

Mennonites turning Quaker were not unusual in the late seventeenth century. The two faiths had much in common: their emphasis on simplicity, their stand on nonresistance, and their interest in ethics. Both the Quakers and the Mennonites were far more concerned about leading a good Christian life than they were about theology. Both Fox and Penn owed much to the teachings of Menno Simons, the founder of the Mennonite Church. Even the essential Quaker belief of the "inner light" was commonly held by the Anabaptists, from whom the Mennonites were descended. It was this marked similarity between the two peoples that led Penn to invite the Mennonites to settle in his colony of Pennsylvania.

In Pennsylvania the Mennonites were fervent supporters of the Quakers, especially in the Quaker opposition to war. Like the Quakers, most of the Mennonites were separated from the Indians by a broad band of churchmen, Lutheran, Reformed, Moravian, and Presbyterian. Yet even in the Revolution most of the Mennonites were treated leniently. The authorities in general recognized that their opposition was to war rather than to the American cause. True, they found themselves in difficulty when they refused to pay the special war tax of £3 10s. that Congress levied. This attitude was roundly condemned by one of their ministers, Christian Funk: "Were Christ here, He would say, Give to Congress that which belongs to Congress and to God that which belongs to God." For this Funk was excommunicated, whereupon he organized several Mennonite congregations loyal to the American cause. It was only in communities where the Mennonites were few in number that they were mistreated. In Berks County several Mennonites were put in Reading jail, and in Northampton County they were classed as Tories by the court. At Saucon in Northampton County all their possessions were confiscated: furniture, stoves, bedding, household utensils, dishes, food, even their very Bibles. The men were ordered to leave the province within thirty days; the women and children, having been made destitute, were permitted to remain. Though such persecution was rare, the Mennonites through much of Pennsylvania were looked upon with suspicion and often with contempt as men who refused to fight for their country.

The memory of this hostile attitude during time of war may have prompted a later generation to emigrate to Canada, where they were promised freedom from military service and where land was cheap. Probably it was this last fact that carried most weight. Beginning in 1793, the exodus to Canada reached its height in 1806–1807. Making their way northward through the river valleys, they crossed western New York to settle on the fertile lands of lower Ontario in what is now Waterloo County. Here, too, life was beset with difficulties. To some of the rascals and cheats of the frontier these unworldly people were sheep ready for fleecing. They were sold tracts of land by men who had no title to the land. When the Mennonites discovered that the deeds to their farms were worthless, they turned to their fellow Mennonites in Lancaster County for help. In the country round about Brickersville $20,000 was raised. In 1802 this money, all in silver dollars, was carted north to Ontario by Conestoga wagon. In the end there was established in Ontario a little island of Pennsylvania Dutch, where the dialect and Dutch customs persist to this day. There the bank

barns and springhouses as well as sauerkraut and chicken potpie show
the race from which the people sprang. In the town of Kitchener there
is even a farmers' market of the sort found in every Pennsylvania
Dutch city.

Later wars have only served to make the Mennonites more convinced pacifists. In the Civil War the North permitted the Mennonites
to choose between hospital service and exemption upon the payment
of $300. In Virginia exemption cost $500 until 1864, when an effort
was made to force the Mennonites into the army, whereupon many of
them slipped through the lines to West Virginia and Maryland. In the
First World War, Mennonites frequently met with persecution in the
army camps if they refused to accept noncombatant service. Although
this abuse was not sanctioned by the War Department, it nevertheless
occurred. In the Second World War the Mennonites met with greater
understanding and fairer treatment. A small number of extreme pacifists who refused to register for the draft were jailed; but most of the
Mennonites, along with Quakers, Brethren, and other conscientious
objectors, were sent to Civilian Public Service camps.

The Mennonites also object to taking an oath, an objection shared
by the Quakers and the Brethren. This was a minor matter that got
them into no serious difficulties. In Pennsylvania they were granted the
right of affirmation as early as 1717. In Maryland "Quakers, Tunkers
and Mennonites" were given this right in the Constitution of 1776.

In so far as possible the Mennonites avoid going to law. Instead
they settle their differences among themselves. Even those Mennonites
who leave the church and take up a profession give law a cold shoulder;
most of them become teachers or doctors. Bankruptcy laws are regarded as new, frivolous, and evil; members of the church are urged
not to take advantage of them. Life insurance is opposed: to insure
life is to show no faith in God's goodness. Yet to soften the blow of
death the Mennonites see to it that widows and children are adequately
provided for: none go to the poorhouse or the orphans' home; none
go on relief.

The Mennonites think of themselves as a peculiar people separate
from the world, a people avoiding worldly pleasures and worldly sins.
This is a view that has come down through the centuries from the
Anabaptists and, to a certain degree, from the Waldenses before them.
It is a part of primitive Christianity that has never wholly disappeared.
Among the Anabaptists the plain and simple primitive church was con-

trasted to the wealth and pomp of Rome. The lowly Christ, born in a stable, who chose as His disciples such plain people as fishermen, seemed far removed from the pope in his jeweled tiara amid the rich pageantry of St. Peter's at Rome. Simplicity marked every day of Christ's life. When He rode it was on an ass; when He spoke, it was the speech of His neighbors and not a learned alien tongue. In their criticism of the magnificence and the involved doctrines of the medieval church, the Anabaptists inevitably met with opposition, just as they did when they expounded their belief in the "inner light" or when they attacked the use of force. By no means all Anabaptists held these doctrines, for under the name Anabaptists forty or more sects were linked together. All of them rejected infant baptism, as the word Anabaptists, meaning to baptize over again, suggests. When a man was baptized and received into the church, he must have reached sufficient years to know what he was about. He must not have his religion forced on him when but a puling infant. This point of view was opposed by the great Reformed leader, Zwingli, who argued, oddly enough, that infant baptism took the place of circumcision. The Anabaptists thought they could dispense with both.

Anabaptism from the start had its strength among the peasants. The terrible slaughter that marked the Peasants' Revolt in 1524 and 1525 only tightened the hold of the Anabaptists on the peasants, for it was then that Luther, in a shocking pamphlet, urged the nobles to have no scruples in putting the rebels to death. By aligning his church on the side of the princes, Luther lost his hold on the peasants. The nobles took his advice seriously enough to kill off at least fifty thousand peasants. As the more militant of their leaders were killed, the Anabaptists turned more and more toward pacifism. With persecution their lot, they stressed humility. Put up with the sufferings of this world, they preached; only make certain your life is as pure and Christlike as possible. Thus the Anabaptists became increasingly unworldly. At the same time persecution and death taught them to look upon the state with fear and suspicion, a lesson all too well learned and never forgotten to this day. In Germany the ruthless suppression of the Peasants' Revolt encouraged the common man to put up with whatever rulers happened to be in power.

Yet in censuring the Mennonites for their suspicions of the state it must be borne in mind that for at least a century and a half in Europe they were a persecuted people cut off from the protection the state

normally gives its citizens. In 1520 the Diet of Spires ordered all Anabaptists to be executed without a trial. Protestant and Catholic alike
looked upon them as disloyal, heretical, rebellious, and untrustworthy
subjects of the state. Even in Switzerland burial in consecrated ground
was forbidden them.

The tendency of the Mennonites to shut themselves off from the
world, even in this century, has sometimes resulted in narrowness;
and occasionally self-righteousness has reared its ugly head. Fortunately,
most of them are far too unassuming, kind, and generous to be self-
righteous. Nor have the Mennonites often been austere, although at
times their condemnation of the innocent pleasures of the world, such
as the celebration of Christmas by hanging up a stocking or decorating
a tree, has struck the rest of us as robbing their lives of color. Furthermore, their suspicion of all formal systems of theology has led to division and subdivision into sects, even to the point of absurdity. Near
Ephrata, for instance, is a small group of Mennonites known as "the
Pikers"—a name given not to brand them with the stigma of stinginess
but because they live along the pike. This is but one of many sub-
divisions. In its most extreme form the church unit is reduced to a
single family—a perfect illustration of the impulse to decide that all
the world is wrong and only I am right.

The Mennonites were not always the simple, unlettered people that
so many of them are today. In the early days they had learned leaders—
this in the time when the Mennonites were still Anabaptists. Especially
noted were Balthasar Hubmaier, professor of theology at Ingolstadt
and cathedral preacher at Ratisbon, and Johannes Denck, the celebrated humanist of Basel; but most leaders of this caliber were put to
death in the persecution that aimed to wipe out the Anabaptists. For a
time Moravia, East Friesland, Augsburg, Worms, and Strasbourg gave
them sanctuary until the higher authorities forced these districts and
cities to join the persecution.

The tragedy reached its climax in the City of Münster, the last
Anabaptist stronghold. Refugees from all of central Europe, especially
from Holland, had streamed into Münster. When the Anabaptists got
control of the city, it was at once besieged by the troops of the bishop
of Münster, who was also a temporal prince of the Holy Roman Em-
pire. Every Anabaptist who could be found was put to death. Under the
duress of the siege the Anabaptists within the city adopted a form of
communism. Even polygamy was practiced during the last months of

the siege. Although polygamy had never been an Anabaptist belief, Jan of Leyden, one of their leaders, persuaded the city, in which there were three women to every man, to decree its practice by law. Every man was ordered to take wives and every woman a husband. Jan of Leyden himself took the text, "Be fruitful, and multiply, and replenish the earth," so seriously as to marry sixteen women. When at last the city was forced to surrender, most of the Anabaptists were summarily slaughtered. No attention was paid to the promise of safe-conduct to leave the town, one of the terms of the conditions of surrender.

In spite of this disaster Anabaptism was not wiped out. In Switzerland a new leader, Menno Simons, appeared. Born the very year in which Columbus discovered America, Menno Simons was a Roman Catholic priest who left the Church in 1536. Rejecting polygamy and returning to the older Anabaptist beliefs, he spent twenty-five years in visiting scattered groups of Anabaptists and in uniting them in the church that bears his name. Although the Mennonites met with severe persecution, the church grew rapidly. The very persecution that scattered the Mennonites spread the movement, particularly in Holland and in the Palatinate, to both of which places many Mennonites had fled.

The long and bitter story of the persecution of the Anabaptists and the Mennonites was compiled by Tieleman Jansz van Braght and published in 1660. This is the *Blutige Shau-Platz* or *Martyrs' Mirror*, commonly known among Pennsylvania Mennonites as *The Martyr Book*. The monks of the Ephrata cloister printed an edition of 1,300 copies of this huge volume of over 1,400 pages for the Mennonite churches of Pennsylvania. The most recent edition of *The Martyr Book* appeared in 1916. Through this book, which is commonly found in every Mennonite home, the sufferings of their remote ancestors have been kept alive for the Mennonites and Amish of this century. For many it has made the past more real than the present. It has served to convince them that the world is evil, that they are right in keeping separate and apart.

All the books in a Mennonite household are religious books. Most important of all is the Bible, on which from early days they put their reliance. When their leaders were killed off and their religion was driven underground, the movement was able to survive as long as there was one among them who could read the Bible. As it soon became the ambition of every Mennonite to be able to read the Bible, illiteracy among them was rare. In Germantown they started a school even before they built a meetinghouse. In 1743, long before the first American edition of the Bible in English, they commissioned Christopher Sauer to print a German Bible, both Old and New Testaments, after the translation of Martin Luther. Three other books widely read by early Mennonites were *The Wandering Soul* by J. P. Schabilie, a Mennonite minister; *The Spiritual Flower Garden of the Inner Soul*, which in 1800 went through its eighth American edition; and *Golden Apples in Silver Shells*, which was printed at Ephrata at Mennonite request as early as 1745.

As the Mennonites are one of the oldest Protestant groups, they have had a wide influence on other Protestant churches. Their view of baptism, that of the Anabaptists, as a rite that could be administered only to a person who had reached years of discretion, crossed the narrow seas that separate Holland from England. The Baptist Church stems directly from the Dutch Mennonites. The very first Baptist church was formed in Amsterdam in 1608, the second in London in 1611. John Smith, the father of the English Baptist Church, was baptized in the Mennonite Church of Amsterdam. In addition, the Baptists borrowed from the Mennonites their belief in universal atonement: that Christ died to save all men and not merely the elect. Even more significant to the history of America was the Mennonite insistence on liberty of conscience; this doctrine, too, the Baptists borrowed. It was this principle that Roger Williams established in the Providence Plantations: complete religious freedom for all for the first time in the history of the world. This is one of the brightest pages in the story of mankind. It could be the proud boast of the Mennonites—if the Mennonites were given to boasting—that it was they who first evolved this principle of religious freedom. The Quaker borrowings from the Mennonites have already been listed; but still another Protestant group, the Congregational Church, is indebted to the Mennonites, and for its most characteristic feature, the large measure of independence possessed by each congregation. The Mennonite influence on other Protestant churches is less obvious, but their interest in working out rules for human conduct rather than in drawing up theological statements had a profound effect on the religious thought of the seventeenth and eighteenth centuries.

In America the Mennonites have been largely a farming people. They lead good Christian lives, for they are a people who live their religion. They are gentle and long-suffering; they are hard-working and practical; they are as stable as the Alleghenies. In Pennsylvania the Church is ultraconservative. Largely because of the uneducated ministry they have clung to the old European ways. Both the Mennonites and the Amish try to live in the eighteenth century; the modern world is not for them. The Franconia discipline, which regulates the conduct of the most conservative group of Mennonites in the state, forbids attendance at political meetings and membership in labor unions. These are put under the same ban that moving pictures, secret societies, horse races, county fairs, excursions, picnics, and surprise parties are. This attitude toward politics is particularly vulnerable. In the early years of the Mennonite Church in Europe there was good reason for forbidding any member of the church to hold political office, since there a magistrate was the tool of the state church and by virtue of his office was compelled to persecute dissenters. That a new country and another century have not changed the Mennonite attitude is one of their most serious defects.

In a government "of the people, by the people, for the people" the Mennonites have ignored the second of these three phrases and put too little emphasis on the first. Except for the most advanced groups among them, such as the New Mennonites, they refuse to take their rightful share in democratic government. The church permits its members to hold only such minor public offices as school director and road overseer. Yet little by little the Mennonites are coming to recognize that whether they like it or not they are a part of the world and that it is necessary to combat rather than withdraw from "the world, the flesh, and the devil." But with evil so strong and flourishing, any compromise with their ancient belief in the wisdom of withdrawing from the world is bound to be beset with difficulties. Expediency is all too often a sweet-smelling name for surrender.

The Mennonite opposition to education is another serious weakness. No Mennonite and no Amishman have ever been prominent in the nation's history, yet many men of Mennonite ancestry have become renowned. Rittenhouse, Pennypacker, Frick, Cunard, Hershey, Landis are all Mennonite names. Young Mennonites of talent and ambition leave the farm to go to the city, and leaving the farm they leave the church as well, for the Mennonite way of life is that of the farm and the small country town.

On the other hand, the Mennonites have achieved a far greater measure of social equality than most groups in America. Almost none are rich, although one Lancaster Mennonite in the feed-and-grain business became a millionaire; and almost none are poor. In the world of the Mennonites one man is as good as another. Among them there is no keeping up with the Joneses. "All men are created equal" is far truer with them than it is with the average run of Americans.

Though the Mennonite way of life may at first sight seem harsh and ascetic, neither of these adjectives is just. True, their family life is marked by a high moral standard seldom matched by other groups. Honesty, integrity, and simplicity have long been and remain Mennonite virtues. Yet there is an unusual gentleness and serenity among them, and among the other "plain people" as well, that sets them off from the Puritans. Their faces and their manner show that they have discovered at leas: one or two of the secrets of the good life. The fundamentals are theirs: they have clothes enough to keep them warm, tight roofs over their heads, and food in the larder. And possibly what is more important, they have stopped with the fundamentals. They have not asked for more. In abjuring luxury they have escaped many ills—above all the great sin of the century, materialism. Yet since they are their brother's keeper, old age, illness, and unemployment hold no terror for them. Hard work they accept cheerfully as the natural lot of man. Although they abstain from smoking and drinking, although they never go to the movies or listen to a soap opera or read a detective story, they have the cardinal pleasures of life. With an unusually fresh enjoyment of visiting, they make many friends. They partake freely of the bounties of the table. The pleasures of the marriage bed they view as natural and right. There is neither smut nor Victorian prudishness here; instead there is a pronounced earthy streak, which is not altogether unexpected in a farming people. Among themselves the young men are fairly frank about sex. They jest about it—sometimes in a fashion surprisingly broad, even Rabelaisian. It may be that their view of sex, which, I venture to say, most doctors and psychologists would judge eminently sound, is the secret of their vitality. Few Mennonite couples produce one child only. Many of their families are large: five or six sturdy boys and girls are common; nine or ten are not unusual. Here, too, they may show more wisdom than more highly educated people.

The Second World War has proved the mettle of this people. Throughout the war they clung tenaciously to their pacifism. Any man accepting service in the army or the navy was expelled from the church. Though this stand would seem to doom the world to Nazi enslavement in a crisis like that of the last war, war is so monstrous an evil that perhaps it is well for the country at large to be brought up short by a group as irrevocably opposed to war as the Mennonites. Their stubborn condemnation of war makes the rest of us consider the evil nature of war more thoughtfully than we would have done otherwise. Like Edith Cavell they would say, "Patriotism is not enough."

In war relief the Mennonites, like the Quakers and the Brethren, have been of great service. The world has long known of the work the Quakers have done; the Brethren, too, attracted attention because of their gift of heifers to war-torn countries. The work of the Mennonites alone has gone virtually unnoticed. This has been by their own choice, for remembering Luke 17:10, "So likewise ye, when ye shall have done all those things which are commanded you, say, We are unprofitable servants: we have done that which was our duty to do," they have shunned publicity. If anything, they have been all too modest in keeping their good works under a bushel.

The great contribution of the Mennonites has been in their gifts of food and clothing. Like the heifer project of the Brethren, the Mennonite work in relief has been intensely practical. Even during the war, before it was possible to ship food and clothing abroad, they had many relief workers in the field. Fully aware of the widespread suffering in the world, the Mennonites looked at their laden shelves at home with troubled hearts. At first there seemed to be no way to share this plenty with the starving. Tin was one of the wartime scarcities and glass is apt to break. Almost as a forlorn hope they sent to Holland a test consignment of thirty-six cases of glass jars, all of the same size and packed in the original cartons banded with wood, which in turn was reenforced with metal strips. If 90 per cent got through unbroken, they decided, they could go ahead and ship food canned on the Mennonite farms. When the report came that the consignment had arrived without a single jar broken, the Mennonites were jubilant. A way to share their food had been opened to them. In later shipments many jars were broken, but never as many as 10 per cent.

With this trial shipment a success, the Mennonite women set to work. From the time the first asparagus poked its spears through the earth in the spring till the last winter pears ripened in the attic, these farm women toiled over their stoves. Jar after jar was filled with all the fruits and vegetables their farms would grow: strawberries, cherries, peas, beans, raspberries, currants, blackberries, plums, tomatoes, corn, peaches, crab apples, pears, beets, applesauce, apple butter, quince chips—right through the calendar from April to November. Much of the food was put up in large two-quart jars, but food for babies was canned in pint and quart sizes. More than 800,000 quarts of food put up at home was the product for the season of 1945. A standard label was pasted on each jar; on the label were written the contents of the jar and the name and address of the woman who had filled it. This personal touch must have meant much to many of the recipients abroad. Here was proof that not all the world was indifferent to their plight. This food went to Holland and France, for under the direction of UNRRA Mennonite relief was centered on those two countries.

Such generosity had its effect on the Mennonites themselves. There was a growing enthusiasm for giving. Many families, often in extremely modest circumstances, gave far more bountifully than anyone would have asked them to. Often they went without things themselves to help feed the hungry abroad. As they worked in their fields growing the food or in their kitchens canning it, there was a broadening of horizons. For many of the Mennonites the larger world had hardly existed; but now, faced with the world's need, they did all in their power to feed the hungry and clothe the cold, and in doing so they felt a sense of brotherhood with them.

During the winter months, when the men had more free time from the work on the farm, they turned their attention to the canning of meat. Fortunately, they were able to get tin cans for the meat. They took over for the winter months a cannery in Smoketown in Lancaster County, one near Franconia Meeting in Montgomery County, and another at Harrisonburg in the Shenandoah Valley. In addition they had two portable canneries, one in Ohio and one in Virginia. Individual Mennonites or several joining together or whole meetings gave or bought steers, hogs, and poultry, which were slaughtered and then cut up, cooked, and canned. Most of this meat was raised on the home farms.

The cannery at Smoketown was run by five men who were appointed as the Food for Relief Committee by the Lancaster Conference consisting of seventy-two churches, Amish and River Brethren as well as Mennonite. It was this committee's duty to supervise the work, to see that there were enough people to help, and to make certain of the supply of meat. Extra equipment for the cannery was bought with money given for that purpose. A company in Lancaster very generously slaughtered all the hogs free of charge, and an equally generous plant in Bird in Hand provided cold storage. Six men worked regularly at the more highly skilled jobs at the cannery in order to keep things running smoothly. All the other help came from Mennonite, Amish, and River Brethren volunteers, men and women. Usually fifty to sixty members of a particular meeting took over for the day. The men performed the heavier tasks, disjointing the steers and hogs. The women cut up the meat into two-inch squares and did much of the cooking and canning. They worked from seven-thirty in the morning till all the work for the day was done—usually well along in the evening, sometimes as late as ten. From the beginning of November to the beginning of March the cannery was in full operation five days a week. For the four months from November 1, 1945, to March 1, 1946, this one cannery produced, all in No. 10 cans holding three and a half quarts each, 21,861 cans of beef, 16,780 cans of pork, 9,036 cans of poultry, and 1,264 cans of fats. Into those cans of poultry had gone 20,308 chickens, 109 turkeys, and 112 ducks.

To look at the larger picture of the Mennonite contribution as a whole instead of just one cannery, 69 shipments of food, weighing 3,259,482 pounds and valued at $210,952.13, were sent abroad between April 10, 1945, and March 1, 1946, a period of less than a year. In addition to the home-canned fruit and vegetables and the meat in tins there were flour, wheat, dried milk, evaporated milk, and raisins. The home-canned food came largely from the East, the dried fruits from the West, and the flour and wheat in carload lots from the Middle West. Except for 6,162 pounds of tools and utensils valued at $1,707.20 all these shipments were food. And except for 17,423 pounds valued at $1,060.29, which went to Puerto Rico, all of this was shipped to Holland and France.

The Mennonites sent clothing, blankets, soap, and medical supplies as well as food. From January 1, 1945, to March 13, 1946, clothing weighing 460,127 pounds and valued at $449,174.82 was shipped abroad. When the Mennonite Central Committee put a small notice in four church papers that blankets were badly needed, the post office and the express office at Akron, Pennsylvania, were snowed under. The postmaster and express agent, in distress, begged the Central Committee to send men to dig them out—figuratively, at least—from under the piles of blankets. Some of the clothing shipped had been worn, some was brand-new. All the used clothing was cleaned, mended, and ironed before it was sent. All sorts of clothing, including layettes for babies and special bundles for hospitals, were made by local sewing groups. Quilts were made by these groups too, while sweaters, scarfs, caps, mittens, and afghans were knitted at home.

One of my friends, a Quaker engaged in work for the Friends Service Committee, told me of her delight in visiting a sewing group, made up that day of Amish women from Paradise. Black bonnets and shawls hung from pegs along the wall. The women in their white house caps and their kerchiefs and bright dresses of violet, green, blue, and wine-red and aprons of black made a picture worthy of Pieter Brueghel. One can't help wondering, though, how the little Dutch and French boys and girls looked decked out in broadfall trousers or bonnets and kerchiefs. Not that the Amish are likely to carry their ideas on unworldly dress that far, but the vision of little Dutch and French children in bonnets and broadbrims is too attractive to be easily resisted.

By the middle of 1947 the various branches of the Mennonite Church, though comprising only one-tenth of 1 per cent of the population of the United States, were sending 40 per cent of all nongovernment relief supplies to foreign countries, a record as magnificent as it is astonishing. No wonder that Bishop John Lapp of the Mennonite Church was able to say, "We no longer live to ourselves nor die to ourselves."

In part the work of the three "peace churches"—the Quakers, the Mennonites, and the Brethren—has been an attempt to justify themselves in the eyes of the world, to demonstrate that though they may refuse to fight they can be of service in binding up the wounds of humanity. But to ascribe the relief work of these churches to an inferiority complex is a mistake. To some degree it is very likely that; but kindness of heart and pity and even a feeling of guilt for what man has done to man all play their part.

One of the most striking features in the history of the Mennonites is the divergent paths taken by the church in America, Holland, and Germany. In Holland the Mennonites from their earliest years have played a prominent part in the government, while their contribution to Dutch culture has been as noteworthy as that of the Unitarians to New England and the Quakers to Pennsylvania. They have furnished many eminent judges and several cabinet ministers to the kingdom as well as a governor general to the East Indies and the first president to the World Court. Oddly enough, they have been so given to finance that many of Holland's most powerful bankers have been Mennonites. In Holland they have been a people of the city rather than of the country, and as an urban people they have long been noted for their intellectual attainments. Painters, physicians, and scientists of the first rank have been Mennonites. The Dutch Mennonite Nickolaus Bidloo was the director of the medical school Peter the Great founded in Moscow. His brother, Gottfried Bidloo, was body physician to William III of England. Rembrandt's famous painting "A Mennonite Preacher and the Widow" portrays the noted Dutch Mennonite Cornelisz Claesz Anslo and his wife. The principal park in Amsterdam bears the name of the Mennonite poet Joost van den Vondel. Beyond any doubt the Dutch Mennonites have been yeast in the dough of Holland—not the only yeast but a goodly portion of it.

In Germany, too, the Mennonites have had a history very unlike that of the Mennonites of America. Since most of the Mennonites of the Palatinate emigrated to Pennsylvania, the German Mennonites of today are largely Holland Dutch in origin. The small meeting at Emden, established in 1530 and the oldest Mennonite congregation in the world, had among its members during the First World War an admiral and a major general. The Krefeld Mennonites, although conservative and simple in their mode of living, included some of the wealthiest people in the country, captains of industry as well as burgomasters and civic leaders. Several German Mennonites became shipowners; several became even brewers. Hermann Sudermann, the dramatist, was the son of an East Prussian Mennonite who combined farming with brewing. Most German Mennonites were set off from the rest of the people by their wealth and conservatism. By the time of the First World War pacifism had completely disappeared among them. In the Second World War their money and conservatism made them ardent Nazis.

The arresting differences of the three Mennonite cultures provides a nice problem for the sociologists. What was it that made the Mennonites of Holland intellectuals and leaders? Why did the Mennonites of Germany set their hearts on wealth? Why did the Mennonites of Pennsylvania eschew it? Why did not the freedom and boundless opportunity of early Pennsylvania bring forth a great Mennonite culture comparable to that of the Mennonites in Holland? What is it that has caused the Pennsylvania Mennonites to lie fallow for two and a half centuries? Perhaps in light of their many fine qualities that phrase, "lie fallow," is overly harsh. Yet like the Puritans, theirs is a world without Shakespeare. Just as the Puritans closed the theaters, broke the stained-glass windows in the cathedrals, and ripped the organs out of the churches, so too the Mennonites have opposed all the arts and even the sciences. Though Mennonite virtues are admirable and many, there has been no place in their world for the intellectual life; and without an intellectual life can a culture, extraordinarily fine though it may be in certain aspects, exist on a truly high level?

The Amish

The reliance the Mennonites put on the Bible, in which each man tended to interpret the Scriptures for himself, as well as the lack of an educated ministry, led to disputes and even division within the church. Even before the emigration to Pennsylvania the Amish had split off from the Mennonites. The principal theological difference which caused this split was the Amish doctrine of *Meidung*—literally *avoidance* or *shunning*. Based on the Pauline injunction "not to keep company," "not to eat" with an unfaithful member (I Corinthians 5:11), but to "put away from among yourselves that wicked person," this doctrine is used to correct and punish an erring member. In 1693 Jacob Amman, a Mennonite preacher in the canton of Bern, began to insist on the strict enforcement of the doctrine of *Meidung*. His followers, splitting off from the Mennonite Church, were given the name of their leader and called Amish. Later this ban was extended by Dirk Philips, an early Amish preacher, to include all social relations and particularly those of bed and board. Today when an Amishman is put "under the ban" it means complete ostracism: business, social, religious, and domestic. He becomes literally "as a heathen man and a pub-

31

lican." None of his fellow church members may buy anything from him or sell anything to him; they may not visit with him or pass the time of day. His wife and his children may not even sit at the same table with him. The Mennonites held that this point of view was too severe, that Paul's injunction "not to eat" was intended only to keep the transgressor from taking Communion. Hence the split.

Footwashing, too, was stressed by Jacob Amman, and this tended to set the Amish off from the Mennonites even more. This rite was later adopted by the Brethren, or Dunkards, and become one of the characteristic features of that church. The holy kiss as an expression of fellowship and brotherly love was also commonly used by the Amish. In essentials, however, the Amish are a branch of the Mennonite Church, which they came to recognize more and more during the Second World War, when they worked with the Mennonites on relief.

Though little by little the Amish built up a culture of their own different in numerous ways from that of the Mennonites and in amazingly complete detail unlike that of "the world's people," in the eyes of most Pennsylvanians it is their use of wagons and buggies and the brilliant colors of their dress that distinguish the Amish from the Mennonites. Vivid delphinium-blue, bright violet, rich wine-red, and shouting winter-wheat green: such are the colors the Amish choose to wear. Mennonites usually dress in black or gray, or at most in a coffee-and-cream tan or a quiet print; but the Amish are a treat to the eye. The gaudy streak in the Pennsylvania Dutch comes out strongly in the clothes of the Amish. These gay colors have become so identified with the Amish in the Dutch country that storekeepers have difficulty in selling material of these colors to ordinary people; they are rejected as being too Amish. Men's and boys' shirts and women's and girls' dresses among the Amish are almost always of these colors. The men and boys except for their shirts wear black—broadbrim hats with low crowns, in winter felt and in summer natural straw; coats without either lapels or outside pockets; vests and trousers. The trousers instead of buttoning or zipping up the front are of the broadfall type often known as "barn-door breeches." It is ironic that this type of trousers is confined to the Amish and—until this year—to sailors, the one group as guarded in their morals as any people in America and the other noted for the freedom of their ways with women. The trousers are kept up by homemade suspenders or by a drawstring around the waist. The men's and boys' clothes are made at home or by a local seamstress. After all, where would you go to buy barn-door breeches or coats without lapels? The hats are made by a hatter in the neighborhood. Hooks and eyes and even zippers take the place of buttons. It was the lavish use of buttons on military uniforms back in the seventeenth and eighteenth centuries that led to the Amish ban on buttons. Neckties, too, are forbidden as worldly; but with the bushy Amish beards they are not missed. In winter an overcoat with a short cape reaching to the shoulders is worn, a garment that might well have kept warm the ancestors of these Amishmen when they landed in Philadelphia in the reigns of George I and George II.

The women, with their brightly colored dresses, wear black bonnets and black aprons and in winter black shawls. The dresses are very like those worn by the Mennonites, a tight bodice with long sleeves, a kerchief brought to a point below the waist both in front and in back, and a long full skirt. Kerchiefs of the same color as the dress are worn by married women, white kerchiefs by unmarried women who have joined meeting. They wear no jewelry except, say, a pin to fasten the shawl. Their hands are plain and unadorned—no diamonds, no painted fingernails. The little girls dress much the same except that their bonnets are brightly colored. Scampering across the fields on their way home from school, the little girls seem all bonnets and shawls, with thin little legs sticking out below. The bonnet worn by the Amishwoman is a commodious one, much larger than the bonnets worn by the women of the other plain sects. It has a full skirt or ruffle in the back, one of the distinguishing marks of an Amishwoman. Under the capacious bonnets they wear simple little house caps of white lawn with long strings, which are usually left untied. These house caps, or prayer caps, as they are sometimes called, are worn by all the women of all the "plain people" throughout the day in order to hide the hair, woman's crowning glory. To display it would be vain, and vanity is sinful. The hair is parted in the middle and combed smoothly with a plait on either side that is wound around the head and fastened in a knot, which in turn is tucked under the back of the white house cap. The hair, worn without combs, is never curled. No Amish woman ever gets a permanent wave; indeed, no Amish woman ever sets foot inside a beauty parlor. For them the world of fashion does not exist.

Even more picturesque than their elders are the children, whose clothes are copies in little of the ones worn by the grownups. The boys have the same broadbrim hats, which they keep on their heads throughout most of the day, even when playing ball. Their black trousers are high of waist and rather short, reaching beyond the middle of their calves. Broad bands of cloth across the shoulders serve as suspenders. In winter or on Sundays black coats and shoes and stockings are worn, but on weekdays in summer all Amish children go barefoot. Sometimes even an Amishwoman, when washing off the porch or raking her smoothly shaven grass plot, goes barefoot as a goose. The skirts of the older Amish girls are not long like those of the older women but, like the boys' pants, stop at the tops of the old-fashioned shoes, which are high-laced. The babies, too, from the time they are born are put into regulation Amish dress—girl babies in bonnets and boy babies in broad-brim hats. On tiny children the costume is unmatched; it is amusing and it is bewitching. They are as quaint and beguiling as the children in the paintings of the old Dutch masters. When a friend of mine— one of the world's people—took his children to Lancaster market, they were so enchanted by the sight of the Amish children that they turned to their father and said, "Daddy, why can't we be Amish too?"

One of the many pleasures of living in the Dutch country is the glimpse every now and again of the Amish. A buxom Amish mother sharing the front seat of a rockaway with her little serious daughter and her even smaller son tucked in between them, a young bearded father in an open buggy with a wide-eyed little boy by his side: such a sight as either of these is enough to set a man up for the day. Yet to catch the flurry of purple skirts it is almost necessary to live in their home county of Lancaster, no very great hardship in itself. One Sunday a number of springs ago I was showing some friends the Dutch country. I had hoped to come upon some "plain people"; but the morning was about gone and we had met with little success. Except for half a dozen Mennonites at Goodville we had seen no bonnets and shawls. Suddenly we came upon a whitewashed Amish meetinghouse by the side of the road with the congregation just coming out. I jammed on the brakes and for ten seconds we sat staring, until I realized how grossly discourteous we were. We moved on, reluctant to leave, and in the next moment stopped again. In the graveyard behind the meeting-house were fifteen or twenty little Amish children for whom the long preachings had been too much. In charge of two girls in their early teens they were picking fat bunches of the largest golden dandelions I have ever seen—shy little girls with rose or blue bonnets and little black jackets and dresses of purple, blue, or green; little solemn boys looking out from under broadbrim hats. There they stood among the tomb-stones, the thick green grass powdered with dandelions. Along the fence row that separated the graveyard from the rich Lancaster County fields were cherries in blossom. Spring and youth and beauty were caught here all together in one picture, and behind it all was the suggestion of death to give it poignancy.

"The Beardy Men" is a name sometimes given to the Amish, and not without reason. An Amishman's beard and his long hair set him off from most of the Mennonites, who almost always are clean-shaven, and from other Americans as well. Only some of the River Brethren and older Dunkards are likely to sport such beards. Among the older Amishmen the beards are long and bushy—fine, magnificent beards. These are patriarchs straight out of the Old Testament. Among the younger men the beards are of scantier growth. Here again the Amish are taking to heart the admonitions of the Bible (Leviticus 19:27 and 21:5). The upper lip is always shaved, since two or three centuries ago the mustache was the pride, almost the hallmark, of the soldier. The young Amishman, however, often shaves before he marries, although he is not supposed to shave once he joins church. Many of the young unmarried men let their beards grow for a few days before church but shave at other times. The elders disregard this as one of the more inno-cent foibles of youth; but if the young Amishman marries and shaves he soon finds himself in hot water. The Amishman's hair is bobbed at the top of his ears with bangs across the forehead and a part in the middle. Parting on the side is a matter for church discipline. The hair-cuts are homemade, a bowl to clap on the head and a pair of shears being all that are needed. Amishmen never pay out a penny to a barber.

The Amish wagons and buggies also distinguish them from the world's people. That heathen invention, the automobile, is forbidden by the church. Sober married folk generally use small boxlike wagons or rockaways open only in front. The tops are of gray, black, yellow, white, or brown, all according to the particular branch of the Amish church to which the owner belongs. There is no dashboard, no mud-guards, no whipsocket. Set high on four wheels, it has a spare and naked appearance. Inside it is usually crowded: almost always three or four little faces peer over the shoulders of the bearded father and bonneted mother on the front seat. The young, beardless bachelors drive topless buggies polished so highly that they shine even on an overcast November day. They drive spirited horses, which they handle with coolness and skill. They are fine-looking animals beautifully groomed. The harness is spotless; each ring and buckle shines. Yesterday there was no checkrein on the bridle, but this vanity is creeping in. When the young men look with envious eyes at the new-model cars speeding along the Lincoln Highway, the elders find it wise to give in on checkreins and mettlesome horses. At the same time there is something pleasingly boyish in the satisfaction these young men take in their briskly trotting horses and even in the recklessness with which they drive. They may not be able to do seventy miles an hour in a sports-model roadster, but they can and do drive like demons down the country pikes. Their elders are unhappy about this. There is the ever present danger that their sons may break their necks. Even more likely is the growth of an overweening pride in the horses; and pride, among the Amish, is a cardinal sin. But what can one do to curb the hot blood of youth? A topless buggy may also be used by a young married couple without children, or by an old couple; but the solid family man drives a rockaway, and the dashing young Amish buck would die rather than drive the boxlike family wagon.

In winter sleighs take the place of the wagons and buggies, but sleighs of one color only. Sleighs of two colors are forbidden; and sleigh bells, too, are looked upon as worldly. This objection to bells is carried so far that on Amish farms a horn is blown instead of a bell being rung to call the men in from the fields to dinner. Naturally, sleighing parties are considered a worldly pleasure. With their preference for the horse and buggy the Amish have only a modified enthusiasm for paved roads. Dirt roads are easier on their horses' feet.

Although most branches of the Amish forbid their members to own automobiles, they may ride in a car if it is not for pleasure. They may take the bus to Lancaster just as they may take the train to Philadelphia. The opposition to cars is not founded on any biblical injunction but is due to their desire to live apart from the world. Since Lancaster County is the heart of the Amish domain and since this county is one of the most thickly settled parts of Pennsylvania and Pennsylvania one of the most populous sections of the Union, to keep the world at a distance is by no means easy.

As in the case of the Mennonites, it was the bitter persecution with which they met in Europe that led the Amish to turn their backs on the world. Seeking religious freedom, they started to migrate to Penn's colony early in the eighteenth century until by the middle of the century practically all the Amish in the world had settled in Pennsylvania. Although a few stray settlers came earlier, the first substantial colony of Amish to come to America arrived in Philadelphia on October 8, 1737, on the *Charming Polly*—a singular name to be associated with this godly people. The newcomers settled along the Northkill Creek in the northwestern part of Berks County, not far from a gap in the Blue Mountains, the very edge of the frontier. The land they took up was a lovely part of the Great Valley in a section where the floor of the valley is very uneven. Little rounded hills shoulder one another for space, and in the little valleys between the hills are brooks. To the north rise the Blue Mountains.

Unfortunately, the Northkill country was a poorly chosen site. With the French and Indian War about to break out, the Amish had selected an extremely vulnerable position. Although the Blue Mountains hemmed them in on the north, there were gaps in the mountains to weaken this natural defense. Soon Indians on the warpath descended through the gaps, raiding the farms to the south. Houses and barns were burned, cattle driven away, and the settlers tomahawked or taken captive. The Amish, like the Quakers and the Moravians, found that their pacifism did not save them from the raids. The Indians did not stop to ask a man's religious beliefs. The wife and two small children of Jacob Hochstetter were killed and he and several sons carried off into captivity. As the raids continued many of the Amish fled to Morgantown in the southern tip of the county. In the end Northkill ceased to exist as an Amish community. Today few of the people who live along the Northkill know that the Amish ever dwelt there.

The leading settlement of Amish in Pennsylvania is in Lancaster County. In the Lancaster Plain near Intercourse and Bird in Hand live the House Amish, who, objecting to churches as worldly, worship in houses or barns. Farther north along the Conestoga from Morgantown to Blue Ball are the Church Amish, who have simple meetinghouses like the Quakers. Farther south, too, near Gap and Honey Brook, live more Church Amish. And up in Mifflin County, in the Kishacoquillas Valley, is another thriving Amish settlement. Elsewhere in the East there are colonies of Amish near Dover, Delaware, and Norfolk, Virginia, as well as a new settlement in St. Marys County, Maryland. Scattered through the Middle West and West are other colonies: in Ohio, Indiana, Illinois, and Iowa, four states in which the Pennsylvania Dutch strain is strong; in Kansas, Nebraska, the Dakotas, Arkansas, and Oklahoma; even in Colorado, Montana, Idaho, and Oregon.

Like the Mennonites the Amish choose their preachers by lot from among their own number. Remembering the simple, godly men Christ chose as his disciples, they look on education as unnecessary for their leaders. The lack of an educated ministry has encouraged each man to interpret the Bible for himself. As a consequence there have been many splits in the Amish churches, often on extremely trivial issues. The chief division is between the House Amish and the Church Amish. Although the House Amish condemn the use of meetinghouses as savoring of worldliness, the two groups in essentials have much in common. The Peachey Amish, who take their name from an Amish preacher, are even less orthodox than the Church Amish. A few years back there was a further division among the Peachey Amish into the King people and the Stoltzfus people. Both groups use tractors and electricity on their farms, but the Stoltzfus people have gone so far as to use automobiles.

The religious services of these groups do not differ much one from another. All are marked by a note of austerity. The services last for two or three hours, during which time the worshipers sit on backless benches. To endure such an ordeal one must be inured to it from early childhood. Among the House Amish the men and boys sit in one room, the women and girls in another. In the central room, where the preaching takes place, the men sit in two groups facing one another with the preachers in between. Each Amish congregation has from two to four ministers and a deacon, with a bishop to every two meetings.

The ordinary service among the House Amish begins about half past eight in the morning or quarter to nine. All the men keep on their hats until the first hymn is announced, when with one swoop they all come off. First there are three hymns followed by a short sermon about half an hour in length. Then the congregation kneels in silent prayer, and after that the deacon reads the lesson for the day from the New Testament. Then comes the main sermon, which lasts for an hour or an hour and a half. This is followed by the brief comments of the other ministers and the deacon on subjects touched upon in the main sermon; then there are a few remarks by the preacher of the main sermon. Then, while the congregation kneels, a prayer is read from the prayer book. After this there is the benediction, the reading of the banns, and finally a hymn.

After the last hymn the men put on their hats and leave; then the young women leave, and last of all the older women.

The service is followed by a dinner at which there are three or four sittings. The old people eat first, the men together and the women together. As at all Amish meals, there is a silent grace at the beginning of the meal and again at the end. In the old days bean soup was served, but the standard meal now is of bread and apple butter, sour beets, pickles, snitz pie, and coffee. There are no plates. The few utensils, which remain unchanged throughout the meal, are used by several people in succession.

Communion among the Amish is held twice a year. A fortnight or so before each Communion there is a fast day, Good Friday in the spring and *Michaelstag,* or Michaelmas old style (October 11th), in the fall. The mornings of these days are spent in meditation. On the Sundays following the fast days questions of discipline are taken up, violations of regularity dealt with, and quarrels and misunderstandings smoothed over.

The Communion service is a long one. Beginning about eight in the morning, it opens with hymns followed by prayers, after which one of the ministers reads long passages from the Bible about the search of the children of Israel for the Promised Land and discusses them in great detail. Then another minister, usually the bishop, speaks of the sufferings of Christ and the significance of Communion and foot washing, also at extreme length. As the bishop's sermon is timed to end at three o'clock, the hour of Christ's crucifixion and the time set for Communion, the congregation slips out one by one before then— usually about noon—for a bite to eat, after which they return to the meeting. As each member partakes of the Communion bread and again when he drinks the wine, he bends the knee. This genuflection is also made at the end of each meeting, when the benediction is pronounced, in accordance with the text, "That at the name of Jesus every knee should bow." Communion is followed by the rite of foot washing, after which each member makes his gift to the poor fund. Finally, about half past four or five o'clock, the service comes to an end.

Baptism usually takes place four weeks before Communion. Before being baptized, each person must be approved by the congregation. At the ceremony, which is trinitarian, the bishop dips a tin cup into a bucket and pours the water over the applicant's head. With almost no exceptions everyone joining church was born into an Amish family.

The Amish do not attempt to make any converts. They hold no revivals; they have neither home missions nor foreign missions. Volun-
tary withdrawals are also exceedingly rare. The Amish have little
difficulty in holding their own people.

Although the Amish speak English with as much ease as many of
the Lutheran and Reformed faiths, their sermons are in German.
Amish children are taught to read and sing in German at a Saturday
afternoon class conducted during the winter months by one of the
members of the congregation. Since German is no longer used by the
"church people" and by the other sects, the Amish use of German in
their services has become still another means of setting them off from
the world. As English has become the mother tongue of most Amishmen, many of the younger preachers find preaching in a language
imperfectly known an almost superhuman task. A further disadvantage
in the use of German is that many of the children find it impossible to
understand the sermons.

The old Froschauer Bible, published at Zurich in the time of Luther,
is still widely used by the Amish, as it is by the Mennonites. Another
book to which they cling is *Enchiridion,* a treatise by the sixteenth century Anabaptist preacher Dirk Philips, which was reprinted for their
use as late as 1910. This book they treasure because of its emphasis on
Meidung and foot washing. The use of *Meidung* is a powerful weapon
to keep the members of the church in line. No Amishman can face it
lightly. The very possibility of being placed "under the ban" helps him
to resist the temptations of the world, be they the lesser evils of going to
see a movie or smoking a cigarette or the more serious ones of speculat-
ing in the stock market or going to law or marrying outside his faith.
Meidung is so severe a punishment that it is employed only with the
utmost caution. The matter is brought up before the whole congregation and the ban applied only with their consent. If an Amishman who
has been banned proves to be unrepentant, he is cast off by the church
and "committed to the devil and all his angels." The threat of a step
so extreme is usually enough to bring the sinner to his knees. For an
Amishman under the ban there is no easy way out. An Amishman in
good standing in the church might leave the House Amish, say, and
join the Church Amish; but a man under the ban would not be
accepted by any other group of Amish. There is nothing halfhearted
in the Amish attitude toward religion. Like most pious Roman Catholics, they believe that man's obedience to God must be absolute. In the

power that the church has over his life the Amishman most closely resembles the Puritan. It is a power that was unsurpassed in seventeenth century Boston and is unequaled outside the walls of a monastery elsewhere in America.

The most notable of all the Amish religious books is their hymn book, the *Ausbund,* the oldest hymn book in use in the country. Published at Schaffhausen in 1583, it contains hymns of an even earlier date. One was written by John Hus, while others were sung by Anabaptist prisoners at Passau in Bavaria as early as 1537. Some of the music to which these hymns are sung is even more ancient. The tune "Hildebrand," to which "Von Herzen woll' wir" is set, has been sung for at least 1,100 years. The *Ausbund* was the hymn book of the Swiss Mennonites and many of the south Germans as well as the Amish, but only the Amish have continued to use it. The first American edition was printed by Chistopher Sauer in Germantown in 1742. The *Ausbund,* which the Amish often call *Das dick Buch* (The Thick Book) because of its size, contains 140 hymns, many of extreme length—several with scores of stanzas—and all of "old, unhappy, far-off things"; all celebrating the sufferings of the early Anabaptist martyrs. As many of the Amish bear the same names as the martyrs extolled in the *Ausbund* and the *Martyr Book,* the sufferings of these men and women who died four centuries ago are brought home all the more vividly to the Amish of Bird in Hand and Blue Ball. These books, along with the draft boards and school boards, have kept alive in many of the Amish the belief that they have been and are a persecuted people.

Since the hymns in the *Ausbund* have always been printed without music, the tunes have been handed down from one generation to another and in certain instances have undergone so great a change as to make them unrecognizable. Even today the same hymn will vary greatly from one congregation to another. The style of singing is slow and doleful. A leader "lines out" the melody, which the others repeat. There is no part singing, for this is ruled out as a worldly innovation. There are no choirs in an Amish meeting and no organs or musical instruments of any kind. Though many of the Amish show astonishing skill in singing, a man who is able to lead the singing in meeting is regarded with real respect. In addition to the *Ausbund* the Amish have a second, or lesser, hymn book commonly known as *Das dinn Büchli* (The Thin Little Book). This is the book used for the Sunday night "singings." Many of its tunes were borrowed from the hymns of other churches, but a score or more are the great-grandchildren of the folk melodies brought over by their English-speaking neighbors. The music of "Wer weiss wie nah" is a variation of that of the familiar balllad "Barbara Allen," while "Nun sich der Tag" is sung to the tune "Dundee" and "In der stillen" to "Aberystwyth." "Wie bist du mir" makes use of the melody "Ortonville"; "O Jesu Christ," of "Rockridge"; "Sei Lob und Ehr," of "Babe of Bethlehem," and "Von Himmel," of "A Frog Went A-Courting"!

Music except that produced by the human voice is condemned as worldly. There are no pianos, phonographs, radios, or television in Amish homes. A small boy with a mouth organ may be excused, but there the line is drawn. This objection to musical instruments is based on Amos 6, beginning "Woe to them that are at ease in Zion," and then going on to describe that "ease":

That lie upon beds of ivory, and stretch themselves upon their couches, and eat the lambs out of the flock, and the calves out of the midst of the stall;

That chant to the sound of the viol, and invent to themselves instruments of musick, like David;

That drink wine in bowls, and anoint themselves with the chief ointments.

To have such a modern invention as the radio banned because of this ancient pronouncement pleases me greatly. Yet to say that the radio is banned is to exaggerate: it is merely restricted to the barn. After all, the weather reports are of use to a farmer. If other programs are heard now and again—well, that sort of thing will happen. Sometimes a man is too busy to turn the radio off.

In many ways the Amish lead a Spartan life. They pass over Christmas and Easter with no celebration except church services. Their houses are large and plain but without central heating, bathrooms, electricity, and telephones. In winter only the kitchen and possibly a sitting room are heated. Much of the family life goes on in the kitchen, where a large coal range dominates the room. The bedrooms are unheated except for one downstairs and the one over the kitchen, in which a microscopic register in the floor takes a little of the chill off the room. All through the house they sleep between blankets, and on the coldest nights they put a hot brick in the bed. The lack of bathrooms may strike most people as the greatest hardship of all. Instead of running water there is a pump at the kitchen sink. Yet the Amish are a very clean people. The women are always spotless, the men in their personal appearance are the tidiest farmers I have ever encountered, and even the children look freshly scrubbed. They may have no bathrooms and they may have to pump their water at the kitchen sink or carry it from the well in the back yard, but the Amish are clean. They may have to work hard to get clean, but no Amishman was ever afraid of work.

The ban on telephones leads to amusing inconsistencies. Since they are forbidden to have telephones on their property, public pay-station booths are erected in Amish communities here and there along the road, always on public property. Amishmen have even been known to contribute toward the expense of a more worldly neighbor's telephone to persuade him to have one in the house. This is but one of several contradictions. Most amusing of all is their attendance at circuses. Since God made the animals, it is all right for man to look at them. As for the rest of the performance—well, you are there and you have paid your money, so why not see it? Permission is not granted but neither is it refused. Attendance at county fairs, on the other hand, is strictly forbidden.

Some of the prohibitions, like the one on large windowpanes in houses, are difficult to account for. I suppose that when large windowpanes were first introduced in the Victorian era they seemed fashionable and worldly to the Amish. At any rate, their houses look all the better for the small panes in the windows. Curtains at the windows are also forbidden. This lack of draperies gives the houses a certain austerity, a quality that is little relieved by the cool light blue with which so many of the rooms are painted. This blue is so widely used by the Amish that among the Pennsylvania Dutch it is often called Amish blue. The walls of the rooms are always painted or whitewashed. Wallpaper, too, is worldly. The only carpets on the floor are rag rugs. Except for the ornamental family records and calendars from the butcher, the baker, the grocer, and the feed-and-grain merchant, there are no pictures on the wall. A calendar is a thing of use rather than a decoration. If a picture comes with the calendar—well, it is possible to put up with the picture. As the Amish are forbidden to have their photographs taken, there are never any family pictures on the wall. Embroidered towels, greatly prized by collectors, sometimes hang on the wall. And potted plants, geraniums, primroses, begonias, and "colies," fill the kitchen windows. The bedrooms, except for the gay patchwork quilts, are as plain as the other rooms. Often a bedroom will have two or more beds, for most Amish families are prepared to house a number of visitors.

Among the House Amish the farmhouses are constructed with movable partitions in the downstairs rooms instead of interior walls so that when meeting is held in that house several rooms can be thrown into one. When a preaching is held at a farm, the whole place is put in apple-pie order. The house is scrubbed and scoured until it is spotless. Even the cellar is whitewashed. The barn gets a thorough cleaning. Cobwebs come down from the rafters above the hay; the wagon shed is swept and the wagons are lined up as though for drill. The houseyard and the barnyard are tidied up. Even the manure pile is banked till its sides are perfectly straight, and then it is covered with fresh straw. Spring house cleaning is nothing to this, for the family knows that it is about to be judged by the whole neighborhood.

Occasionally, if the weather is mild, church will be held in a barn. The Church Amish worship in meetinghouses. These, with their whitewashed walls and unpainted backless benches, are as simple and plain as can be; if anything, they are even simpler than Mennonite and Quaker meetinghouses.

Yet the Amish do not think of their lives as Lenten in their austerity. Possibly more than any other people in America they have realized their hearts' desire. Look at the faces of the women or men behind the stalls at Lancaster market or as they drive along the pike at Paradise or Goodville. The serenity of their faces—and that word "serenity" above all others best describes them—bespeaks the good life. They are at peace with the world. They are at peace with themselves. They live in a fat land. They have more than enough: sausages and hams in the smokehouse, bolts of broadcloth and yard goods in the attic. Their lives are simple, temperate, and regular; although filled with labor, they are beautifully uncomplicated. Their marriages are untroubled by the threat of scandal or divorce. Their sons are cheerful, husky, hard-working boys who will till the soil after them; their daughters will settle down on neighboring farms, sew, clean, bake, and bring Amish babies into the world. There are no loafers, no drunkards, no gamblers, no ne'er-do-wells among the Amish. These are contented, self-respecting people, unworldly, clannish, yet kindly and friendly. Even Henry Miller, who has hardly a good word to say for anyone or anything in America, is impressed by the great peace and silence of the land of the

Amish. In "Good News! God Is Love" (Fragment from *The Air-conditioned Nightmare*) he praises the Amish for having converted the Pennsylvania earth into a garden of peace and plenty. Just the same, a non-Amish family living in an Amish community may have a lonely time of it, largely because an Amishman has such a vast number of friends and relatives among the members of his own faith that he seldom gets around to the rest of the world. Yet there is a warmth and friendliness in the Amish that is undeniably attractive. See them in Lancaster market as they help a customer pick out a plump immaculate fowl or explain to him the taste of the apple named Fanny or direct him to a stall where he can find the first sauerkraut of the season. It is not only the wonderful food the Amish sell or the Old World dress they wear that makes going to Lancaster market a pleasure; even more it is their cheerful, friendly attitude. The Amish are the quintessence of country ways and country life. As Clare Leighton has so happily put it, "These bearded Amish farmers and bonneted Amish women bring with them the color of ripening barley and the scent of clover fields in flower."

Almost all of the Amish today are direct descendants of the Amish immigrants of the eighteenth century, probably only five hundred in number. As marriage outside the church is forbidden, the Amish have intermarried to an amazing degree, until today there are only about thirty surnames among them. Indeed, most of them have one of a dozen surnames. There is a school in Lancaster County in which for the last ten years 95 to 100 per cent of the children, and the teacher as well, have been named Stoltzfus. Small wonder that they resort to almost every personal name in the Bible: Aaron, Abner, Abram, Amos, David, Elam, Enos, Isaac, Jacob, Jesse, Job, John, Levi, Mahlon, Milo, Moses, Naaman, Stephen, Urie. Even so, six or seven men in the same community may bear the same name. Since more than a name is needed to tell them apart, six Jacob Zooks may be known as Big Jake, Hickory Jake, Henner's Jake, Red Jake, Turkey Jake, and Smoketown Jake. Incidentally, titles of respect are not used by the Amish. These are plain people who prefer to be called by their first names or, if a stranger is addressing them, by their full names. With all this intermarriage the health and vigor of the Amish today speak well for the soundness of the original stock. On the other hand, close intermarriage is not encouraged. A young Amishman from Lancaster County will often visit another Amish community—down Dover way, perhaps, or up in the Kishacoquillas Valley, or one of the western settlements—to seek out a wife.

The Amish insist on a rural way of life for all their people. Although a few of them may live in small villages, the church forbids them to live in towns and cities. Nor does a single Amish family live off by itself among more worldly people; they always settle in colonies. When a new settlement is made, enough families move to the new colony to form a religious unit and to a lesser degree a self-sustaining economic unit as well. In this way their ancient customs and beliefs are preserved.

The family farm is usually inherited by the youngest son. By the time a man is ready to retire, the older sons are usually settled on farms of their own; the youngest son is the one who stays at home. Even when an Amishman retires, he does not move into town. A part of the spacious farmhouse is set aside for him. This is the *Grossdawdy* (Grandfather) house, where he has his own separate establishment. The farm has been his life, and he very wisely stays there. A horse and wagon are always reserved for his use so that he can be free to come and go as he wishes. From time to time he may help with the work on the farm just as his wife may lend a helping hand with the sewing. Living in a house of their own yet surrounded by grandchildren, an aged Amishman and his wife spend the latter days of their life in quiet and happiness. When they have enough of grandchildren and relatives, they can retire into their own part of the house and need not emerge for a week of Sundays. As the *Grossdawdy* house has its own kitchen, the elderly Amishwoman can prepare a favorite dish for her husband or whip up a batch of cookies for her grandchildren whenever the fancy strikes her. Beyond the shadow of a doubt the Amish have hit upon the perfect solution for the care of the aged. Even in the case of a man with no children, a part of the farmhouse is reserved for his use when he sells the farm. No Amishman ever goes to an old people's home.

With each farmer hoping to settle all his sons on farms of their own, there is an eager and everlasting search for land. Almost all farms put up for sale in the Amish country are bought by the Amish. Especially great is the rivalry where House Amish meet Church Amish. There land values have doubled. Since there are not enough farms to go around and since urban life is out of the question, the Amish have been forced to seek out farms elsewhere. Hence the recent colonies in Lebanon County and in Berks.

The Amish farms along the two branches of the Conestoga or those farther south on the Lancaster Plain are paragons of neatness. Hardly a weed is to be seen in the fields. The houses and barns and tobacco sheds have all been painted; the fields are plowed right up to the fences, the ground harrowed so fine that it looks as though it has been gone over with a currycomb. Many farms elsewhere are rich and prosperous, but none but the Amish farms have been scrubbed behind the ears.

An intense love of the land distinguishes the Amish and Mennonites from other American farmers. Others may boast of the number of bushels of wheat they harvest, of the fertility of the soil; so do the Amish and Mennonites. Yet the Amish and Mennonites never dream of selling out and retiring to Los Angeles in their old age. They are wedded to their farms for life.

One of the most valuable heritages that the Amish and the Mennonites brought with them to America was their method of farming. In their efforts to make a living on the poor soil of the Swiss mountain valleys in which they found refuge, they were the first people in central Europe to experiment with new crops, new feed for their cattle, new ways of fertilizing the land. When they moved down to the Rhineland, they were able to apply these new methods to rich soil. Different communities tried different experiments, of which they kept one another informed so that all might benefit from the success of one. This gave the early Amish and Mennonites a broader point of view than that of the ordinary farmer, whose horizon was bounded by the hills of his own parish. Such advances in farming as diversified farming, rotation of crops, and improving the soil by fertilizing it with barnyard manure and by growing red clover were first put into general use in America in southeastern Pennsylvania and were more widely practiced on Amish farms than on any others. Furthermore, their stock was well housed. In fact, to this day the stock is better housed on the farms of southeastern Pennsylvania than anywhere else in America.

All the Amish farms are family farms worked by a man and his sons; they are never "factories in the fields." Oddly enough, though very few Amish smoke, tobacco is the big money crop on many Amish farms. Not all the Amish are easy in their consciences about growing tobacco, and in recent years many have replaced it with tomatoes, potatoes, or peas; yet tobacco is still generally grown by most Amish farmers. The crop is carefully rotated so that it does not wear out the soil. With the

Amish the land comes first and the tobacco crop second. An Amishman who does not give his land proper care is brought up before the church. He who robs the soil sins against both God and man. Impairing the fertility of the soil is as undoubtedly a sin as adultery or theft. In the Amish country the abandoned fields so characteristic of the old tobacco plantations of tidewater Maryland and Virginia are unknown. This is one part of America in which the land is as fertile as it was two or more centuries ago, when the forests were first cut down. The House Amish in their concern for the land even go so far as to reject tractors for use in the fields. Ingenious though tractors may be, a farmer gets from them no manure to put on the land. Instead three horses abreast pull the plow and five the disk harrow. There is considerable dis-satisfaction on the part of some of the Amish with the ban on tractors, especially when they see the excellent use made of them by non-Amish farmers. There is a wide use of most other machinery, such as culti-vators, self-binders, and sprayers, although none of it may be run by electricity. The ban on the use of electricity is hard on the Amish engaged in dairying or poultry raising, both of which have been on the increase on Amish farms in recent years. They do not mind putting up with coal-oil lamps in the house, but they would like to use elec-tricity in the cowsheds and henhouses. There is likewise some objection among the House Amish to the ban on trucks for farm work. Once more they see how useful trucks are to their more worldly neighbors. In Ohio a group of Amish go to the extreme of rejecting mules for farm work on the ground that they are "unnatural" animals. The Lancaster County Amish, however, use mules with equanimity. On the other hand, the Amish are undeniably superior farmers and are generally eager to adopt modern farming methods. Contour plowing, though, has made slow progress among them, possibly because so many of the Pennsylvania Amish live on the flat Lancaster Plain or in rela-tively level valleys. Yet they are no longer as far in advance of the ordinary farmer as they once were. Their extreme conservatism has held them back.

Sometimes the unworldly attitude of the Amish strikes more mate-rialistic men as incredible. For instance, the Amish refuse to ship out milk on Sunday. No arguments the Philadelphia milk dealers have been able to think up have made them change their minds. Since they refuse to permit their milk to be picked up on Sunday morning, there is a Saturday evening collection of milk an hour or two after milking time. The Sunday morning milk is used on the farm, while that of Sunday evening is combined with Monday morning's milking.

When the New Deal went in for restriction of crops, the Amish grew less wheat and raised fewer pigs but declined to accept any money for the smaller yield of wheat or the lesser number of porkers. Diogenes could not have been more startled when he found his honest man than the officials in Washington were when the Amish refused to pocket the money the government was eager to pay them. The Amish fear of the "unequal yoke," of joining with people of the world, was responsible for this decision—though in the end a few broke down and accepted the government's money. This principle of the "unequal yoke" also prevents the Amish from joining farmers' cooperatives when farmers other than Amish are members. To a cooperative supported only by the Amish, such as the Lancaster County Swiss cheese plant, they have no objection, for there the principle of the "unequal yoke" does not apply.

The Amish have the social security that the government desires for all the people. The specters of unemployment and poverty in illness or old age have been successfully laid by generosity, common sense, and hard work. Their belief in the brotherhood of man is not mere lip service reserved for Sundays; they live their religion. If a man with a wife and four or five small children is taken sick, his neighbors come to his help. They do his chores and the farm work until he recovers his health. Enough will turn up to harvest a crop in a single day. Or suppose he dies. What happens to his wife and children? If the wife's parents are still living, she will very likely move back home; or she may move in with her husband's parents or a brother or brother-in-law, an uncle or an aunt. Even in those rare cases when there is no relative to take her in, the Amish will provide a place for her and for her children.

If a man's barn burns down, that is an act of God. The Amish decline to oppose God's will by putting lightning rods on their barns, although if they buy a farm with lightning rods on the barn they generally let them stay. They will not take out fire and storm insurance with a company that might "yoke" them with worldly people; instead they have formed an Amish aid society, to which most of the Amish in Lancaster County, the Kishacoquillas Valley, and Delaware belong and which effectively takes the place of the commercial companies. Life insurance, however, is absolutely forbidden. Who are they to stand in the way of the Lord? It is God's right to end a man's life when He sees fit. Yet they believe that man should treat with tenderness one whom the Lord has smitten. If a man's barn burns down and his cattle and crops are destroyed, his fellow Amishmen—and often his more worldly neighbors as well—gather from all over the countryside to clear away the charred timbers and raise a new barn. They come not singly but by the hundreds. By evening the barn is virtually built, all except for a handful of nails still to be driven or a few finishing touches that a man can do by himself. In the days before the Amish aid society was formed, they contributed money, cattle, and grain as well; all shared in the loss. Plows, harrows, and the essential farm machinery were bought. Horses and cows replaced the ones lost—not as many, perhaps, as before, since a man must bear a part of his misfortune himself. But it is the community as a whole, and not the individual, who bears the burden. The wind is tempered to the shorn lamb.

This is clearly not the policy of rugged individualism, of each man for himself and the devil take the hindmost. This is the kingdom of God on earth—or at least as close to it as the Amish have been able to come. Competition has not been ruled out: it has been combined with cooperation. To rugged individualism has been added brotherly love. As far as possible each Amishman supports himself, his wife, and his children.

The Amish attitude toward the accumulation of wealth is in direct contrast to that held by most of their fellow Americans. In moderation wealth is good, but by moderation they really mean moderation. Enough money to enable a man to give each of his sons a farm or help him acquire one is as much as anyone should desire. The accumulation of wealth as such is sanctioned nowhere in the Bible: a truth that the Amish alone among Christian churches seems to have recognized. Many of the more usual ways of making money, such as investments in stocks and bonds, are regarded as sinful by the Amish. This attitude has helped them to weather financial depressions with greater ease than their fellows who tried to make a killing in the stock market.

The Amish believe in hard work. In their interpretation of the seven deadly sins, tremendous emphasis is put on sloth. The Amish farmer gets up between four and five, and after a few chores he has breakfast at five-thirty. From six until dinner at eleven he works in the fields in spring and summer and fall and in the barn stripping tobacco in winter. During the hot sultry days of summer he may rest for half an hour or even an hour after dinner before going out to the fields again. Supper at four-thirty is followed by the evening chores and often more work in the fields until dark; then to bed at eight-thirty or nine. Few people in America work so hard.

His life, though, is not without its joys. He finds pleasure in his work: in seeing the wheat sprout, in watching the tobacco leaves grow more gigantic day by day, in rubbing down his sleek horses, in whitewashing the springhouse, even in hauling manure to his fields. The thousand and one tasks of the farm give him a solid satisfaction. He takes time out for fun, too—not for movies, pinochle, or bingo—but for auctions, for weddings, one might almost say for funerals, and above all for visiting back and forth. Visiting is the Amishman's chief diversion. He is so extraordinarily fond of visiting his relatives and friends that church is held only every other Sunday. Half the Sundays in the year are "off" Sundays reserved for visiting. This is the time for the *freindschaft* [1] to get together. Out in the barnyard the boys play corner ball and *blum-sock* [2] or try their skill at wrestling. On the pavement by the grape arbor the girls skip rope. The women, sitting in the shade of the porch or hugging the stove, have time for a good talk. The men go out to the barn to look over the stock and talk crops. These are simple pleasures but very real ones. Thanksgiving, Christmas, Second Christmas, Good Friday afternoon, Easter Monday, and Whitmonday are other favorite visiting times. In winter or sometimes in August, when there is a lull in field work, long visits are common. These may last for several days or even several weeks. This is the time to visit other Amish communities, to go up to the Kishacoquillas Valley or down to Dover or even out Indiana way. Or there may be a barn-raising in his own township. The cornhusking bees, threshing bees, apple-butter cookings, and quilting parties are largely things of the past. Only the barn-raisings are as common in this century as they were in the last. With a huge dinner served to all the workers, this occasion is turned into a frolic. Quite as much as the family gathering and the barn-raising the Amishman loves an auction. These are usually held in February and March, when farm work is light. The Amish gather from miles away for a country sale. Even if he doesn't want to buy anything, it's too good a chance to see old friends to stay away.

The young people have a somewhat gayer time than the settled married folk. The young men and women growing up together have ample opportunity to get to know one another. The innocent country

[1] The whole relationship.
[2] A game played with a knotted grain bag.

pleasures of the Amish youth are those of early America. Although the cornhusking parties followed by supper and games on the threshing floor are rarely held today, games are often combined with the Sunday evening singings. These folk games, Skip to My Lou, Twin Sisters, There Goes Topsy Through the Window, O-h-i-o, Six-Handed Reel, and others, often involve kissing. The Sunday-night singings are the principal diversion of Amish youth. The young folks of the House Amish usually meet early on a Sunday evening at the village of Intercourse, where they learn at which farm the singing is to be held. At Intercourse, too, they pick up their partners. A young Amishman will drive his sister to Intercourse, but there he swaps her for somebody else's sister. After the singing, which breaks up before midnight, he drives the girl of his choice to her home. The singings start soberly enough with the singing of hymns. About ten o'clock, though, the old folks go to bed and the young people turn to the games. In the "pickings" with which the games start the girls pick the boys and the boys pick the girls until rows of them, first a girl and then a boy, fill the benches on the threshing floor. Suddenly they all stand up, and each boy kisses the girl on his right and then the girl on his left. After that fun the "pickings" start all over again. Sooner or later they take time out for other games and for cider or coffee, cookies, and snitz pie.

The singings are not exactly decorous. In the kissing games the young men find that pretty girls have the same effect on them that they have on young men the world over. The Amish blades cut up and show off. On the way home the young bloods show their girls—and the other fellow—how much speed their horses have. Not that the Amish boys are mired in sin; they are not. It is only that the Amish are such a godly people that it comes as something of a shock to find even an Amish youth of sixteen going in for high jinks.

No myth about the Pennsylvania Dutch has established itself more firmly in the public mind than the one of the Amishman painting his gate blue to tell the world that he has a daughter ready for marriage. Picturesque though this legend may be, there is not a grain of truth in it. Some gates, it is true, are painted blue. Blue is a favorite color of the Amish. The Amishman's kitchen and his farm wagon are likely to be painted blue; his shirt and his sons' shirts, too, may be blue. Furthermore, Amishmen do at times have daughters ready for marriage. But there is no connection between their daughters, the color blue, and the front gate. This is merely a legend that has caught the public fancy

Amish courting customs are sufficiently curious to stand in no need of legendary additions. Most of the courting is done on the sly, with all the secrecy of courtly love of medieval days. Never do you see an Amish boy and girl buss one another openly on the streets. The boy goes courting only by night. When late evening has come and the girl's parents are safely in bed, he goes a-wooing. In the old days a handful of pebbles or corn tossed against the pane of the girl's bedroom window let her know that her suitor had come; now a flashlight turned on her window informs her of her lover's presence. Usually the girl, who has only pretended to go to bed to hoodwink her parents, comes down and lets the young man in. Today most of the courting takes place in the kitchen, where a coal fire is burning in the range. In the past, however, the young couple often resorted to bundling just as they did in New England. It is possible that bundling may linger on in some Amish communities, although everywhere the church fathers condemn the practice. Even in bundling the Amish were characteristically moral. There were no shotgun weddings. Amish children born out of wedlock are as rare as the phoenix. There may be one every hundred years but no oftener than that. If accused by his friends or his family of paying suit to a girl, a young Amishman lies blatantly. This is regarded as a white lie wholly justified.

When finally the youth has made his choice and won the girl's consent, he sends an older man, a *Schteckleimann*,[3] usually a deacon of the church, to ask the approval of the girl's parents. If they consent, the intentions of marriage are announced in church at least a fortnight before the wedding. As soon as the banns are read, the prospective bridegroom leaves the meeting and drives directly to the girl's home, where on that particular Sunday she is awaiting him.

Nowhere does the individual quality of the Amish way of life appear more clearly than in their weddings. These are always big affairs. They take place in the fall after the harvest is in, for the farmers have more leisure at that time and there is an abundance of food. The weddings are held only on Tuesdays or Thursdays. Wednesday is believed to be an unlucky day and so is Friday. There is not enough time to get ready for a Monday wedding, since no unnecessary work may be done on Sunday; and Saturday is too close to Sunday. No engraved invitations are sent out. Instead the groom calls in person on all the people to be invited. As there are sometimes two hundred or more guests, for

[3] A secret intermediary

often the whole meeting and most of the relatives on both sides are asked to the wedding, this is no light chore.

Often friends of the family are asked to help with the baking and the cooking. There may be fully a score of helpers, since both a wedding dinner and wedding supper are served. Sometimes the marriage ceremony may be performed at a neighbor's house because all the available space at the bride's house is needed for the extensive tables for the wedding dinner.

At the wedding there is the usual Amish order of service. With the announcement of the first hymn, the bride with her two bridesmaids, known as "waiters," and the groom with his attendants, also known as waiters, accompany the preachers to the stairs. The waiters stay below while the bride and groom go upstairs with the ministers, there to receive instructions on the duties and ethics of marriage. When the bride and groom come downstairs, their waiters rejoin them and they all take their places on two benches before the ministers, the three women facing the three men. The main sermon preached is a standard wedding sermon that is preached at all Amish weddings. Among the House Amish the preachers dwell upon the marriage of Tobias and Sarah from the Book of Tobit. At the end of the sermon the wedding ceremony is performed.

In other particulars as well an Amish wedding differs from the usual church wedding. There is no bride's bouquet, no wedding ring, no one to give her away. The bride is dressed in the traditional garb of the young, unmarried Amishwoman—black cap, white kerchief and apron, and her dress of any of the usual Amish colors, but never white. The white kerchief and apron will be put away to be kept for her shroud. Only when she is dead can she wear them again.

The wedding dinner is a bountiful one, thanks to the biblical example of the wedding feast at Cana. There are roast chicken, stewed chicken, fried ham, mashed potatoes, sweet potatoes, bread and butter, apple butter and jellies, and numerous pies and cakes. The wedding supper is almost as ample: cold turkey, stewed chicken, ham, roast beef, bread and butter, jellies, cakes, stewed and canned fruit, and wine. The most elaborate cake is placed in front of the bride.

The seating arrangement for the wedding dinner is an unusual one. Tables are placed together to form a large hollow square with one side open. The bride and groom are seated at one of the outer corners, which is known as the bride's corner. On the bride's left are her waiters with the young unmarried women beyond them; on the groom's right are his waiters and still more unmarried women beyond them. On the other side of the table are the young unmarried men. Beyond the young unmarried people are the young married women, with the young married men across the table from them. The middle-aged married people follow next and finally the old people. As it is not often that all these can be seated in one room, tables for the old people, and usually for the middle-aged couples as well, are set up in the downstairs bedroom and in the kitchen. At the wedding supper they all sit in couples.

After the wedding dinner the three traditional marriage hymns of the Amish are sung. These are followed by more hymns, which finally give way to conversation. About four o'clock the young people go out to the barn to play the usual folk games. This is the last day on which the bride and groom may play these games. After this day they are a sober married couple. Sometime or other during the day the young men get hold of the groom and toss him over a fence to show him that they have cast him out from among them, that he is now "on the other side."

After the wedding supper there are more hymns. Then the cooks come in with brass dippers to collect money for their work. They put on quite an act, extolling their skill, exaggerating their labor, and beseeching the guests to take pity on their poverty. The guests feign reluctance to pay, but in the end each one permits himself to part with a coin or two. The money collected is divided among the cooks, and with it each buys some little memento to mark the day. Finally there are more games on the threshing floor until late in the evening the bride and groom slip away to their room. This is the signal for the guests to leave.

A day or two after the wedding the groom brings the bride to his own home. Instead of a honeymoon they start on a round of visits, staying overnight at the home of each uncle and aunt and often cousins as well and calling on every person who had been invited to the wedding. At every house at which they stay a bountiful dinner is served to them, and at this time many of their wedding presents are given to them. After a fortnight or more of such visits, they at last move into their own home.

The parents of both the bride and groom do their utmost to give the young couple the best possible start in life. It is the dream of every Amish farmer to give each of his sons a farm. If the home farm is large

enough, it will be divided and a new house built for the young couple;
or if the groom's father has enough money he will buy a farm for his
son. At the very least the father will give his son some money toward
a farm; and usually some other Amishman will advance the rest of the
money, accepting a mortgage at low interest and far beyond what any
bank would consider the margin of safety. This is done partly from the
Amishman's desire to keep his money in land but even more from the
wish to help young members of his faith establish themselves. Nor do
the young couple go empty-handed to their farm. All through his youth
the groom has worked on his father's farm without wages, and now his
father does what he can to set him up as a farmer and head of a household. He gives his son a horse and harness, a cow, a plow and harrow
and possibly some other farm machinery, a pig or two, some furniture
for the house, and probably some dishes and linen. The bride as her
dower may bring a cow and some chickens, a stove, a cupboard, a
table, a bureau, a bed and bedclothing, six chairs and a rocker to
match, linen, dishes, hams, potatoes, and a barrel of flour. Between the
two families the house will be fairly well furnished. The wedding gifts
from their relatives and friends include not only such usual presents
as dishes, clocks, lamps, and linen but also such eminently practical
gifts as axes, hammers, wrenches, and other tools necessary on a farm.

Amish funerals are as distinctive as the weddings. They are always
held in the home, never at funeral parlors. They are the acme of
simplicity. There is no crape at the door and no flowers at the funeral.
The coffin, usually of plain walnut boards, is made by a local carpenter.
Until the state law required embalming, the body, instead of being
handed over to an undertaker, was washed and dressed by two members
of the same sex. For a woman the shroud is always white—cap, kerchief, apron, and dress; for a man, a white shirt and a black suit. For
this occasion not only the family but almost all attending the funeral
wear black. Four friends of the family dig the grave and act as pallbearers. It is they, too, who make the round of friends and relatives and
invite them to the funeral; and it is they who take the meeting benches
to the house for the funeral. The coffin is hauled to the graveyard in
the *Todtenwagen* (hearse), a spring wagon very like the Amish carriages but somewhat larger, or one of the farm wagons may be used.
Friends come in to prepare the funeral dinner, which, like the old-time
funeral dinners so common in many country sections, is more of a feast
than a plain dinner. At the funeral service no hymns are sung. There is

an introductory sermon, then silent prayer and reading from the Scriptures; then the main funeral sermon, which never takes the form of a eulogy; and finally a prayer from the prayer book and the benediction. At the cemetery there is a short service at the grave. Then the pallbearers fill in the grave while the family remains. When the mound has been rounded off, the minister reads a hymn, after which they all repeat the Lord's Prayer silently. Then the minister speaks a few more words and pronounces the benediction.

Amish graveyards are very plain. Among the Church Amish the graveyard is usually next to the church; among the House Amish it is down a lane, off in the fields. The tombstones are simple ones with rounded tops, bearing usually only the name and dates of birth and death. No shrubs, neither box nor yew nor rose, are planted in the graveyard; no flowers are ever placed on the graves. The Amish very seldom visit the graveyards. Once a year the men of the meeting will set aside a day to fill up sunken graves, set up fallen tombstones, and if necessary mow the grass; but often a few sheep are kept in the graveyard so that the grass is always well clipped. The graveyard is owned by the whole meeting. Individual members are never charged for lots. If more land is needed to extend the graveyard, it is bought by the whole congregation.

It is in their views on education and politics that the Amish, like the Mennonites, are most open to criticism. Except for a mastery of the three R's they are opposed to education. They maintain that book learning is not needed to make a good farmer or a farmer's wife. High school is bad for a boy or girl, they insist, and college even worse. The knowledge acquired is of little practical value, while the way of life there makes an Amish boy or girl soft and lazy. They are ruined for hard work on the farm. Better to know the rotation of crops, or how to make a man's shirt or cook apple butter. The years a boy spends in high school are the very ones in which he should be trained for the work he is to do. And the only way a man can learn a job, the Amish maintain, is by doing it. This is the theory behind the old apprentice system that worked successfully for centuries.

The Amish look around them and see the deserted Episcopal and Presbyterian churches, the abandoned Quaker meetinghouses—all of them belonging to people who believed in education. Once there were thriving communities supporting these churches; now the Episcopalians and Presbyterians and Quakers have vanished, and Amish and Mennonites farm the land these people once owned. Even land owned for generations by Lutheran and Reformed families is now being bought up by Poles and Italians and by the Amish and Mennonites as the sons and daughters of the "church people" drift into the towns and cities. The Amish think they know the moral of this. If they are to perpetuate their way of life, if their children are to plow the fields their fathers plowed before them, education beyond the three R's must be resisted. The Amish believe that it was God's intention for man to till the soil and tend his flocks. God put man on the land, and man is right only as long as he stays on the land. Certainly the most superficial examination of the Amish and Mennonite farms shows that their ability to cling to their farms has been a positive benefit to American agriculture. On the other hand, the Amish must depend on people of other faiths for their doctors, dentists, and veterinarians.

The Amish belief in the little red schoolhouse is a part of their attempt to maintain their way of life. As the Amish form self-contained communities in which they work with other Amishmen, go to Amish meetings, and visit back and forth with other Amish families, they naturally want their children to go to school with Amish children. If the children go to a one-room country school, most of the other children there will be Amish; but if they go to a large consolidated township school, the Amish are likely to be seriously outnumbered. Not only must they ride in busses, to which their elders object, but the other children are likely to poke fun at them. They are exposed daily to worldly ways, for most consolidated schools pride themselves on being modern: they have entertainments and dances and plays; they have bands and orchestras; they put emphasis on sports. Of none of these can the Amish approve. From the Amish point of view the little red schoolhouse is far better and much less expensive.

The ambitious youth desiring an education has a hard row to hoe if he is born an Amishman. He must rebel. He may even have to break all family ties and religious ties too. Usually such a person ceases to be an Amishman. But such a youth is extremely rare among the Amish. Most Amish boys and girls have no desire to rebel; they fit into the life easily. As the Amish have been farmers for centuries, farming is in their blood. From his early childhood the Amish boy has been brought up with the expectation of becoming a farmer. At eight or nine he is helping with the chores and able to take a hand at milking. He has a calf of his own and possibly a pig and some chickens to raise and market.

He has a little garden in which to grow some vegetables. When he is a little older, he is given a small plot of land on which he raises a highly profitable crop of tobacco. Not that he works all the time. Like other boys he will go swimming, not in a public pool, but in a near-by creek or mill dam. Between sixteen and eighteen he gets his own horse and buggy. These children do not have a bad time of it, as their roguish faces clearly show. If the Amish didn't love children, they wouldn't have so many of them. And among the Church Amish, at least, the size of the family is a matter of choice.

When it comes to politics, the Amish try to live apart from the world. They keep in mind the biblical admonition to "come out from among them" and be separate (II Corinthians 6:17). In general they neither vote nor hold office themselves, nor will they serve on a jury. It is only when they are faced with the shutting down of their one-room schoolhouses or the neglect of the roads leading to their farms that they will turn out to vote. Then they come in droves, bringing their wives with them. Even then they will vote only for school director or road supervisor; never for a county office, much less for a state or federal one. But if worst comes to worst, they will serve on the school board or become road supervisors themselves. Normally they are exemplary and law-abiding people. As far as the Amish go, the Lancaster County police can sleep the year around. But if they have to choose between conscience and jail, conscience wins every time. Their refusal to accept the rights and duties of citizenship fills many of their fellow Americans with misgiving. One cannot help wishing that they had for the country as a whole some of the same feeling of responsibility they have for the members of their own sect. But to the larger issues of the nation they close their eyes, as they do almost invariably to those of the state and even the county. For the most part they see no farther than the township. Others may make the laws; if their consciences permit, they will obey them.

One last point: the place of the Amish women. Broadly speaking, it is in the home, as it was for women generally during the Victorian Age. There is no belief in the equality of the sexes. That the men should sit in front in meeting and the women behind is characteristic. The Bible puts it very clearly in I Corinthians 11:7-9: "He [man] is the image and glory of God: but the woman is the glory of the man. For the man is not of the woman; but the woman of the man. Neither was the man created for the woman; but the woman for the man." That, for the Amish, settles the matter. As the Amish woman is the domestic type, she does not demur. There are no career women among them. The Amish women stay in their homes busy with household duties, with the care of their husbands and children. Occasionally they may "stand market" or go shopping in Lancaster or Reading. Although their families are usually large, this is as they would have it. In an Amish home babies are genuinely welcome, whether the first or the twelfth. The peace and happiness in the faces of the Amish women show that this is the life they want for themselves. There is no hint of rebellion. Fortunately there are few spinsters among the Amish, for this way of life has no place for the unmarried. A very few become schoolteachers or nurses, but most live the life of an "aunt" in the home of a married brother or sister.

Probably the Amish are best summed up in a remark once made by Oliver Allston, which perhaps should be chalked up to the credit of his creator, Van Wyck Brooks. "All the old sects have not gone," he wrote. "Remember Pennsylvania, and thank heaven for the Amish." To which I can only say "Amen!"

The Brethren, The Schwenkfelders, and Other "Plain People"

The Brethren, or Dunkards, are the last important group of "plain people." Although they prefer to call themselves the Church of the Brethren, or more simply, the Brethren, their fellow Pennsylvania Dutchmen use the more vivid terms of Dunkard and Dunker. These popular names, meaning one who dips, seize upon the central tenet of their faith that sets them off from other churches, baptism by immersion in a flowing stream. In general the Dunkard ideas of baptism were derived from the early Anabaptists and the Mennonites, but to these they added the further refinements of trine immersion and a flowing stream. Their leader was Alexander Mack, a native of the Palatinate, who was one of a small group of deeply religious men who met together for study of the Bible and worship. Having come to the conclusion that trine immersion in the name of the Father, the Son, and the Holy Ghost was of paramount importance, they went down to the river and, kneeling in the stream, baptized one another. Thus was founded the Church of the Brethren in 1708 in the town of Schwarzenau on the banks of the river Eder in Westphalia.

This new religion immediately attracted much attention and soon began to make converts. Since many of the early Brethren had been members of the Reformed Church, this older Protestant church was bitter and resorted to persecution to stamp out the new sect. Many of the Brethren fled to Krefeld on the lower Rhine; but hearing of the religious freedom of Penn's new colony, twenty families consisting of one hundred and twenty people set sail for America. Arriving in Philadelphia in 1719, they settled in Germantown. On Christmas Day, 1723, the first congregation was organized with seventeen members who had been baptized in Germany and six converts baptized that day in the Wissahickon. At this first baptismal service in America they had to break the ice on the creek before the new members could be baptized. After the ceremony they held their first love feast and communion at the home of Johannes Gumre, one of their members. The following year a second congregation was formed at Coventry and a third at Conestoga. In 1729 their leader, Alexander Mack, came to America, bringing with him most of the other Brethren. As the few who were left in Europe returned to the Reformed Church, the whole church may be said to have been transferred to Pennsylvania.

Like the Quakers, the Brethren were a church without a creed. Later in the century, when Franklin suggested to Michael Wohlfahrt, an Ephrata Dunkard, "that it might be well to publish the articles of their belief and the rules of their discipline," Wohlfahrt replied:

When we were first drawn together as a society, it had pleased God to enlighten our minds so far as to see that some doctrines, which were esteemed truths, were errors, and that others which we had esteemed errors were real truths. From time to time He has been pleased to afford us further light, and our principles have been improving and our errors diminishing. Now we are not sure that we have arrived at the end of this progression and at the perfecting of spiritual and theological knowledge, and we feel that if we should once print our confession of faith, we should feel ourselves as if bound and confined by it, and perhaps be unwilling to receive further improvement, and our successors still more so, as concerning what their elders and founders had done to be something sacred—never to be departed from.

Franklin's reply shows the admiration he felt for an attitude so modest and reasonable:

This modesty in a sect is perhaps a single instance in the history of mankind. Every other sect, supposing itself in the possession of all truth and that those that differ are so far in the wrong, like a man traveling in foggy weather, those at some distance before him on the road he sees wrapped up in the fog, as well as those behind him, and also the people in the fields on each side, but near him all appears clear, though in truth he is as much in the fog as any of them.

Like the Quakers, too, the Brethren believed in nonresistance, which in those early days they took with the utmost seriousness. One of their members, Jacob Neff, had built a flour mill in a lonely spot north of the Blue Mountains. During the French and Indian War he was attacked by the Indians, and after killing two of them he fled to his neighbors for help. By the time he got back, his mill had been burned to the ground. But it was the taking of life, even in self-defense, rather than the burned mill that troubled his fellow Brethren. Neff was expelled from the church, and when he rebuilt his mill the Brethren were forbidden to carry their grain to it.

The Brethren's emphasis on the simple life also endeared them to the Friends. This insistence on plain and unpretentious living, which became almost the hallmark of the "peace churches," was borrowed from the Mennonites and the Quakers. The Brethren were the most eclectic of the churches of colonial Pennsylvania. Except for their belief in trine immersion there was little that was original in their religion. Like the Mennonites, they were congregational in church government. Their dress closely resembled that of the Mennonites and Quakers: for the men, broadbrim hats, coats without lapels, and bushy beards; for the women, small white house caps and for outdoors slightly larger bonnets, simple dresses with high necks and long sleeves, and capes instead of coats. As gold was regarded as a "signal to Satan," jewelry was forbidden. Their churches were plain meetinghouses, again like those of the Mennonites and Quakers, in which the congregation sat on backless benches. They followed the example of the Mennonites and Quakers once more in forbidding their members to take an oath. And last of all, they disapproved of going to law. Only when he had the sanction of the church was a Dunkard permitted to bring suit.

It is their method of baptizing that sets the Brethren apart from other Protestant sects. No other religious body insists on dipping, three times face forward, in a flowing stream. Baptism usually takes place in the spring of the year; but sometimes, as in that first Christmas Day ceremony in the Wissahickon, it is in the winter and the ice must be broken, not once but two or three times, before the ceremony can be performed. The person to be baptized and the bishop usually wade out into the stream until the water is well above their knees. Then the candidate for baptism kneels while the bishop prays—nor are his prayers always marked by brevity. The immersion is complete. The bishop places his hand on the aspirant's head and three times dips him face forward under the water. Once baptized, the newly made Dunkard hurries to a farmhouse, sometimes a full mile away, to change into dry clothes. Tradition among the Brethren has it that no one ever catches cold, let alone pneumonia, from this experience.

Another feature of the worship of the Brethren that has attracted much attention is the love feast. The service begins with the singing of hymns—vigorous, warmhearted singing unaccompanied by an organ or any other musical instrument. After half an hour of singing one of the Brethren rises to offer testimony to the divine power and love of the Lord in the manner of the old-fashioned "experience meeting." Intermingled with this are more hymns, which are followed by sermons, one by the bishop and several by other preachers. After this is the foot washing, which begins on the men's side of the church. With a towel tied around his waist, one of the men, usually the bishop, washes and dries the feet of the man next to him, who in turn performs this rite for the man beside him, until each man has washed the feet of another man and has had his own feet washed. In a similar fashion the women on their side of the church wash one another's feet.

Although this strikes many Protestants as a curious ceremony, none of the rites of the Christian church is more fully sanctioned by the words of Christ. The puzzle here is not why foot washing is an important rite among the Brethren but why it is not practiced by all Christian churches. The thirteenth chapter of St. John shows what emphasis Christ put upon foot washing:

Jesus knowing that the Father had given all things into his hands, and that he was come from God, and went to God;

He riseth from supper, and laid aside his garments; and took a towel, and girded himself.

After that he poureth water into a bason, and began to wash the disciples' feet, and to wipe them with the towel wherewith he was girded. . . .

So after he had washed their feet, and had taken his garments, and was set down again, he said unto them, Know ye what I have done to you?

Ye call me Master and Lord: and ye say well; for so I am.

If I then, your Lord and Master, have washed your feet; ye also ought to wash one another's feet.

For I have given you an example, that ye should do as I have done to you.

The rite of foot washing is followed by Communion, and this by a handshake symbolizing "the right hand of fellowship" and by "the holy kiss of charity" on the cheek. Each man shakes hands and exchanges kisses with the man whose feet he washed and the man who washed his feet, and so does each woman. Sometimes this kiss is given to other members of the congregation of the same sex as a sign of Christian fellowship.

Finally there is a supper in commemoration of the Passover, at which the main dish is a stew of the paschal lamb. Tables are set up in the meetinghouse or under the trees outside. Often four Brethren eat from a single bowl. Sometimes, too, there are as many as three sittings at the tables, in which case the bowls and spoons are unchanged. To ask for a clean dish or spoon would be thought a mark of pride and also a reflection on the one who had just used them. At the larger Dunkard meetings the love feast may last two days. Usually the meetinghouses have kitchens in the cellar and sometimes even sleeping quarters in the attic.

Another peculiarity of Dunkard belief is the anointing of the sick with oil in the name of the Lord. Here the Brethren have in mind James 5:14: "Is any sick among you? let him call for the elders of the church; and let them pray over him, anointing him with oil in the name of the Lord."

As in the case of the Mennonites and Amish, the Brethren ministry was uneducated. The ministers, who served without pay, were elected by individual ballot by all members of the congregation. Usually the most gifted young men were chosen. Among the Dunkards were some men of undoubted ability. Christopher Sauer, the eminent printer, was one of these. At Sauer's house in Germantown, Ludwig Hoecker in 1738 started his Sunday afternoon services for the young people of the meeting, more than forty years before Robert Raikes set up the first Sunday school in England. Conrad Beissel, the founder of the Ephrata community, was a Dunkard preacher at Conestoga for four years. But the Brethren by and large were mostly farmers, although there were a number of artisans among them, especially in the first colony in Germantown. To this day most of the Brethren are farmers.

Like so many of the other Pennsylvania Dutch, they knew good land when they saw it. Many of them settled in Lancaster County, which even in this century has more Brethren than any other single county in the country; but the growing population of southeastern Pennyslvania and the high land values led the Brethren to search for good land elsewhere. In the latter part of the eighteenth century they began to move down into Maryland and the Shenandoah Valley of Virginia, as well as farther west in Pennsylvania to the fertile valley of Morrison's Cove. In the nineteenth century many of them settled in the Miami Valley in Ohio and later in Indiana, Illinois, Iowa, and Kansas. Wherever they went they chose good land. Today a full five-sixths of their membership lives in the open country or in small country towns.

In the last half-century the Brethren have undergone a great change. Many of the peculiarities they borrowed from the Mennonites and the Quakers are disappearing, as they disappeared among the Quakers last century. Except among some of the older people in the more conservative meetings of southeastern Pennsylvania, the plain dress is vanishing. The Dunkards still dress simply, the women in quiet prints, but the plain somber colors, the white prayer caps, and the small skirtless bonnets are seldom seen. Nor are the broadbrim hats and the buttonless, high-neck coats worn very often by the men. Ornate churches with organs are replacing the simple meetinghouses. The ministers, most of whom are college-bred, are paid for their services. There are even Dunkard colleges—Juniata in Pennsylvania and Manchester in Indiana, to mention two. Nor are nearly so many of the Brethren pacifists as in former years. Each man decides for himself whether or not it is right for him to fight. Consequently, there were many Brethren, just as there were many Quakers, in the armed services during the past war. Divorce, too, is becoming more frequent among the Brethren. They still disapprove of gambling, drinking, and smoking; but in spite of their belief in "quiet moderation in all things" the Brethren are no longer a "separate" people in the sense that most of the Mennonites and all of the Amish are. Through most of their history the Brethren have been less suspicious of "the world's people" than the other "plain people." And now they are becoming one of "the world's people" themselves.

This is by no means a criticism of the Brethren, since in sloughing off many of their peculiarities they have been careful to preserve the essence of Christianity. Their heifer project is proof of that. Under this program heifers have been shipped to the war-torn countries of Europe to restore the depleted herds. This was done so that the new-born infants and mothers with babies might have milk. It was Dan West, one of the Brethren relief workers in Spain, who hit upon this idea. During the civil war in Spain he saw the disastrous effect of the lack of fresh milk on babies and nursing mothers. Long before the Second World War ended, the Brethren started to raise heifers to be shipped abroad. A group of four or more farmers would band together to provide a shipment of four or more animals, caring for them until they were from eighteen to twenty-five months old, when they were sent to Union Bridge, Maryland, to await shipment abroad. Churches in towns and other urban groups often bought calves, placing them with local farmers and paying for their care. Many others contributed money for this project. All heifers were bred before they were shipped so that on their arrival or shortly afterward there would be two heifers instead of one, or a heifer and a bull calf. Before the heifers were shipped, the Brethren made certain of the need for these cattle and the presence of enough fodder and shelter to maintain them on their arrival. The Brethren also provided men to care for the heifers during the voyage. These "seagoing cowboys" were usually ministers, school-teachers, farmers, and high-school youths. All the heifers were freely given to the people abroad; none were sold.

Before it became possible to ship heifers across the Atlantic, some were sent to Puerto Rico and Mexico and a few to some poverty-stricken areas of Arkansas, but most of the heifers were held to await the end of the war in Europe. The first European shipment was the one to Greece in June, 1945. Before the ship sailed, the heifers were consecrated in an impressive ceremony by a Greek Orthodox priest. By March, 1946, 1,138 heifers had been sent to Poland, Belgium, Czecho-slovakia, France, and Holland as well as to Greece.

In the heifer project the Brethren were soon joined by other churches, notably the Reformed Church, the Quakers, the Mennonites, and the Northern Baptists. In some places as many as twenty-five Protestant denominations joined them. Through much of the country other groups, sometimes statewide, followed this excellent Dunkard example.

The aid of the Brethren to war sufferers was not confined to heifers. Like the Mennonites and the Amish, the Brethren found themselves with plenty while people in many parts of the world were dying from hunger and cold. The Brethren, too, felt a deep shame and made up their minds to do whatever they could to provide people in need with food and clothing. Food and clothing and money for relief were collected in all sorts of ways. Often they were joined by friends and neighbors and even strangers who belonged to other churches or no church at all. In a section of Ohio where the farmers grew only enough wheat for their livestock, with perhaps a few bags left over to sell, it occurred to a farmer's wife that these people might be willing to give those few bags of wheat for relief instead of selling them. A day was set to collect the wheat, and in this one community alone a whole carload was given by the end of the day. By March, 1946, the Brethren Service Committee had shipped abroad 69 carloads of wheat, flour, corn, and oats, most of it wheat; 32 carloads of clothing and bedding, including thousands of pairs of shoes and 180,000 diapers, these last to Russia; and 8 carloads of "other commodities." Among these "other commodities" were a carload of rice; a carload of seed potatoes sent to France; 5 tons of dried milk; 10,475 packages of seeds, also to France; 24½ tons of soap to France, Holland, and Italy; 22 boxes of thread to Greece; 1,240 pounds of tools and household utensils to France; 10 large boxes of toys to Holland; and 6,750 Christmas boxes. Canned goods were sent to Finland, and 56,800 eggs for hatching to Poland. Clothing, shoes, and bedding went to France, Belgium, Holland, Italy, Greece, Russia, China, and the Philippines.

Eisenhower's mother was a member of the Church of the Brethren. At least several of the qualities the world has so much admired in Eisenhower are a part of his inheritance as a son of the "plain people": his simplicity and naturalness, his modesty and serenity, and above all his integrity. These are no small virtues, whether they be found in a man or a people.

Yet another group which may be included among the "plain people" are the Schwenkfelders, who even more than the Dunkards have lost most of their plainness. Of ancient lineage, they are the followers of an Anabaptist mystic, Kasper Schwenkfeld von Ossig, born in 1490 of an old aristocratic family in the Duchy of Leibnitz. Schwenkfeld, who was an early supporter of the Reformation in Silesia, corresponded with Luther, with whom he soon found himself in disagreement. Rejecting Luther's emphasis on the Bible, Schwenkfeld believed that the Scriptures in themselves were not enough: to them must be added the living word, or what he called "the spirit of Christ in man," better known as "the inner light," the term the Quakers gave this conception. Although this idea of "the spirit of Christ in man" or "the inner light" was an old one in the medieval church, Schwenkfeld was one of its chief proponents in the sixteenth century. In his rejection of baptism and Communion as a means of grace he also took a point of view later adopted by the Quakers. But in the importance he attached to the worship of Christ he resembled the Moravians. The Roman Catholics were mistaken in their worship of the Virgin Mary, he maintained; Christ was not from Mary but from God.

When Luther understood how radically he and Schwenkfeld disagreed, he looked upon him as a dangerous heretic. Lutherans and Jesuits vied with one another in their attempt to convert the Schwenkfelders. To escape persecution Schwenkfeld fled from one place to another, gathering around him a devoted band of followers yet making no attempt to found a separate church. It was persecution rather than any desire to form a new religion that forced the Schwenkfelders into separatism. Under the pressure of persecution they scattered throughout Silesia, Bohemia, Moravia, Swabia, Switzerland, Italy, and Holland. By 1700 all were wiped out except a remnant of fifteen hundred in the Görlitz and Liegnitz sections of Silesia. In 1720 the emperor Charles VI, through a Jesuit mission formed for the purpose, decided on their extermination. Many of them fled to Saxony, where for a time they found refuge at Berthelsdorf on the estate of Count Zinzendorf. When they were ordered to leave Saxony within a year, they determined to go to America. Zinzendorf tried to persuade them to go to Georgia, but wishing to make certain of religious freedom they came to Pennsylvania instead. Like the Amish and the Brethren, a whole religious group moved to Pennsylvania; none were left behind in Europe. On September 24, 1734, all that survived the ruthless persecution, about forty families, arrived in Philadelphia. So grateful were they to be at last in a land where they were permitted to worship as they pleased that they have observed ever since then the anniversary of the day of their arrival as *Gedächtniss Tag*, or Remembrance Day, their Thanksgiving.

In Pennsylvania the Schwenkfelders settled in what is now upper Montgomery County, mainly along the Skippack and Perkiomen, with a few in the Goshenhoppen (now Bally) section of eastern Berks and in upper Bucks and lower Northampton counties. There they live to this day, less than a dozen congregations in all—one of the smallest religious bodies in the United States.

The Schwenkfelders were so accustomed to being a hunted people, so used to remaining hidden, that for their first fifty years in Pennsylvania they built no meetinghouses or churches, though they did set up schools. There was no official ministry; instead the heads of families conducted services in one another's houses. For many years there was little attempt to organize, but in 1762 a general conference was held and a catechism and hymn book adopted. This hymn book, printed for them by Christopher Sauer, the Germantown printer, included a number of hymns by Schwenkfeld and by his followers in Pennsylvania and also some borrowed from the Moravians. The organization into a separate church did not come until 1782. For a long time brethren served as ministers without pay.

In the past two centuries the Schwenkfelders have lost most of the characteristics that set them off from the "church people." Once upon a time the women wore white caps, white kerchiefs, and long aprons; but like the Moravians and the Quakers their plain dress has long since been abandoned. Their early meetinghouses were plain and simple like Mennonite and Quaker ones; today their churches are like those of any of the "church people." Their pacifism, too, has given way to the more usual attitude toward war. During the Revolution the Schwenkfelders often got cold looks from their rebel neighbors, but since that time the Schwenkfelders have fought in every war in which America has been engaged. Even mixed marriages, which once they frowned on, are taken as a matter of course today.

Despite the loss of many of their old peculiarities the Schwenkfelders look upon themselves as a religious group different from all others. The publication of the monumental *Corpus Schwenkfeldianorum,* in which all the works of Kasper Schwenkfeld von Ossig have been collected, has served to make them aware of this difference. They are still mostly a country people with country ways. They are generous toward their poor and unfortunate. The fund early set up for the aid of their poor has never been exhausted. *Gedächtniss Tag* with its simple feast of home-made bread, butter, and apple butter has by the very choice of its foods the flavor of a country festival. This is a homecoming day for all Schwenkfelders. On this day the exiles in Philadelphia, New York, and Washington go back to Salford and Goshenhoppen, to Skippack and Worcester and Towamencin. The apple butter alone is worth the trip. Knowing housewives in near-by towns seek out a Schwenkfelder farmer to make sure of good apple butter. Yet even more noted is the Schwenkfelder cakes served at their marriage feasts. This is a raisin cake, flavored with saffron and sprinkled with sweetened crumbs, baked from an old recipe brought from Silesia, where it was known as *Streuselkuchen*. Wide as the oven door, it is baked in an old-fashioned bake oven attached to the kitchen or in a separate building near by. Another old Schwenkfelder custom, and one that deserves to be widely copied, is their gift of baskets of food to the poor on the occasion of a wedding.

These are by no means all the "plain people." Division and sub-division among the Mennonites have given rise to numerous tiny sects. One of the most important of these is the River Brethren, or Brethren in Christ, founded about the time of the Revolution. They differ from the Mennonites chiefly in their adoption of the Dunkard belief in trine immersion. As most of them live close to the Susquehanna, they were early dubbed River Brethren. The Old Order, or Yorker Brethren, most of whom live in York County, split off from the River Brethren. They have no churches or meetinghouses but, like the House Amish, hold their services in houses or barns. The United Zion's Children, or Brinserites, are a group who because of a difference of opinion over a church building left the River Brethren to follow Matthias Brinser and form a sect of their own. The River Brethren, the Yorkers, and the United Zion's Children all have in common a strong strain of mysticism and a desire to withdraw from the world. Like the Mennonites and the Amish they are strongly opposed to the use of force. All of them wear the plain dress of former centuries.

The "Church People"

It was another religious group, the "church people," Lutheran and Reformed, who gave the Pennsylvania Dutch their characteristic way of life. These two churches form the main stream of Pennsylvania Dutch culture. By and large they have made the Pennsylvania Dutchman what he is today. They gave him his ways of celebrating Christmas and Easter; they gave him his folk art, whether dower chest, *taufschein*,[1] or barn sign; to a large degree they gave him his ardent patriotism; and to nine out of every ten they gave religion.

To the Pennsylvania Dutchman not given to theology there was little difference between the two churches. The country people sometimes said, rather dryly, that the chief difference was that the Lutherans began the Lord's Prayer with *Vater unser* and the Reformed with *Unser Vater*. Very often the two churches occupied the same building. If there is a lone church out in the country or if there is only one in a town, the chances are that it is a union Lutheran and Reformed church. This was so common in the early days as to be almost the rule, and

---

[1] The decorated baptismal certificate.

even today it is quite usual. Members of the two faiths intermarried freely; people passed easily from one church to the other. That the Lutheran Church accepted the actual presence of Christ's body and blood in the bread and wine of the Communion service and that the Reformed Church regarded the bread and wine merely as symbols seldom disturbed the Pennsylvania Dutch layman. A Lutheran was a Lutheran largely because he was born and raised a Lutheran. If he married a woman of the Reformed faith, he too might become Reformed, or he might not. Having been born a Lutheran, he would probably stay a Lutheran. As a rule, though, he was well disposed toward the Reformed Church; it was the only other church to which he might conceivably belong. Often the clergy of the two churches were on friendly terms. The great Lutheran leader Mühlenberg preached the funeral sermon of the Reformed pastor Steiner. He even permitted a Reformed congregation to worship in one of his churches when it was not in use by the Lutherans. Together the two churches founded Franklin College in 1787, an experiment not wholly successful, as the Lutherans recognized when they relinquished its control to the Reformed Church. Sometimes the close association of the two churches was marred by petty criticism and bickering, an unhappy condition not unknown today.

In the early colonial period in Pennsylvania the Reformed Church was the stronger of the two. During the first half of the eighteenth century it established more congregations in Pennsylvania than the Lutheran Church. The Lutherans had been spared the religious persecution that led many of the Reformed faith to emigrate. The Peace of Augsburg in 1555 followed the principle "like master, like man." It stipulated that the religion of the subject must follow the religion of the ruler. As many of the German princes were Lutherans, there was relatively little persecution of that church. Until kindled by the mass impulse to emigrate to Pennsylvania that swept through the Palatinate like wildfire, the Lutherans for the most part were satisfied to stay at home. Members of the Reformed Church, however, were not permitted to practice their religion with the liberty they desired. In the Palatinate they were forced to share their church buildings with the Lutherans and the Roman Catholics. The use of their catechism was denied them, and Jesuits were appointed to the faculty of the University of Heidelberg, a stronghold of the Reformed Church. As a consequence the members of the church left the Palatinate by the thousand, thus converting that province from a Reformed land into a Catholic country, which it remains to this day. On the other hand, the flood of Palatine Protestants helped to make Pennsylvania a Protestant colony. By 1730 the Reformed numbered more than half of the German population of Pennsylvania. It was not till the latter half of the century that they were outnumbered by the Lutherans. Most of the Lutherans who came to Pennsylvania came to better themselves economically, not for religious reasons. Württemberg and Alsace, both of which sent many immigrants to Pennsylvania, were dominantly Lutheran; but Baden, Hesse, Nassau, Zweibrücken, Hanau, Anhalt, Lippe, and Bremen, as well as the Palatinate, Switzerland, and Holland, were Reformed centers.

Though a knowledge of the Lutheran Church may be taken for granted, many an American looks blank when the Reformed Church is mentioned and asks, "Reformed from what?" To this the Reformed theologian would reply that it is the Catholic Church reformed of abuses. In so far as the Reformed Church made a more radical break with Catholicism, it is more thoroughly Protestant than the Lutheran Church, which it thought imperfectly freed from medieval error. Because of its widespread influence on other churches, the Reformed Church has been known as "the mother of sects." While not precisely that, it has had so momentous and so pervasive an effect on other Protestant churches that few are unmarked by its influence. It was largely the Reformed view of the sacraments that Wesley expressed in his Articles of Faith. And it was the Reformed conception of the Communion, first borrowed by the Mennonites, that was adopted by the Baptists. Indeed, it is this Reformed view of the bread and wine as symbolic that has become the usual Protestant one. Furthermore, it is the Reformed system of church government that set the pattern for most Protestant churches. Though the Reformed Church with its synods, as well as the Lutheran Church with its bishops, exercised control over the individual congregations, the laymen in the Reformed Church shared this authority with the clergy. This part of the congregation in the government of the church was one of the most notable contributions of the Reformed Church to Protestantism. It was far more democratic than the authoritative government of the Roman Catholic Church or the Church of England or even the Lutheran and Moravian churches. Less shaped by the teachings of one man than Lutheranism, the Reformed Church put less emphasis on creed. This made it more flexible—an advantage when science began to affect the hold of religion on man.

The Lutheran Church is so well known that it needs only a cursory description. In middle Europe it became the dominant Protestant body. Still the most important Protestant church in Germany, it was also the state church in all three Scandinavian countries. In the United States it is one of the largest Protestant churches. In his break with the Roman Catholic Church, Luther stressed man's direct access to God as one of his chief tenets. He insisted that it was not necessary to approach God through a priest. Another essential part of Lutheran belief was the doctrine of ubiquity, in which Luther maintained that Christ's glorified body was to be found in the bread and wine of the Communion, in the table on which man wrote, even in the stone thrown by a boy—in fact, everywhere. Possibly most important of all was Luther's emphasis on the grace of God, which alone could purify sinful man. "By faith alone, without works," was a center of Luther's theology.

The Lutheran Church was more ritualistic than the Reformed Church and more conservative. Except when a wave of rationalism swept the church during the late eighteenth and early nineteenth centuries, the Lutherans have clung to the Augsburg Confession of 1530 and 1531 and to Luther's Small Catechism. The conservatism of the Lutheran Church has been most marked since the middle of the nineteenth century. Today, just as in the time of Luther, great emphasis is placed on God's grace and mercy. In the Pennsylvania graveyards of the old Lutheran churches there are none of those great mounds in which were buried the unbaptized infants, supposedly doomed to hell, that are occasionally found in the old Puritan burying grounds of New England. Yet the Lutherans had a firm belief in sin, mitigated, however, by their conviction of God's love and grace. The Reformed Church had neither as hearty a belief in the sinfulness of man nor as sure a faith in the mercy of God.

The Reformed Church had its origin in Switzerland early in the sixteenth century under the leadership of Ulrich Zwingli, born in the same year as Luther. The important conception of a free church in a free state was largely Zwingli's. The most radical difference between the Lutheran and Reformed churches was in their conception of Communion. This was dramatically revealed at Marburg in 1529 at the meeting of Luther and Zwingli. "This is my body," declared Luther, insisting on the actual presence of the body and blood of Christ in the bread and wine. Zwingli, less literal, defended his view that the bread and wine are merely symbols. When Zwingli offered his hand at the close of the meeting, Luther rejected it. "You have another spirit," he said. Zwingli's work was continued and in a sense completed by Calvin. But in Calvin's extreme views on predestination the Reformed Church of Switzerland, the Rhineland, and Holland as well as Bohemia, Hungary, and Poland parted company with the Huguenots of France, the Scotch Presbyterians, and the Puritans of England. As a whole the Reformed churches were more militantly Protestant than the Lutheran and more conscious of their difference from Rome. Another difference was the more intellectual approach to religion. Reformed theology was a closely reasoned system of belief. The Heidelberg Catechism of 1563, which was drawn up by the scholars, Olevianus and Ursinus, is evidence of this.

Of the Reformed churches the French Huguenot suffered most from persecution. After the Massacre of St. Bartholomew, the Palatinate was crowded with French Huguenot refugees. The elector Frederick III sent a military expedition under the command of his son, John Casimir, to aid the Huguenots. With the revocation of the Edict of Nantes in 1685, a still larger number of Huguenots fled to the Palatinate and other parts of Germany where the Reformed Church was powerful. Since the Reformed Church in Germany resembled the French Huguenot Church so closely, the refugees almost automatically became members of the Reformed Church.

In Switzerland and Holland, however, the Reformed Church became the national church; but since the Reformed Church believed in "a free church in a free state," its connection with the state was seldom as close as that of the Lutheran Church. In Holland the influence of Erasmus and Humanism on Zwingli and the church he founded helped to make the Reformed faith popular. In Scotland the Presbyterian Church throve mightily. In England the Puritan Church disappeared, to be succeeded by the Congregational Church and other Protestant groups. Later in Germany, where the Hohenzollerns were members of the Reformed Church, a forced marriage united the Lutheran and Reformed churches in a single national church. In Bohemia and Poland the church was wiped out by persecution; but in Hungary, despite bitter attacks, it maintained its existence. In these last three countries many of the followers of John Hus had joined the Reformed Church, those in Poland as early as 1532.

The Reformed and Lutheran churches and all the other Protestant churches of Dutch Pennsylvania were greatly influenced by the Pietism of the seventeenth and eighteenth centuries. Pietism stressed Christianity as a way of life rather than as a creed. This movement was a revolt against the dry formalism in worship and the emphasis on dogma that had become so pronounced in Germany in the latter part of the seventeenth century.

In early America the Reformed Church flourished in New York and Pennsylvania, yet even in colonial times people were puzzled by the name Reformed. Often they referred to it as the Dutch or German Presbyterian Church. Though the Reformed Church and the Presbyterian Church are sister churches, they are not one and the same. Yet when John Knox withdrew from Scotland on the accession of Mary, he preached for a time to Reformed congregations in Frankfort-on-Main and Geneva. At Geneva Knox came into contact with Calvin, by whose ideas he was so greatly influenced. It was the enthusiasm for Calvin's ideas that distinguished the Presbyterian Church from the Reformed. On Knox's return to Scotland he also introduced into the Presbyterian Church the government of the Reformed Church, which is so marked a characteristic of the Presbyterian Church that it has given that church its name. In the Reformed Church the synod, made up of clergy and elders from all the congregations, is the main governing body. A classis is a subdivision of the synod. The first synod was formed at Bern in 1528, and the first general synod met at Paris in 1559.

Lutheran and Reformed churches had been established along the Delaware for many years before the German settlers organized churches of their own. The early Swedish churches had all been Lutheran, while the Dutch founded a Reformed church at New Castle as early as 1642. Neither church was expressly invited by Penn as the "plain people" were, yet both had reached the shores of the Delaware before the Quakers. Penn looked askance at the Lutheran and Reformed churches just as he did at the Church of England; yet the Church of England was the church of his father, and the Reformed Church, for a time at least, that of his mother.

Throughout the colonial period both the Lutheran and the Reformed churches, and the Moravian as well, kept their Old World connection. In the case of the Reformed Church the connection was with the Reformed Church of Holland, which as the state church was powerful, rather than with the Reformed Church of the Palatinate, a persecuted church. Until 1793 the Reformed Church in Pennsylvania was under the cure of the Classis of Amsterdam. Only at that late date did it become an independent American church. In 1743 the Reformed synods in Holland proposed that the Dutch Reformed Church in New York, the Reformed Church in Pennsylvania, and the Presbyterian Church be united. The Presbyterians refused even to consider the union, while the Pennsylvania church, though grateful for the aid received from Holland, politely asked to be permitted to retain the old Heidelberg Catechism and the church order of the Synod of Dort. In recent years the Reformed Church in the United States, into which it grew, merged with the Evangelical Synod in North America under the name Evangelical and Reformed Church; and in 1949 the resulting body voted to join with the Congregational Christian Churches of the United States to form the United Church in Christ. This proposed merger has been forbidden by the court, on the grounds that in the Congregational Church authority rests with the congregations and not with the central governing body. This decision is being appealed.

The real founder of the Reformed Church in Pennsylvania was John Philip Boehm, a layman, who organized three churches within a few years: Falckner's Swamp, Skippack, and Whitemarsh. But it was Michael Schlatter, sent to America in 1746 by the Reformed synods of Holland to organize the Pennsylvania churches, who became the leading German Reformed clergyman of the colonial period. To prove to the people his disinterestedness, he "neither required nor received any salary for the first year." During his first years in America Schlatter assiduously visited all the scattered congregations of the church: Winchester and Woodstock and Rockingham in Virginia, as well as such nearer places as Goshenhoppen, Oley, and Tulpehocken. From 1747 to 1751, Schlatter journeyed over 8,000 miles on horseback, preaching 635 times and organizing 46 congregations into a synod. In 1751 he returned to Holland to put Pennsylvania's need before the church authorities there. In Holland, the Palatinate, and Switzerland he raised £12,000 for the churches in America in addition to securing 700 Bibles and 6 young clergymen, who were examined by the Classis of Amsterdam, ordained and commissioned for work in "the forsaken vineyard of Pennsylvania." The Reformed Church was extremely for-

tunate in having so devoted and able a leader as Schlatter; but unluckily his association with William Smith in the scheme to educate
German immigrants impaired his usefulness by making him suspect in
the eyes of many of his people. Saddened by the attacks on his motives,
he resigned and went into retirement, to emerge only during the
French and Indian War, when he served as chaplain in the 2nd Pennsylvania Battalion of Colonel Henri Bouquet's Royal Americans.

In its early years in Pennsylvania the Reformed Church seems to
have specialized in the warrior-priest. John Conrad Bucher, educated
at the University of Marburg, came to America as an officer of Dutch
troops to serve under Braddock and fought through the War of Pontiac's
Conspiracy. Ordained in 1767, he served congregations at Carlisle,
Middletown, Hummelstown, and Chambersburg and went on missionary trips as well. Bucher was the first clergyman to preach in German
beyond the Alleghenies. In the Revolution he served as chaplain in the
German Regiment under Baron von Arnt.

Though not a soldier, John Weikel of the little Wentz Reformed
Church near Kulpsville was even more bellicose. When feeling over
the Stamp Act ran high, he took as his text, "Better is a poor and a
wise child than an old and foolish king, who will no more be ad-
monished," and preached a rip-roaring sermon against George III.
Not only did he urge his parishioners to accustom their horses to gunfire
so that they would be ready for service when war broke out, but he
even showed them how to do it. Holding his horse by the bridle with
one hand, he shot off his pistol with the other. When the authorities
forced his church to dismiss him as pastor, he continued to live in the
parsonage, where passers-by were sometimes startled to see him appear
at an upstairs window and fire his gun over the head of a horse tethered
on the lawn.

A Reformed clergyman of colonial days who nearly brought the
church to grief was John Peter Miller, sent to Pennsylvania in 1730 by
the Classis of Heidelberg. His conversion to the mystical religion of
Ephrata was a severe blow to the church. Miller's devotion to his congregation at Tulpehocken coupled with his unusual learning had won
for him so great a reputation throughout the province that his conversion threatened for a time the very existence of the Reformed Church
in the colony. Only through the faithful work of many less noted men
was the church able to recover from his defection.

Since the Revolution the Reformed Church has gone its quiet way.

Although the number of its communicants is considerable, it was not until its union with other churches that it became in point of size one of the great churches of America. Still guided by the principles of the Reformation, it interprets these ideas liberally rather than literally. Possibly no other church is so fully representative of Protestantism as the Reformed Church. It may have attracted so little attention in the rest of the country because it is so typical. In a sense it is the archetype Protestant church.

The Lutheran Church was fortunate in the character of the clergy sent to minister to the early German settlers. The greatest of these was Heinrich Melchior Mühlenberg, who came to America in 1742 to be the pastor of the united congregations of Philadelphia, Trappe, and Falckner's Swamp. Nine years before his arrival these congregations had asked that a minister be sent out to them; but the authorities in Germany insisted that before a clergyman was sent the three Pennsylvania churches promise to support him. This the Pennsylvania churches refused to do; to their way of thinking it was buying a pig in a poke. Only when Zinzendorf attempted to persuade the Lutherans to join with the other Pennsylvania Dutch churches was a minister dispatched post haste to save the Pennsylvania Lutherans from Moravianism. No word of Mühlenberg's coming had preceded him. Upon his arrival he was forced to exert his powers in order to win the acceptance of all three congregations. It was well that Mühlenberg was a man both of infinite tact and of zeal. With untiring ardor he worked early and late to lay stable foundations for the church in America. Though riding a hundred miles each week to visit the three churches, he soon added a fourth, that of Germantown. Unable to find schoolmasters for the parochial schools attached to the churches, he undertook for a time the instruction of the children himself, giving a week to each school in turn. The picture of this man, educated at the University of Göttingen and one of the most erudite men in the colony, able to preach in English and Holland Dutch as well as German, teaching little boys and girls to read and write and cipher, is almost fantastic. There was no limit to Mühlenberg's devotion. He struck farther afield to visit congregations at Tulpehocken, Hanover, Monocacy, and elsewhere. These he was able to save both from the followers of Zinzendorf and from the vagabond ministers they had taken up with in want of anyone better. Within six years he organized the Ministerium of Pennsylvania, the oldest Lutheran body in America, by joining seven other churches to the three original "united congregations." He drew up a model for a church constitution and compiled a liturgy, one of great dignity, for use in these churches. The liturgy adopted was patterned after an old, conservative form then in use in the Savoy Chapel in London as well as in northern Germany and Scandinavia. In his wife and children Mühlenberg was particularly blessed. His wife was the daughter of Conrad Weiser, who was in fact if not in title Pennsylvania's ambassador extraordinary to the Iroquois and other Indian nations; while two of his sons, Peter, the general, and Frederick, the first speaker of the House of Representatives, became almost as eminent as their father. Mühlenberg's piety was so natural and sincere and his life so thoroughly Christian that he became the inspiration of Lutherans throughout the province.

Although the greatness of Mühlenberg tended to overshadow the fame of other early Lutheran ministers, Mühlenberg was by no means alone in his labors. The John Casper Stoevers, father and son, were untiring itinerant missionaries, violently orthodox, who visited one country parish after another in Pennsylvania, Maryland, and Virginia. Justus Heinrich Christian Helmuth, one of the numerous preachers trained at the University of Halle, and John Christopher Kunze, Mühlenberg's son-in-law, were but two of the many learned clergy of this period. Kunze knew Arabic and Italian in addition to the more usual Latin, Greek, and Hebrew.

Both the Lutheran and Reformed churches took pains to obtain the best clergy possible and to conduct their services with dignity. John Adams wrote of these churches from York on October 25, 1777:

The town is a small one, not larger than Plymouth. There are in it two German churches, the one Lutheran, the other Calvinistical. The congregations are pretty numerous, and their attendance upon public worship is decent. It is remarkable that the Germans wherever they are found, are careful to maintain the public worship, which is more than can be said of the other denominations of Christians this way.

The position of the Lutheran Church in colonial America was an advantageous one because of its close connection with the Church of England. As early as 1692 St. Mary's Church in the Savoy, generally known as the Savoy Chapel, had been founded in London. Lutheran influence in England was strengthened by Prince George of Denmark, consort of Queen Anne, when he endowed the German court chapel at St. James. With the death of Anne the throne passed to a Lutheran family, the house of Hanover; and Lutheran pastors from Halle occupied the pulpit at the Royal Chapel. At the accession of George I, a group of English and German divines carefully examined the doctrines of the Lutheran Church and those of the Church of England to determine wherein they differed. Episcopacy was the one great difference; otherwise the two churches were found to be very much alike. The Thirty-nine Articles agreed with the Augustan Confession so perfectly that it was decided that a Lutheran minister might preach in an Episcopal pulpit and vice versa. The Reverend Richard Peters, an Episcopal divine, preached on occasion in Mühlenberg's church at Trappe. The Reverend Mr. Duché of Christ Church took part in the consecration of Zion's Lutheran Church in Philadelphia in 1769. To enable Mühlenberg's son, the famous Peter, to preach in Virginia, where the laws of the colony refused to recognize any clergyman who had not received Episcopal ordination, he was ordained by the Bishop of London; yet he remained a Lutheran and while in London preached in the Savoy Lutheran chapel. Another Lutheran clergyman ordained in England was Bernard Michael Hansihl, who served as pastor in Lutheran churches in Frederick and Reading. After Yorktown he went into exile in Nova Scotia, where at Halifax he was able to officiate as an ordained clergyman of the Church of England, though in Pennsylvania he had been a Lutheran. Even in the early days of the Republic this attitude was unchanged. When a Lutheran joined the Episcopal Church, Bishop White of Philadelphia did not feel it necessary to repeat the rite of confirmation.

Both the Lutheran and Reformed congregations insisted on an educated clergy. Though they themselves might be simple farmers and artisans, they demanded education in their pastors. Once satisfied of the learning of their ministers, they held them in honor. In most Pennsylvania Dutch communities the clergyman stood first—higher than the "squire" or justice of the peace, the doctor or the president of the bank. Only a wealthy ironmaster would be given a place of greater respect. With his position in the community assured, the pastor was given considerable leeway in his life. Even a preacher who took to drink was looked upon by his flock not only with toleration but sometimes also with amusement.

One Lutheran pastor with a charge in eastern Berks was accustomed to stopping at the local hotel to prepare himself for his catechetical class with what he was pleased to call a "hot toddy." At a preparatory sermon to a class to be confirmed the next day it was apparent to the congregation that their pastor had imbibed so deeply that he was unable to find his way out of the morass of his sermon. He droned on and on until as it began to grow dark the congregation started to slip out of the church, whereupon one of the elders climbed into the pulpit and timidly suggested that the pastor bring his sermon to a close. "I know my business!" roared the tipsy preacher and proceeded relentlessly on with his endless sermon.

An even more extraordinary incident occurred in Bucks County at Springfield Church, which also had a preacher who had taken to drink. Things were at length in such a sorry pickle that the pastor was dismissed; but very unwisely he was given the privilege of preaching a farewell sermon. This presented him with a beautiful opportunity to tell his congregation what he thought of them. To show how mean and stingy they were, he read off a list of their paltry gifts to him. In no time at all the congregation was in such an uproar that the pastor was no longer able to make himself heard. He climbed down from the pulpit and started to walk out of the church; but by the aisle his eyes lighted upon a man he had failed to mention. "And you," he shouted, pointing his finger at him, "you gave me only half a loaf of bread!" "And *that* was too much, you rascal!" shouted the accused man in turn as he reached out and caught hold of the preacher's coattails. With a mighty lunge the pastor struggled to free himself. There was a rip, and the angry parishioner was left with the coattails in his hand.

Often the shortcomings of the clergy were looked upon with some degree of pride. At their worst they had the advantage of making the ministers seem more human. Of course wit in a pastor was better than sin, but absent-mindedness did almost as well. A great favorite of the stories told at the expense of the clergy is the one of the absent-minded minister who was called upon to conduct a funeral and a wedding on the same day. Pronouncing the couple man and wife, he turned to the congregation and said: "Es werd nau en Gelegenheit gewe den Leichnam zu sehne." (There will now be an opportunity to view the remains.)

Occasionally in these stories it was the preacher who emerged triumphant. This story has all the earmarks of a folk tale. In an old stone church no very great distance from the Blue Mountains the congregation had begun to weary of their minister's sermons, so the elders went to him and said: "You've been preaching all these years on texts you have chosen; now we would like a chance to choose the texts for you for a while."

"All right," assented the preacher. "Pick out a text and write it on a piece of paper, and every Sunday put it on the Bible in the pulpit, and I'll preach on that text for you."

This the elders did, and for several Sundays everything went well. The pastor preached very good sermons on the texts they had chosen. Then one Sunday the elders were tempted to put the minister to a further test; instead of a text they placed a blank piece of paper on the Bible in the pulpit. That Sunday the preacher picked up the paper, looked at it, and said, "Here is nothing." Turning it over, he added: "And here is nothing. And out of nothing God created heaven and earth." With that he proceeded to preach a bang-up sermon, much to the admiration of the elders.

Today services are conducted in a more seemly fashion. Elders no longer play tricks on the pastor. Times have changed. The old *klingelseckli,* the little bag with a bell at the bottom, which hung from the end of a long pole, has given way to the collection plate. Literally *klingelseckli* means tinkling little bag. In the old Dutch churches collection was always taken in these. The purpose of the bell, I presume, was to wake up those who had fallen asleep during the long sermons. Now no one sleeps in church except small children.

Yet both the Lutheran and the Reformed churches continue to play a prominent part in Pennsylvania Dutch communities. In many a village the whole town goes to church. No one is outside. As a consequence much of the social life centers about the church. The Ladies Aid Society or the Daughters of the Church or the Women's Bible Class are everlastingly having a church supper, a strawberry festival, or a cake sale to pay off the debt on the old church—almost no Pennsylvania Dutch congregation is satisfied without a church debt—or to start a building fund for a new one.

The other leading church of the Rhineland, the Roman Catholic Church, played only a small part in Pennsylvania Dutch life in early days. There were only two Roman Catholic churches in the Dutch country in colonial times. The older of these, at Conewago, was founded by the Jesuits about 1721 and is the mother church of all

Roman Catholic parishes in Pennsylvania. Here is buried Joseph II's envoy, Baron de Beelen Bertholff, who followed the Continental Congress to York and died there. The second Roman Catholic church was at Goshenhoppen in Berks County. Mennonites and Moravians had already settled at Goshenhoppen when the Jesuits arrived in 1743, and the Mennonites are still there, as are the Roman Catholics. Under the direction of its first pastor, Father Theodore Schneider, an alumnus and former Rector Magnificus of the University of Heidelberg, and the able priests who succeeded him, this church became an important missionary center. Later on in the eighteenth century Roman Catholic churches were established in Philadelphia and Lancaster. Today there is a Jesuit seminary at Wernersville and many Roman Catholic churches in the cities and some of the towns of the Pennsylvania Dutch, but their parishioners are drawn largely from the nineteenth century Germans and Irish and the more recent Italians and Poles. The old stock Pennsylvania Dutch are still fervently Protestant.

There were few Jews in Pennsylvania in colonial times except for a thriving congregation in Philadelphia. Yet one of the first eleven families to settle in Easton was Jewish, and in Lancaster there were Jews from the first years of the town. A Jewish cemetery in Lancaster dates from 1747, but there was no synagogue. The Jewish colony at Schaefferstown in Lebanon County, if it ever existed, which seems doubtful, is shrouded in mystery. What probably happened was that a few Pennsylvania Dutchmen to whom religion was as strong drink became convinced of the truth of the old dispensation and decided to become Jews—as far as abjuring Christianity and circumcising one another could make them Jews. They ate no pork (a hardship for any Pennsylvania Dutchman) and stretched the prohibition against eating swan to include goose, probably because they had no swans but did have geese. They built a synagogue of logs, the first among the Pennsylvania Dutch, and set off a graveyard of their own. Such heady fanaticism died down as rapidly as it had flared up, leaving little more than the legend of this strange community. An alternate theory, with less color, is that a small number of Jews from Lancaster established a fur-trading post at Schaefferstown in the early days of the eighteenth century and lived there long enough to build a synagogue and start a graveyard. Today there are synagogues in almost all the Pennsylvania cities, where the Jews are frequently merchants. There are almost no Jewish farmers in the Dutch country.

Very like the "church people" are the Pennsylvania Dutch religions which, so to speak, have not gone plain. Most important among these is the Evangelical United Brethren Church, until 1947 two churches instead of one, the Church of the United Brethren in Christ, usually known as the United Brethren, and the Evangelical Association. These two churches were Pennsylvania Dutch products of the Methodist revival of the late eighteenth and early nineteenth centuries. To call them Pennsylvania Dutch Methodists, while not wholly accurate, is nevertheless fairly close to the truth. The older of the two, the United Brethren, looks upon Philip Otterbein as its founder. Otterbein was one of the young clergymen Schlatter recruited in Germany to minister to the Reformed congregations in Pennsylvania. Arriving in America in 1752, Otterbein first preached in Lancaster, where he was noted for the fervor of his sermons and the stress he put on the spiritual life. In addition to caring for his charge in Lancaster he went about the country preaching to other congregations and also to those unreached by any church.

Another preacher of this time, Martin Boehm, was a Mennonite bishop of the village of Willow Street in Lancaster County who held services in a large barn not far from Lancaster. Martin Boehm was one of the most pious of Mennonites. Chosen for the ministry by lot in accordance with the Mennonite practice, he was greatly distressed by his failure in his first attempts to preach. Since the lot had fallen to him, he could not doubt that God had called him. Plowing in his field, he prayed at the end of each furrow; then, sinking to his knees in the middle of the field, he appealed to God for help. At last the certainty of God's love and help filled his soul, and he rose from his knees to hurry to the house to share this great moment with his wife. The next Sunday he told the congregation how God had come to his help, whereupon many wept. So deeply affected was he by this experience that he became a most persuasive preacher, warm, earnest, and deeply spiritual. Finally he felt moved to carry the gospel to those outside the Mennonite fold; and he began to hold "great meetings," as he called them, here and there through the countryside, often in large barns. It was to one of these meetings that Otterbein went to hear him preach. In Boehm, Otterbein immediately recognized a kindred spirit; both men had the same piety and fervor. At the end of the meeting Otterbein threw his arms around Boehm and said, "Wir sind Brüder." (We are brethren.)

From this time on these two men worked together. Neither man was at home in the church in which he found himself. The Mennonites, frowning on Boehm's "great meetings" and his concern for the people of the world, at length expelled him from the church. Otterbein went on to become the pastor of an independent Reformed church in Baltimore that gave him great latitude for his beliefs. Yet he was not satisfied with the Reformed Church: its religion he thought too staid and formal. There were no prayer meetings in the Reformed Church, not even much family worship. To make up for this want he organized a group of six Reformed clergymen, who held semiannual meetings to promote piety in the churches, largely through greater warmth in preaching, the inauguration of prayer meetings, and the promotion of family worship. In all this Otterbein had the example of the Methodists to encourage him. His friendship with the great Methodist leader Francis Asbury, at whose consecration as bishop he had assisted, incited him to even greater zeal. Naturally there were many in the Reformed Church who looked on all this as excessive.

Up to this time Otterbein had worked within the Reformed Church; but in 1789 a new church, the United Brethren, may be said to have been born. In that year he called a meeting in Baltimore of fourteen clergymen, nine of them Reformed and five Mennonite. This was the first conference of the church and one at which a confession of faith and rules of discipline were adopted. The Bible was accepted as "the only rule and guide," "the true way to salvation." The importance of repentance and salvation through Jesus Christ was stressed. The sacraments adopted were largely a compromise between those of the Reformed Church and those of the Mennonites: each group was free to follow its own way. The Mennonite Church believed only in adult baptism, whereas the Reformed Church practiced infant baptism. Therefore the mode of baptism was left to "the judgment and understanding of each individual." The Reformed view of Communion as a symbolic act was the one chosen. The rite of foot washing, which was practiced by some of the Mennonite churches, was permitted to those who desired it. The next conference was held two years later, in York, by which time seven more clergymen had joined the group. Even at this early date some of the pastors began to make missionary tours into "the territory of the United States northwest of the Ohio," where the new church gained a stronghold in the Miami Valley. At the third conference, held in 1800 in Frederick, both Otterbein and Boehm were elected bishops and a name for the church was chosen, the United Brethren in Christ.

Since that day the church has continued very much as it started. At first all the services were in German, by which the church lost many of its converts to the Methodists; today they are all in English. Methodist influence has been strong from the start: the organization of the church is very like that of the Methodist Episcopal Church; the pastoral supply is that of the itinerant system; there is an insistence on a thorough conversion and a godly life—penitent sinners can be saved only by faith in Christ and not by "works." In many ways this is what is sometimes referred to as "the oldtime religion." There is a complete acceptance of the Bible, both the New and the Old Testaments, as the Word of God; the Fourth Commandment, to keep the Sabbath holy, is faithfully obeyed; indulgence in intoxicating liquor is "strictly prohibited," and abstinence from tobacco is "kindly advised." Revivals or camp meetings to promote conversion are frequently held. The Church of the United Brethren in Christ has become strong in a number of the Dutch counties of Pennsylvania, Maryland, and Virginia and also in parts of West Virginia, Ohio, Indiana, and Illinois. In 1947 it joined with the Evangelical Association to form the Evangelical United Brethren Church.

The Evangelical Association, too, was a Dutch form of Methodism. Its founder, Jacob Albright, was born in Pottstown in 1759 and later moved to Lancaster County, where as a maker of bricks and tiles he was known as "the honest brickmaker." Although baptized and confirmed a Lutheran, he was little affected by religion until the death of several of his children and the funeral sermon of a Reformed minister moved him to repentance and brought about a conversion. In his own church, the Lutheran, he found too little of the evangelical spirit to satisfy him. "We knew nothing of true conversion; no trace existed of prayer meetings, Bible studies, family prayers, Sunday-schools, or revivals. Hardly a show of godliness remained. The power thereof was outlawed as fanaticism. The salt had lost its savor." As the Methodist Church was more to his liking, he set out to learn English so that he might enjoy the full benefit of that form of worship. Troubled by the plight of the Pennsylvania Dutch, whom he found uncared for and sinful, he had a call to preach to them. For a long time he hesitated; he feared that he lacked the true gift of a preacher and, in addition, he felt the want of education. Finally he yielded to the call and, although he had not been ordained by any church, began his work as an itinerant preacher, organizing classes in the Dutch counties of Pennsylvania and Maryland and in the Shenandoah Valley. At the first council of his followers in 1803 the Bible was accepted as the true Word of God and Albright as the leader of the group. Soon after this Albright was consecrated by two of his associates after the fashion of the consecration of Barnabas and Saul. The first annual conference was held in 1807 at Kleinfeltersville and the name, The Newly Formed Methodist Conference, adopted. About this time a union with the Methodist Church was seriously considered, but this was abandoned when the Methodists found it inexpedient to permit the new group to establish circuits in the Pennsylvania Dutch districts and to hold their own conferences. In 1809 a new name, The So-called Albrights, was chosen; a church organization, like that of the Methodists, set up; and a discipline adopted. The religion they desired was a fervent Methodism, a muscular Christianity. Their early leaders have been described as "men of much prayer," who "wrestled with God by day and night." What they lacked in education they made up in fervor. Shouts of praise and demonstrations of joy by the congregation were common in the early meetings. Revivals and camp meetings were held to bring about conversions. Temperance was insisted on; indeed, there was strict discipline to curb all worldly indulgence.

In 1891 there was a bitter quarrel and a split in the church. A part of the seceding group rejoined the Evangelical Association in 1922, but about 25,000 refused to come back to the mother church. This independent group took the name of the Evangelical Congregational Church. The larger group, the Evangelical Association, went out of existence in 1947, when it merged with the United Brethren to form the Evangelical United Brethren Church.

Still another Pennsylvania Dutch church, the Church of God, was a part of the revival movement of the early nineteenth century. This church was founded by a Reformed preacher, John Winebrenner, born in Frederick County, Maryland, in 1797. Baptized and confirmed in the Reformed Church, he was ordained as a clergyman and called to a charge at Harrisburg. There he became so earnest in his preaching that one part of his congregation became seriously alarmed about their spiritual condition while another part complained to the synod. Withdrawing from the Reformed Church, Winebrenner gathered about him a group of followers and continued to preach in the country round about Harrisburg. Revivals of the camp-meeting type were held to procure conversions. The Reformed view of Communion was retained, but infant baptism was rejected. Immersion and foot washing were borrowed from the Dunkards.

Here and there through the Dutch country, especially in the cities, are churches of other religions that, like Roman Catholicism and Judaism, are not characteristically Dutch. In all the larger cities, and occasionally in a smaller town of English origin, there is an Episcopal church, invariably the most fashionable church, though seldom the strongest. The Methodist Church, too, thrives in the larger cities, as does the Presbyterian Church, the Baptist, and even the Christian Science and the Greek Orthodox churches. There are practically no Congregational or Unitarian churches in the Dutch country, and only a few Quaker meetings have managed to stay alive.

The Moravians

The Moravians are the third of the three principal Pennsylvania Dutch cultures. Theirs is a position somewhere between "the plain people" and "the church people": in the early days close to "the plain people," today almost indistinguishable from the Reformed and Lutherans. An emphasis on plain living, a dislike of war, and—at least in part—a conception of themselves as a peculiar people gave them a resemblance to such bonneted sects as the Mennonites, Amish, Brethren, Schwenkfelders, and the Quakers too. Yet their emphasis on church ritual made them like the Lutherans and the Reformed. In their plain living also, for all its idyllic simplicity, there was an elegance, a sophistication, that put the Moravians on the side of the world's people.

The historic Moravian Church, usually regarded as the most ancient of the Protestant churches still in existence, can trace its origin back to John Hus, who was burnt at the stake on July 6, 1415. The Moravian Church has been known by a confusing number of names: the original Bohemian name of Jednota Bratrska, the Latin name of Unitas Fratrum, and such other names as the Brethren's Church, the Bohemian and Moravian Brethren, the Church of the United Brethren, and the Moravian Church. This last name was adopted to distinguish the Moravians from the Church of the Brethren, commonly known as the Dunkards, and the United Brethren.

In 1457 a number of Hus's followers calling themselves "the Brethren" found refuge near Kunwald on the domain of Lititz in northeast

Bohemia. Lititz was the property of George Podiebrad, who became King of Bohemia the following year. But at Lititz, too, they suffered from the persecution of Rome, for with the growth of the Brethren Rome forced the king to withdraw his support. This time they fled to the mountains of Reichenau. To ensure apostolic succession, one of their leaders, Michael Bradacius, was consecrated as bishop in 1467 by Stephen, an aged bishop of the Waldenses who was able to trace his ordination back to the Roman Catholic bishops at the Council of Basel. Two years later, in 1469, Rome burned Stephen at the stake for this act. Another leader, Matthias of Kunwald, was ordained by Michael. Thus the episcopate was established in this group of the Brethren. Except for the Episcopal Church, the Moravian Church is the only Protestant church with an apostolic succession.

During the latter half of the fifteenth century the Brethren continued to increase. By 1517 they had nearly 200,000 members in Bohemia and Moravia. Their first collection of hymns, the earliest of all Protestant hymnals, had been published in 1501. By 1520 three out of the five printing presses in Bohemia belonged to them. The Bohemian version of the Bible, on which eight of their most learned scholars had labored for fifteen years, was published at Kralitz in 1593. The sixteenth century, however, brought further persecution. In 1549 many of them were driven into exile by Ferdinand I; but the real attempt to wipe them out did not come until the Counter-Reformation of the seventeenth century. Ferdinand II, who ascended the throne of Bohemia in 1617, had promised his Jesuit preceptor to blot out Protestantism in Bohemia. With the disastrous defeat at the battle of White Mountain on November 8, 1620, the Protestant cause in Bohemia was lost. The bishops and ministers of the Moravian Church were banished, its churches and schools were closed, its property confiscated. June 21, 1621, is still remembered among the Moravians as "the day of blood" because of the slaughter of prisoners on that day. At first the persecution was centered on the Moravians, but soon the Reformed Church and a little later the Lutheran had their turn. Thousands fled, for the choice was exile or death. The Protestants who stayed and who were true to their faith were tortured and killed. The population of Bohemia shrank by two-thirds. Ferdinand fulfilled his promise to the Jesuits: the Moravian Church in Bohemia was wiped out. Many members of the church, however, were in exile: in Poland, Silesia, Hungary, Holland, and even in England. At the University of Oxford money was raised for the relief of the Moravians. Under the leadership of their eminent bishop Comenius, probably the greatest scholar of the age, the most important group of exiles settled at Lissa in Poland, only to be scattered anew by the war between Sweden and Poland. Not many of the congregations survived. After the sack of Lissa in 1656, Comenius, impoverished, fled to Holland, where he died in 1670. Most of the Moravians in Poland, especially after 1670, joined the Reformed Church, with which they felt a sense of kinship. Yet here and there in exile, and even in Bohemia and Moravia, there were a few "hidden seed" through which the church continued an underground existence. Even the episcopal succession was preserved when it was passed on from Comenius to Jablonsky, his grandson.

Because the Moravian Church in separating from Rome, unlike the Lutheran and Reformed churches, had been careful to guard the episcopal succession, its position as "an ancient Protestant Episcopal Church" was formally recognized by the Parliament of Great Britain in an act passed on May 12, 1749, "for encouraging the people known by the name of Unitas Fratrum or United Brethren to settle in his Majesty's colonies in America." In this act Parliament declared the doctrine of the Moravian Church "to differ in no essential article of faith from that of the Church of England, as set forth in the Thirty-nine Articles." Thus the Moravian Church was given Parliament's blessing, an advantage enjoyed by no other church except the Church of England and to some extent the Lutheran.

In 1722 Nicholas Louis, Count Zinzendorf and Pottendorf, offered a remnant of the Moravians a refuge on his estate, the domain of Berthelsdorf in Saxony, which he had just acquired from his grandmother, Countess Henrietta von Gersdorf. There the Moravians built the village of Herrnhut to house three hundred members of their faith.

Count Zinzendorf was a young, idealistic nobleman who was much excited by the ideas set afloat by Pietism. He had always been sensitive to mystical influence. At the age of six he had spoken of Christ as his brother. At the University of Halle he had helped to establish the Order of the Grain of Mustard Seed, whose members were pledged to walk worthily in the steps of Jesus and to exercise charity toward their neighbors.

The more dubious features of the Moravian religion were the ones that most attracted Zinzendorf. The emphasis on Christ's sacrificial death, the blood atonement, moved him deeply. Like many other

Moravians, both at Herrnhut and later at Bethlehem, he dwelt upon the blood and wounds of Christ with too exuberant a fancy. To other Protestants much of this extravagance seemed fantastic and even shocking. The language of love when applied to Christ seemed both irreverent and in bad taste. When Zinzendorf likened the true Christian's relation to Christ to that which exists in marriage; when he declared that all souls, which he described as essentially female, were married to a "conjugal Lord Jesus"; when he insisted that the relationship between Christ and the saved soul was the most intimate possible in all human relationships, most Protestants were genuinely puzzled, while a few of the more sinful were vastly amused. Communion, too, took on a sensuous coloring: the Lord's Supper was described as an "embrace" in which Christ pressed the communicant to His heart and kissed her with His pale lips.

Yet Zinzendorf, despite his vagaries, was a man with some measure of greatness. He had character. He had boundless energy. He was ruled by the heart, it is true; he was so generous and forthgiving that he was willing to spend every penny he had to turn his ideals into reality.

Zinzendorf's fondest dream was the union of all Protestant churches, each church to preserve its distinctive character yet to unite for the common good. In examining the Augsburg Confession of 1530, the articles of the Reformed Synod of Bern of 1530, and the German reissue of the confession of the Brethren of Bohemia and Moravia published under the direction of Luther in 1533, he came to the conclusion that all Protestant churches could reach a Christ-centered point on which all could agree. In the Synod of Sendomir in Poland in 1570, the Moravian and Reformed and Lutheran churches had joined together to form an evangelical federation. Later the three churches had entered into a similar agreement in Bohemia. This had permitted three distinct modes of worship and discipline, yet the members of one church were encouraged to attend services at the other two. Zinzendorf thought of himself as a Lutheran and believed that he had been authorized by the University of Tübingen to serve as a Lutheran minister. The Moravians, he thought, might be used as a connecting link, since they considered themselves close to the Reformed Church, and yet in Germany they were recognized as belonging to the group united by the Augsburg Confession. This seemed proof to Zinzendorf that there was no essential difference between them and the Lutherans. Later, in Pennsylvania, he attempted to unite these three churches and the Mennonites, Dunkards, Quakers, Schwenkfelders, and the Ephrata community as well. "In each religion," he wrote, "lies a thought of God which cannot be received through any other religion. . . . Not any religion has the whole; she must take the best out of other religions to assist her if she wants the whole."

In 1736 Zinzendorf was banished from Saxony for ten years for harboring fanatics and promoting views contrary to Lutheranism—or, as Frederick William I of Prussia put it, "because he wished to live piously though a count." He was ordered to sell his estates and leave the country. The Moravians and Schwenkfelders were banished with him. The next year, however, the banishment was revoked and the Moravians were permitted to remain at Herrnhut. But in the meanwhile their attention had turned to America. As early as 1732 Moravian missionaries had been sent to St. Thomas in the Virgin Islands. In 1733 a mission was established in Greenland and another dispatched to St. Croix in the Virgin Islands; early in 1734 one was sent to Lapland and late that year, one to Georgia; and in 1735 one was set up in Surinam. The Moravians were busy with foreign missions long before other Protestant denominations got started. It was not until 1806, when five students at Williams dedicated their lives to the spreading of light in the "darkness of Asia," that the Moravians were joined by other Protestant churches in America.

When the Moravians were faced with exile, Georgia looked like a hopeful site for a colony. Zinzendorf had first tried to persuade the Schwenkfelders to settle there, but when they insisted on going to Pennsylvania a group of Moravians went instead. The place chosen for the colony was part of the present site of Savannah. Headed by Spangenberg, a bishop endowed with wisdom and also with common sense, this little band of Moravians proposed to convert the Cherokees and the Creeks as well as found a colony. At first their prospects for success were bright. Spangenberg, a graduate of the University of Jena, was all they could hope for in a leader. And from the beginning the Moravians had friends in high places. On the voyage Spangenberg had made a favorable impression on his fellow passengers, General James Oglethorpe and John and Charles Wesley.

At first things went well. A school for Indians was opened the following year, 1736, on an island in the Savannah River five miles above the settlement. The same year, on March 10, Bishop Nitschmann ordained Anton Seiffert at Savannah, the first ordination by a bishop of the Christian church in the thirteen colonies. In fact, Nitschmann, who had been consecrated as bishop in 1735 by Bishop Jablonsky, court preacher to the King of Prussia, was the first bishop to come to America to perform his episcopal duties here. But disaster followed on the heels of this happy start. A number of the settlers came down with fever, some of them dying. War broke out between England and Spain. The Moravians, who disapproved of war, refused to fight and were consequently looked upon with disfavor. Some of them returned to Europe, while the rest gratefully accepted the offer of the Methodist missionary, Whitefield, to go with him on his sloop to Philadelphia. The freedom of religion in Pennsylvania and the pacifism of the Quakers made Penn's colony particularly attractive to them. On April 13, 1740, they sailed from Savannah; this was the end of the Moravian colony in Georgia.

The Moravians were invited by Whitefield to settle on "the Barony of Nazareth," a five-thousand-acre tract of land near the forks of the Delaware and the Lehigh. The deed to this tract carried with it "the Franchise, Royalty, Right, Privilege, Liberty and Immunity to erect the said 5,000 acres of land, or any part or parts thereof, into a manor, and to have and to hold Court Baron therein with all things whatsoever which to a Court Baron belong." The dignities and privileges of the manor were to "be holden of the said John Penn and Thomas Penn in free and common socage as of the Seigniory of Windsor free and discharged of and from the debts and legacies of the said William Penn, Sr., yielding and paying therefor one Red Rose on the 24th day of June yearly, if the same shall be demanded, in full of all services, customs and rents." Although the Moravians never attempted to exercise any of the rights of this charter, the only manor in Pennsylvania sold by the Penns with the rights and privileges of a court baron attached to it, it was rendered invalid only by the Revolution. It had been granted originally in 1682 by Penn to his daughter Letitia.

On the Barony of Nazareth, Whitefield intended to found a school for Negroes and a village for destitute Englishmen. Early in May, 1740, the Moravians set to work to clear the land and to build a log house for shelter from the winter. Unfortunately, Whitefield and the Moravians did not see eye to eye on religion. Even in Georgia he had begun to argue in defense of predestination with Peter Boehler, a Moravian clergyman who had been educated at the University of Jena and who had later taught there. As Whitefield could not speak German and

Boehler could not speak English, the argument was conducted in Latin. For all that, it was hot and furious. Finally Whitefield lost his temper and ordered the Moravians off his land. When he cooled off he permitted them to stay in the log house they had built, for winter had already set in; but the Moravians, to be on the safe side, bought five hundred acres of land where the Monocacy flows into the Lehigh, the present site of Bethlehem. In the following spring Whitefield discovered he was unable to pay for his barony and offered it for sale to the Moravians, who promptly bought it. The large stone house named Ephratah, which Whitefield had started, was left unfinished. A band of brick in the stone shows how much had been completed when he sold the barony to the Moravians.

The first Moravian Christmas Eve service in Pennsylvania was celebrated in the log house at Nazareth. The Reverend Peter Boehler had prepared a choral liturgy with verses of his own composition, which was followed by a love feast of corncake and coffee made of roasted rye. After the Christmas Eve vigils there was Communion, the first Moravian Communion in Pennsylvania.

The next year, 1741, the first building at Bethlehem was erected. This was a log structure, half house, half stable, twenty feet by forty, one story high, with sleeping quarters under the steep-pitched roof. Here were held the famous Christmas Eve vigils of 1741, when Zinzendorf, inspired by the singing of an old carol, named the settlement in honor of the birthplace of the Christ child.

With Count Zinzendorf's arrival real progress began to be made; Bethlehem began to take form as a community. The congregation was organized in 1742, the same year as the one in London. The Gemeinhaus, a community house, had been built the year before. A large log building, forty-five feet by thirty, it was enlarged in 1743 and is still standing. A grist mill was built in 1743, and the large stone structure known as the Bell House was started in 1745. This last building, with its bell tower, was a most ambitious edifice for so young a settlement. The first town clock was placed in the graceful belfry, which was crowned with an unusually beautiful weathervane of a lamb with a banner, the historic emblem of the Moravian Church. At the same time other buildings were erected, while the clearing of the forest went steadily ahead.

But from the very start missionary work came first. At one time Zinzendorf went so far as to decide that it was more important to convert the heathen than to sow grain to keep themselves alive. Yet all work was looked upon as religious. In 1742 they divided their number into two groups, the Pilgergemeine, who were to work among the Indians and the whites; and the Hausgemeine, who were to erect buildings and put the settlement on its feet, to tarry "by the stuff" (I Samuel 30:24). Some of the members volunteered to serve in one group or the other; the rest were chosen by lot. Some of the itinerant workers known as "Fishers" sought out places in need of attention; others going from house to house visited a circuit known as the Pennsylvania Wheel (Ezekiel 1:15 and 20) and also as the Pennsylvania Chariot (Acts 8:26–39). Far and wide through the American colonies these missionaries wandered: they reached isolated parts of Maryland, Virginia, the Carolinas, and Georgia where no Christian minister had ever been seen; they penetrated the Alleghenies; they went as far north as Canajoharie in New York and Broadbay in Maine; they visited New Haven, Newport, Long Island, Staten Island, and near-by New Jersey.

The lot of those who tarried "by the stuff" was not an easy one. Besides the arduous labor of clearing the land and erecting buildings, they had to put up with the deep mistrust of the Scotch-Irish Presbyterians in the neighborhood. A crisis arose in the summer of 1746, when one rainy day after another prevented them from harvesting their grain until at last there came a perfect day, the Sunday of July 31. The Moravians decided to make use of the good weather and get in their grain, only to be charged as "Sabbath breakers" by the incensed Scotch-Irish. Although the Moravians were finally exonerated, the Scotch-Irish came to the conclusion that Moravian ways were not Presbyterian ways and continued to view these queer people from abroad dourly.

In 1742 Zinzendorf made a zealous attempt to draw the Pennsylvania Dutch Protestant churches and the Quakers together into a union. He called a series of conferences, as many as seven in six months. At the first of these, thirteen faiths were represented, but to the fourth only the Lutheran, Reformed, and Moravian churches sent representatives. The smaller religious groups such as the Mennonites, the Dunkards, and the society of Ephrata were especially suspicious of Zinzendorf's intentions. They strongly suspected that his purpose was to bring them "under his own hat." In this they were less than fair to Zinzendorf, who had in mind not so much the creation of an overhead authority as the nurturing of spiritual ties between the sects. Yet Zinzendorf's choice of Moravian hymns and his frequent use of the lot laid him open to suspicion. The Lutheran and Reformed groups were more interested, understandably so since Zinzendorf paid them the compliment of treating them with respect as two historic churches. Both the Lutheran and the Reformed churches had been neglected by the mother churches abroad; both were in desperate need of clergymen. As Zinzendorf put it, "It had become proverbial, respecting anyone who cared not for God and His Word, that 'he was of the Pennsylvania religion.'" In Europe both the Lutheran and Reformed churches became alarmed and sent ministers to save their congregations from the designs of Zinzendorf. Zinzendorf's brave plan came to naught. Its only effect was to intensify suspicion among the various churches.

In other ways as well Zinzendorf showed himself a visionary and a utopian, particularly in the government he organized to get the pioneer colonies of Bethlehem and Nazareth started. This was a communistic society. Known as the General Economy, it was in full force from 1745 to 1762 at both Bethlehem and Nazareth, the two settlements being governed as one unit. Every man, woman, and child became part of one household; everyone worked for the good of the whole. They gave their time and labor, receiving in return shelter, food, and clothing. No one was paid any wages. The church owned all the land, all the buildings, even the very tools with which the people worked. Yet no one was forced to surrender his private property. Anyone who disliked the system was free to leave. As it was pointed out, there was no wall around Bethlehem.

Bishop Spangenberg and his wife were at the head, with committees set up to manage the details of government. There was a committee on building, a committee of domestic supplies, a food committee, a clothing committee, a committee on medicine and sanitation, a committee on education, even a police committee. Bishop Spangenberg's wife was in charge of female industry: the spinners, weavers, knitters, seamstresses, milkmaids, laundresses, nurses, teachers, even the mothers. Some women helped to herd the cattle, though this and carrying water were tasks usually allotted to the old men and boys. Visitors to Bethlehem in 1761 spoke of being awakened "by one hundred cows, a number of them with bells, a venerable goat and two she-goats, driven in town by two sisters." There was a general steward to do whatever buying was necessary, which was very little since to a great degree

Bethlehem and Nazareth relied on the products of their own fields and orchards, their cattle and their poultry.

In manufacturing, too, Bethlehem became as nearly self-supporting as it was possible for so small a place to be. There was no private industry; everything was directed and owned by the community. By 1747 there were thirty-two different industries, which together with the farmlands were able to support the two settlements and fifty itinerant missionaries as well. Twelve years later, in 1759, though Bethlehem had only 618 inhabitants and Nazareth 268, there were 2,454 acres of land under intensive cultivation and nearly a hundred different industries and trades. Many of the products were sold in other parts of the colony. Bethlehem, which was designed as a center of industry and trade in contrast to Nazareth, which was intended as an agricultural community, was a busy workshop. There was a gristmill, a sawmill, a fulling mill, a tannery, a pottery, a hattery; there were blacksmith and carpenter shops; there were spinning wheels and linen looms—even a silk mill; there was a bleaching yard and a washhouse. At Bethlehem they made even their own buttons for their coats, their organs for their churches, and their bells for their belfries. By 1759 there were ninety-seven buildings: seventeen choir houses in which people were housed by age groups, five schools, twenty buildings where trades were carried on, five mills, two inns, and forty-eight farm buildings.

Spangenberg was head of the church in temporal affairs and also in charge of the missions to the Indians and to a large extent of those to the West Indies and Surinam. For a time his power suffered an eclipse and Bishop Cammerhoff succeeded him—an unfortunate choice, for Cammerhoff was one of the most enthusiastic and sentimental of Moravian visionaries. He may have had some of Spangenberg's godliness but he had none of his common sense.

Visitors to Bethlehem and Nazareth were greatly interested in these novel settlements. Hannah Callender, a Quakeress, who visited Nazareth in 1758, mentions the waterworks there, the milkhouse, and the fine oxen; yet—a very human touch!—she most admired the trout in the spring, so tame that they were fed by hand. A communal feature at Bethlehem that caught the fancy of a later visitor, Isaac Weld, was the spring house. In November of 1796 he wrote:

The spring house in Bethlehem is common to the whole town: a shelf or board in it is allotted to each family, and though there is no watch placed over it, and the door be only secured by a latch, yet every person is certain of finding, when he comes for it, his plate of butter or bowl of milk, etc., exactly in the same state as when he put it in.

The whole community was divided into age groups called choirs, each living apart. The children were placed in the nursery as soon as they were old enough to be taken from their mothers' arms. There they were taken care of by widows and single women and sometimes by married women who were not strong enough for other work. At three years of age they were put in the choirs for little boys or little girls. After 1762 only the children of missionaries who had to be away from Bethlehem and Nazareth were placed in the nurseries. If the parents were living in Bethlehem or Nazareth, they cared for the tiny children themselves. Older boys and girls, however, were placed in separate choirs, which were actually boys' and girls' boarding schools. In 1755 there were nearly three hundred children in the various Moravian schools, with eighty teachers and helpers instructing them. There was a choir for the single sisters, one for the single brethren; there was a choir for the married sisters and brethren, though these commonly lived in houses; there was a choir for the widows.

Each choir had its own house with a life devised for that particular group even to its own hymns and liturgies. Although every detail of life had been thought out, there was a certain amount of freedom. In the older girls' choir the rising bell rang at five, for this was the eighteenth century, with only candles, the stars, the moon, and the sun for light. Morning prayers were held before breakfast, which was at six; there was a further "piece" to stay the appetite at nine; dinner was at eleven-thirty; there was a love feast or tea or some social relaxation of one kind or another between three o'clock and vespers; supper was at five; evening prayers were at eight; and at nine the house was locked for the night.

The love feast mentioned above was a term used loosely by the Moravians to describe informal gatherings with light refreshments. It was partly devotional in character and partly social. A love feast could take the form of a treat for children, a welcome or a farewell to a guest, or simply an afternoon get-together; it could be part of a wedding or a funeral, or even a harvest-home festival. Some sort of food was always served. Probably it was these love feasts that brought Moravian baking to such a high state of excellence. The love feasts were graced with the delicious Moravian buns and butter semmels—or if it was near Christmas, the white or brown Christmas cookies, or both —with a cup of chocolate, mint tea from the garden, or some imported bohea from China. Bishop Spangenberg looked upon love feasts with favor as a means of offsetting the hard pioneer life. They were a good builder of morale.

Dress, too, was regulated. The women dressed in gray or brown, with white for gala occasions. The dresses were plain with tight-laced bodices, white kerchiefs, and full skirts. Capes were worn outdoors when the weather was cool. The close-fitting white caps, known as *Schnepplehaube,* came to a point in the middle of the forehead and were tied under the chin with bows: red bows for little girls, rose bows for older girls, pink bows for unmarried women, blue bows for married women, and white bows for widows. At Nazareth the caps had a crimped border with scallop shells to cover the ears. The men, all of whom were clean-shaven, wore broad-brimmed hats with low crowns, straight dark coats without lapels, and the eighteenth century knee-buckled breeches.

In the years of the General Economy zeal was at its height. In the early years there were prayer bands to maintain "hourly intercession" as introduced at Herrnhut in 1727. Nineteen classes were organized for prayer turns or watches from five in the morning to midnight, with the turns from midnight to five taken over by the night watch. On Saturday the prayer turn was kept by a band that closed the watch on Sunday morning by going out to the graveyard and singing a hymn in commemoration of the Resurrection. Returning they sang hymns at the choir-house doors and then went to the chapel for prayers. In these early years, too, Saturday was looked upon as the Sabbath and observed as a day of rest; but Sunday was regarded as peculiarly the Lord's Day, at which time there was preaching and public worship. During the eighteenth century the rite of foot washing was practiced, especially on Maundy Thursday. These were years of enthusiasm, hard work, and sacrifice that enabled the Moravians to build a Christian community in the wilderness and to do notable missionary work in converting the Indians. It was one of the most successful experiments in communal living that America has ever seen. Although abandoned by general consent in 1762, the General Economy gave Bethlehem and Nazareth their start. During this time each person got the necessities of life, his children were educated, and he was cared for in sickness and

old age. There was security for all, poverty for none. There was even
a considerable measure of social equality, despite the fact that Zinzendorf was a count and his daughter a countess.

Oddly enough, this little settlement in the Dutch country had an
unusual concentration of nobility. Among the nobles there in the early
days, in addition to Count Zinzendorf and his daughter, were the
Baroness von Seidewitz; Anna von Pahlen, a pious young Livonian
baroness who was the wife of Bishop Cammerhoff; Baron Johannes
von Watteville, who married Zinzendorf's daughter, the Countess
Benigna; the Baroness Anna Dorothea von Watteville, who became
the wife of Hans Christian von Schweinitz; and Juliana Benedicta von
Gammeru, the daughter of Baron Christian von Raschan. Still another
member of the nobility, Anna von Marschall, the daughter of Baron
Frederick von Marschall, became identified with the Moravian settlement in North Carolina.

Perhaps it was the presence of such nobles that accounted for the
high degree of culture at Bethlehem from the beginning. These people
refused to be mere backwoodsmen. Although the life at a settlement
that was in the process of being carved out of the wilderness had to be
plain and unpretentious, gentle manners and high standards in education and the fine arts, especially music, were not permitted to lapse.
As early as May, 1746, a summerhouse was built on Wunden Island in
the Monocacy with a rustic footbridge over to the island. The women
worked with their hands, but a fair number of them sat for their portraits too. It is always possible to get along without some of the necessities of life as long as there are a few of the luxuries.

For the Moravians music was a must. The children in the choir
houses ate their dinners off wooden trenchers, but they were taught to
play the violin, the viola da gamba, or the flute or French horn, and
to sing in a chorus. This was quite as important as the three R's and
even more so. The first settlers brought musical instruments with them.
On January 25, 1744, a spinet, brought over on *The Little Strength*
from London, reached Bethlehem. "In dulce Jubilo" was sung at a
love feast on August 21, 1745, in thirteen different languages: Bohemian, German, Latin, Greek, English, French, Swedish, Dutch,
Wendish, Gaelic, Welsh, Mohawk, and Mohican; and there were three
persons there of three more nationalities, Danish, Polish, and Hungarian, who did not sing.

On October 27, 1745, Spangenberg composed a hymn for the spin-

ning sisters. Soon all the other crafts had their own songs: the shepherds, the plowmen, the reapers, the threshers, the knitters, the seamstresses, the washwomen—all of them. Everyone worked; everyone
sang. The Church Diary for July 8, 1754, has the following entry: "Our
musicians of the church choir, performing hymn tunes, accompanied
the harvesters as far as the river, on their way to cut the rye on the
new farm, which was put under cultivation last fall near the *Crown*;
as the weather was fine, all who could assist, repaired to the fields,
men, women, and children." This was no uncommon thing; this was
the way things were done in Bethlehem. The same year a band of
women, each with a sickle, went to the harvest fields to cut grain to
the music of flutes and French horns. Friendly Indians escorted the
women to ensure their safety. The men, working in a group elsewhere,
also went to work to the accompaniment of music. Before the oxen or
horses drawing the harvest cart loaded high with sheaves of wheat or
rye went a small band of musicians with French horns, flutes, and
cymbals sounding hymns of jubilation and thanksgiving for God's goodness, songs in which the workers joined as they brought home the
harvest. No one day was set aside for music; there was music every day.
If they set out to cut timber, or dig a cellar, or raise a barn, a band
of musicians went with them. They sang as they went to work in the
morning and as they came home in the evening. Even the early immigrants at the end of their long journey from Saxony or Bohemia or
Holland or England or some other far-off land sang hymns of thanksgiving to the sound of the oars as they rowed across the Lehigh, their
eyes on their goal of Bethlehem.

The impromptu evening concerts of the young men became a regular feature of the life. In fine weather during the summer months the
young men entertained the rest of the community, sometimes with a
small orchestra, sometimes with a chorus. For nearly a hundred years,
from 1744 till well along in the nineteenth century, these concerts were
given, first on the balcony of the Bell House, then on the roof terrace
of the Brethren's house, the people sitting on the grass under the
trees, listening to the music and watching the fireflies in the meadows
by the river. In winter the concerts were held indoors in the Single
Brethren's house; there the married people went to hear the music and
to play or sing. Music was the life of the town.

At the start much of this music was religious, but as taste developed
secular music became more and more popular. Occasionally lighter

music was played, especially by the young men in their serenades. A particularly sober young clergyman took it upon himself to reprimand the young men for descending to music of this character. One night at dinner he turned to them and asked, "Do you use the same instruments in church to play sacred music which you used last night?"

"Yes," the young men admitted; "we do."

"What do you think, brother," the young clergyman asked, turning to an elderly clergyman at the table. "Is it proper to do so?"

"Well, you will use the same mouth to preach with tonight that you now use in eating sausage, won't you?" inquired the old clergyman.

Bethlehem seized on any excuse for music. Visitors to the town were often greeted by a band of musicians playing outside the inn. Even the night watchman as he made his rounds sang out the hour. There was a couplet set to music for each hour from eight to six:

> Past eight o'clock! O Bethlehem! do thou ponder
> Eight souls in Noah's ark were living yonder.

> 'Tis nine o'clock! Ye brethren, hear it striking,
> Keep hearts and houses clean to our Savior's liking.

> Now, brethren, hear! The clock is ten and passing,
> Now rest but such as wait for Christ's embracing.

And so on till five:

> 'Tis five o'clock! Five virgins were discarded,
> When five with wedding garments were rewarded.

> The clock is six and I go off my station,
> Now, brethren, watch yourselves for your salvation.

The original, of course, was in German, with better rhyme and meter.

The great ado with which the Moravians celebrated birthdays also added to their enjoyment of life. The "birthday child" was awakened by singing outside the door of the room in which he slept. Often a birthday hymn was sung at the breakfast table as well, and always in school. There was a small birthday table arranged with flowers and simple home-made gifts: a painted box, an illuminated text, a silk pincushion, a little basket of fancy paper, and often a poem of sorts written by some friend or relative. In the afternoon there would be a love feast with a birthday cake, or if the weather was good a picnic on Calypso Island in the river.

Death, too, was marked by ceremony, though there was no mourning. The trombone choir in the belfry announced the death of any member of the community. Three chorales were played, the second indicating the choir to which the dead person belonged, for each choir had its own chorale. The trombone choir led the funeral procession from the church to the grave. When the Indian convert John Wasamapah, often known as Tschoop, died, the *Memorials* of 1746 record that "the remains were conveyed to the graveyard amid the strains of solemn music."

Despite the many quaint features Bethlehem was one of the most progressive towns in the American colonies. Its waterworks, built in 1754, were the first public waterworks anywhere in the country. By the use of three force pumps, water was pumped up seventy feet to a tower. The pipes were made of carefully selected trunks of hemlock that had been floated down the Lehigh from Gnadenhütten. A fire company, now the Perseverance, was organized in 1762. Its fire engine, bought in London at a cost of £43,12s., was the earliest in the United States. At its first trial, on November 22, 1763, it sent a jet of water over the Single Brethren's House. Bethlehem has still another first, *die Apotheke*, or apothecary shop, opened in 1743 by Dr. Frederick Otto and now the oldest drugstore in America. Bethlehem's main hostelry, the Sun Inn, was one of the best and one of the most famous in the country. It had private suites consisting of a sitting room and two bedchambers, with a servant in attendance on each suite. The inn boasts that all the Presidents of the United States from Washington down to Lincoln stayed there. Though Bethlehem was in the wilderness, so to speak, it was by no means a backwater.

The Moravians even had ships of their own to bring their people to America. There were no redemptioners among the Moravians. The first of these ships was the *Catherine,* purchased for £600 and specially fitted out to transport the first "sea congregation," which sailed from London on March 16, 1742. This first sea congregation consisted of 56 people in addition to the minister at its head: 16 married couples, 2 married men without their wives, and 22 single men. Throughout the voyage "hourly intercession" was maintained night and day by prayer bands.

The second sea congregation sailed from Cowes on September 17, 1743, in *The Little Strength,* a ship the Moravians had bought and fitted out in England. All the crew except one sailor and two boys were Moravians. This sea congregation was made up of 56 married couples, 4 single men, 1 single woman, 1 widow, and 1 infant. Thirty-three young couples, thirty of them just married, were headed for Nazareth. Of these, twenty-four had been married at the same time at "the great wedding" at Marienborn on May 27, 1743. After a voyage of ten weeks and one day *The Little Strength* docked at New York on November 27th. At once the passengers set out on foot overland to Bethlehem, a great undertaking, especially for the women, many of whom were weak from the long voyage. Eight days later the first of the travelers reached Bethlehem. This was a youth who had given out on the way and for whom a horse had been procured. During the evening service of the next day the rest straggled in, one group after another, all hardly able to take another step. Everyone at Bethlehem was up waiting for the new arrivals, and when the last one finally got there a love feast was held in the chapel. "The chapel was quite filled," it is recorded; "and all rejoiced like children at this new influx to our little manger. The Bethlehem brethren served the newcomers, and bathed their galled and weary pilgrim feet, for they had bad weather, roads, and lodging, and often scarcity of food on the journey."

After the capture of *The Little Strength* by a Spanish privateer on May 1, 1744, a third ship, the *Irene,* was purchased. The *Irene* was a brave ship—"as strong as a tower," declared Spangenberg—with a lion as her figurehead. She was a square-rigged vessel of the sort called a "snow," with a keel of 85 feet. She was of 80 tons burden, and so commodious that a person could walk upright between her decks. Though the Moravians were pacifists of sorts, the *Irene* was mounted with two guns. In addition to a master and two mates, she carried a crew of nine men, two of them Jean and Jacobus van der Bilt. The *Irene* was launched on May 29, 1748, near Port Richmond on Staten Island at a cost of nearly £1,800. The third sea congregation arrived at London in the *Irene* on January 11, 1749, and put out to sea on March 1st, bound for Pennsylvania. The *Irene,* too, was eventually captured—by a French privateer off Cape Breton on November 30, 1757. She was succeeded by a fourth Moravian ship, the *Hope,* launched on November 21, 1760. Of 120 tons burden the *Hope* carried four cannon and a crew of thirteen men.

One of the most glorious and one of the saddest of chapters in Moravian history is their attempt to convert the Indians. In this they had far greater success than any other Protestant church. Here their courage, self-sacrifice, humanity, and endurance are shown at their finest. Only the greed, the ruthlessness, the "manifest destiny" of the white man prevented the success of the Moravians in Christianizing the Indians. Possibly the common belief that the Indians were descended from the ten lost tribes of Israel added to the Moravians' zeal. Be that as it may, the Moravian missionary society, the Society of the United Brethren for Propagating the Gospel Among the Heathen, organized on August 19, 1745, is the earliest missionary society in America; yet even before that the Moravians, both in Georgia and Pennsylvania and elsewhere too, had been working among the Indians. Zinzendorf had met deputies from the Six Nations in August, 1742, at the home of Conrad Weiser in the Tulpehocken settlement and persuaded them to consent to the Moravian missionary plans. He had met with other Indians at Shamokin, the Indian village that stood on the present site of Sunbury; here Madame Montour acted as his interpreter. He had journeyed through the forests to the mission at Shekomeko, about twenty-five miles from Rhinebeck on the Hudson. On September 15, 1742, he baptized the first Indian converts at Bethlehem: Wanab, to whom he gave the name David; and Tassawachamen, whom he called Joshua. Joseph Bull of Oley, a white man, was also baptized at the same time. The three converts knelt around a tub from which water was dipped out with a bowl and poured on their heads. Earlier, on January 12th of the same year at the conference Zinzendorf had called in Oley, three Indians had been baptized: Shabash, Otabawanemen, and Kiak. At this ceremony, performed in the barn of Isaac De Turck, the Indians had been given the names of Abraham, Isaac, and Jacob.

All the Indians were dealt with generously. Indians as well as white people were paid for whatever lands the Moravians occupied. The Moravians never attempted a "walking purchase." At Nazareth the Indians were paid for their huts, a peach grove, and a little field of wheat that were on the land of the Moravian settlement. In 1744 a school for the study of Indian languages was opened at Bethlehem under the direction of Christopher Pyrlaeus. In New York, however, Moravian missionary efforts met with disapproval. The New Yorkers believed that such success among the Indians could be accounted for only if the Moravians were French agents. Consequently all Moravians were banned from the colony in 1743. Two missionaries, Christian Frederick Post and David Zeisberger, who had gone to live with the

Mohawks in order to learn their language, were arrested on February 23, 1745, and locked up in the New York jail until April 10, when through the efforts of Conrad Weiser and Governor Thomas of Pennsylvania they were released to take part in negotiations with the Indians. Even the French and Indian War did not stop the Moravian attempt to convert the Indians. The missionary work was extended year by year until it covered most of the tribes east of the Mississippi, especially the Algonquins and the Iroquois.

Indians were always made welcome at Bethlehem. A stone tavern or lodge for the entertainment of Indian visitors was built in 1752 on the west bank of the Monocacy. Farther up on the Lehigh, on the present site of Lehighton, was the mission of Gnadenhütten. The massacre at Gnadenhütten on November 24, 1755, when the Moravian missionaries there were either killed or taken captive, was a terrible blow to Moravian hopes. After the destruction of this mission many of the Indian converts fled to Bethlehem, where the Moravians gave seventy of these "brown hearts" shelter for a year and then built the Indian village of Nain for them.

With the outbreak of the French and Indian War, Bethlehem doubled in size: 556 refugees, both white and red, were housed there by January, 1756. Friendly Indians acted as guards for the town and rangers in the woods. They brought in game from the forest, sometimes three deer a day; they set up bush nets in the river and caught shad and rockfish by the thousand. Even this did not provide enough food for the greatly increased population, for the harvest of 1755 had been unusually poor. Between the first of the year and the fall of 1756, the Moravians bought five thousand extra bushels of grain for their own needs and those of the refugees. For this the provincial government reimbursed the Moravians only in part. Fortunately clothing and food were collected in Philadelphia and sent to these "displaced persons."

There is a tradition that hostile Indians had planned to attack Bethlehem on Christmas Day, 1755. The Indians were about ready to start the attack when the trombone choir on the belvedere of the Brethren's House broke the silence of the dawn with the playing of the Christmas chorale. The startled Indians lurking in the forest listened to the solemn strains of the melody thrice repeated and took it for the voice of the Great Spirit warning them away. Only months later did Bethlehem learn of its escape when a Minsi convert told them what had happened. This is one of the town's most cherished traditions. It may be merely a fanciful story; it may be the truth.

All through the French and Indian War the Moravians were in an unhappy position. Although liable to attack by hostile Indians, they were regarded by other white colonists with mistrust because of their friendliness to the Indians. Some of this suspicion was fantastic. The calendar they used, which was the modern one instead of the antiquated English one commonly in use then, though eleven days behind the time, was advanced as proof that they were secretly papists and in league with the French—this because it was a pope who had corrected the calendar and brought it up to date.

Though in many ways the outbreak of hostilities was a far greater blow to the Moravians than to any of the other white settlers, Bethlehem took the war more quietly than most of the other frontier settlements. There was none of the panic in Bethlehem that there was in Reading. The outlying Moravian villages of Christianbrunn, Gnadenthal, Friedensthal, and even Nazareth and Bethlehem were all threatened. The Moravians appealed for soldiers to save these settlements and also prepared to defend themselves. In this respect they differed from the Quakers, the Mennonites, the Brethren, and the Amish. As they put it, they were not *kriegerisch* (warlike), but neither were they *Quäkerisch* (Quakerlike). Although they rejected all aggression, they believed in defending themselves. Throughout the war they kept the authorities in Philadelphia informed of the movement of any considerable band of Indians that came to their knowledge. Furthermore, some of the Moravian missionaries, especially Christian Frederick Post, were invaluable in winning the support of the Indians.

Much of the success of the Moravians in converting the Indians was due to the fact that they looked upon the Indians as fellow human beings. They treated them with absolute justice. They translated their hymns and religious books into the Indian languages. They taught them their music. They took such pains that at Friedenshütten on the upper Susquehanna the Indians were able to set up on Christmas Day, 1767, a spinet made by the Mohican, Joseph, with the help of the missionary, John Jacob Schmick, and to use it to accompany the Moravian hymns that they sang in their own tongue. The Moravians received the Indians into their churches. Occasionally they intermarried with them. Christian Frederick Post twice took an Indian wife, largely because he believed it would help him in his missionary work. When their Indian converts died, the Moravians buried them in their grave-yards side by side with their own people. One hundred and thirty-six Indian converts are buried in the old Moravian graveyard in Bethle-hem. The Moravians well deserved the thanks of George Washington for their "disinterested endeavors . . . to civilize and Christianize the savages of the wilderness."

The old Moravian graveyard at Bethlehem, in which many of the Indians were buried, is one of the more fascinating burying grounds of the country. It is a peaceful spot shaded by old trees with stones flat on the ground—the "breaststones" that mark the Moravian graves instead of headstones. To show the equality of all in the eyes of the Lord, each stone is the same size. In the Moravian graveyards the dead are buried, not family by family, but pretty much in the order in which they die, though the little boys are buried in one section and the little girls in another, while the single men have a section to themselves, as have the single women, the married men, and the married women. The tombstone marking the grave of each unbaptized boy is inscribed with the word *Beatus* (blessed), that of each unbaptized girl *Beata*—a singu-larly gracious custom. Sometimes there are epitaphs on the stones, but none to match the tender one on the tombstone of a little boy in the Moravian graveyard at Nazareth:

> Thy little suff'rings now are o'er,
> Thy little head shall ache no more;
> Thy little race on earth is run,
> Farewell but for a time, my son.

Bishop, plowman, Indian convert, organ-maker, seamstress, missionary, locksmith, miller, dairymaid, shepherd, choir leader, baker: here is a cross-section of early America. There are men and women from every position in society, from all occupations. There are men and women from the Rhine, from England and France, from Moravia, from Switzerland, from Norway and Sweden and Denmark, from the shores of the Baltic, from the three corners of the world; and there are Indians from the Loyalhanna, Shamokin, and the Chenango. This was an eighteenth century melting pot, a pattern in little of the America to come.

Bethlehem and Nazareth were not the only Moravian settlements in the American colonies. In 1753 a tract of a hundred thousand acres in the Yadkin Valley of North Carolina was purchased from the Earl of Granville and named Wachovia after one of Zinzendorf's estates. Here the villages of Bethabara, Bethania, Hope, Friedland, and Salem were founded. Bethabara was intended to be the chief town, but it was soon surpassed by Salem. Today Bethabara is a quiet village with a fine old Moravian church of stone and brick with a dunce-cap steeple, while Salem as part of Winston-Salem is a bustling city. Winston-Salem is still one of the principal Moravian centers. A heritage from its past are the fine old buildings, almost as many as at Williamsburg. Originally the steep roofs were covered with red tiles, only one mark of their continental origin. The onion-shaped dome crowning the cupola of the church, arched hoods over doorways, and vaulted cellars are wholly unlike the prevalent Georgian architecture of the South.

In 1756 a little settlement in northern Lancaster County was named Lititz in honor of the barony in Bohemia that had been the ancient refuge of the Moravians. A *Gemeinhaus* had been built in 1748 and the congregation organized in 1749; but it was not until 1754, when George Klein gave the church 491 acres, that a village was formed. A Single Sisters' House was started in 1758 and one for single brethren the following year. By the "lease system" only Moravians were permitted to live in Lititz. Although the General Economy was never adopted at Lititz, it was essentially a *Landgemeine*, a country congregation. Life at Lititz was almost as idyllic as that at Bethlehem. The church diary for July 3, 1763, records that the rye harvest commenced "and the Single Sisters were busy cutting it (with sickles)." An entry for April, 1774, reveals something of the placid nature of the town: "A meeting of the Brethren was held to consider the question whether anything could be done to prevent the running at large in the streets of cows." In the main, life was earnest. The single sisters engaged in spinning and weaving in addition to taking a turn in the harvest fields; they knitted and embroidered and made lace; they made dresses and wove chip hats; they fashioned little boxes and made confectionery. A small store was opened to sell the products of their labor. Frivolous pastimes such as checkers and chess were forbidden, and even "fig-mill," a game played with yellow and red grains of corn on a board, was frowned on. A regulation of 1765 forbade the smoking of "segars" on the street, but this was because of the fear of fire that haunted

Lititz rather than a concern for morals. It was also ordered that live coals must be carried in a covered pot when taken from one house to another. A further regulation directed that chimneys be swept three times a year (a shilling and fourpence for two-story houses, ninepence for one story) with the exception of those on the Gemeinhaus and the two choir houses, which must be swept every eight weeks (a shilling and sixpence per chimney).

With the end of the General Economy in 1762 the communistic features of the life at Bethlehem and Nazareth were discontinued. The various industries were sold to individual members, who bought the stock and fixtures and leased the buildings; but a number of the farms, the store, and the Sun Inn continued under the control of the church authorities. Both Bethlehem and Nazareth remained church towns, little Christian republics, in which only members of the church were permitted to reside permanently. Municipal affairs were handled by the congregational council, which made many of the appointments to the various positions, including the postilion to carry the mail to Philadelphia, the nurse to assist the physician, the night watchman, the sexton, the almoner, and a dozen or more others. Many of these positions were filled by lot, for the Moravians made use of the lot more than any other Protestant church.

The excessive use of the lot is one of the more curious features of Moravian life. The rest of the world may believe that marriage is a lottery, but only the Moravians took this truism literally. The theory behind the use of the lot in marriage is clear: thus man was assured of divine guidance in choosing a wife. A scoffer might suggest that in marriage by lot man was able to blame God for the choice of his wife rather than take the blame himself. In Bethlehem the two sexes were separated from early childhood: boys and girls grew up seeing very little of one another. Most emphatically the Moravians did not believe in coeducation. The young men and the young women lived in separate choir houses. Even in church they were assigned to different sides of the building, for in the Moravian church, like many another of the day, the men sat on one side and the women on the other. Rarely did the two sexes mingle. One such occasion was the snitzing bee held on fall evenings in the Snitz House, a little log structure that had been built in 1749. Here the single sisters pared the apples and cut them into slices or snitz, while the single brethren placed the trays of snitz in the drying oven. Even then they were well chaperoned. The chances are that when a young Moravian came to marriageable age and wished to take a wife, he knew no girls. Of course, if he had been smitten by one of the single sisters he met at a snitzing bee or saw in church, he could submit her name; but very often he left the choice of the girl to the proper authorities, the *Bruder-Pleger,* or caretaker of the single brethren, and the *Schwester-Pleger,* or matron in charge of the single women. Together they would consider the young man's character and choose a proper mate for him. But whether he submitted a name or left the choice to his elders, the next step was the use of the lot to determine whether or not his name might be presented to the girl. This was a fifty-fifty chance. If the lot went against him, his hopes of marrying that particular girl were dashed; he was never given a second chance. If he wished he could ask the authorities to choose again for him, or he could wait until another girl took his fancy, or he could go to Nazareth or Lititz and try his luck there. Even if the lot was in his favor, it was up to the young woman to decide whether or not she wished to marry him. Although she was under no compulsion to take him, so much weight was attached to the divine element in the use of the lot that she often let herself be guided by the lot. These marriages seem to have turned out well, to have been as happy as those made for more romantic reasons.

Yet the Moravians did not take marriage as a matter of course. To them marriage was part of the good life; it made for contentment in man. Earthly marriage was. regarded as a preparation for heavenly marriage. Sex relations were natural, right, and even holy. The married man who lived in the world was their ideal, not the ascetic who withdrew from it.

This utopia in Pennsylvania had come into being largely because Zinzendorf, who was a wealthy man, was willing to advance large sums of money to the church. It was Zinzendorf's money that enabled the Moravians to purchase large tracts of land and erect substantial buildings on them. This early advantage turned into a liability when the church in Europe followed the lead of impractical enthusiasts to attempt a new settlement at Herrnhaag and to embark on ambitious manufacturing and trading ventures in England. To save the church Zinzendorf stepped into the breach in 1753 with all his property and credit. On Zinzendorf's death in 1756 the church found itself indebted to his heirs. Though the church paid $90,000 to the heirs for their interest in the Pennsylvania estates, far more onerous was the enormous debt that had been contracted. By 1764 about $550,000 had been paid off, with $773,162 still owing. Of this debt the Moravians in Pennsylvania had to shoulder a large part. Not until 1801 was the church rid of this burden.

In spite of the heavy debt Bethlehem continued to progress. In 1770 the Widows' Society of Bethlehem was founded, probably the oldest existing beneficial society in the United States. The same year John Martin Mack was consecrated bishop, the first Moravian bishop—in fact, the first bishop of any Christian church—to be consecrated in America.

The Revolution found Bethlehem in the thick of things. It was on the line of march from Pennsylvania to New York. In July, 1775, Pennsylvania troops passed through on their way to New England; these were soon followed by troops from Virginia. Then came British prisoners on their way south. On January 30, 1776, four sleighs filled with the wives and children of prisoners captured at St. John's pulled into town. Their suffering in the bitter cold so moved the Moravians that they collected warm clothing and blankets for them. This was only the start. The Moravians, often counted with the "peace sects" of Pennsylvania, had hoped to sit out the war in quiet. The church had decided that all its men would take the same stand, to refuse absolutely to have any part in active military service but to pay any fine levied upon them. This position did not endear them to their militant rebel neighbors, the Scotch-Irish and the Lutherans and Reformed among the Pennsylvania Dutch. In near-by Emmaus twenty-five Moravians were imprisoned and put on bread and water for a month.

Bethlehem and Nazareth did not have to go to the war; even though these towns saw no fighting the war came to them. Nowhere else in the colonies were buildings so perfectly suited for use as hospitals as those at Bethlehem. Furthermore, Bethlehem was just the right distance behind the lines. In December, 1776, the general hospital of the Continental Army was moved to Bethlehem. On December 5th the first wagons loaded with wounded, shivering in the piercing cold, came rolling into town. These poor men were quickly moved into the Single Brethren's House. Here they were nursed by the Moravians, Bishop Ettwein serving as chaplain in the hospital. At first all was in disorder, with no food and the wounded men famishing. These the Moravians fed from their own stores until the commissary supplies reached Bethlehem three days later. On December 15 General Gates, the ranking division commander under Washington, arrived; and on December 17 General Sullivan, with three thousand to four thousand troops. Even before the army came, the town had been filled to overflowing with refugees from Philadelphia, but with the army pouring into town all was at sixes and sevens. Every house, every barn, every shed was packed with men. The Sun Inn was jammed with high-ranking officers: Generals Arnold, Glover, and Sterling were all there. The church at the Christmas Eve services was crowded as never before. Most of the soldiers were forced to encamp outside the town, where they burned up the fence rails for miles around. Later on Bethlehem put in a bill for this wood: 17,000 fence rails, 200 posts, and 594½ cords of firewood—and was awarded £1,750 in Pennsylvania money. In all fairness to the Moravians it must be pointed out that this £1,750 was the total amount of Bethlehem's war claims. It never made any attempt to collect a penny for the use of its buildings as hospitals or for its citizens' services as nurses. That much Bethlehem was glad to give free. Fence rails, however, were another matter.

Crowded though it was, Bethlehem went its unruffled way. The coolness, the absence of all hysteria, made Bethlehem invaluable as a hospital site. There was no demoralization. In February, 1777, large quantities of military stores were brought to the town. On March 27, 1777, the hospital was moved, and Bethlehem breathed a sigh of relief. One hundred and ten dead were left behind, buried on a bluff across the Monocacy.

All that summer many members of Congress visited Bethlehem: Henry Laurens, soon to become president of Congress; John Hancock, John Adams, Samuel Adams, Richard Henry Lee, and ten other members. On September 7 there arrived 218 prisoners, mostly Scotch Highlanders. Then came the defeat at Brandywine, and once more Bethlehem became the general hospital for the Continental Army. The most noted patient was the wounded Lafayette. For a time it looked as though the whole town might be taken over by the army and the Moravians forced out. To guard against this the members of Congress who were then in Bethlehem made their wishes known to the army:

BETHLEHEM, September the 22d, 1777.

Having here observed a humane and diligent attention to the sick and wounded, and a benevolent desire to make the necessary provision for the relief of the distressed, as far as the powers of the Bretheren enable them We desire that all Continental Officers may refrain from disturbing the persons or property of the Moravians in Bethlehem, and particularly that they do not disturb or molest the Houses where the women are assembled. Given under our hands at the time and place above mentioned.

Nathan Brownson	Richard Henry Lee
Nath'l Folsom	Wm. Duer
Richard Law	Corn'l Harnett
John Hancock	Henry Laurens
Samuel Adams	Benj. Harrison
Eliph't Dyer	Jos. Jones
Jas. Duane	John Adams
	Henry Marchant
	Wm. Williams

DELEGATES TO CONGRESS.

Yet the town was grossly overcrowded, especially after the battle of Germantown, when wounded in vast numbers were brought to Bethlehem. Some, it is said, were "laid upon the ground in the rain to die" —a statement more shocking than true, since the Moravians were doing everything in their power to give shelter to the men, to nurse the wounded and alleviate their pain. The Moravians went through the town again and again, collecting all possible blankets and clothing. Some of the soldiers were housed temporarily in tents. All these were moved to the garret of the Brethren's House when hard rains came on at the end of October. Another hundred were in a frame building that had been thrown up to give them shelter. When there was no longer a place to put another man, fifty wagons loaded with sick and wounded arrived from Princeton. In the Brethren's House, where it had been estimated two hundred men could be properly cared for, seven hundred had been jammed. Though the facilities were the best the army could obtain, they were woefully inadequate. It was impossible to keep the men or the place clean under such crowded conditions. The stench was frightful, especially in the attic, which was virtually without ventilation. A malignant fever known as "putrid fever" broke out and spread rapidly. Men died—five, six, even as many as twelve a night.

So unsanitary were the conditions that Dr. William Smith of the hospital staff later declared that four or five patients had died on the same straw before it was changed. At first the Moravians aided by soldiers made coffins for the dead, but soon men were dying faster than coffins could be built. Many of the civilians died, too, nurses and orderlies in the hospital and people in the town. At dawn each day the dead-cart piled high with bodies left the Brethren's House for the hill across the Monocacy, where the dead were buried in trenches. There unnamed, even unnumbered, they lie among the cedars on a bluff above the creek. There may be as many as five hundred soldiers buried there; there may be more. No one knows.

In addition to all the sick and wounded, nine hundred wagons of baggage and munitions with all their wagoners had come to Bethlehem. Washington's baggage and the bells of Christ Church in Philadelphia were among these. Even the Liberty Bell on its way to Allentown passed through the town. And, to top it all, two hundred and eighteen British prisoners were quartered there. The military population was forever shifting, for the town was a thoroughfare for troops. Bethlehem had become the crossroads of America. Fresh regiments that had not yet smelled powder came marching jauntily into the Platz, buttons shining, banners flying; others, battle-stained and weary, plowed grimly through the streets of the town. For Pulaski the Moravian sisters embroidered a handsome crimson-silk guidon, which he still carried as his standard when he fell at Savannah. Martha Washington visited Bethlehem and accompanied by a group of American officers attended the services in the church. George Washington, too, came to town and worshiped in the Moravian church. One general after another turned up in Bethlehem: Greene, Knox, Sterling, Schuyler, Gates, Arnold, Armstrong, Reed, De Kalb, and von Steuben. There was even a captured Hessian general and his wife, Baron Riedesel of the Brunswick corps. Later on, in the summer of 1783, John Paul Jones came to Bethlehem and stayed for a month.

After the Revolution a period of tranquillity set in. Bethlehem was known throughout the Republic for its schools and its music. In a sense it was a large, quiet cloister, yet it was not unaware of the world; to a certain degree it was even cosmopolitan. Many of its inhabitants were people of culture. Moreover, the influx of visitors during the Revolution had made a knowledge of English common. Practically everyone in Bethlehem was bilingual. By 1783 there was English preaching in the church every Sunday. There was a steady stream of visitors, from Philadelphia and the greater world. The Duke de la Rochefoucauld, the Duke of Saxe-Weimar, the Prince of Wied, and Joseph Bonaparte were some of the visitors with the most dazzling titles.

Yet pleasant though the town was, it was stagnating. More and more it was becoming an agreeable country town where Philadelphians could escape the heat of a Philadelphia summer. It was quiet, it was inexpensive, it was cultured, it was even quaint. Its inhabitants had good manners; there was almost an Old World courtesy. Its inn was one of the best in America. Its only rival in the neighborhood was the Gasthof zur Rose, better known as the Rose, at Nazareth. The British officer Aubury, in his *Travels in America,* published in London in 1789, speaks of the Sun Inn as "equal to the first tavern in London" and praises it for its excellent wine. Many of the brief notations of the guests made by the clerk are tantalizing vignettes of the days of the early Republic:

July 12, 1801.—A lady dressed in black.

July 15, 1801.—A company of French gentlemen with a servant. Four suppers, 4 breakfasts, 4 dinners, 5 bottles porter, 2 bowls punch, 1 pint Lisbon.

August 12, 1801.—A gentleman in a Windsor chair.

August 26, 1801.—A company from Maryland in chairs, viz: one gentleman, two children, and one negro servant. Six suppers, 3 breakfasts, 3 dinners, 2 glasses brandy, $2\frac{1}{4}$ pints Teneriffe, $1\frac{1}{4}$ glass sangaree.

August 28, 1801.—A company of actors. Twelve suppers, 12 breakfasts, 9 dinners, 12 gills brandy.

September 12, 1801.—A gentleman and a lady in a phaeton.

November 28, 1801.—General Lee, 6 horses and 4 servants. Five dinners, 1 bottle Madeira, 5 quarts beer, $5\frac{1}{4}$ pints brandy.

October 3, 1802.—A gentleman in a "Sopus wagon."

The coming of the nineteenth century meant little to the quiet, sleepy town. With its women still wearing the Schnepplehaube, with marriages still arranged by lot, with the whole town turning out on Whitmonday for an excursion to Calypso Island down the river, the town seemed anchored in the eighteenth century. Bethlehem was a place where time stood still. But for all that it was not an American Cranford; it had more life than that. The Philharmonic Society produced oratorios; the girls' school was still the best in the country, and there were men of eminence living in Bethlehem (Moravians, too!):

Lewis David de Schweinitz, the botanist, and John Heckewelder, the missionary to the Indians.

What brought about the change? What had transformed Bethlehem from a vital, stirring town to a sleepy backwater? In large part it was the decision made at the synod of 1769 at Marienborn that the church in America was merely a subordinate, outlying branch of the Unity, to be managed by a board responsible to the elders' conference in Europe. For eighty years no American synod was empowered to convene. Thus the American church was effectively hamstrung. Everything had to be referred to the European church for decision, to men who knew little of America or American conditions. Their view was a narrow, conservative view, timid and completely out of keeping with the spirit of the growing Republic. Their eyes were fixed on the exclusive closed church village of Herrnhut, not on the vastness of a continent. This was the great opportunity and the great failure of the Moravian Church. If it had seized this chance boldly, its members today might be numbered by the million instead of by the thousand. In its ideas there was much that was good. Wesley borrowed some of them; Schleiermacher and Goethe felt their influence. Indirectly the world has been affected by them, but directly the impress of the Moravian Church since the end of the eighteenth century has been slight.

Two specific features to which particular objection was raised by the Moravians themselves were the excessive use of the lot, especially in marriage, and the regimentation of the choir system. The contagion of independence infected the quiet town. The great facts of the American and French revolutions could not be denied—even in a cloister. As a result of these protests the Single Brethren's House was given up on April 16, 1814. More surprising was the revolt of the women, who had seemed to be occupied with their work or such mild diversions as apple-butter cookings or carpet-rag parties. Suddenly in 1815 they informed the authorities that henceforth they were going to wear English hats instead of the traditional Schnepplehaube. No permission was asked of anybody; it was a blunt statement of fact. Before such a revolt the authorities were helpless. Shortly thereafter, in 1818, the use of the lot in marriage was abandoned. The Moravians of Bethlehem and Nazareth and Lititz were becoming increasingly aware of their American citizenship; they were no longer thinking of themselves as a "peculiar people" set off from the rest of the world. These growing pains were accompanied by a loss of members: small Moravian settlements such as

Donegal in Pennsylvania and Hope and Woolwich in New Jersey had to be abandoned. On the other hand, the mission for the Negroes at Salem met with encouraging success until the North Carolina legislature passed a law that forbade all education of Negroes.

Year by year the revolt went on. The American separation of church and state prevailed in the Moravian towns as well as elsewhere in the nation. Membership in the church and the town were no longer one and the same. The towns were "opened up." Anybody could move in: Lutheran, Reformed, Roman Catholic, or Greek Orthodox. At the same time the Moravian Church in America was freeing itself from the church in Europe. Practical independence was established by 1848, absolute independence by 1857. Once more the church began to branch out: churches were founded at Green Bay, Wisconsin, and Utica, New York. A mission was sent to the Eskimos in western Alaska.

As the century wore on, Bethlehem lost much of its distinctive character and became simply one more small American town. Railroads were built, and the outside world was much closer than it had ever been before. Then in the fifties steel moved in and Lehigh University was founded. The town began to grow until by the end of the century it had been transformed into a city. At first the Moravian community looked askance at the great steel mills and the university on the other side of the river, but by 1918 it had become reconciled to living in the same world with them and the two settlements were joined to form one city, the Bethlehem of today. This is the city of Moravianism and the Bach Choir, and of miles of steel mills along the Lehigh.

A Hotbed of Religions: Ephrata &
Other Curious Religious Societies

In 1782, when Comte de Ségur visited Philadelphia, it was the religious toleration that excited his admiration rather than the fine proportions of the State House, or the markets along the High Street, or the handsome country houses with gardens dipping down to the Schuylkill. That Quakers, Episcopalians, Mennonites, Dunkards, Lutherans, Reformed, Presbyterians, Moravians, Roman Catholics, Jews, Methodists, and Baptists could all worship amicably together, each in his separate church or meetinghouse, each in his own fashion: that to him was the miracle.

The religious toleration established by Penn in his colony is in part the explanation of the large number of churches and sects in early Pennsylvania. In the rich soil of Pennsylvania, which produced bountiful crops of wheat and tulip trees nearly two hundred feet high, religions transplanted from Europe struck root and newer sorts of native growth sprang up. Such was the welter of religions in colonial Pennsylvania that Mühlenberg wrote, "There is no sect in the world that has not followers here." From the Society of the Woman in the Wilderness in the late seventeenth century to Buchmanism today, Pennsylvania has been blessed with a bumper crop of religions, many of them Pennsylvania Dutch. Undoubtedly the religious freedom of the colony attracted to its forests religions persecuted elsewhere, for at that time persecution on religious grounds was almost invariably the rule. Only in Holland, Rhode Island, and Pennsylvania could a man worship as he pleased; and because Pennsylvania afforded greater economic opportunities than such a thickly settled country as Holland or such a small colony as Rhode Island the oppressed of Europe swarmed to it. One cannot but wonder, though, if there may not have been something in the air of colonial Pennsylvania, something right about the atmosphere—perhaps a sort of celestial yeast—to give rise to bizarre and freakish religions, just as there was in New York State in the nineteenth century and just as there is in southern California today.

The Ephrata Society was in several ways the most curious of the early Pennsylvania Dutch religious groups. This religious order was largely the creation of Johann Conrad Beissel, the posthumous son of a drunken baker of Eberbach in the Palatinate. Beissel became a baker like his father and drifted to Mannheim. There he quarreled with his employer's wife, and it was "deeply impressed upon his heart that a man who intends to devote himself to the service of God must, at the beginning of his conversion, renounce Adam's regenerative work," as the *Chronicon Ephratense* so circumspectly puts it; "for which reason he bade good night to earthly women at the very commencement." At this same period he came into contact with Pietists and was attracted by their ideas. In the Palatinate he went from Mannheim to Heidelberg, where he was arrested and finally banished. Passing from one Rhineland city to another, he at length set sail for America. In Germantown he learned the weaver's trade in the home of a Dunkard elder. Then he withdrew to the woods near Conestoga to try the life of a hermit, only to find such a life unfruitful. His next step was to have himself baptized a Dunkard and become an elder in the Conestoga meeting. In 1732 he broke with the Dunkards to found a religion of his own, the Ephrata Society. Into this new religion he led most of the members of the Dunkard church at Conestoga.

Two main ideas set off the Ephrata Society from the other Pennsylvania Dutch churches. First was the observance of the seventh day as the Sabbath, an idea Beissel borrowed from the Keithian Quakers. This was the chief point of difference between Beissel and the Dunkards. Second was his dislike of marriage and disapproval of the sex relation. Celibacy, though not required, was decidedly stressed at Ephrata. The two celibate groups, the Order of Spiritual Virgins and the Solitary Brethren, were the backbone of the community. Complete celibacy was the ideal, although it was never attained by the whole community. Marriage, looked upon as a state far short of perfection, was at best but tolerated. Married couples joining the "Economy" at Ephrata were pledged to continence. Shortly before his death Beissel drew up a list of the many blessings he had received from God, one of the first of which was that God had "preserved him from the allurements of the female sex." At the third religious conference at Oley, where Zinzendorf was attempting to unite the various Pennsylvania Dutch religions, the Ephrata view of marriage was presented by Beissel's followers and vigorously attacked by Zinzendorf. On the surface alone did the two communistic societies of Ephrata and Bethlehem have much in common; fundamentally they were unlike. The Moravians believed in a rich, full life; Ephrata in abnegation.

Joined to Beissel's suspicion of sex was a disapproval of the human body. Both sexes wore a monastic garb designed to "muffle the mortal body," to conceal "that humiliating image revealed by sin"—white for the Spiritual Virgins and the Solitary Brethren—linen or cotton in summer and wool in winter. The men wore a long gown, to which was fastened a pointed monk's hood, over shirt, trousers, and vest; the women wore a rounded cowl and long skirts. Both men and women went barefoot in summer and wore shoes of wood and hide in winter. The secular members with families wore gray instead of white. Both sexes were tonsured, and the men were bearded. The garb adopted was almost precisely that of the Capuchins or White Friars, which Ephrata chose to regard as a coincidence. "The Solitary at Ephrata felt flattered that they should have the honor to dip water from the same well with so venerable, famous, and ancient an Order." These white-garbed Protestant monks working in the fields or moving about the austere gabled buildings must have been one of the stranger sights of colonial Pennsylvania.

The first buildings at Ephrata were erected on Mount Zion, a hill rising above the Cocalico, a site soon abandoned for the meadow below. Two of the strange, severe structures built by Beissel and his followers still remain: Saron, the sisters' house built early in the 1740's, and Saal, the chapel. Bethania, the brethren's house, to which there was a chapel attached, was torn down during the last century. Even earlier was Kedar, a three-story structure for the brethren on Mount Zion. On the first floor of Kedar was a refectory and on the second a curious circular room with no windows but only a light in the center. Around this lamp the brethren slept on pallets placed like the spokes of a wheel. On the third floor was a room to which brethren retired for forty days and nights of prayer and study in an effort to gain for themselves, through various mystical experiences, a limited immortality of 5,557 years. Sustained only by dry bread and rain water that fell during the month of May, many of them saw visions; some even took leave of their senses and had to be flogged to restore them to their right minds.

Ephrata had smaller buildings as well, among them an almonry, a granary, and a bakehouse in back of Saron, and here and there cottages for the married couples in addition to the barns and mills of several kinds. As Beissel had scruples about the use of iron, the brethren substituted wood for iron wherever possible. Saal was built without any iron, wooden pegs being used in place of nails. This was in obedience to the injunction given by Moses in Deuteronomy 27:5: "Thou shalt not lift up any iron tool upon them." Furthermore, iron was symbolic of evil and darkness. The trenchers from which they ate were naturally of wood, but so were the knives and spoons and even the Communion goblets. Blocks of wood were used to iron their clothes.

Much importance was attached to symbolism. In determining the size of one of the larger buildings, they were guided by the symbolism of the numbers designating the length of the building. They believed that in any number a circle represented God and the downstroke man. The number 66 was rejected because in each of the 6's man was put over God; 100 was rejected because there man was put before God. Finally 99 was approved because in each 9 God was put above man.

The monks and nuns at Ephrata occupied tiny cells, with only one small, high window to a cell. There were two monks or two nuns to each cell. In Saron the older sisters lived on the lower floors, the younger ones in the upper stories. The doors throughout were low—to teach humility; the passageways were narrow—to bring to mind the straight and narrow way. They slept on wooden planks with small wooden blocks for pillows. A bed or even a pillow of goose feathers was forbidden as contributing to man's luxurious indulgence. A small hanging cupboard for each monk or nun was the only furniture besides the planks on which they slept. Their diet was largely a vegetable one, for in the early years of the community it was considered sinful to kill any animals or eat of their flesh. Although later Beissel left the eating of flesh to the conscience of each disciple, few of them ate meat. Many of their contemporaries remarked on their pale, bloodless faces. Whenever they appeared in public they walked with "a solemn, steady pace," with their eyes fixed upon the ground. On a journey they walked one behind the other. The spectral sight of these strange bearded men from the banks of the Cocalico, dressed in white from head to foot and walking in Indian file, made a deep impression on all who saw them. At first the brethren thought it sinful to compel horses to work for them. The monks put the harness on themselves and dragged the plows through the fields or hauled home the wood. In later years they made use of horses and oxen, yet their consciences were troubled because of this and they tried to make it up to the horses and oxen by treating them with extreme gentleness.

It was an ascetic life from start to finish. On joining the order they left behind their worldly names and adopted new ones, some fantastic and others biblical or classical: Beno, Arnella, Zephaniah, Obed, Keturah, Agabus, Iphigenia, Jonadab, Syncletica, Euphrosina, Jael, Flavia, Persida, and others of a like nature. The sloughing off of the names they had borne ever since they were christened was but a minor change that marked the new life they led on entering the Cloisters, a life of complete regimentation. At midnight the bell rang for prayer. In the early years of zeal and enthusiasm many of the families dwelling in the surrounding countryside rose up at the sound of the bell to hold family prayers. In the first flush of enthusiasm the midnight vigil lasted from twelve to four until they were forced to admit that lack of sleep was an obstacle that even enthusiasm could not surmount. Then the vigils were cut to two hours and finally to one. This was only one part of the constant battle against the body and its demands. After a vigil, let us say, from twelve to two, the Ephrata monk or nun rose at five for an hour of meditation; then followed three hours of work and a fourth of rest, at which time he or she might eat a frugal breakfast if food was necessary to keep body and soul together. Then there was another hour of work and still another hour of meditation. At noon a light lunch was eaten. The afternoon was given over to work, with supper, the main meal of the day, at six. The two hours after supper were occupied by reading, writing, or singing, with bedtime at nine. Every Friday each member had to present to Beissel a written confession of his or her spiritual state. These were read to the whole meeting on Saturday.

It was a life of hard labor to which these monks and nuns sentenced themselves. Ephrata was a workshop as well as a religious community. There was a flour mill, a sawmill, a paper mill, a fulling mill, a flaxseed-oil press, a printing press, and a book bindery. The printing press was one of the most noted of colonial America. The Mennonite *Martyr Book* of this press was the most remarkable accomplishment of colonial printing. During the Revolution, when Philadelphia was occupied by the British, it was this press that printed the Continental dollars for the Congress then sitting at York. The nuns copied hundreds of volumes of music and spent hours illuminating texts—the famous *Fraktur* of Ephrata. Oddly enough, they made sulphur matches, paper lanterns, and artificial flowers too; and especially during the Revolution, when the Cloisters became a hospital, they nursed the sick. Furthermore, the community conducted a school that attracted pupils from as far away as Philadelphia and Maryland. Latin was taught with enough skill to enable teachers and pupils to write to one another in that language. In addition to all this there was the everyday work essential for the well-being of any community: the felling of timber, the construction of buildings, the tilling of fields; or even such lesser tasks as gathering wood for the fireplaces, spinning flax and weaving cloth and fashioning it into garments, making shoes, cooking food, and washing clothes. As the two sexes were kept apart as much as possible, to each sex fell work ordinarily performed by the other. The men washed their own clothes and kept their quarters clean as well as cooking and baking for themselves. The women split their own firewood. It is amazing how much so few people accomplished, for Ephrata never had more than eighty monks and nuns. In 1740 there were thirty-five brethren and thirty-four sisters; in 1770 these had decreased to fourteen brethren and twenty-eight sisters; and in 1785 there were only seven men and nine women.

Ephrata was a communistic venture with Beissel as the manager. All property, whether of the monks and nuns or the families that joined the community, was at Beissel's disposal. Everything belonged to the community; everyone worked for the good of the whole group. Economically Ephrata was a success. There were even branch monasteries at Germantown and Snow Hill in Franklin County, though Ephrata was always the center of the society. But so far were they from materialism that surplus money was given away.

There can be no doubt that Beissel was in many ways an extraordinary man. He had great personal magnetism. According to the *Chronicon Ephratense* he was followed through the streets by women enthusiasts singing hymns as they went, some so exhausted they had to be carried, "so that people ran to the street to behold the wonder." It is ironic that a man with the ascetic views of Beissel should have been so successful in drawing women to him. A number of women were so infatuated that they had to be forcibly restrained by their husbands. A few such who outlived their husbands joined Beissel as soon as they became widows. One young woman of Oley was so moved that she left her bridegroom to follow Beissel and become a nun at Ephrata. These women with ardent temperaments often gave Beissel trouble, although as a rule a vegetable diet and midnight vigils helped to tame them. One especially spirited nun, Anna Thomin, fell so madly in love with a handsome young redemptioner whom Beissel had acquired that she was permitted to marry him. Beissel, however, did not give up hope. At the very wedding he persuaded her to return to the convent, where she repented with vigor. Later the world attracted her once more, and she left Ephrata to marry John Wister, a prosperous merchant of Philadelphia. The most prominent of the women drawn to Ephrata by Beissel was Maria Sauer, the wife of Christopher Sauer, the printer. As Sister Marcella she served for a time as subprioress. At length, however, her sons persuaded her to return home. Her desertion of his bed and board undoubtedly helped to make Sauer one of Beissel's bitterest enemies. Beissel's relations with these women were purely platonic. His hatred of sex was so extreme that when one of the women of the community fell into sin he had the house in which she had lived torn down and the wood chopped up for firewood.

Beissel also attracted men. His two most famous converts were John Peter Miller, the Reformed clergyman of Trinity Church at Tulpehocken, and Conrad Weiser, the province's negotiator with the Indians. John Peter Miller was one of the most learned theologians in the colony. He was a linguist of note who was later employed by the Continental Congress to translate the Declaration of Independence into several European languages. Miller not only joined the Ephrata community but he brought ten families from his congregation with him. For the rest of his life he labored long and earnestly at Ephrata, finally succeeding Beissel as prior. The translation of *The Martyr Book* and the printing of it, a task almost superhuman, rested chiefly on his shoulders. Some indication of the measure of the man is shown by his appeal—and a successful one—for the life of his bitterest enemy, Michael Widman, a Tory who had been sentenced to death by the patriots. Conrad Weiser was even more eminent then Miller. Fascinated by religion, he passed easily from one denomination to another. For a time he tried resolutely to submit himself to Beissel's views and to live an ascetic life; but the constant sight of his wife was too much for the call of the flesh. His wife gave birth to four children while they were members of the Ephrata community. Beissel's despotism and extravagant ideas also alienated Weiser, who had too sturdy an independence and too much common sense to fit into so fantastic a society as Ephrata.

The extreme asceticism at Ephrata led quite naturally to fanaticism. The desires of the Ephrata virgins were so repressed that their only outlet was in fervent songs of union with the Redeemer in which the love described sometimes passed beyond the bounds of the purely spiritual into the realms of the erotic. The printing of these hymns had been entrusted to Christopher Sauer. One day a printer's devil who was at work on them asked Sauer if he didn't think that the Redeemer mentioned in the hymns was Beissel rather than Christ. Sauer at once wrote asking if this was true, whereupon Beissel flew into a rage but failed to answer to Sauer's satisfaction. Sauer replied to the insults with the accusation that Beissel had the effrontery to portray himself as Christ. To this charge Beissel answered with such fury and vituperation that Sauer declared that he got "from Mars his strength, from Venus his influence over women, and from Mercury his comedian tricks." There was some truth to Sauer's criticism. Some of the Ephrata disciples did look on Beissel as divine. Although he never made this claim himself, it was not one he took pains to discourage. Very clearly it appealed to his vanity.

This was but one of the extravagant fancies entertained at Ephrata. Another was baptism by proxy to save the souls of the dead, a rite later adopted by the Mormons. Emmanuel Eckerling was thus baptized by Beissel on behalf of his mother. No wonder that the country people believed that Prior Onesimus walked at midnight on the ceiling of the Saal, where his footprints are still pointed out. Some notions were even more extreme. The *Chronicon Ephratense* mentions an A. W. and D. C. of Oley who circumcised each other and blasphemed against Paul because he did away with circumcision. Most absurd of all were those Ephrata disciples who attempted to follow the doctrines of Jakob Böhme, who declared that Adam before he ate of the apple had not performed the grosser physical functions. These foolish people believed that if they could hit upon the proper diet the body would absorb everything. Their valiant efforts to check the action of the bowels only resulted in dire cases of constipation.

The half-baked ideas of Ephrata were a product of the religious ferment of the times, of the fantastic notions adopted by a number of religious sects in the seventeenth and eighteenth centuries. So many of the fancies with which Ephrata flirted were so lacking in realism that the community left little mark on American life and thought. Though we are grateful to Ephrata for its printing press, its *Fraktur,* and its care of the wounded during the Revolution, we look upon this strange order as one of the oddities of colonial America.

Quite as curious as the experiment at Ephrata was the earlier colony on the Wissahickon, the Contented of the God-Loving Soul. This was better known as the Society of the Woman in the Wilderness because of its belief that the Woman in the Wilderness, mentioned in Revelation 12:14–17, foretold the second coming of Christ. Led by Johannes Kelpius, a mystic of the University of Altdorf, the Contented of the God-Loving Soul reached Bohemia Landing on the Chesapeake on the 12th of June, 1694. Clothed in coarse pilgrim garb or in the dress of German university students, they struck out for Philadelphia, arriving there the 23rd. That night, only a short way out of Penn's new city, they built a bonfire on a hill to celebrate Midsummer Night's Eve and scattered the burning brands down the hillside. The next morning they went on to Germantown, there to await the millennium. On the Ridge, a wooded hill above the Wissahickon, they built a log structure forty feet square, with a large room to serve as a chapel and small cells as bedrooms for the brethren. On the top of the building was an observatory equipped with a telescope or perspective glass. There each night one of the brethren watched the heavens for some celestial sign of the Bridegroom's coming "that their lamps might be trimmed and burning." Near-by, in a small cave to which he could retire and meditate, Kelpius set up his hermitage. In a small clearing by the monastery they planted a garden of medicinal herbs, possibly the first botanical garden in America.

Theirs was a monastic settlement; the brethren took vows of celibacy. Many of the votaries were learned men who had been driven from the German universities because of their unorthodox religious views. A smell of alchemy hung about this colony in which horoscopes were cast and the use of the divining rod was not unknown. When the year 1700 came and went, and the millennium on which they had counted did not take place, some of the brethren lost heart. Yet the following year they felt for a short time that their hopes were about to be realized. In this particular year they attached great importance to their celebration of Midsummer Night's Eve because it was their seventh Midsummer Night's Eve in America. According to a legend recorded later at Ephrata, the brethren saw a vague white moving figure in the air just as they were about to light their fire. As it came closer to them they saw that it was an angel, gloriously fair. Receding for a moment into the deep shadows of the hemlocks that towered above, it reappeared so that again they were able to see that it was an angel, "the fairest of the lovely," before it melted away into the forest. The enthralled votaries fell to their knees, feeling certain that the Heavenly Bridegroom was about to appear. Prayers were held until midnight, when the fires were lighted. Then with incantations the brethren flung the fiery embers down the hill. Throughout the rest of the night the brethren prayed. On the third night the apparition was seen once more and then it vanished forever.

After this the brethren lost hope, and the community began to diminish until Kelpius's death in 1708 at the early age of thirty-five brought it to an end. Kelpius was buried in the garden at sunset to the chanting of *De Profundis*. As his body was lowered into the grave there was let loose a white dove that flew to the heavens and vanished over the hemlocks. Within a few years the abandoned monastery fell into ruins. Today the Society of the Woman in the Wilderness is only a memory.

There were other curious plants in the German hotbed of religion in early America. The *Neu-gebornen,* or Newborn, who settled in the Oley Valley in Berks County early in the eighteenth century, were one of the most fantastic of all these groups. Declaring that they were like Adam before the Fall, they believed themselves to be free of sin and even incapable of sinning, an advantage Adam never possessed. The Newborn left little mark on the religious life of their day: few people were simple-minded enough to take them seriously.

Other groups such as the small band near Ephrata known as the New Mooners, who believed that for prayers to be effective they must be made during the new moon, or the Inspirationalists, who thought themselves gifted with prophecy, left equally little impress on the times.

The Millerites of the nineteenth century gained adherents in many parts of the country. Their faith rested on the belief that the year one thousand eight hundred forty-three would usher in the millennium. In Pennsylvania a hundred or more of them from Middletown gathered on Hill Island in the Susquehanna on the designated night to await the Bridegroom's coming. When dawn came and with it no millennium, an uncertain and somewhat sheepish band of people made their way back to the mainland. This was but one of many such incidents. In many parts of the state people went forth that night to meet their God only to find themselves on the morrow in the same old workaday world.

Most extraordinary of the nineteenth century enthusiasts were the followers of a New England prophet, Theophilus R. Gates. Preaching views on sex far from orthodox, Gates gained some adherents among the Dutch farmers in the country back of Pottstown. No wife, he declared, should lack a husband brisk in bed; no husband should lack an "attentive" wife. The emphasis was on sexual satisfaction rather than marriage, for if a woman came upon a man unhappily married it was her right to offer herself to him to console him. This was a religion suited to strongly sexed people with inhibited spouses. Tied in with this was "planned parenthood," no doubt a wise precaution in a religion in which sex relations were so free. In addition there was a measure of communism in that all worldly goods were to be shared. A colony called Free Love Valley, where both free love and nudism could be practiced, was established not far from Pottstown. As soon as the local authorities discovered what was up, they arrested Gates and his followers, charging them with adultery. Apparently religious fanaticism could be carried too far, even in Pennsylvania.

The only Pennsylvania Dutch religion of the twentieth century is Buchmanism, or, as some prefer to call it, the Oxford Group movement. The latter term may lend some kudos to the religion; but it makes it difficult to distinguish from the Oxford Movement of the nineteenth century. Why the movement should have borrowed the name of Oxford is not entirely clear, for it is the child of a Pennsylvania Dutchman, Frank N. Buchman, born in Pennsburg in the Dutch section of Montgomery County and educated at the Lutheran college of Muhlenberg. Few of its adherents are Pennsylvania Dutch; for the most part they are the wealthy and socially prominent of Europe and America.

Part Two

THE PAST

The Broad Atlantic

The mass emigration from the Rhineland to Pennsylvania was in full tide during the first half of the eighteenth century. So great was it that for a time it looked as though the whole Palatinate—indeed, the whole Rhineland—would be depopulated. Year after year vessels packed to the gunnels with emigrants sailed from Rotterdam bound for Philadelphia. Only the French and Indian War was able to check this exodus.

There was good reason for this wholesale emigration: war and religious persecution. The Thirty Years' War from 1618 to 1648 had devastated the Palatinate. Then in 1674 and 1675 the terrible raids of the French Marshal Turenne brought further tragedy to the Rhineland. A few years later occurred the War of the Palatinate (1688–1697), in which the ruthless order of the French minister Louvois to General Melac to make the Palatinate uninhabitable was carried out with horrifying thoroughness. In 1689 Mainz, Worms, Mannheim, Speyer, and Heidelberg were sacked and burnt. The castle of Heidelberg, the chief residence of the electors of the Palatinate, was left in ruins. Villages and farmhouses were burned and the people driven from their homes in the dead of winter. Fruit trees were cut down and even the vines in the vineyards rooted up. This war is so well remembered in the Palatinate that to this day people call a worthless cur Melac.

The Palatinate was not the only province to suffer; Württemberg and Alsace among other places were hard hit. To make matters worse, the people had to put up with excessive taxation. The German princes tried to emulate the French court by building palaces and gardens to match Versailles. All this was in addition to the religious persecution that was visited upon many. The electors of the Palatinate changed their religion four times in as many reigns. With each change the people were expected to follow suit. For some the severe winter of 1709 came as the last straw. "It was so cold that the birds froze in the air and the wild beasts in the forest," reported Löher. It was then that men looked in one another's eyes and said, "Let us go to America; and if we perish, we perish."

Penn, who had visited the Rhineland in 1671 and again in 1677, had expressly invited the inhabitants to come to Pennsylvania. His prospectus, *Some Account of the Province of Pennsylvania,* was written for the purpose of attracting settlers. Translated into Dutch, German, and French, it had a wide circulation throughout the Rhineland. A little later Queen Anne, in an attempt to draw settlers to the lands along the Hudson that the English had taken away from the Dutch, painted America in colors so glowing that the prospectus issued in her name came to be known as *The Golden Book of Queen Anne.*

The start of the immigration was slow. The vanguard of the Germans to accept Penn's invitation arrived at Philadelphia in the ship *America* on August 20, 1683. Francis Daniel Pastorius headed the small number of German Mennonites on this ship. On October 6, 1683, the *Concord,* with the first shipload of German settlers, docked at Philadelphia. These were the people who founded Germantown.

The first mass emigration of the "church people," the largest single emigration to America in the colonial period, was directed not toward Pennsylvania but toward New York. Accepting the glowing terms of the *Golden Book* at their face value, the long-suffering inhabitants of the Palatinate started down the Rhine by the thousand. More than thirteen thousand eager immigrants crossed to England between May and October in 1709. The British government had invited these Germans to go to America with the design of establishing them in colonies in New York to manufacture naval stores. All the commons and fields about London were filled with their tents; several thousand were on Blackheath alone. All London came out to gaze at the curious sight. There were far more of these Palatines than were needed for the proposed settlements; something had to be done. First, the Roman Catholics were weeded out and sent back to Holland. Nearly three thousand others, many of them linen weavers, were sent to Ireland, where their descendants still live. The Duke of Sussex settled several hundred on his estate; and John Law, whose name was made infamous by his grandiose scheme of the Mississippi Bubble, got several thousand for a colony at Biloxi on the Gulf of Mexico, where he left them to perish in the fever-laden swamps. A settlement on the Scilly Isles was attempted and a colony of six hundred sent to North Carolina. Thus the thousands of Palatines who crossed from Holland were whittled down till in the end only 2,814 started for New York.

Although the Palatines embarked in December, 1709, the ships hung off the southern coast of England all through the winter. Not until the 10th of April, 1710, did the ten vessels finally hoist sail and leave the shores of Devon. Packed on board the ships for months before leaving England, the wretched immigrants came down with "ship fever" and died in large numbers. There was no sanitation worth speaking of, no chance for the passengers to wash. Some of those below decks had neither light nor fresh air. In view of these appalling conditions it is surprising that only 446 died on the way over.

The first ship arrived at New York on June 13, 1710; several other vessels reached port the next day. One was wrecked on Long Island, and the last did not arrive until August 2. More dead than alive, the Palatines were landed on Governors Island, where they were housed in tents. Typhus had broken out among them. Almost all of them were seriously weakened by the ordeal they had been through. Two hundred and fifty more died that summer from the effects of the voyage, while it was months before many of them recovered their health.

Meanwhile Governor Hunter had been busy. Children whose parents had died on the way over were bound out. John Peter Zenger, later renowned for his defense of the freedom of the press, was one of these orphans. Even many children whose parents were living were taken from their families and bound out. As soon as the Palatines were able to work they were established in seven villages along the Hudson: at Hunterstown, Queensburg, Annsburg, and Haysburg on the east side; at Elizabethtown, Georgetown, and New Village (the site of Saugerties) on the west. Others were pressed into the army to fight against the French in the War of the Spanish Succession. A few of these engaged in the capture of Port Royal in Acadia, and three hundred or more took part in the expedition against Canada.

The experiment on the Hudson to manufacture naval stores was a dismal failure. It was not until fall that the Palatines reached the seven villages—villages in name only. Shelter had to be provided against the oncoming winter; and the people had to have food. Furthermore, the trees had to be cut and barked to concentrate the sap and then two years had to pass before they could get the pitch the navy needed.

The patroon, Robert Livingston, Inspector of the Palatines and President of the Palatine Court, had almost unlimited power. He could sentence the Palatines to be flogged. The meat he gave them was so salty it could hardly be eaten; the bread was short weight. Later the Palatines were in such a sorry state that the Reverend John F. Haeger wrote in a letter dated July 6, 1713, that "they boil grass and ye children eat the leaves of the trees." Governor Hunter had made the mistake of trusting Livingston, who cheated the Palatines. Both Livingston and Hunter were blamed by the Palatines, and this angered Hunter, who thought them basely ungrateful since he had been supporting them out of his own pocket. The ministry in London refused to reimburse him because they were suspicious of his connection with Livingston. At last, when winter was coming on and the men were without food and without work, Hunter was forced to let the Palatines shift for themselves. Leaving the seven villages, they scattered from Rhinebeck to Germantown on the east bank and on the west bank from Newburgh to Schoharie.

About a fourth of them, the most adventurous—the troublemakers, as Governor Hunter put it—went to Schoharie. Later, some of them settled in the Mohawk Valley at German Flats and Palatine Village (afterward Herkimer), and some at Minden and Canajoharie. The Schoharie refugees met with further trouble because they had no legal title to the land on which they settled. A group of English and Dutch in Albany, known in history as the Seven Partners, all of them belonging to the governor's party, set out to obtain titles to the land the Palatines had cleared at Schoharie and to the villages they had built. Buying up old titles of dubious legality, they ordered the Schoharie pioneers to pay up or get out. Governer Hunter went so far as to order them to stop cultivating the land they had cleared, but as this would have meant

starvation the settlers ignored the order. In 1718 the Schoharie Palatines sent John Conrad Weiser and two other delegates to London to
appeal to the king. Here, too, fortune was against them. Robbed by
pirates on the voyage, the delegates were arrested for debt when they
reached England. Furthermore, Governor Hunter, who had newly
arrived in London, easily prevailed against these friendless foreigners.
When he stooped to falsehood and claimed that the Schoharie Palatines
had taken up land already granted to others, the government ordered
them to be moved elsewhere.

Some went to Stone Arabia (later Palatine Bridge) to start anew
the work of cutting a settlement out of the wilderness. Others stayed at
Schoharie and submitted to the cheat of the Seven Partners. Still others
in a more rebellious mood deeply resented their unjust treatment and
determined to leave the colony of New York. When an invitation came
from Governor Keith of Pennsylvania to settle in that province, some
of the bolder of the Palatines made up their minds to accept. In 1723
fifteen families made their way down the Susquehanna to the Tulpehocken region. Two years later there were thirty-three families in the
new settlement, and in 1729 fifty more families joined the isolated
settlement in Berks County.

The sorry experience of the Palatines in New York was soon known
throughout the Rhineland. Thereafter New York was avoided like the
plague. Per Kalm in his *Travels in America* speaks of this: "It sometimes happened that they were forced to go on board of such ships, as
were bound for New York, but they were scarce got ashore, when they
hastened on to Pennsylvania, in sight of all the inhabitants of New
York."

Many of the early Palatines were of the Reformed faith, but soon the
desire to be on the move had infected the Lutherans as well. Even a
number of Roman Catholics left the Palatinate; instead of going to
Pennsylvania they went east to Banat and Bachka along the lower
Danube, there to form a bulwark against the Turks. At Philadelphia
the Palatines arrived in such numbers that the good people of that
city got the idea that there were nothing but Palatines in Germany and
applied the name Palatine indiscriminately to immigrants from Württemberg, Alsace, and Switzerland as well as to the legitimate Palatines.

So many ships crammed with Palatines docked at Philadelphia that
the English inhabitants began to fear that these people might attempt
to form a separate nation, especially since the new immigrants were,

as the Provincial Council put it, "ignorant of our language and laws and settling in a body together." To guard against this and to keep an exact tally of the number of Germans arriving, the Provincial Council, meeting in Philadelphia on September 14, 1727, ordered all captains of ships conveying these immigrants to submit passenger lists. In addition all foreign immigrants were ordered to take "the Declaration of Fidelity and Abjuration"—fidelity to the king and abjuration of allegiance to the Stuart pretenders and the rights of other foreign princes, prelates, and so forth, within the realm of Great Britain or the Dominions. To Pennsylvania Dutch genealogists these lists are an invaluable source.

No group of pioneers who came to America in the colonial period suffered on the voyage as much as did these forefathers of the Pennsylvania Dutch. Compared to what the German immigrants went through, the Pilgrims on the *Mayflower* and the Quakers on the *Welcome* had crossings of ease and luxury. Many of the immigrants from the Rhineland were victims of dishonest ship companies and land agents. Many others owed their poverty to the trickery and rapacity of British promoters and ship captains. For the sake of fat commissions from the shipping merchants "soul snatchers" went through the Rhineland to persuade the inhabitants to take passage on one of their ships.

Many of the families who decided to try their fortunes in America believed they had enough money to pay for their passage, but from the day they started they were fleeced right and left. On the journey down the Rhine, with its thirty to forty customhouses, they were held up so often that it took five to six weeks to reach Rotterdam, the port for the whole Rhine Valley. At Rotterdam there was often a further delay of a month or more until a ship sailed for Philadelphia. By the time the ship left, many were short of money and sold themselves as indentured servants to pay for their passage. Three or four or even five hundred passengers were packed into the small ships. Food and water were scanty and often contaminated; ventilation was bad; and rats and lice abounded. Mühlenberg in his journal speaks of the rats on the ship so driven by thirst that they licked the sweat from the faces of the sleeping passengers and gnawed holes in the tops of the water vessels, into which they stuck their tails and then licked off the water. The voyage was especially dangerous for small children and old people, many of whom died before the shores of America were sighted. Though occasionally a ship crossed the Atlantic in five weeks, a voyage of two or three months was more usual. *The Good Intent,* which sailed late in 1751, hung off the American coast for weeks waiting for a sea calm enough to make port. After twenty-four weeks at sea the vessel put into harbor in the West Indies with nearly all of her passengers dead.

Nor were these the only perils. Whittier's poem, "The Tent on the Beach," tells of a ship wrecked on Block Island by flares the inhabitants lighted to bring it on the rocks. After looting the vessel, the Block Islanders set the ship on fire. It is small wonder that there is a legend that those seas are haunted by the flaming ship. Especially during the early nineteenth century the ghostly flames of the specter ship are supposed to have been seen, always by night, off the northwest shore of the island.

There was also a real danger of being captured by pirates and sold into slavery. Mühlenberg on his voyage in 1742 notes in his diary the precautions taken on board ship: "Towards evening the captain ordered that every male person in the vessel should come on the quarterdeck and drill. They all came together, received their sabres, pistols, muskets, guns, and powder. The captain showed each one the place where he should stand in case a hostile attack should be made."

A much happier glimpse of life on shipboard occurs in the account that John Naas, an elder of the Church of the Brethren, left of his voyage to Philadelphia in 1733. Even at this day two entries bring to life the jubilation the passengers felt at each sign that America was near and the long, weary weeks of the voyage were coming to an end:

On the 17th, a small land bird which they call the little yellow wagtail in German, perched down several times on our ship. This caused great rejoicing and the people clapped their hands with joy.

On the 18th, a ship from Rhode Island came up to us. It had a cargo of sheep and other things in order to sail to the West Indies, to which our Captain spoke through a speaking tube; after they had made their arrangements they reefed their sails on both ships since there was but little running anyhow, and our Captain had a boat lowered into the water and rowed with four seamen to their ship. When they had drunk their welcome together, he returned and brought with him half a bag of apples, a goose, a duck and two chickens, and distributed the beautiful apples at once among the people. That caused great rejoicing to get such beautiful American apples on the high sea, and those which were still left over he threw among the people to grapple for them, and they fell in heaps over one another for the beautiful apples.

For the most part, though, the picture is a dark one. Many of the ships brought fever with them. Infected ships remained in quarantine down the river from Philadelphia, where they anchored in midstream. The evils of the system were plain to see, but the Assembly did little to correct them. In 1742, however, a "Pest-House" was built to which "all sick and infectious persons" could be sent; but not for a long time were there any laws to prevent the gross overcrowding of the vessels and to ensure ventilation and food and decent treatment for the immigrants.

To the inhabitants of Penn's city these ships presented a golden opportunity of getting servants cheap, since many of the Palatines were forced to sell themselves. Often they had been robbed by seamen, or sometimes even by the captains, of whatever goods they possessed. Sometimes their chests with all their possessions were put in other ships or left behind. To us today the most shocking feature of colonial immigration is this sale of immigrants for a term of years to pay the ship captains for their passage, a system next door to slavery. In Pennsylvania the larger part of the redemptioners, as they were called, were German and Swiss, with a goodly number of English, Scotch-Irish, and Welsh and a few French. This system was not confined to Pennsylvania but was prevalent throughout the colonies, where it continued even after the Revolution. As late as 1790 a cargo of redemptioners was sent to Chester, then stricken by yellow fever, and a market for nurses opened.

At first the term of service was for seven years; later it was reduced to four. But even the latter figure was an exorbitant price to pay for a passage across the Atlantic. When the ship reached port, the captain placed an advertisement in the local paper, offering the redemptioners for sale. Those not bought within a few days were sold at bargain rates to speculators, or sometimes the speculator went on board ship and bargained for the whole lot. Then the redemptioners were taken from town to town, "like a parcell of sheep," till all were disposed of. Conrad Richter in his novel *The Free Man* draws a vivid picture of this pretty proceeding. Most of the men, ranging from sixteen to forty years in age, brought from £10 to £24, though the first price was more usual than the second. Women brought two-thirds the price of men. Children under five could not be sold, but those over five could be bound out until they were twenty-one. Indentured servants were provided with food, clothes, and lodging during the years of service and "freedom dues" at the end of their indenture. These "freedom dues" varied from time to time. In the late seventeenth century they consisted of "a year's provision of Corn" and fifty acres of land; about 1700 they were two suits of clothes (one of them new), an ax, a grubbing hoe, and a weeding hoe; after 1750 a suit of clothes and a horse for a man, a new dress and a cow for a woman. Redemptioners could not marry without the consent of their master except on payment of a large sum of money—which obviously they did not have.

Many of the redemptioners were simple farmers or laborers. A smaller number were skilled workmen, and a few were well educated. All the trades and many of the professions were represented. Though the great majority were of humble birth, a few were well born. Of these latter many had good reasons, usually political or religious but sometimes less creditable, for leaving the country of their birth.

Probably the most romantic tale was that of the Irish peer James Annesley, Lord Altham, who was seized as a boy of thirteen, shipped to America, and sold as a redemptioner. This was part of an evil plot by his uncle, Richard, who, desiring to get possession of the estate and title, had had the boy shanghaied by an American ship sailing from Dublin. In Philadelphia the boy was bought by a Dutch farmer who lived near the fortieth milestone along the Lancaster road. He worked as a common laborer for twelve years until one day two fellow countrymen, John and William Broders, stopped at the farm and, getting into conversation with the young man, discovered that all three were from Dumaine in county Wexford. To them Lord Altham told his tale and enlisted their help. They notified the authorities, and eventually the young peer returned to Ireland and brought suit against his uncle. Unfortunately, the story has a sorry ending: the villain emerges triumphant. While the case was still pending, young Lord Altham died, and the wicked uncle got the title and the estate as next in line. This is the tale that forms the basis of the plot of Charles Reade's novel *The Wandering Heir*.

In Pennsylvania many redemptioners were treated fairly well, and some with consideration and kindness. Yet the fact that so many ran away is proof that they did not look upon their lot as a happy one. The newspapers of the day are full of advertisements like the one below that appeared in the *Pennsylvania Gazette* for April 3, 1760:

Run away on the 15th Instant, from the Subscriber, living in Lower Dublin Township, Philadelphia County, a Dutch Servant Man, named Paul Clem, about five Feet high, has tender Eyes: Had on when he went away, a new Hat, good Buckskin Jacket, lined with striped Flannel and an old blue Jacket under it, good Buckskin Breeches, brown Stockings, and half worn Shoes, with large Brass Buckles. Whoever takes up and secures said Servant, so as his Master may have him again, shall have a Pistole Reward, and reasonable Charges, paid by

JAMES BUCHANAN

As I read this advertisement I can only hope that Paul with the "tender eyes" made good his getaway.

Redemptioners who met with ill treatment were given the right to apply to the nearest magistrate, a step few of them dared to take. Instead they ran away—at least, the boldest spirits among them. Not many took kindly to serfdom, no matter how temporary. During the wars the army encouraged indentured servants to enlist, despite the bitter opposition of the Assembly. And enlist they did—in large numbers.

The most encouraging feature of the redemptioners, and indeed of all the Dutch immigrants, was their recuperative powers. By and large they lived simply and worked hard. Their souls' desire was to till their own land or set up for themselves in business. They hated debt as they hated the devil, and sometimes even more so. In less than a century some of the finest farms in colonial America were theirs and some of the most thriving industries. Nor were the farms and industries operated by slave labor. Having tasted of serfdom, the redemptioners had little love for slavery. By 1780 there were more free Negroes in Pennsylvania than there were slaves. Today many of Pennsylvania's leading families have the blood of these redemptioners in their veins. Nor need they apologize for it. The sufferings, the courage, and the industry of their redemptioner forefathers had few parallels elsewhere in the thirteen colonies.

White Man, Red Man

More than any of the other twelve original colonies, Pennsylvania from the early days of its settlement has been a melting pot. It set the pattern for the America of today. The very diversity of its population made it more characteristically American than its sister colonies of Virginia and Massachusetts. When the new immigrants from the Rhineland and Switzerland arrived in Pennsylvania, they found a large number of English settlers, a fair number of Welsh, and a handful of Swedes, Finns, and Dutch already there. Though the Swedes and Finns had reached the shores of the Delaware in 1638, the common view that Pennsylvania was not settled until 1682, when the English arrived, has a certain justice to it. The settlements made by the Swedes and Finns, and later destroyed or taken over by the Dutch, were never strong. The number of settlers was small. Except for the log cabin that the Swedes and Finns introduced, their imprint on Pennsylvania was negligible, while the influence of the Holland Dutch was even slighter. As the few Swedes and Finns and Dutch living in the province were soon engulfed by the English migration, the colony was virtually English as the seventeenth century passed into the eighteenth. Though there was a fair number of Welsh, they had little effect upon the colony.

They intermarried freely with the English and later with the Germans as well. But the Germans and Swiss and Scotch-Irish came in numbers far too great to be swallowed up by the English. Pennsylvania became a melting pot once more. With the Germans came the French Huguenots, many of whom had fled to the Rhineland and become infected with the passion to migrate to Pennsylvania.

The large number of French Huguenots among the early Pennsylvania Dutch is seldom realized. This is because many of the French had lived in the Palatinate or Württemberg for two or three generations and thus had lost much of their French coloring. Occasionally they were still sufficiently conscious of their nationality to settle in colonies by themselves. Such was the one established in 1712 on the Pequea Creek by Madame Ferre and the one a few years later in the Oley Valley. But as a rule the French Huguenots were scattered among the Germans. Intermarriage was so frequent that within two or three generations only the French surnames betrayed the large admixture of French blood in the Pennsylvania Dutch. One of the commonest of all Dutch names is Boyer, while Lefevre, Demuth, Bertolet, Benedum, De la Plaine, Le Van, De Turck, Boileau, and Fortineaux are a sample of other French names that clearly show their origin. Often, however, the name has been so changed through the years that its French nature is much less obvious. Le Shur became Lesher; Vesqueau, Wesco; Tournet, Dorney; Vautrin, Wotring; De la Cour, Dellicker, and Chresmere, Griesemer. The French Christian names disappeared almost at once. The original settler may have borne such a name as Pierre or Jacques but as likely as not he named his son Johannes or Friedrich.

Though Pennsylvania had as many French Huguenots as any other colony and possibly even more, it was not the French but the English, the Germans, and the Scotch-Irish who made up much the larger part of the population. By the time of the French and Indian War Pennsylvania was roughly one-third English, one-third German, and one-third Scotch-Irish. Of all the colonial stocks of Pennsylvania, the Scotch-Irish were the last on the scene. Even a few Irish Quakers, early assimilated by Quakers of English blood, had preceded them. Although the Scotch-Irish and the Germans became neighbors on the frontier, there was little intermarriage between them. Yet there are good Pennsylvania Dutchmen with such patronymics as Buchanan and Campbell.

Between the English and the Germans there was considerable intermarriage. In Philadelphia especially, the more prosperous German families intermarried with the Quakers. Some of these German families became so thoroughly Quaker that their German origin was almost forgotten. Wister and Wistar, Gummere, Shoemaker, Lukens, and Yerkes are good Quaker names that were once Pennsylvania Dutch. Up-country, however, it was the Quakers who were assimilated by the Dutch. Such old English names as Boone, Adams, Lincoln, and Lee all occur to this day in Berks County, yet families bearing them are generally as Dutch as their neighbors with such names as Eisenhower, Spatz, Schlegel, or Wagner. The tendency to translate a German name into English, by which Zimmerman became Carpenter, Yeager became Hunter, and König became King, may lead a stranger to exaggerate the magnitude of the English strain in the Pennsylvania Dutch of today. Many German names were changed to adapt them to English spelling or pronunciation, changes often relatively slight. Thus Johst became Yost; Snaebele, Snavely; and Huber, Hoover. Their German origin, however, remains unmistakable.

In much of southeastern Pennsylvania originally settled by people of German blood, the German strain has been dominant from the start. It has been estimated that in 1800 90 per cent of the inhabitants of Reading and 75 per cent of those of Lancaster were Pennsylvania Dutch of German and Swiss descent. York at this time had a strong English and Scotch-Irish flavor, yet was predominantly German. Berks and Lehigh counties had a higher proportion of Rhineland Germans than the other counties; Lancaster and upper Montgomery more Swiss. Appenzeller, Zug, Hunzicker, and Oberholtzer are but a few of the many Swiss names. Where there are "plain people," there is Swiss blood.

There was also a small admixture, often so slight as to be infinitesimal, of other nations. Such was the strain of Moravian and Bohemian blood in the old families of Bethlehem, Nazareth, and Lititz.

Most surprising of all is the gypsy strain. As early as 1750 the gypsies of the Palatinate began to migrate to Pennsylvania. Often they sold themselves as redemptioners in order to make the voyage to Philadelphia. Most of them settled in Lancaster, York, Reading, and Lebanon, in so far as they settled at all—for, like gypsies everywhere, they spent most of their time on the road. They became a familiar sight on turnpike and country lane and even on old Indian trails along the streams. They visited the farms and the towns and villages to sell the baskets they made and to tell fortunes. At first they rode on horse-back; then later they traveled in caravans of wagons, and later still in automobiles. Gayly dressed in the traditional gypsy garb, they were gypsies to the core except that most of them spoke Pennsylvania Dutch with a few words of Romany thrown in and a few other words bor-rowed from the French Huguenots and Indians.

After the Revolution some of the Hessians who had been imprisoned in one or another of the Pennsylvania Dutch cities stayed there. How many, it is impossible to say, because few people boast of Hessian ancestry. There is no society to glorify the descendants of the Hessians and to compile genealogies. It is doubtful if the number of Hessians who settled in Pennsylvania was great; yet it is very likely more con-siderable than is generally believed, for nearly 5,000 of the 30,000 or more Hessians in the Revolution stayed in America. Of the 1,100 prisoners brought to Reading only 300 returned to Germany. Where the rest went is anybody's guess. Some stayed in the Dutch country and in a generation or two were completely swallowed up by the rest of the population. Only now and again, as in the case of General Custer of "Last Stand" fame, is one of their descendants brought to light.

For almost a hundred years after the Revolution the Dutch country got relatively few of the immigrants coming to America. With all the new land opened up in the West, most of the newcomers avoided a section so thickly populated as southeastern Pennsylavnia. In these early years of the Republic, however, the Pennsylvania Dutch extended their holdings within the state as they bought up one farm after another from the Scotch-Irish, who were following the frontier west. During the latter half of the nineteenth century, a fair number of arrivals from Germany settled in the Dutch country, but most of the 1848 emigrants headed for the Middle West. Some Irish Catholics moved in, but not in large numbers. A few Negroes came up from the South and in a generation or two were speaking Pennsylvania Dutch along with every-body else in the Dutch country. Toward the end of the nineteenth century and up to the First World War there was a large influx of newer immigrants into many Pennsylvania Dutch cities: Poles, Italians, Hungarians, Czechs, Russians, and Greeks. Pennsylvania became more of a melting pot than ever before. Yet even today the Dutch country is still largely Dutch—to a far greater degree than New England is Yankee. Though many Pennsylvania Dutch have left their homeland, most families—until the day before yesterday—were so large that there were enough sons to plow the land and man the factories of the Dutch country, with some left over to seek fortunes in the West.

In addition to the Swedes, Finns, Dutch, English, and Welsh, the German settlers found Indians in Pennsylvania, though these were largely in the unbroken forests to the north and west. The white settlements were all confined to the southeast corner of the province along the lower Schuylkill and the tidewater Delaware. Penn had ventured north into the wilderness only as far as Molatton, a journey less than fifty miles from Philadelphia. Of the Indians inhabiting the Pennsylvania forests, the Lenni Lenapes, or Delawares, played the largest role in the early history of the colony. The Lenni Lenapes were a tribe of the Algonquin family, which was the most extensive of North America. Tribes of the Algonquins were found from Labrador and Hudson Bay south to North Carolina, and from the Rockies to the Atlantic. The Lenni Lenapes were kinsmen of the Narragansetts and Pequots of New England, the Mohicans of New York, the Shawnees, the Miamis, the Chippewas, the Blackfeet, the Cheyennes, and about thirty other tribes. Of all the Algonquin tribes the Lenni Lenapes were regarded as the "grandfathers" of the family, the parent stock from which the other tribes had sprung. Heckewelder, the Moravian missionary, records that there was a tradition among the Lenni Lenapes that a long time ago they had come far from the West, from beyond the Mississippi.

The Lenni Lenapes, or Delawares, were divided into three subtribes, the Minsi (or Munci), the Unami, and the Unalachtigo, each with its own totem: for the Minsi, the wolf; for the Unami, the turtle, and for the Unalachtigo, the turkey. As it was believed that the turtle was the oldest of all created beings and bore the earth on its back, the totem of the turtle gave the Unami a special place of honor. In times of peace its chief was the head of the whole tribe. As the Minsi lived in the mountains north of the Lehigh, they were at first little known to the white man. It was the Unami, who lived along the Schuylkill and the Delaware south to Wilmington, and the Unalachtigo, who inhabited the lower reaches of the Delaware, with whom the Swedes and Dutch first came into contact. Like all the Eastern Indians their state of civilization was primitive. Although they lived largely by hunting and fishing, they grew some of their food. They raised corn, beans, pumpkins, probably sweet potatoes, and a few other vegetables. They collected maple sap in gourds and boiled it into sugar, a practice the white man early borrowed from them. Penn speaks of them as "tall, straight, and well built, and of singular proportion." They had great self-control and fortitude as well as extraordinary endurance. They kept their word and were loyal in their friendships. They were friendly to the white man when he first appeared and remained friendly for more than a century. They had no intoxicating liquor, a fault the Swedes and Dutch took upon themselves to correct. The Swedish traveler, Per Kalm, in writing later on of the Lenni Lenapes, remarked that although small-pox had been the death of many, "brandy had killed most."

In the late seventeenth century and the first half of the eighteenth the Lenni Lenapes were in the ignominious position of a conquered people. It was long the custom to look upon these Indians as a craven tribe of old women and their conquerors, the Iroquois, as a mighty warrior race. Yet nothing could be more mistaken than this point of view. It was a mere accident of history that enabled the Iroquois to subdue the Lenni Lenapes. As early as 1609, when Champlain attacked the Mohawks at Ticonderoga, an Iroquois tribe had learned the effectiveness of firearms. From that time on their chief desire was to obtain these deadly weapons. As the French and the Dutch were willing to exchange guns for furs, the Mohawks and the Senecas and other Iroquois were soon armed with guns. With these weapons the Mohawks and later the Senecas turned against their traditional enemies, the Mohicans and the Minsi group of the Lenni Lenapes as well as the Susquehannocks and the Eries, Indians no less vigorous and warlike than the Mohawks and Senecas but armed only with bows and arrows and tomahawks. The outcome was certain from the start, yet the Minsi fought so desperately that it took a full twenty years for the Iroquois to overcome them.

The Susquehannocks, who like the Lenni Lenapes had only bows and arrows, were conquered by the Senecas about 1674. The Susquehannocks inhabited the Susquehanna Valley north of the Chesapeake and south of the Juniata. Captain John Smith left an account of his meeting with them on the Sassafras River in the summer of 1608:

Sixty of these Susquehannocks came to us, with skins, bowes, arrowes, targets, beeds, swords, and tobacco pipes for presents. Such great and well proportioned men are seldom seen, for they seemed like giants to the English, yea, and to the neighbors, yet seemed of an honest and simple disposition. They were with much adoe restrained from adoring us as gods.

Another early writer, George Alsop, also speaks of their great stature. Alsop describes them as "a people cast into the mold of a most large and warlike deportment, the men being for the most part seven foot high in latitude and in magnitude and bulk suitable to so high a pitch; their voice large and hollow, as ascending out of a Cave, their gate strait and majestick." A nice Paul Bunyan touch! Yet possibly these accounts are not only figments of the imagination. It may be that the skeletons of unusual size unearthed in the lower Susquehanna country are those of Susquehannock warriors. In the eighteenth century the Susquehannocks disappeared as a tribe, unless the Conestoga Indians were a remnant of this once powerful people.

Toward the end of the seventeenth century Shawnees moved into Pennsylvania, some to settle along the Pequea near the Conestogas, but most to join the Minsis at the forks of the Delaware, at Fishing Creek and Catawissa, and along the Swatara and at Paxtang. But it was the Lenni Lenapes, and only to a lesser degree the Shawnees, whom the Pennsylvania Dutch and the Scotch-Irish faced on the frontier of the Blue Mountains. In view of the vast expanse of the United States to the west, it is difficult to realize today that in the middle of the eighteenth century the frontier was, roughly speaking, only seventy miles north of Philadelphia. Then the West was not California and Montana nor even Ohio and Kentucky, but the line of settlements just beyond the tidewater ports. In Pennsylvania the frontier was formed by the Pennsylvania Dutch settlements between the Delaware and the Susquehanna and by the Scotch-Irish ones west of the Susquehanna. The long line of the Blue Mountains was a natural boundary, but by 1750 the whites were pushing north through the gaps the rivers made in the mountains: along the Delaware to Minisink, up the Lehigh to Gnadenhütten, through Schuylkill Gap to Brunswick. The stage was set for the French and Indian War.

The French and Indian War

War between England and France had broken out twice before in the eighteenth century. In the War of the Spanish Succession, or Queen Anne's War, some of the newly arrived Palatines had found themselves on an expedition against Canada. In the later War of the Austrian Succession, or King George's War, from 1740 to 1748, one of the four Pennsylvania companies that joined in the attack on Canada contained so many Pennsylvania Dutch that it was known as the German Company. But it was the French and Indian War that in the most literal sense brought war home to the Pennsylvania Dutch. In this war Pennsylvania was the worst sufferer of the thirteen colonies. Nor was it the Quakers and the Anglicans in Philadelphia who suffered; it was the Pennsylvania Dutch and the Scotch-Irish on the frontier. These two peoples formed a protecting band for Philadelphia and its home counties.

For a long time the province of Pennsylvania had lived at peace with the Indians. In the beginning much of this was due to Penn's fair dealing; later on it was largely owing to the wisdom and skill of Conrad Weiser, who was in a sense the colony's ambassador to the Six

Nations. Weiser was one of the Schoharie pioneers who had moved south to the Tulpehocken region. As a youth he lived for a winter with Quagnant, the Iroquois chief, to learn the Mohawk tongue and the Indian way of life. Later, in Pennsylvania, Weiser became a close friend of Shikellamy, the Iroquois agent in the province. Trusted and respected by the Indians as was no other white man in the colony—or, for that matter, in the other twelve colonies—Weiser became the greatest Indian agent of colonial days. Believing that only the support of the Iroquois could check French expansion in the West, he was able to persuade James Logan, then a rising statesman in the province, of the soundness of his views. As a consequence Pennsylvania in 1731 recognized the Six Nations' sovereignty over all Indians in the colony, in return for which the Iroquois were expected to keep the Indian tribes in order. In June, 1744, the Treaty of Lancaster, probably Weiser's greatest achievement, was signed. This treaty, which bound Pennsylvania, Maryland, and Virginia on one hand and the Six Nations on the other with a "chain of friendship," was a serious diplomatic defeat for the French. Weiser's ability and fairness were recognized by the Iroquois when they gave him the great name of Tarachiawagon, an unparalleled honor, as this name, meaning the Holder of the Heavens, was that of the chief god of the Iroquois.

An incident that occurred in 1754 shows how friendly Weiser was with the Indians. A fine rifle carried by Weiser was greatly admired by Shikellamy, the Iroquois chieftain, who was filled with a desire to possess it. The next morning he told Weiser of a dream he had had in which Weiser made him a present of the rifle. Weiser was caught, for Indian etiquette compelled him to give the rifle to Shikellamy. Weiser handed over the rifle, but several days later he too had a dream, in which Shikellamy had given him the beautiful Isle of Que in the Susquehanna. Shikellamy gave Weiser the island, but as he did so he said, "Tarachiawagon, let us never dream again."

Weiser's policy had the serious disadvantage of turning the Lenni Lenapes to the French. Resentful of the dominance of the Iroquois, they had been acquiring firearms and were almost ready to put their valor to the test. Nor did the fraud of the Walking Purchase endear the white man to them. Though white lawyers might justify this as a stratagem rather than a cheat, the Indians remembered that a way for the "walkers" had been cleared through the forest ahead of time and that riders had been hired to carry "Rum, Sugar, and Lime Juice" to fortify the "walkers"—probably the daiquiri's first appearance in American history. Weiser foresaw the coming war but he was helpless to head it off. Shikellamy had died in 1748, and with his death Weiser lost a good deal of his influence.

Braddock's defeat was the signal for the opening of the war. From its very conception Braddock's expedition was badly managed. The first mistake was to route it through Virginia, for in that colony the horses and wagons he needed were not to be obtained. Turning to Pennsylvania for one hundred fifty wagons, he got all of them and fifty more within three days. Some of the Pennsylvania farmers offered their wagons, to be sure, with the idea of profit in mind; some as a means of defending their homes; and some because they felt that if they refused them the government would take them anyway. But only in Pennsylvania were the wagons forthcoming.

With the stupid and disastrous defeat of Braddock, the whole frontier was open to attack. The white settlements beyond the Blue Mountains were wiped out almost at once. Everywhere from the Delaware to the Potomac the tale was of burning houses and barns with men, women, and children tomahawked and scalped or carried off into the woods. On October 16, 1755, occurred the massacre at Penn's Creek near Shamokin, with fourteen killed and eleven taken captive. The raid at Great Cove, in what is now Fulton County, was a repetition of the Penn's Creek massacre. Most of the settlers in the Congohego Valley fled for their lives. In the middle of November the settlements on the Tulpehocken and the Swatara were attacked. Thirteen more people were killed and many houses and barns burned. Governor Morris made no effort to defend these settlers except to write to General Shirley of New York to send some troops down from Albany. The attack on the Moravian settlement of Gnadenhütten on the Lehigh on November 24, 1755, was one of the worst. Usually, however, the story was one of an attack on an isolated pioneer and his family rather than the slaughter of an entire settlement.

Refugees crowded into the towns. Bethlehem, with less than six hundred people, took in 208 refugees in eight days. A stockade was hastily constructed to protect the town from the Indians. Near Bethlehem, Mühlenberg met an old woman of eighty-eight who had had to leave behind all of her earthly possessions except a little bundle of clothing. "She wept bitterly at being compelled to journey into a strange land at her great age," Mühlenberg wrote in his *Journals*, "but took comfort in God's word and desired the dear Lord would take her out of the harsh world to everlasting peace." The people of Reading, who could see in the skies the glare of the burning buildings at Tulpehocken, were so badly frightened that they were about to pick up their skirts and run. Only a command of Scotch Highlanders summoned to the town and stationed there put some spunk into them.

Many of the settlers had good cause to be frightened: the Indians had broken through the barrier of the Blue Mountains and were raiding almost at will the farms of Allemengel, Berne, Tulpehocken, Bethel, and Swatara. In Lancaster the courthouse bell rang almost constantly throughout the day of October 28 to call the people together to defend themselves. From Carlisle, too, came reports of people fleeing in terror. Sauer in the November 16 issue of his paper declared that between Lancaster and Carlisle all was in confusion. Women were carrying children on their backs as they fled to the more thickly settled sections.

Fortunately, many of the settlers displayed presence of mind and courage. Companies of men were formed to resist the Indians and to build blockhouses at strategic points. On October 26th Conrad Weiser's call for volunteers at Tulpehocken was answered by 300 men and within a few days by 400 more. But the Indians had slipped away as suddenly as they had appeared. Disappointed in finding no Indians, many of the men returned to their homes.

When the massacres were reported to the Assembly, the only action this body took was to ask the governor if he knew of any injury to the Delawares and Shawnees that could have alienated their affections. This tenderness and concern of the Quakers for the Indians filled the frontiersmen with fury and disgust. General Amherst marveled at "the infatuation of the people [of Pennsylvania] who tamely look on while their brethren are butchered by the savages." Not from the Dutch and the Scotch-Irish alone but from all the thirteen colonies the harshest criticism was leveled at the Pennsylvania Assembly.

At length the Assembly, seeing that some defense would have to be made, proposed to lay a tax on land. To this the Penn heirs promptly objected that their land should be tax-free. The quarrel dragged on for a fortnight, as though there were all the time in the world in which to talk. Nothing was done. Finally the patience of the frontiersmen was exhausted; they decided to compel the authorities to defend the province against the French and Indians. News was brought to Governor Morris that "a body of five hundred Dutch from Berks" and another group of Chester County farmers were marching on the city. Philadelphia sent out the sheriff to turn them back, but they calmly took him prisoner and forced him to lead the way to the governor's house. Morris was able to show them a letter from the Penns offering £5,000 for their defense. The Assembly was not so fortunate; it was unable to explain away its procrastination. A special night session was called with rules suspended, while the Dutch frontiersmen waited outside to make sure of action. A militia bill for an army to defend the frontier was quickly passed; but in it the Quakers quietly inserted a joker that exempted all Quakers and conscientious objectors from service and even from taxation for defense. Furthermore, troops could not be compelled to serve in any campaign that lasted more than three days, nor could they be garrisoned at any place for more than three weeks, nor could they serve more than eleven consecutive months; nor could a man under twenty-one be enlisted in the militia, nor an indentured servant. Clearly the Quaker members of the Assembly were more interested in making certain that no Quaker could be forced into the militia than in providing protection for the Dutch and Scotch-Irish settlers on the frontier.

It was this act that broke the Quaker hold on the "church people" among the Dutch. Only the "plain people," all of them pacifists, still held to their old alliance with the Quakers; but the Dutch of the Reformed and Lutheran faiths from this time on joined with the Scotch-Irish Presbyterians to bring to a close the Quaker control of the colony.

Two weeks after the Militia Act was passed another German procession moved on Philadelphia, one of a very different kind and possibly the most dramatic the Quaker City has ever seen. It was a silent German funeral procession with a wagon bearing the bodies of new victims of Indian massacres. As it passed through the streets before the sympathetic but angry spectators, it attracted crowds of excited citizens who followed it to the statehouse, where the procession came to a halt. There the wagon was drawn up at a spot where the bodies of the victims could be seen by the assemblymen meeting inside.

Early the following year a series of forts from ten to twelve miles apart were erected along the frontier from the Delaware to the Susquehanna. Stockades of heavy planks were built about an open space in which there were from one to four blockhouses pierced with loopholes through which the riflemen could shoot. Franklin was in charge of the construction of the forts in Northampton County and Weiser in Berks. Although the forts were not a complete defense, for the Indians were able to slip through the lines in the country between the forts, they did succeed in checking the Indian raids. Yet at some of the forts the forest was so close to the stockade that the Indians with their rifles were able to pick off men who ventured outside. At Fort Henry, where the Shamokin Trail crossed the Blue Mountains, a touch of horror was added when wolves dug up the shallow graves in which the men killed by the Indians had been buried. That the shedding of blood did not cease with the building of the forts is shown by the account of a raid made by Indians crossing the mountains at Swatara Gap that was published by Christopher Sauer in his paper on October 15, 1757:

News comes from Quittobohille that in Lancaster [now Lebanon] county on October 1 Indians came to Peter Wamfflers house, while he and his wife were in the fields, bringing in a Wagon with hay. The Indians took 5 Children off with them, 4 girls and one boy; the smallest Child is scarce a Year old and cannot walk yet; they took from the House all they could carry; the rest they destroyed, scattered the flour, spilled the honey, broke the pots and windows and tore up the beds.

Earlier that year, on July 5, an impressive service was held in the graveyard of Christ Church, Tulpehocken, at the burial of three men and four children who had been slain by the Indians. Led by the pastor, the bereaved families and the assembled friends and neighbors sang Luther's great hymn, "Ein' feste Burg ist unser Gott," the solemn words striking home as seldom before.

In the Dutch country bordering the Blue Mountains these raids have never been forgotten. The farmer tilling the soil looks up from his plow to the mountains on the north and remembers his forefathers who fled for their lives or fell victims of the tomahawk. Among the Dutch carried off by the Indians was one who became a folk hero. This was Regina Hartman—or Leininger. There are two schools of thought as to her identity. Mühlenberg's original account does not mention her name. Later she was believed to be one of the Hartmans from the country near Orwigsburg, just north of the Schuylkill Gap. More recently scholars have tended to identify her with Regina Leininger of Penn's Creek. The very uncertainty of her identity makes her more of a legendary figure.

The Leiningers were one of the families who had ventured up the Susquehanna to Penn's Creek. On October 16, 1755, the whole settlement was wiped out. Regina's father was shot, and her older brother tomahawked. Regina, ten years old at the time, was one of a group of children who were carried off by the Indians. Her mother and younger brother had taken some grain to the gristmill and thus escaped only by chance. On the way to the Ohio country a little girl of two was given to her to carry on her back. For a hundred miles the ten-year-old girl with a child on her back plodded up hill and down on the Indian trails over the Alleghenies. Finally an Indian encampment deep in the forest was reached, and Regina was handed over to a squaw. The little girl she had carried on her back was placed in her care. Other work, too, was given to her: tanning the hides the braves brought back, grinding meal, gathering fagots in the woods.

Winter came on, and then spring and summer, and then winter again. One year followed another. The braves with war paint on their faces went out to fight, and those who returned brought fresh scalps with them. As the years passed, Regina forgot her native speech till she could remember only a few fragments of Dutch. The memories of the little white settlement on Penn's Creek became dim until that early life was only a strange dream of far away and long ago. The real things were the deerskin she fashioned into moccasins, the pike she broiled on a spit, the bitter January cold.

For nine long years Regina lived among the Indians. Her freedom came only with the victory of Bushy Run, when Colonel Henri Bouquet decisively defeated the Indians. The Lenni Lenapes, the Shawnees, the Wyandots, the Mingos, and the Mohicans all were compelled to surrender the whites remaining in their hands. By November, 1764, there were 206 white captives assembled at Fort Pitt. Some of them knew their names—Christopher Tanner, Joseph Studibacker, Sarah Boyd; but some knew only a first name—Peter, Jemmy, Kitty, Christina, Phoebe; and some knew neither first name nor last but only a nickname or perhaps an Indian name—Crooked Legs, Flat Nose, Pompadour, Tawanima. From Fort Pitt the prisoners were brought east to Carlisle so that they might be identified and united with their families. The news that the whites carried away by the Indians were at Carlisle soon spread through all the villages along the frontier. It reached Regina's mother at Tulpehocken, where she had taken refuge. After these many years she continued to nurse a hope that her daughter was still alive. At once she set out for Carlisle. It was New Year's Eve, 1764, when she reached the town. Colonel Bouquet had the girls and women among the captives drawn up in a long line. Regina's mother went up and down the line, peering into the face of each one in turn; but there was none she recognized.

"I don't see her anywhere," she faltered.

"Are you sure?" Colonel Bouquet asked. "Remember, it's a long time. She wouldn't be a little girl any more. Was there a birthmark by which you could know her?"

"No, no."

"Maybe there was a pet name you gave her that she would remember?" Bouquet suggested.

"No, no pet name," said the mother sadly.

"A song, perhaps, you used to sing to her?"

At once the mother's face lighted up. In a thin, tremulous voice she started to sing the old German hymn she and her daughter had sung together many times in the years gone by:

> "Allein und doch nicht ganz alleine.
> Bin ich in meiner Einsamkeit."

Hardly had she begun to sing when a young woman stepped forth from the line, her face transfigured as she took up the words:

> "Denn wenn ich ganz verlassen scheine,
> Vertreibt mir Jesus selbst die Zeit,
> Ich bin bei ihm und er bei mir,
> So kommt mir's gar nicht einsam für."

But she could not finish the verse. With tears of joy the mother took her daughter in her arms. With Regina was the girl she had carried on her back nine years before. No one had come to claim her; no one knew her name. Pitifully she begged to go with Regina. The mother could not refuse this child, who was just about the age that Regina had been when the Indians took her away. Together the three set out for Tulpehocken. In the old graveyard of Christ Church, Tulpehocken, where sheep graze among the thyme, Regina and her mother lie buried, a spot so peaceful that the Indian massacres seem a distant, evil dream.

There was poetic justice in the fact that it was Colonel Henri Bouquet's Royal Americans who helped to bring about Regina's release, for this regiment was largely Pennsylvania Dutch. Colonel Bouquet had been placed in command of the Royal Americans because he was Swiss and could make himself understood to the Pennsylvania Dutch under him.

Bouquet and his men were paid by the Pennsylvania Assembly. No other colony contributed a single farthing. It was the Royal Americans with their "Kentucky" rifles manufactured in Pennsylvania that made Washington realize what these men from the Pennsylvania frontier could do. Years later, when he was made commander of the American forces at Cambridge, he was to recall what fine shots they were. Hence his appeal to the Continental Congress for riflemen.

Forbes's expedition against Fort Duquesne in 1758 was one of the great triumphs of the war in Pennsylvania. At Bedford he assembled a force of 350 Royal Americans, 1,200 Highlanders, 1,600 Virginians under Washington and other commanders, and 2,700 Pennsylvanians. General Forbes's second in command was Colonel Bouquet. For ninety miles westward a road was cut over the mountains. Once again most of the wagons and horses were supplied by the Pennsylvania Dutch. Forbes himself was so ill that he had to be carried in a litter. Four months later he died and was buried in the chancel of Christ Church, Philadelphia.

In this expedition the Moravian missionary, Christian Frederick Post, was invaluable in winning over the Indians. Post, who had gone in advance of General Forbes's army, was so successful in loosening the French hold on the Indians that the French abandoned Fort Duquesne and set fire to it before Forbes could attack.

In 1763, when Pontiac's conspiracy caused the war to break out anew, the three forts of Presque Isle, Le Bouef, and Venango, all of them to the north of Fort Pitt, were captured by the Indians; and Ligonier and Bedford were attacked. Once more the Indians came through the mountain passes to burn houses and barns and kill settlers. Berks and Northampton counties, along with the rest of the frontier all the way down to the Shenandoah, were again the scene of bloodshed and fire, though this time they suffered much less than before.

With the close of the French and Indian War the frontier moved westward. Only a few of the Pennsylvania Dutch moved with it. It was the Scotch-Irish and not the Dutch who became the characteristic people of the frontier. Yet the Dutch, in the few years in which their country and the frontier were one and the same, left an ineradicable mark on the frontier. The Kentucky rifle, the log cabin, the covered wagon, and even the "shivaree" were all Dutch contributions to the frontier pattern of life.

The Eve of the Revolution

From the time of the Civil War until Roosevelt's election in 1932 Pennsylvania was blatantly Republican, yet a few Dutch counties, Berks and Northampton in particular, were Democratic islands in that Republican sea. The dumb upcountry Dutch were still voting for Andrew Jackson—that was Philadelphia's explanation. For once Philadelphia underestimated the Dutch. It was not Andrew Jackson that started these counties voting the Democratic ticket: it was the French and Indian War.

When the German and Swiss and French Huguenot immigrants first came to this country, they were not much interested in politics. They had had little experience in self-government. In their early years in Pennsylvania they were thankful to the Quakers for the peace and quiet they found in the colony. Compared to the rest of the world Pennsylvania was making a magnificent success of government. Furthermore, there was the language barrier. To hold office a knowledge of English was necessary. For a long time the Dutch took a back seat and kept their mouths shut. Then came the French and Indian War, with the Quaker reluctance to use force to defend the frontier. Suffering and fighting side by side, the Scotch-Irish and the "church people" among the Dutch joined forces to wrest the power from the Quakers. Such an aim was not accomplished overnight; but all through the years from the French and Indian War to the Revolution it was the prime end in view.

The Quakers were able to stay in power for so many years only because of the gross inequality of representation in the Assembly. In 1760 Quaker Bucks had eight members in the Assembly and Dutch Berks only one, yet each county had virtually the same number of taxable inhabitants. This was an injustice bitterly resented. Again and again the Dutch and Scotch-Irish counties petitioned the Assembly for an increase in members, but without avail until 1771, when Berks and Northampton counties were each given one more member—insult added to injury.

The eve of the Revolution found the Pennsylvania Dutch and the Scotch-Irish demanding full representation within the colony just as Americans generally were insisting on rightful representation from Great Britain. In Pennsylvania the Revolution was both local and national. The Dutch and Scotch-Irish embraced the Revolution with ardor partly because in it they saw a means of ridding themselves once and for all of the Quaker-dominated Assembly. When the growing resistance to Great Britain gave birth to the Continental Congress, there was at last a national body to which the Dutch and Scotch-Irish could appeal over the heads of the Assembly. In the months to come the Assembly gave ground little by little to the rebels on the frontier; and finally, on March 15, 1776, in an attempt to save its skin, it added seventeen new members. Although this reform helped to correct the glaring inequality of representation, the frontier counties were still without their fair number of members. The danger of leaving a great colony like Pennsylvania in the control of the Quakers and their allies, the conservative Anglicans, was apparent to the Continental Congress. As Washington moved from one defeat to another, a faction so unsympathetic to the patriot cause might well be tempted to treat with Great Britain. In *Common Sense* Thomas Paine pointed out the danger of permitting colonies to be governed by men who did not represent the majority of the inhabitants. Pennsylvania could not take its rightful place on the patriot side unless the people freed themselves from the

Assembly and the provincial constitution that kept the conservatives in power.

On June 8, 1776, the Pennsylvania delegation to the Continental Congress voted 5 to 2 against Lee's resolution "that these united colonies are, and, of a right ought to be, free and independent states." But the Dutch and Scotch-Irish were so set on independence that they refused to accept this verdict. Day by day tempers grew hotter. On June 19, at a meeting in Carpenters' Hall, delegates approved by the various county committees declared the government of the colony incompetent and called for a provincial conference to form a new government "on the authority of the people only." To do this they revived William Penn's "Great Law" of December, 1682, which gave every taxpayer the right to vote. The Pennsylvania delegates to the Continental Congress now attempted to win the favor of the rebel element by changing their vote on Lee's resolution to 3 in favor and 2 opposed, with 2 delegates absenting themselves. The vote in Congress had stood 6 to 6 until Pennsylvania cast the deciding vote for independence. It was a proud moment for Pennsylvania and for the Scotch-Irish and the Pennsylvania Dutch. The effect of the Pennsylvania vote on the delegates to the Continental Congress from the other colonies was tremendous, for meeting as they did in the heart of Philadelphia they could feel the full force of the revolution that was taking place within the colony against the conservative Quakers and Anglicans.

The great majority of the members for the new Pennsylvania convention elected on July 8 were naturally radicals—from the British point of view both radicals and rebels. On July 15th that eminent radical and rebel, Benjamin Franklin, was chosen president of the new body. Delegates to represent Pennsylvania in the Continental Congress were also chosen. Later that summer a new state constitution was adopted, the most thoroughly democratic in the thirteen colonies. The opposition to this constitution was strong and bitter. Later, in 1789, a compromise was reached and some measure of harmony restored.

But Pennsylvanians have long memories. That is why in any normal election year Berks and Northampton and some other old-frontier counties can be relied on to vote Democratic. Ask a Berks or Northampton County Dutchman what his politics are, and even today you may get as an answer the proud words, "Luderisch un Demegraudisch verdollt sei!" [Lutheran and Democratic, I'll be damned!].

After the Revolution the temper in the counties that had formed the Old West continued radical. All for independence and for having their own way, they were opposed to a strong federal government. On the other hand, the "plain people" of Lancaster County and upper Montgomery, fearing these radicals, counted on a strong federal government to keep them in check. In the administration of John Adams trouble broke out in Northampton and Berks in the fiasco known as Fries Rebellion. When a direct tax on real property was passed in 1798 and tax collectors came to count the windows in houses, the opposition reached a head. Liberty poles were set up in Northampton and Berks, and it became great sport to shout, "Dämn die President, dämn die Kanggress, dämn die Arischdokratz!" It was sport, too, to drink French brandy and shoot off a gun to scare the tax collectors out of town. It was an extremely minor rebellion, if it can be called a rebellion at all; but Adams took it seriously enough and sent militia to put it down. The soldiers came and cut down the liberty poles and arrested Fries. In Reading they seized the editor of the local paper, the *Adler,* who had published some inflammatory editorials, dragging him to the market and there publicly flogging him. Fries was eventually pardoned, for most people realized that this was in no sense treason; it was not a deed to hang a man for. If anything could increase the opposition of the old-frontier counties to the Federalists, it was this assertion of force. Even the declaration by the National Republicans that Adams could talk Dutch did not appease them. They welcomed Jefferson with enthusiasm, recognizing him as a far truer democrat than Adams. With rare exceptions they have been loyal to his newly formed Democratic party ever since.

For a number of years, however, the Pennsylvania Dutch did not pull their weight in state and national politics. Perhaps their distrust of lawyers had something to do with this. A story they like to tell in Berks County is a mark of this feeling. An old Berks County farmer, Jake Paffenberger, from over Bernville way died and went to heaven. At the gate he found St. Peter, who looked up in a bored sort of way. "Go right in, Jake," he said, jerking his thumb. Jake went in as directed; but just as he got inside the gate he heard a tremendous blaring of trumpets, and such a crowd of angels rushed out that he was nearly blown over. Jake went outside to take a look and see what all the hullabaloo was about. There he saw St. Peter clapping a man on the back and crowing with delight while all the angels sang loud hosannas. Jake felt a little hurt when he saw the welcome this man was getting.

His own reception had been pretty matter-of-fact. When at last the crowd of angels had taken the newcomer into heaven, Jake turned to St. Peter and said: "What's all the fuss about? You didn't put on such a show for me."

"Now, now, Jake, you mustn't mind that," said St. Peter, smoothing him down. "After all, we get your kind all the time. Pretty near every day one of you Berks County farmers comes up here—maybe from Maxatawny, maybe from Oley, maybe from up near Bethel. We get them right along from all over the county. But this is the first time, Jake—the very first time—we've ever had a Berks County lawyer."

The Revolution

In the years between the close of the French and Indian War and the outbreak of the Revolution the Pennsylvania Dutch were little affected by King George's attempts to intimidate the colonies. If they chose to drink tea, it was mint tea from the kitchen garden they imbibed and not store tea, which had always been somewhat of a rarity among them. Roasted rye took the place of coffee. Their wine was homemade, not imported from abroad; nor had they forgotten how to brew ale and beer. If rum from the West Indies was cut off, they could turn to Monongahela whisky. They could get glass from Manheim in Lancaster County or from Jersey or Maryland, and iron from the Pennsylvania forges and furnaces. Their log cabins and stone houses needed little paint; if need be, they could shift with whitewash: they had plenty of lime. Yet George III's acts of repression quickly stirred the Dutch to anger. Though the gentry along the coast were more moderate in their indignation, one town after another in the Pennsylvania back country passed resolutions condemning the closing of the port of Boston. Dutch farmers raised money for the relief of the poor of Boston, "who are immediate Sufferers by means of the Port being

Shutt up." In York it was resolved: "That the recent action of the Parliament of Great Britain is iniquitous and oppressive. . . . That in the event of Great Britain attempting to force unjust laws upon us by force of arms we leave the cause to Heaven and our Rifles."

The Pennsylvania Dutch had no sentimental attachment to England, no feeling that England was their second home. Nor had their life in the principalities along the Rhine or in the Swiss mountain valleys been so happy that they longed to return there. America was their country, whether it was Pennsylvania, Maryland, the Valley of Virginia, or the North Carolina Piedmont. They had a fierce attachment to the valleys and hills among which they lived. Though they had been transplanted, they had sent down roots.

Except for Bethlehem the Dutch cities possessed few of the amenities and graces of Philadelphia, Boston, New York, and Charleston; but neither was there the division of loyalties so characteristic of the older cities along the coast. With the exception of the "peace churches" the Pennsylvania Dutch were ardent in support of the patriot cause. The Moravian superintendent of the church store at Bethlehem who acidly remarked that he had enough rope to hang all the members of the Continental Congress was typical neither of the Moravians nor of the Pennsylvania Dutch as a whole. Nine out of every ten Pennsylvania Dutchmen supported the Revolution heart and soul, and the tenth man was either Mennonite, Amish, Brethren, Schwenkfelder, or Moravian. Trevelyan rightly speaks of them as being "almost to a man, devoted adherents of the popular party"; while Bancroft points out that although the Germans constituted only one-twelfth of the population they formed one-eighth of the patriot army.

The gulf between the Old West of the frontier, of which much of the Dutch country was a part, and the older civilization of the coast was partly social and economic but sometimes religious as well. The contrast between the older and newer sections was more marked in Pennsylvania, Maryland, Virginia, and North Carolina—in all four of which colonies there was a strong Pennsylvania Dutch element in the stock along the frontier—than it was in New England. In Pennsylvania the cleavage between the two sections deepened after the Quakers lost their hold on the "church people" among the Pennsylvania Dutch. Confronted by the alliance between the Scotch-Irish and the Dutch, the Quakers and the Anglicans turned to one another for support as never before. Trevelyan probably exaggerates when he declares that the Quakers and Anglicans of Pennsylvania "already held between them most of the property in the colony, and all of the privileges"; but the statement has a bottom of truth. Despite the differences in their views on theology the Quakers and the Anglicans were natural allies: the Anglicans had no wish to bear arms against the king, the Quakers had no desire to fight at all. The Revolution in Pennsylvania was consummated not by the Quakers and Anglicans but by the people of the back country, Dutch and Scotch-Irish, with the help of the mechanics of Philadelphia.

These two peoples, the Scotch-Irish and the Pennsylvania Dutch, were ready to back up their words with arms; and that they were soon called upon to do. It was Pennsylvania that bore much of the brunt of the Revolution. After New England was cleared of the enemy, the Yankee troops were disinclined to fight in the other colonies. Ever finding it difficult to look beyond the borders of New England, the Yankees were not much concerned with what happened west and south of the Hudson. And after the enthusiasm of the first year of war had cooled, the Southern troops showed little readiness to go to the aid of the North. Nor did much help come from New York. New York was one of the most sparsely settled of the thirteen colonies. There were settlements only at the mouth of the Hudson and in the narrow Hudson Valley and west along the Mohawk. The enormous land grants to the patroons and the unhappy fate of Queen Anne's Palatines had deterred other settlers. In 1770 the colonies of Connecticut, Maryland, and North Carolina all had a larger population than New York. Furthermore, New York was a hotbed of Tories. It furnished more soldiers to George III than to George Washington. Pennsylvanians were forced to defend themselves against the loyalists from New York. It was John Butler's Tory Rangers and Barry St. Leger's Loyal Greens who with the Mohawk Indians descended into Pennsylvania and massacred the inhabitants of the Wyoming Valley. When the Revolution centered in Pennsylvania, the Yankees and the Southerners were inclined to let the Pennsylvanians and the British fight it out. Pennsylvania was far too much alone in those bleak and terrible days when defeat at Brandywine was followed by defeat at Germantown and that succeeded by defeat at Whitemarsh, and all crowned by the bitter ordeal of Valley Forge. Though Washington and his troops spent more time in Pennsylvania during the Revolution than in any other colony, few of those days were ones of hope.

The Pennsylvania Dutch were in the war almost from the start. Berks and York counties are still quarreling over the honor of having the first company of riflemen to reach Washington at Cambridge. Congress, by its resolution on June 14, 1775, had called for six companies of expert riflemen from Pennsylvania, two from Maryland, and two from Virginia. These were the first troops ever to be raised by authority of Congress. It was by no accident that riflemen were called for. The rifle had been introduced into Pennsylvania by the Palatines and Swiss, and there the gunsmiths of Lancaster and Berks and one or two other Dutch counties had vastly improved the model. At the time of the Revolution the rifle was used only in Central Europe and on the American frontier from Pennsylvania south to the Carolinas. Congress well knew that these backwoodsmen with their rifles would be far more deadly than the men from the coast of New England or tidewater Virginia. The common report of their prowess was noted by John Adams in a letter he wrote at the time: "These are said to be all exquisite marksmen, and by means of their firelocks, as well as their skill in the use of them, to send sure destruction to great distances."

Within sixty days after Congress had authorized the formation of these companies 1,430 backwoodsmen had joined the army before Boston, yet not a penny had been paid to one of them. Virtually all these men were by origin or ancestry from the back country of Pennsylvania. The two Maryland companies were both from the Dutch county of Frederick, and the two Virginia companies were made up of Scotch-Irish and Dutch who had moved south from Pennsylvania into the Valley of Virginia. Even the Carolina companies, which were raised later, were of Pennsylvania stock. With rifles lighter in weight than the awkward regulation army musket, the heavy brown Bess imported from England or some local variation of it, these riflemen traveled with speed. Though handicapped by bad weather, Morgan's riflemen made the six hundred miles from Winchester, Virginia to Cambridge in twenty-one days.

The riflemen fought in almost every battle of the war from Long Island to Yorktown. At the battle of Long Island, Colonel Peter Kichlein and his regiment from Northampton County, though suffering seventy-one casualties out of less than a hundred men, hung on long enough to permit Washington to evacuate his forces. At Saratoga they were especially effective in picking off enemy officers. At King's Mountain they were largely responsible for the victory. The skill of the riflemen was famous throughout the colonies and in England as well, for they delighted in putting on shows of their marksmanship. To send at a distance of forty yards or more eight bullets through a small board, five by seven inches, that a comrade held in his hand or between his thighs, was one of the feats that thrilled the townspeople of Frederick and Lancaster. On the common at Cambridge they had shown that they could stand two hundred and fifty paces from a pole seven inches in diameter with a fair chance of hitting it. No other gun of the time could shoot that far.

The uniforms the riflemen wore, if they can be called uniforms, were thoroughly backwoods like the men themselves. The hunting shirts were of coarse linen or linsey-woolsey, or buckskin for winter, often with a double cape fringed along the edges and fastened around the waist by a belt, sometimes of wampum, in which was thrust a hunting knife or even a tomahawk. Some men wore buckskin breeches; but others, even more picturesque, instead of breeches wore a breechcloth with the thighs bare and buckskin leggings reaching above the knee. Captain Morgan, even on a midwinter march, wore a breechclout like many of his men. On their feet were buckskin moccasins, often decorated with beads and porcupine quills. From the shoulder belt hung the powder horn, bullet pouch, and canteen. The officers, to distinguish themselves from the enlisted men, wore crimson sashes over one shoulder and around the waist.

In the weeks after Lexington, company after company was formed in the Dutch country. In Berks County one composed of men over forty was known as the Company of Old Men. The same county of Berks proudly claims that it sent a larger proportion of its men to fight in Washington's armies than any other area of similar size and population in all the thirteen colonies. Though this may not be cold, sober truth, it is not far from it. Elsewhere in the other Dutch counties where the "church people" made up the bulk of the population, the story was much the same. All through the Dutch country men flocked to the colors.

One unexpected virtue of the Dutch was pointed out by Morgan when he was asked about the difference between the various stocks making up the American army: "As for the fighting part of the matter, the men of all races are pretty much alike; they fight as much as they find necessary, and no more. But, sir, for the grand essential in the composition of a good soldier, give me the 'Dutchman'—he starves well."

The Pennsylvania Dutch country was almost untouched by the fighting. There were no battles fought on its soil. Although Valley Forge is on the edge of the Dutch country, the only British soldiers who marched along the roads of the home counties of the Dutch were prisoners. The Dutch country was the arsenal, the commissariat, and the hospital of the Continental Army. Here was Washington's main source of supplies during the darkest days of the Revolution. Although the British occupied Philadelphia and much of the Quaker country, Washington could go on fighting as long as the country to the north and west was in patriot hands: it was for this reason that he took his stand at Valley Forge. Here were the forges and furnaces and foundries to smelt the ore and cast the balls and cannon, here were the gunshops to make the rifles, here were sulphur and saltpeter for gunpowder, and here were the wheat and corn from the richest farms in colonial America. Here too were the horses and wagon trains that gave Washington's army its mobility. The British, not daring to move from their base of supplies, were anchored to the ports; but Washington, with the wagons and horses of the Dutch at his command—and almost all the teams of the army were supplied by the Dutch—was able to move almost at will through the back country, checking the advance of the British at no matter which port they appeared.

Though Washington's forces at Valley Forge were badly off, that was not wholly the fault of the Dutch. It was owing, at least in part, to the commissary department's ignorance of Pennsylvania and the rich supplies in the back country. Moreover, some of the agents could get nowhere with the Dutch farmers because they could not speak Dutch and the farmers in turn could not speak English. When agents who could talk Dutch took on the job, supplies began to move toward Valley Forge. Some of the farmers, it is true, were slow to respond: they were afraid their horses and wagons would be seized by the army once they reached Valley Forge; others hesitated to accept the Continental paper money with which they were paid; and a few were out to make as much money as possible—they would sell their goods to the highest bidder, be he American or British. Nevertheless, supplies moved down the Schuylkill Valley from Reading, the provision center of the Continental Army. The farms fifty miles around were stripped of all they could spare: flour and grain and hay, salt pork and flitch, dried fruits, homespun for clothing, leather, even axes, picks, and shovels. These were carried down to Valley Forge by six-horse Conestoga wagons, many of which were seized by the army just as the farmers had feared. Yet most of the farmers from the near-by Dutch country took their products to the markets set up in the camp. There the ragged soldiers would crowd around a Dutch farmer and chip together to buy a duck, a bag of apples, some smoked sausage, a keg of cider, or a jug of applejack.

A great many of the army stores were assembled at Bethlehem, which for a time became the chief ordnance center. On September 17, 1777, a train of thirty-eight wagons arrived in the town; on the 18th, twenty-four wagons; and on the 19th, nine more. These carried sulphur, gunpowder, cartridges, provisions, and whisky. Then, on the 24th of September, a gigantic train of seven hundred wagons, bearing the entire heavy baggage and stores of Washington's army, reached the town. When these wagons were unloaded, they were ordered to Trenton to bring the army stores there to Bethlehem.

Bethlehem, of course, was even more noted during the Revolution for its hospitals. The best equipped hospitals were the Moravian ones at Bethlehem and Lititz, but military hospitals were set up in many of the Dutch towns and cities. Easton, Allentown, Reading, Lancaster, Sunbury, Ephrata, Trappe, Manheim, Skippack, Falckner's Swamp, Schaefferstown, and other places as well helped to care for the sick and wounded. For miles north of the fighting zone almost every church and meetinghouse, almost every public building was turned into a hospital at one time or another. At Reading patients were housed in the courthouse in the square. At Trappe the little Lutheran church was crammed with wounded and sick. The medical supplies were kept in the pulpit. It is only a slight exaggeration to say that for many of the months during the bitterest part of the war the Pennsylvania Dutch towns were the hospitals of the Revolution.

One of the towns used as a hospital center was the Moravian settlement of Lititz. The first sick, about eighty in number, reached Lititz on December 19, 1777, and were put in the Single Brethren's House. The following days fifteen more wagonloads arrived. "Putrid fever" broke out, killing off almost every other man. Some of the convalescent soldiers, fearing for their lives, became so alarmed at the appalling death rate that they fled from the hospital, only to be forced back by a blizzard raging outside. The hospital at Lititz was finally closed on August 28, 1778, when the last patients were moved to Lancaster and Yellow Springs.

These hospitals had able surgeons—in so far as there were able surgeons in those days. One of the best was Dr. Bodo Otto of Reading, a graduate of the University of Göttingen, who served as senior surgeon of the middle division of the Continental Armies in the hospitals at Trenton, Bethlehem, and Yellow Springs. Though sixty-five years of age, he had joined the American forces in 1776 as surgeon in the Battalion of the Flying Camp.

Yet another use was made of the Pennsylvania Dutch cities, that of prison camps for the Hessians captured at Trenton and Saratoga. The captured Hessians were so pleased with their fate that those taken at Trenton were permitted to find their own way to prison quarters in the Shenandoah Valley. Washington could not spare the men to go with them. At first the Hessians were confined at Winchester, Virginia; later they were moved to Frederick, Maryland; and still later, as their numbers increased, they were sent to the Pennsylvania cities of Reading, Lancaster, and York. In Reading one of the sections of the city is still known as Hessian Camp. As all five towns were largely Pennsylvania Dutch, even though one was in Virginia and one in Maryland, the Hessians were guarded by local militia able to speak their language. The choice of Pennsylvania Dutch communities as prison camps was by no means an advantage to the Hessians. The Pennsylvania Dutch, even more than the rest of America, cordially detested them. Recognizing the blood ties that bound the Hessians to them, the Dutch looked upon the Hessians as kinsmen who had come to fight against them. The Dutch hatred of the hired Hessians was so intense that to this very day the epithet "du verdammter Hess" remains one of the worst insults in the Dutch country.

Yet it is possible to feel sorry for the hapless prisoners. General Riedesel, in command of the Brunswickers, caught the pathos of their plight in the passage in his journal describing the Hessians bivouacked in the woods of Loudoun County, Virginia, on New Year's Eve, 1778:

Here Germany's sons lay in the woods, wet and cold, in snow a foot deep, with a gloomy future in store for them. Perhaps each of them thought of his home in the distant fatherland, of dear relatives and friends, of the days of his boyhood, and of the joys of former New Year's Eves, past, never to return.

The fires, which were kept going with green wood, gave off scarcely any warmth. All was cold and cheerless. In that dreary primeval forest nothing was heard except the forlorn moaning of the wind among the old tree tops; and while some lay on the snow-covered ground to rest their tired and aching limbs, others meditated sadly beside the camp fires.

A more notable prisoner than any of the Hessians was Major André. After his capture at St. John's, André made the round of the Dutch towns: Bethlehem, Reading, Lancaster, York, and finally Carlisle.

Only one of the generals of the Revolution was Pennsylvania Dutch, John Peter Gabriel Muhlenberg. The most dramatic episode in his life was the one known to every American schoolchild. Pastor of a Lutheran church in a Dutch settlement at Woodstock in the Shenandoah Valley, he rose in his pulpit one Sunday at the outbreak of the war, not to preach the usual sermon, but to plead with his congregation to join the fight for freedom. Throwing aside his ministerial gown, he showed himself dressed in the uniform of an American officer. Buckling on his sword, he urged all the able-bodied men in the congregation to follow his example:

"To every thing there is a season," he declared, "and a time to every purpose under the heaven . . . a time of war and a time of peace." Thus he went on, building up to the climax that thrilled the hearts of his people: "In the language of Holy Writ there was a time for all things—a time to pray and a time to preach—but those times have passed away; there is a time to fight, and the time to fight is here!"

As one man the congregation rose to sing Luther's stirring hymn, "Ein' feste Burg ist unser Gott." Outside, at the church door, the drums began to roll as men turned to kiss their wives and then walked down the aisle to enlist. Within half an hour 162 men were enrolled. This regiment commanded by Muhlenberg fought at Brandywine and Germantown, suffered through the winter of Valley Forge, fought again at Monmouth and Stony Point, and survived to take part in the surrender at Yorktown. As for Muhlenberg, the name the Hessians gave him, Teufel Piet (Devil Pete), gives some notion of the fear with which he inspired the enemy.

One of the folk heroes of the Revolution who was Pennsylvania Dutch was Molly Pitcher, whose maiden name was Mary Ludwig. So much in love that she insisted on accompanying her husband to the wars, she won a place for herself in American story by her bravery at the battle of Monmouth. When her husband fell wounded beside the cannon he was firing, she took his place and for the rest of the day kept the cannon in action against the British.

An honor greatly prized by the Pennsylvania Dutch was their selection as Washington's bodyguard. The original bodyguard had to be dismissed in 1777, when it was discovered that some of the guards were planning to assassinate Washington. As his new bodyguard Washington chose the Independent Troop of Horse, made up largely of Pennsylvania Dutch recruits from Pennsylvania and Maryland. At the close of the war this guard accompanied Washington to Mount Vernon. They were the last of the Continental Army to leave him.

Many incidents of the Revolution live on as winter tales in Pennsylvania Dutch farmhouses, whether it be of the farmer who drove to Philadelphia to market and came back with the Liberty Bell in his wagon to stow it away in the cellar of the Reformed church in Allentown, or the patriot refugees who fled from Howe at Philadelphia to crowd the towns of Reading and Lancaster and York. Or the tale may be of Sergeant Everhart, who carried Lafayette to safety when the French officer was wounded at Brandywine; or of Peter Humrichouse, who by his dash from Philadelphia supplied Washington with ammunition at Yorktown when he needed it most. But when the winter wind sweeps down from the Blue Mountains and old men draw closer to the kitchen range, it is the stories of Valley Forge above all that they delight to tell.

All the fall preceding the winter of Valley Forge the army moved about in the Dutch country from one village to another. Just behind them was the defeat at Brandywine. After this battle the army had retreated north to the safety of the Dutch country, there to rest and lick its wounds. On September 22 Washington set up Camp Pottsgrove a few miles back from the Schuylkill at Falckner's Swamp, where he was in a position to intercept Howe in case he moved against Reading to capture the supplies there. At Falckner's Swamp the Dutch farmers and their wives rallied to feed the army. When the baker-general, Christopher Ludwick, complained that there were too few bake ovens to bake enough bread, Ensign Willie Antes, glad to be back home and determined that his native village should not lose face before his comrades, built an enormous bakehouse, paying for it out of his own pocket. And Willie Antes was right in thinking well of Falckner's Swamp, for the village did itself proud as host to the American Army. Cattle and pigs were butchered; chickens, ducks, geese, and turkeys were killed.

The whole harvest of wheat, rye, buckwheat, corn, and oats was turned over to the army. Everything went for the soldiers. When the army pulled out the country was bare: no cattle in the barns, no wheat in the bins, no butter in the springhouse, no snitz in the attic, no honey in the hive—but the soldiers were new men. Falckner's Swamp had put some starch into them.

On September 26 the army moved to Pennypacker's Mills along the Perkiomen. Here too the army ate the countryside out of house and home. Every duck, goose, chicken, and guinea hen was eaten except one old half-mad *klook* [1] that had stolen away to hatch out a brood come winter or the American Army. Then, just before the attack at Germantown, a temporary camp was made along the Skippack and a few days later another at the village of Worcester. With the defeat at Germantown on October 4, the British pursued the Americans as far as Blue Bell Tavern. For three days the army returned to Pennypacker's Mills and Skippack; then, hearing of supplies at Kulpsville and Towamencin Meeting, Washington moved there on October 8, the defeated men miserable and cold in the falling rain. Unfortunately the report of supplies was much exaggerated. On the 16th the army was on the move again, from one Dutch crossroads village to another. Only the account of the British debacle at Saratoga lightened their gloom. A new advance to Center Square, with the idea of retaking Germantown, was beaten off. Then, after an engagement at Whitemarsh, the army settled down at Camp Hill for more than a month's stay. After this series of defeats the morale of the men had sunk so low and the army was so greatly outnumbered by the British that it was decided not to make another attack but to go into winter quarters. On November 30 Valley Forge was selected—largely to ensure the safety of the supplies at Reading. Finally, on December 12, the army crossed the Schuylkill at Swedes Ford and with snow whirling in their faces marched along the country roads till three in the morning, when at last they made camp on the bleak slopes of Gulph Mills.

In Reading the quartermaster general, Mifflin, was plotting against Washington. This was the Conway Cabal, in which a determined effort was made to relieve Washington of his command. To many the American cause seemed doomed. The British had captured Philadelphia. Even the remnant of the defeated army that Washington had been able to hold together had little courage left.

[1] A broody hen.

At Valley Forge all was far from well. The men were now housed in a thousand little log huts, eighteen by sixteen feet, and six feet high at the eaves; but these had neither fireplaces nor windows. In the bitter cold the men had worked with amazing speed to provide shelter for themselves, yet it was not until the end of the first week in January that the whole encampment of eleven thousand men had roofs over their heads. The misery at Valley Forge was made worse by the bungling of the commissariat and the quartermaster corps. With the men next door to starvation, hundreds of barrels of flour were left on the banks of the Susquehanna to spoil from exposure to the weather. And while four thousand men at Valley Forge went without blankets, six thousand blankets were sent to the west of Lancaster. Furthermore, Congress seemed to be unperturbed by the wretchedness of the soldiers at Valley Forge. Faced with starvation, the men foraged for themselves and cleaned out the farms for miles around. Much of the food sent down from the Dutch country failed to get through, for with the coming of winter many of the great Conestoga wagons bringing the food were frozen in the mud. The Reading road was lined with them. To make matters worse, the winter was one of exceptional cold. Ordinarily the winters in southeastern Pennsylvania are fairly moderate, but the winter of 1777–1778 was a Maine winter that had slipped south into Pennsylvania. Not a fence rail was left for miles around. Despite the cold the need for food was so desperate that before the winter was over the soldiers had scoured not only southeastern Pennsylvania and much of southern Jersey and practically all of Delaware but also a good part of Maryland and even the upper part of Virginia.

The most memorable day was the one early in spring when schools of shad came swimming up the Schuylkill—thousands upon thousands of beautiful, fat shining shad. The whole camp turned out to catch shad. The river so swarmed with fish that each haul of the net brought in hundreds. That night for the first time since the army had moved to Valley Forge there was not a hungry man in camp; each soldier went to bed with a belly stuffed with shad.

In spite of the underlying misery Valley Forge had its lighter moments. Just before St. Patrick's Day some skylarking Pennsylvania Dutchmen hung up a grotesque effigy labeled "Paddy." As the figure had been hung up during the night, the furious Irish, though out to skin the perpetrators alive, did not know on whom to turn until the jubilant Dutchmen sicked them on the Yankees. Then the row began

in earnest, to be ended only when Washington stepped in and pro-
claimed a holiday. Other sports were more innocuous. There was bowl-
ing on the green with cannon balls—with a swig from the opponent's
canteen for the winner. There was shooting with bows and arrows and
there was "playing at base," possibly the great-great-grandfather of the
great American game. During the winter there were even a few dances,
at the King of Prussia Tavern or some other near-by inn or farmhouse
—these in spite of the fact that the serious Lafayette frowned on
dancing in wartime as frivolous. Yet Valley Forge had little of the
gaiety of Reading and York, both of which towns were bursting with
refugees; and compared with Philadelphia and its Mischianza, possibly
the most elaborate party in all of American history, it was drab and
sober enough.

On May Day, however, Valley Forge put on a show to celebrate the
treaty of alliance with France and Holland. Since it was May Day there
were Maypoles, but the principal feature of the celebration was a
grand review of the army. After the weary hours they had suffered on
the parade grounds under von Steuben, the troops made a smart
appearance. The climax came with a fusillade from right to left in the
first line of troops, then from left to right in the second line, and so on
through the whole army of ten thousand men. After the review refreshments were served in the marquees that had been set up. Although
there was not much food, there was plenty of hard cider and rum. The
day ended with a production of that superlatively dull play, Addison's
Cato. It is a pity that the play was not Farquhar's *Recruiting Officer*,
which the officers were rehearsing when the encampment broke up, or
Washington's favorite play, *The Beggar's Opera*; but at least *Cato* was
better than no play at all: it made the day more of an occasion. And
after the winter at Valley Forge the audience was hardened to suffering.
After all they had been through, *Cato* was merely the bite of a gnat.

"Johnny Reb"

It is ironical that Pennsylvania, the Quaker colony, should have seen more of war than any of the other forty-eight states. During the French and Indian War Pennsylvania suffered more than any other colony; during the Revolution it was both literally and figuratively the keystone of the young Republic; and during the Civil War it was the only Northern state to suffer invasion.

At first the Civil War was unpopular in Pennsylvania, nowhere more so than in the newspapers. Although Pennsylvanians had little love of slavery, the "plain people" and the Quakers were pacifists; and on much of the rest of the state the Democratic party had a firm hold. Many Pennsylvanians believed that this "brothers' war" was a tragic mistake that should be settled by arbitration instead of bloodshed. Nevertheless, three days after Lincoln's call for volunteers five companies arrived in Washington. These were the Ringgold Light Artillery from Reading, the Allen Rifles from Allentown, the Washington Artillery and the National Light Infantry from Pottsville, and the Logan Guards from Lewistown. As the first Union troops to reach the Capital, they proudly dubbed themselves "The First Defenders." Although the federal government had called for only fourteen regiments from Pennsylvania, enough men volunteered within a fortnight to make up twenty-five regiments. Green recruits were trained at Camp Curtin near Harrisburg. In addition to serving as a training center, Camp Curtin was a depot for military stores, a hospital for the sick and wounded, and even a prison camp for Confederate troops. During the course of the war three hundred thousand Union soldiers passed through this camp. Much the most important camp in Pennsylvania, it was also one of the principal training centers in the entire North.

Today the name of Camp Curtin is largely forgotten; but the names of two Pennsylvania Dutch towns, Chambersburg and Gettysburg, became known throughout the world. Though the name of Chambersburg may some day be forgotten, since the evil men do does not always live after them, the name of Gettysburg is forever famous.

Chambersburg first came into the limelight when it was captured by Jeb Stuart in his surprise raid on Pennsylvania in October, 1862. Crossing the Potomac on the 10th of October, his troops pressed on to Mercersburg, where they arrived in advance of rumor. In the stores of Mercersburg, Stuart's men bought all the shoes that would fit. It was not until the soldiers proffered Confederate quartermaster's receipts instead of good hard cash that the guileless storekeepers realized that these were not Union soldiers. The farmers were equally innocent. The rebels simply walked in and helped themselves to the horses. As the fields were wet, most of the farmers were busy in their barns, many of them threshing wheat. There was never a thought of the Johnny Rebs in their minds. Jubilantly the soldiers took possession of the huge farm horses, powerful draft animals of the breed that had hauled the Conestoga wagons. Having good sense as well as dash, they took the horse collars at the same time: no Confederate quartermaster could have produced collars big enough for these animals. By the time Stuart's men reached Chambersburg the alarm had spread. The money in the bank was moved to safety. At the army depot the Southern troops had better luck: there they found five thousand excellent new rifles as well as many pistols and sabers and also a store of army overcoats, underwear, socks, and other odds and ends of clothing. They helped themselves to what clothing they wanted and burned the rest. They also captured about two hundred and eighty sick and wounded Union soldiers; these they paroled. Burning the railroad shops in the town, Stuart then boldly led his troops east instead of retreating to the west as the Northern leaders expected him to do. Skillfully avoiding one hundred thousand Union soldiers near-by, Stuart with his eighteen hundred men crossed the South Mountains, headed into Maryland, and soon had put the Potomac between his small band and the Northern army. They took twelve hundred horses back with them, as well as thirty-seven civilians of prominence as hostages for Southern civilians in Northern hands. The government and railroad property they destroyed was worth at least $250,000. On the 11th and 12th they had been on the march continuously, covering eighty miles in twenty-seven hours. Naturally Stuart's raiders were picked men mounted on strong horses. Two stragglers had been lost, but not a soldier was killed. Seldom in war is it the lot of any body of troops to thumb their noses at the enemy in quite so spectacular and satisfying a fashion.

A month earlier in the summer of 1862 the Southern armies under Stonewall Jackson had crossed the Potomac to invade Maryland. Instead of being welcomed with open arms, however, the army was made to feel that Frederick County was hostile or at best indifferent. Stonewall Jackson attended the Reformed church in Frederick, where the minister boldly prayed for the President of the United States, though Jackson put the minister in his place by sleeping throughout the sermon. A few days later two battles were fought in the heart of the Maryland Dutch country, the Battle of South Mountain on September 14th and that of Antietam on September 17. Antietam was one of the bloodiest battles of the war, with the Confederate forces losing about ten thousand men and the Union armies even more. Antietam was not a clear-cut victory for either side but was costly to both. Although the Union Army was unable to drive Lee back across the Potomac, he found it wiser to withdraw and leave Maryland in McClellan's hands. One of the wounded men on the Northern side was young Captain Holmes, later justice of the Supreme Court. This episode became famous in the story, "My Search for the Captain," written by his father, Oliver Wendell Holmes.

The next year, 1863, the Pennsylvania Dutch country was invaded again, this time late in June by the Southern armies under Lee. The Confederates were amazed by the fatness of the land. "It's like a hole full of blubber to a Greenlander," wrote General Ewell. On their side the Bible-reading Pennsylvanians thought of the scourge of locusts in the land of Egypt as they watched the soldiers feasting on the ripe cherries hanging from the trees along the country turnpikes. Once again the troops helped themselves to horses and cattle at the farms. Nor did the towns escape; they were forced to hand over the greater part of their food. At Caledonia, fifteen miles west of Gettysburg, it gave Jube Early particular satisfaction to burn Thaddeus Stevens's ironworks. One Dutch town after another fell to the Southern armies with barely a struggle. Gettysburg was taken by Early and on June 27 York. "Extra Billy" Smith's men marched through York to the tune of "Yankee Doodle" and "Dixie." Early forced York to turn over $28,000 in cash to him before he left the town to attempt to cross the Susquehanna at Wrightsville. But here the Confederate plans misfired: by burning the bridge at Wrightsville the Union troops prevented Early from crossing the river. Confederate strategy called for a rear attack on Harrisburg by Early while Ewell was making a frontal attack. Meanwhile Ewell's men had taken Chambersburg and moved on to Carlisle. As he approached Carlisle, Ewell sent back three thousand head of cattle for the two corps behind him. At Carlisle, with some ceremony, he raised the Stars and Bars on the old Carlisle barracks. Balked of crossing the Susquehanna at Wrightsville, Early's forces joined Ewell's to attack Harrisburg from the west. The vanguard was only three miles from Harrisburg, the farthest north the Confederate forces ever penetrated, when Ewell received Lee's orders to rejoin the main army at Chambersburg. The Federal Army was reported to have crossed the Potomac and to have reached Frederick. Later Ewell got new orders to proceed to Gettysburg instead of Chambersburg.

While the main Confederate Army was converging on Gettysburg, Jeb Stuart's cavalry was off on a raid. On the morning of June 30th, from the hills above Hanover, Stuart spotted Union cavalry in the town below, whereupon the rebels charged and with a yell Hanover has never forgotten chased the men in blue through the streets of the town. Outside the town Brigadier General Elon J. Farnsworth was able to stop the fleeing cavalrymen and turn them on their pursuers. This time it was the Confederates who fled headlong through the streets of Hanover, with the Union cavalry at their heels. The rebel forces were so completely routed that Stuart, unable to halt his men, escaped capture only by forcing his horse to take a desperate leap across a gully fifteen feet wide. Only when the Confederate field guns were brought into play was the Union cavalry halted and Hanover retaken. But Stuart did not linger in Hanover; he pressed on to Carlisle, arriving there on July 1. He had started to shell the town when news reached him that fighting had broken out at Gettysburg. Stopping only long enough to burn the cavalry barracks, Stuart hurried to Gettysburg, arriving there on the 2nd of July but with men so weary they could hardly sit in the saddle.

It was lucky for the North that the Army of the Potomac was advancing from the south, where there was a clear road, and not from one of the other points of the compass. East, west, and north the roads were jammed with refugees fleeing before the Southern armies. Troops going to reinforce the Union armies could hardly get through the hordes of refugees. Wagons and carts of every description and even wheelbarrows, each piled high with pots, mattresses, and other household goods, crowded the roads as throngs of frightened people fled from the invading army. Overnight the horse had become man's most valuable possession. Lame, halt, or spavined, every nag was roused from the stall and put upon the road. Even more panic-stricken than the whites, and with good reason, were the Negroes who had escaped North and thought themselves free once they had crossed Mason and Dixon's line. With slavery hanging over their heads once more, they fled to the wooded hills and mountains.

The battle of Gettysburg is too well known to need further description here. In this bloody battle ten thousand more men died than at Waterloo. To the Pennsylvania Dutch particularly this battle struck home, for here they were fighting on their native soil. This was a battle to defend their villages and towns and cities, their houses and barns and fields. Furthermore, about a third of Meade's army was made up of Pennsylvanians, and of these a goodly number were Pennsylvania Dutch.

The last raid on Pennsylvania took place the following year. In early July Confederate forces led by Jubal Early moved up the Shenandoah Valley and then turned east toward Washington until on July 11 they could see the Capitol across the Potomac. Forced by the advancing Federal Army to withdraw, Early crossed to Maryland, where he levied $200,000 in cash on Hagerstown and $200,000 more on Frederick, two Dutch towns that had strayed south of the Mason and Dixon Line. In order to get the money the town of Frederick borrowed it from the banks, a loan on which it had paid well over $300,000 in interest by the time of the Second World War. Frederick will at last be rid of its debt in 1951.

With the money in his possession, Early turned back to Virginia, destroying bridges as he went. But almost at once he turned north again, this time on a raid of reprisal for houses burned in Virginia by General Hunter. It may be that Chambersburg was selected because it was in this town that John Brown planned his raid on Harpers Ferry. John Brown had appeared in Chambersburg in the summer of 1859 and lived there quietly for six weeks or more. No one in the town had any idea what he was up to. But it is far more likely that Chambersburg was chosen not because of John Brown but simply because it was within reach. The Confederate forces under General John McCausland, acting under Early's orders, entered Chambersburg at five-thirty in the morning of July 30, 1864. Early remained behind on the Potomac to keep open a line of retreat. McCausland at once presented a demand for $100,000 in gold or $500,000 in greenbacks, with the threat to reduce the town to ashes if the money was not paid. The town council firmly rejected these demands; as a matter of fact, all money had been removed from the banks. At nine that morning McCausland set fire to the town. Colonel William E. Peters of the 21st Virginia Cavalry protested violently against this action, pointing out that the only people left in Chambersburg were women and children. Rather than obey such an order, Peters declared, he would break his sword and throw it away. Faced with such mutiny, McCausland had Peters placed under arrest. Many of the soldiers set to firing the town with pleasure and turned with even greater gusto to looting. The looting was later confirmed by Brigadier General Bradley T. Johnson, whose brigade and McCausland's burned the town. Johnson's report in the *Official Records of the Union and Confederate Armies* is a particularly blunt statement in light of the fact that General Johnson was a Confederate officer: "Every crime in the catalogue of infamy had been committed, I believe, except murder and rape. Highway robbery of watches and pocket-books was of ordinary occurrence. . . . Pillage and sack of private dwellings took place hourly."

About two-thirds of the inhabitants of Chambersburg were left destitute and homeless by the burning of the town. It was a stupid act for which the South paid heavily. Many a Southerner was to hear the grim cry "Remember Chambersburg!" as Union soldiers set fire to his dwelling.

The Civil War has often been called a brothers' war. Where the Pennsylvania Dutch were concerned it was precisely that. In Pennsylvania and Maryland the Pennsylvania Dutch fought on the side of the North; but their cousins in the Valley of Virginia and in the Carolina

Piedmont—men of the very same blood—fought for the South. It is one of the ironies of history that many of the soldiers who made up the army of Lee and who followed Jeb Stuart and Jube Early on their raids were the descendants of the Pennsylvania Dutch who a hundred years before had poured south into the Shenandoah Valley and down into the Carolinas. When many of these men in gray crossed the Mason and Dixon Line to see before them the wooded hills and fat valleys and red-brick towns of Pennsylvania, they were back in the land of their forefathers.

Few of them had any qualms about this. Colonel John F. Neff of the 33rd Virginia, though the son of a Dunkard minister, was one of the ablest of Stonewall Jackson's colonels. Yet some of the men of the western part of North Carolina believed it wrong to carry the war into the North; they had volunteered to resist invasion, not to invade. Other Southerners discovered that Northern troops fought best on Northern soil. "I believe that the confounded Yankees can shoot better in the United States than they can when they come to Dixieland," wrote one disgusted rebel.

The Valley Dutch in Virginia suffered even more than the Dutch in Pennsylvania. The Shenandoah Valley was Lee's granary and as such was put to waste by Sheridan "so that crows flying over it . . . will have to carry their provender with them," as it was aptly phrased by General Early. Grain and hay, whether in barn or field, were either destroyed or seized. Cattle, too, were driven away or slaughtered. Barns and mills were burned and some houses, too; and railroad tracks were torn up. But even more deeply resented than the devastation wrought by Sheridan's army were "the burnings" of General David Hunter, a Virginian fighting for the North. Virginia Military Institute and many houses through the Valley were burned, not from military necessity, but out of hate. It is small wonder that the South retaliated in kind with the burning of Chambersburg.

It was by way of the Valley that the South made its two great invasions of the North, the first stopped at Antietam in 1862, the second at Gettysburg in 1863. No part of the country saw so much fighting as the Shenandoah Valley. The town of Winchester changed hands seventy-two times during the four years of the war.

Part Three

BY THE SWEAT OF THEIR BROW

The Fat Earth

From colonial days to the present the Dutch country has been noted for its fine farms. By the time of the Revolution Pennsylvania was the granary of the colonies, and a little later the descendants of the Pennsylvania Dutch made the Shenandoah Valley the granary of the South. In 1789 Benjamin Rush had written: "The German farm was easily distinguished from those of others, by good fences, the extent of orchard, the fertility of the soil, productiveness of the fields, the luxuriance of the meadows." Even today Lancaster County produces more per acre than any other county in the country, while back in the days of the Civil War Oliver Wendell Holmes, the essayist and poet, found words of high praise for the farms of southeastern Pennsylvania:

Much as I had heard of the fertile regions of Pennsylvania, the vast scale and the uniform luxuriance of this region astonished me. The grazing pastures were so green, the fields were under such perfect culture, the cattle looked so sleek, the houses were so comfortable, the barns so ample, the fences so well kept, that I did not wonder when I was told that this region was called the England of Pennsylvania. The people whom we saw were, like the cattle, well nourished; the young women looked round and wholesome.

The excellence of the Pennsylvania Dutch farms was no accident; they were the result of good judgment, hard work, and superior methods of farming. To a large degree the Pennsylvania Dutch were the founders of the agricultural prosperity of America.

At the very start they chose good land whenever possible. It has often been said that they hunted out the land where the trees grew tallest, for there they knew the soil would be most fertile; that they looked for the black walnut, which grew best in limestone soil; or that they sought out blue stones streaked with white—in other words, limestone. Whatever their method of judging the fertility of the soil, they chose some of the richest land in America. Coming from one of the most fertile agricultural sections of Europe, the Rhineland, the early German settlers undoubtedly had an eye for good land; and, once having come into possession of it, they kept it. But in some sections, where the English, mostly Quakers, and the Scotch-Irish had already pre-empted the best farmland, they had to take what was left and only gradually were able to get hold of the good lands, and then only because the Quakers had a hankering for the easier money of trade and the Scotch-Irish an itching heel. On poor soil the Dutch had no more success than the English and the Scotch-Irish, as is shown by the poor farms of many of the Dutch hill dwellers of Pennsylvania and by the Southern mountaineers of Pennsylvania Dutch blood.

In 1799 Thomas Hill described the Pennsylvania Dutch farmers as "the most early rising, hard working people I ever saw." Many of them, especially the "plain people," are still that. They have never been afraid of hard work or of getting their hands dirty. In the early years they deliberately chose to cut down the tall forest trees instead of girdling them and leaving them to die. And this they did with their own hands. There were no slaves on Dutch farms, and few of the Dutch were gentlemen farmers. The Dutchman was a dirt farmer who guided the plow and sowed the grain himself.

Possibly the greatest difference between the farms of Pennsylvania and those of the other colonies was brought about by the firm belief of the Dutch in the necessity of conserving the fertility of the land and, if possible, increasing it. The wasteful methods that wore out the good earth of the tidewater tobacco plantations in Maryland and Virginia were avoided. In the first decades the Dutch permitted the fields to lie fallow for a time to regain their fertility. Or sometimes plaster of Paris was used to build up the soil. This was good for the first time it was tried, but with each application the benefit became less. Later on lime took the place of plaster of Paris, and the limekiln became a familiar feature of the Dutch landscape. But the most important ways to keep the land fertile were the use of manure and the rotation of crops. The Dutch have always had a strong faith in both. Even in the early years there was some rotation of crops, though the usual four-year rotation of corn, oats, wheat, and hay—clover and timothy mixed—was not developed until shortly after 1800. But white clover was planted as early as 1748, and by 1780 the more important red clover was grown on almost every Dutch farm. To the Amish depleting the land, as was done in the South, was literally sinful; to the other Dutch farmers it was stupid. With his idea of permanency the Pennsylvania Dutch farmer thought of himself as holding the land in trust, as being honor-bound to pass it on to his sons as rich and fertile as he received it from his father. In their attempt to be good farmers the Dutch were greatly aided by the early German newspapers of Pennsylvania. In the eighteenth century they printed the best articles on agriculture to be found in the country.

Fortunately even the earliest settlers had a clear idea of a good farm. At the back of their mind they had the model of the Palatinate farm, which when not despoiled by war was exceedingly rich. Wheat, rye, oats, barley, and buckwheat were the principal grains on the Palatinate farm. Potatoes, introduced early in the eighteenth century, were widely grown. Hemp and flax were important crops. Almost every farm had its orchard of apples and pears, a line of cherry trees, and a vineyard on a hillside. There was a herd of cows and a sty or two of pigs; there were chickens, geese, and ducks. There was a row of beehives in the orchard. This idyllic picture represents the ideal rather than the actual, for in the war-torn Palatinate a farmer seldom made this dream come true. Yet it was this conception of what a farm should be, well ordered and self-sustaining, that the Palatine farmer brought with him to Pennsylvania and handed on to his sons. By the last quarter of the eighteenth century farm after farm in the Pennsylvania Dutch country showed that this ideal had been attained, that in Pennsylvania the Palatine farmer's utopia had been realized.

Naturally the new conditions in Pennsylvania forced some slight modifications of the Palatine immigrant's original plans. He could no longer build his house in a country village as he had commonly done back in the Rhineland. When each farm had many acres, the distances became too great to make living in a village practicable. Since land was so cheap, the early farms were of large size. Many were 300 or 400 acres, while 600 or 700 acres were not uncommon in the original grants. Most of this was in forest, and for a long time the clearings were relatively small. The early settler's greatest disappointment, however, was not that he had to forgo the friendly life of the village—the enormous number of acres he owned made up for that—but in his failure to start a vineyard. Unable to induce the grapes of the Rhineland to grow in Pennsylvania, he had to give up the wines to which he had been accustomed for centuries. Happily all the other fruit he had grown along the Rhine throve in Pennsylvania. The peaches were even finer than those back home and needed much less pampering. The grains and vegetables of Europe also grew well in Pennsylvania. Furthermore, there was corn, an invaluable new grain, and several new vegetables—squash, pumpkin, sweet potatoes, and lima beans. Even the climate was not greatly unlike the one he had known on the other side of the Atlantic. The summers were far hotter and the winters somewhat colder, but the mean temperature was much the same. Both regions had about the same number of frost-free days.

The basic pattern of the farm in Pennsylvania, that of the single farmstead with the family forming the unit, was the one on which the American farm was molded. In New England there was a tendency to settle in villages instead of on individual farms, while in the South the plantation worked by slaves became the rule. In addition the Pennsylvania Dutch farmer of the eighteenth century combined general farming with the raising of livestock. This is still the pattern of many farms in the Dutch country, especially in Berks County; and it was this method of farming that spread to the prairie states of the Middle West. By growing diverse crops the farmer was able to rotate them and thus preserve the fertility of the soil; and by selecting his crops wisely he could keep himself and whatever help he had busy round the calendar.

These farms were as self-sustaining as it was possible for them to be. A large variety of fruit and vegetables was dried for winter use, for this was long before the sealed glass jar had been thought of, and only the richest preserves would keep in crocks covered with paper. Meats were smoked over hickory or salted in brine for the winter. Honey and maple sugar took the place of "store" sugar. Even the clothes on their backs and the cloth stretched over the hoops of the Conestoga wagons were spun at home from flax and hemp grown on the farm or the wool of their sheep. Their very shoes were often made on the farm. Candles and soap were home-made, too. Every farmer was a Jack-of-all-trades and so was his wife. Only salt and pepper, molasses, spices, occasionally a little coffee, and perhaps some rum or Monongahela whisky were bought at the country store. Strong beer and ale made of barley malt sold at the crossroads tavern for twopence a Winchester quart. Practically everything else came from the farm.

In colonial days wheat was the main crop, the money crop, as it very often is today. A decade or two before the Revolution, and for some time after it, great quantities of wheat were collected at Reading each winter to be sent down the Schuylkill when the river rose in the spring. For the better part of a century Pennsylvania topped all other colonies —or states—in the amount of wheat it harvested from its fields. Not only was there enough to take care of Pennsylvania's growing population, but there was some left over to export to the West Indies and to New England. At that time wheat was sown broadcast by hand, usually in September, and cut with sickles early in July. The sheaves were stored in the barn to be threshed by flails in the fall or winter. In a year of severe drought, or in a rainy year when the grain sprouted in the sheaves, the Dutch farmer was saved by his other crops. Corn was grown more and more widely, until today it is first in acreage although not in value. It never became the money crop wheat was but was used chiefly for feeding the stock, and so it is today. Barley, oats, buckwheat, and rye and also potatoes, and even a bit of tobacco for home use, were grown too. Rye was more widely grown in Pennsylvania than anywhere else in the colonies. The whisky was made from rye, and so was the daily bread. Much hay was grown too, for the climate proved to be right for it. Every farmer tried to include some meadow land and a brook in his property, for almost every farmer had a small herd of cows. The irrigation of meadows, which had begun by 1750, was general practice fifty years later. Only when clover and timothy began to be grown on uplands was less importance attached to meadow land.

Of the lesser crops hemp was one of the more widely grown, since it did better in the richer soil and hotter summers of Pennsylvania than in New England. Hempfield Township in Lancaster County took its name from the common crop of that countryside. Flax, too, was much cultivated; the seed was exported and the fibers used largely at home. The flax plants were pulled up by the roots in July, tied in bundles, and dried in the sun. When the seed had been removed, the bundles were stacked in a pool and left until the pith between the fibers had rotted. Then they were dried in a flax kiln, an E-shaped stone wall with poles across the top on which the stalks were laid. An anonymous traveler in the Dutch country in 1829 remarked on this practice: "All along my rides, I noticed everywhere fields strewed with flax laid to dry—for everywhere German women still use the spinning wheel! Cheapness of manufactured goods will not allure *them* from their older habits of making home-made stuffs." Hops were grown for the beer that replaced the wine of the Rhineland, although many a farmer stuck to cider—or, if he was ambitious, applejack or cider royal—or made wine from elderberries, currants, blackberries, wild cherries, or wild grapes; or he might make some mead from honey or even attempt brandy—peach, plum, cherry, or persimmon.

Every farm had its orchard of apples, a grove of peaches, and cherry trees along the lane or in a fence row dividing the fields. In the house yard were a few pear trees, several plum trees, and usually a quince tree or two. Today Pennsylvania is one of the few parts of America in which the quince is still common. With the increase of insect pests in the last fifty years, the farm orchards began to disappear. More and more farmers bought their apples and peaches from the large commercial orchards. In the past wood was freely burned, and even today almost every farm has its bit of woodland, where some wood is cut for the kitchen stove; but coal from the mines to the north is generally used during the winter months.

All the farms had some chickens and perhaps ducks, geese, guinea hens, and turkeys as well. There were pigeons on many farms, then and now, not to keep the table supplied with squabs but "for nice," because pigeons cooing on the barn roof are part of the proper farm atmosphere. Like the painted barn signs or the ancient oak in the middle of the corn field, they are "for pretty," "for fancy," "for nice." Choose whichever phrase you will.

An outstanding feature of the Pennsylvania Dutch farm was the great bank barn. In none of the other colonies, except in the Dutch sections of Maryland and Virginia, were there barns comparable to them. On the ground floor the livestock was stabled, snug, warm, and protected from the winter's coldest blasts; on the floor above were ample stores of hay in the mows and grain in the bins to keep them well fed till the Easter grass was green in the meadow. Far more than the settlers of English blood the Dutch were aware of the necessity of housing their stock in winter. In the milder climate of England there had not been needed the shelter necessary in Switzerland and in much of the Rhineland. The early Dutch farmers built good stout barns for the stock, though they themselves had to put up with makeshift log cabins. The huge barns that the German and Swiss settlers regarded as essential the English and Scotch-Irish thought a luxury.

The horses, like the barns, were huge and splendid. These were the Conestogas, the favorite draft animals of the Pennsylvania Dutch. This was the breed that early ousted the oxen from Pennsylvania. Though oxen lingered on in New England till after the Civil War, in Pennsylvania they were seldom seen after the Revolution. Not that the early oxen were not large and powerful enough; one giant exhibited at Elizabethtown in 1796 weighed 2,884 lbs. By modern standards the cattle were a poor lot. They were a mixed breed in part descended from a few animals brought over by the Swedes in the first years of the colony and in part from later importations from the Dutch of New York and the Yankees, these last being part English cattle and part Danish. Except in winter the cattle were permitted to graze in the clearings and in the forest. Branding was not uncommon. For instance, Conrad Weiser's brand was a C over a W, the C a little to the left of the W. Sheep were numerous, and in those happy days remarkably free from disease as well as prolific. They, however, were not housed in the barn, nor were the razorback hogs that ran wild in the woods and fed on acorns.

The barn was but the most important of the farm buildings. Next came the house, and then a baker's dozen or more of other buildings: tenant house, summer kitchen, bakehouse, springhouse, smokehouse, washhouse, woodshed, privy, wagon shed, chicken house, corncrib, pigpen, tool shed, and later pump house: a little village in itself. All was plain, simple, functional, and unmistakably Pennsylvania Dutch. The value of these buildings was often three or four times that of the land.

The Dutch farms were models of neatness. The fields were fenced in, at first with the snake or worm fences and later with the familiar post-and-rail fence. These last were often whitewashed; even the trees in the house yard were whitewashed. The theory was that whitewash helped to protect the trees from disease and insects, but it was done more to make the house yard look trim than for any other reason. With the passing of the chestnut trees from which the wooden fences were made, unfenced fields became common. Today there may be a single strand of wire charged with electricity closing in the pasture; that is, if the farmer is not an Amishman. Yet post-and-rail fences are still seen; but almost all of the old snake fences, which the white man borrowed from the Indian, have rotted away.

Very often the Dutch will combine the old and the new. Silos have been enthusiasticaly adopted, yet each July finds a few Berks County farmers building ricks of straw in the ancient manner. A cluster of these beautifully shaped conical ricks is one of the more picturesque sights of the Dutch country. Sometimes the persistence in clinging to old ways is amazing. Wheat was sown broadcast, cut with sickles, and threshed with flails on at least a few farms until the dawn of the twentieth century.

Many of the products of the early farms were marketed in the near-by towns of Lancaster, York, Reading, and Lebanon. Almost before there were roads eggs, butter, cheese, salt meat, and poultry as well as fruit and vegetables were taken to market. Women rode along the forest trails with a butter pail on each side of the fat farm horses and bags of dried snitz behind them. On an evening in May, 1795, François de La Rochefoucauld-Liancourt encountered some girls near Quakertown as they were setting out on the forty-mile ride to Philadelphia so as to arrive at market by break of day:

I met on the road some girls of eighteen on horseback, travelling to Philadelphia, and carrying forty pounds weight of butter, with some cheese and poultry. Some of them travel alone; and their youth and beauty, for the greater part of them are very pretty, gives them no disturbance in a journey so long, so often repeated, and the greatest part of which is made in the night time: no person thinks of injuring them.

Then, as now, tending market was largely the women's business.

The farmers' markets have long been a characteristic feature of the larger Pennsylvania Dutch towns. They are a survival of the days before the railroad, when many of the farm products had to be disposed of locally. These markets were to the advantage of the farmer in that he sold directly to the consumer—and at good prices. The middleman was eliminated. With good rail lines and trucking facilities the Dutch farmer is no longer dependent on the market houses of the Dutch cities. Philadelphia, New York, Baltimore, and Washington are all within reach. Yet tradition dies hard in the Dutch country. Whether it is a matter of habit or a desire to stand well with his own people, many a farmer sends his choicest products to the local market. Lancaster, York, Reading, and Lebanon still eat at the first table; Philadelphia, New York, Baltimore, and Washington at the second.

Although general farming is still the rule in the Dutch country, certain counties specialize in specific crops. In Lancaster County tobacco, with yields of 1,400 pounds to the acre, has become the most profitable crop. But in many fields there are steers from the West, largely shorthorns, being fattened for beef; yet since Lancaster is so far from the great ranches and since corn can be grown more cheaply in Iowa than in the East, the fattening of beef cattle is no longer as common as it once was. Even so, the stockyards of Lancaster are the largest east of Chicago. Lancaster County has fattened cattle from the West ever since 1804 or 1805, when cattle from the Monongahela and Ohio country were driven across the mountains. In a county as intensely conservative as Lancaster old ways die hard—even if there is little money in them. But little by little the old does give way to the new. In recent years Lancaster County has taken to growing heavy crops of tomatoes. And the rise of cooperatives likewise marks a change. Although the local cooperatives are still insignificant when compared to those of Wisconsin and California, they are growing in size each year. Farmers, even in the Dutch country, are learning to work together.

Certain other counties have their specialties too. In Lehigh County potatoes are the big crop; and in Adams, York, and Franklin, apples. Elsewhere the farming is well diversified. Wheat is still grown throughout the Dutch country, the only part of the East that has been able to face the competition of the vast farms of the Middle West and Canada. Fortunately for the Dutch farmers the winter wheat of southeastern Pennsylvania brings a high price, since it is particularly good for pastry and cake flour. All the Dutch counties grow corn, and oats too are pretty much of a standard crop. Barley and buckwheat are little grown. Dairy cows and poultry are important in most of these counties because these districts are within easy shipping distance of four great Eastern cities, while the western edge of the Dutch country ships some of its milk, chickens, and eggs to Pittsburgh. Although quite a little cheese, particularly cup cheese, cottage cheese, and even Swiss cheese, is made in Lancaster and York counties, cheese is not as important as it once was; nor is butter. The demand for milk in the near-by cities is so great that it does not pay to turn much of it into butter and cheese. As a consequence many farms specialize in dairying, while chickens are raised in such numbers that Pennsylvania is first among the states in egg production. The cattle most favored are Holstein, Guernsey, and Jersey, with some Ayrshire and even a few Black Angus. White Leghorns and New Hampshire Reds are the two most popular breeds of poultry. Swine are raised on many farms, usually Berkshires and Chester Whites. Sheep are not common, but they are not as rare as they were twenty years ago. Apples and peaches are the two principal fruit crops. Belle of Georgia, Elberta, and Hale are among the more widely grown peaches. The Winesap is the apple held in highest esteem in the Dutch country and along with the York Imperial is the apple most extensively planted.

The apple deserves a word or two more, for the Dutch have a number of varieties of their own that are hardly known to the outside world. Though the York Imperial is a Dutch apple, since it is a native of York County, this apple has been borrowed by other sections. A much more delicious apple, the Smokehouse, the Dutch have kept pretty much to themselves. One of the best of all apples, with a distinctive flavor of its own, the Smokehouse ripens in September but is at its best before fully ripe, for it soon becomes mealy. Two other Pennsylvania Dutch apples that are fairly well known are the Fallawater and Smith's Cider, while the Monocacy is a Maryland Dutch apple of recent origin. There are a host of other apples, little planted today but occasionally turning up at market in one or another of the Dutch cities: Evening Party, Blue Mountain, Fanny, Ewalt, Hiester, Klaproth, Susan's Spice, Paradise, Water, Winter Sweet, and Mama Beam or Belmont. At Nazareth the Countess's Own, named for the Countess Benigna, was a favorite in colonial days. The Summer Rambo is an apple the Dutch got from the Swedes of the Delaware valley. The Keim is an Oley Valley apple, green and so late in ripening that it can be eaten only after New Year. The Doktor is another winter apple, long popular in Germantown. A large honey-colored sweet apple ripening in July—unfortunately, I do not know its name—is much sought after for *snitz un knep*.[1] Between apple pies and apple tarts, snitz pies, snitz un knep, apple dumplings, apple sauce, and apple butter, not to speak of cider and applejack, apples are much in demand among the Pennsylvania Dutch. And with good reason, for the Dutch country (in which for the moment I include western Maryland and the Shenandoah Valley) grows some of the finest apples in America. While not as large nor as handsome as the Western apples, they are a delight to the palate; they are filled with juice and not with sawdust. When you bite into a Pennsylvania Winesap, you realize that Pennsylvania is

[1] Dried apples and dumplings cooked with ham.

a part of the world that God designed for growing apples. It is high time that more Dutch farmers tumbled to this fact and stopped piddling around with oats and beef cattle and put more of their acres into apples.

In much of southeastern Pennsylvania the land is as intensively cultivated as it is in Europe. In the period between the two world wars, farms often brought from $200 to $300 an acre or even more, and after the Second World War considerably more than that. As in colonial days, the farms are as fine as any in the East. Most of the fat land the Dutch cleared in the eighteenth century is still in Dutch hands, and in addition they have taken over most of the limestone soil originally occupied by the Quakers, Episcopalians, and Presbyterians. This has been notably true in the Cumberland Valley, which in colonial days was dominantly Scotch-Irish and which today is largely Dutch. Most of the Quaker holdings in Berks and Lancaster counties have also passed to Dutch ownership. But how long the Dutch will hold their own is difficult to say. Although they have not yet been displaced by more recent immigrants as have the Yankees in the Connecticut Valley, Poles and Italians have begun to buy up farms that have come down for generations in Dutch families of Lutheran or Reformed faith. This tendency, though not yet common, is more pronounced in the Cumberland Valley than elsewhere. The "plain people," with their insistence on hard work and their opposition to higher education, have not only succeeded in holding their own but are even expanding.

Still another factor is decreasing the number of farms in the Dutch sections. Since the advent of the automobile more and more farms have been bought up as country residences by city people. Businessmen, lawyers, and doctors from Bethlehem, Allentown, Reading, Harrisburg, Lancaster, and York, eyeing the old stone farmhouses with admiration, have bought many of the finer farms around those cities. For a few years some of them attempt to carry on as gentlemen farmers or worry along with tenant farmers, but many find the struggle too much for them and abandon all efforts to farm, letting the land grow up in weeds and brush.

Pennsylvania Dutch farmers have been criticized *ad nauseam* for working their women too hard. That most women on Pennsylvania farms work hard is undeniable; so do the men. For the most part the women work willingly; they recognize that there is work to be done and they pitch in and do it, just as the men do. Few women on the farm view marriage as a relationship in which the husband works and the wife fritters away her time. That is a suburban attitude, not a country one. Most Pennsylvania Dutch wives look on marriage as a partnership and act accordingly. If it is necessary, they can take a turn in the hay fields or bind sheaves of wheat at harvest, but their work in the fields is pretty well confined to harvest time. The heavier and the more unpleasant work is done by the men as a matter of course. The chickens, unless the flock is a large one, are usually the women's charge, though the men and not the women generally clean the roosts. Often, too, the kitchen garden is cared for by the women; but if the work it too onerous the men will help out. On the Pennsylvania Dutch farm everybody works, men, women, and children. Yet there is no brutal driving of women and children. The children are given tasks suitable to their age, the girls usually helping their mother and the boys their father. This was the American way for more than two centuries, and on the Dutch farms it is still the way. In view of the widespread employment of women in factories it is difficult to understand the criticism of the Pennsylvania Dutch for the hard lot of the farm women. One look at the Dutch countrywomen should dispel that notion. See how buxom most of them are; notice the contentment in their faces. These women, happy and healthy, are in no need of sympathy.

Forge and Mill

The highly skilled workman, as well as the good farmer, has been a characteristic type among the Pennsylvania Dutch for more than two centuries. Today the Dutch section is divided between industry and agriculture, with even more skilled mechanics than there are farmers. Great mills and industrial plants, as well as small industries by the hundred, fill the towns and cities. Even in the eighteenth century there were almost as many artisans as farmers. A high proportion of the Germans who came to Pennsylvania in the eighteenth century were skilled workmen, as well they might be, since the Palatinate was one of the busiest industrial areas of Europe. Speyer was noted for its woolens and linens, Donnersberg for iron, Lambrecht and Mannheim for their cloth industries, and Rheinzabern for its potteries and tileworks. Quarries and limekilns and charcoal houses were common in many parts of the Rhineland. Small wonder that the men who had worked at one or another of these industries abroad should desire to pursue the same occupation in Pennsylvania.

There was a large range of skills among the early immigrants. Among the Palatines who arrived in London between the middle of April and the middle of July, 1709, all the more usual crafts were represented, and in addition there were such skilled workmen as linen weavers, stocking weavers, hatters, lime burners, brickmakers, glass blowers, and even silversmiths and engravers.

Though some workmen moved on to Lancaster, Reading, or York, the first Pennslyvania Dutch manufacturing center was Germantown, which early turned to the manufacture of linen and knit goods. Stockings were made on rude frames that the Mennonite weavers set up in their houses. This was the true start of American textiles. By 1756 the Dutch of Pennsylvania were manufacturing 720,000 pairs of stockings a year. These sold over the counter for four shillings a pair. And to this day Pennsylvania has gone on making stockings; it is still the hosiery center of the country. Textiles in general got off to a good start in Pennsylvania because the early German distaff and spindle, or rock, as it was known, was superior to that of the handwheel employed by immigrants of English blood.

Much weaving, of course, was done at home in Pennsylvania, as in other colonies. Flax was woven into linen, flax and wool into linsey-woolsey. More rarely, cotton and flax were woven into fustian or cotton and wool into jeans. Indigo was the dye most commonly used. Bought at the country store or from a peddler, it was mixed with urine and poured into the dye pot. It was woven into checks or sometimes into stripes for dresses, aprons, shirts, spreads, or bed ticks. The bark of black oak or hickory made a good yellow, and so did the juice of jewelweed. Sassafras bark gave quite a good orange, pokeberries a rich red, sumac berries a red-brown, and the hulls of black walnuts a yellowish brown. Whiteness in cloth was more difficult to achieve than color. To ensure a fair degree of whiteness for homespun linen, thirty to forty bleachings were necessary.

In Germantown, in 1690, the first paper mill in America was established by William Rittenhouse on Papermill Run, a branch of the Wissahickon. By the middle of the eighteenth century, Germantown had become an important printing center for the Pennsylvania Dutch. Here Christopher Sauer ran the printing shop from which were issued the books, pamphlets, and almanacs that circulated throughout the Dutch country.

Germantown was by no means the only Dutch manufacturing town. The cities to the north and west had almost as many industries. Many of these industries came into being in the Dutch country at such an early date because of the difficulties of transportation. The Dutch country was not a river settlement like the towns along the Hudson, where ships from Europe could tie up at the docks; nor was it on tide-water like much of New England and the South. For the most part it had to make its own iron and cloth and glass or go without. Most of the early factories were small, little more than incipient factories; yet combined with the industry of Philadelphia they made Pennsylvania the chief center of manufactures in America in the eighteenth century. Once started, the manufacturers soon discovered that Pennsylvania was an advantageous site for trade: it was in the very heart of the English colonies. Furthermore, Pennsylvania was rich in natural resources: it had the most fertile ground east of the mountains; it had the richest supply of minerals; and in Philadelphia it had one of the great ports of the eighteenth century.

Almost from the start the manufacture of iron was one of the chief industries of Pennsylvania. The first forge in the colony was the one Thomas Rutter opened for business in 1716 on the Manatawny Creek in Berks County. The first blast furnace in the colony was Rutter's Colebrookdale Furnace, also in Berks County, which lighted its hearths about 1720. In 1725 Pool Forge, Pine Forge, and Glasgow Forge, all three on the Manatawny, began operation. In 1729 they were joined by Spring Forge, and in 1744 by Oley or Spang's Forge. In 1752 Pottsgrove Forge, followed ten years later by Pottsgrove Furnace, was built on the Manatawny, while in 1760 Oley Furnace started up on Furnace Creek, a little stream emptying into the Manatawny. In addition two other forges and another furnace, all either on the Manatawny or its tributaries, antedated the Revolution. It is one of the curiosities of American history that this gentle, idyllic Manatawny region, where today cattle browse in lush meadows, where the rattle of a car crossing the covered bridge interrupts the country quiet, should have given birth to American heavy industry.

Not far away, on French Creek in Chester County, a smaller iron center developed. There in 1718 Coventry Iron Works was built, in

1733 Reading Furnace, and in 1737 Warwick Furnace. In 1744 Hopewell Forge was opened just across the border in Berks. Along the Schuylkill to the south was Valley Forge (1742), and to the north the forges at Birdsboro (1744). Still farther north, on the Tulpehocken, there started up in 1742 the forge with the wonderful, mouth-filling name of Tulpehocken Eisenhammer, better known by its later name of Charming Forge. To the south the Perkiomen was a minor iron center with Green Lane Forge (1733), Mount Pleasant Furnace (1737), and Hereford Furnace (1745). By 1750 so many forges and furnaces had been built in the Schuylkill Valley that it, rather than the Manatawny section alone, had become the iron center of America. By the time of the Revolution at least three dozen forges and furnaces had been built in this small district.

There were other important forges near-by in other parts of the Dutch country. In Lebanon County, Peter Grubb had opened a bloomery on Furnace Creek in 1737, which was followed in 1742 by the important Cornwall Furnace. In Lancaster County were the Windsor forges on the Conestoga (1743), Stiegel's Elizabeth Furnace on Middle Creek (1750), and Martic Forge on the Pequea (1755). In upper Bucks County the Durham Iron Works on the Delaware dated from 1727. The forges west of the Susquehanna were concentrated in York and Cumberland counties. Probably Mary Ann Furnace, founded in 1762, and the Codorus Iron Works, opened three years later in 1765, were the most important of the York County forges. In Cumberland County there were four forges, and just outside Carlisle was an armory that during the Revolution turned out sabers, muskets, and cannon for the Continenetal forces.

Many of these furnaces made stove plates for stoves of various types, the stove for heating houses being yet another Pennsylvania Dutch "first." Elsewhere in the colonies fireplaces alone supplied the heat. In addition to the boxlike stoves, Franklin fireplaces or stoves were manufactured at Warwick Furnace, for Franklin gave a model of his stove, which he called "the new Pennsylvania fireplace," to his friend Robert Grace, who had castings made of it. The first cookstove, too, was made in the Dutch country—at Mary Ann Furnace in 1765. Stoves were exported to Boston and elsewhere, as they were during the nineteenth century and as they are today.

The ironworks of early Pennsylvania were of different types. The bloomery forge, of which there were only a few in Pennsylvania, was a primitive type that had been developed in Catalonia about the tenth century. The iron it produced was very impure because of the large amount of slag in it. Much more usual in Pennsylvania were the blast furnaces of a type common in England during the reign of Henry VIII. These produced on the average twenty-five tons of pig iron each week, as well as stove plates, firebacks, pots, and kettles. The refinery forges, of which there were many in Pennsylvania, fashioned the pig iron into bars of wrought iron of the sort sold to blacksmiths. From this iron the blacksmiths made axes, shovels, hoes, chains—indeed, most of the iron tools and implements commonly used in colonial America. A good-sized forge, such as Charming Forge, produced about three hundred tons of bar iron anually. Steel was made at Coventry, Pottsgrove, and Vincent furnaces and at Birdsboro, as well as in Philadelphia. There were slitting mills, which made slit iron for nails, at Pine Forge, Charming Forge, and Birdsboro; and there was a wire mill in Cumru Township, Berks County. All of these were in existence by the time of the Revolution.

Pennsylvania was rich in iron ore. Visitors from abroad marveled at the quantity of iron ore in the colony. It was so close to the surface that it was not necessary to mine the ore; it was simply dug out of the ground. At Oley or Spang's Forge, at Warwick Furnace, and at Reading Furnace the mine holes were only twenty feet deep. Even such important ironworks as Durham and Cornwall had not gone deeper than fifty feet by the middle of the century. At Oley Furnace alone there was a shaft mine like those common in Europe. There a galley three hundred feet in length had been driven into the side of a hill, and then a shaft sixty feet deep had been sunk. With iron so close to the surface few miners were needed. Two or three were enough to keep a furnace supplied with ore, although Oley Furnace, with its more laborious shaft mining, employed six miners in 1783. Almost invariably the ore was mined close to the forge or furnace for which it was intended.

Charcoal was used by all the forges and furnaces to smelt the ore. The wood was cut down in the near-by forests and charred for fuel in much the same way that Pliny describes the ancient Romans as charring their wood. An enormous amount of charcoal was consumed by the furnaces: Warwick Furnace used from five to six thousand cords of wood annually during the periods it was in blast. At Oley Furnace more than four hundred bushels of charcoal were used to produce a ton of iron. Consequently a large number of wood choppers, colliers, and teamsters were needed to keep up the supply of charcoal. The great quantity of timber needed explains the large tracts of woodland purchased by the early ironmasters: for Durham Furnace, 5,600 acres; for Colebrook, 7,684 acres; for Elizabeth Furnace, 10,124 acres; while Cornwall Furnace and Hopewell Forge split 9,669 acres between them. Many of the forges and furnaces were finally abandoned because there was no more timber near-by to supply them with charcoal. Reading Furnace and Colebrookdale were two such that shut down right after the Revolution. Others were more fortunate; in some charcoal was burned almost up to the time of the Civil War.

At the forge or furnace itself most of the labor was highly skilled, although the number of ironworkers needed to keep a furnace running was not large. Usually a furnace would be in blast for not more than nine months at a stretch, shutting down in the winter or during the hottest part of the summer. Two shifts of men, each twelve hours long, were needed to keep the furnace going.

Very often the ironmasters found it difficult to get the necessary labor. Negro slaves, redemptioners, and in the early days even Indians were pressed into service. They were never able to get much work out of the Indians, who slipped away into the woods when work became hard or boring. Most of the slaves in the Pennsylvania Dutch country were those on the iron plantations. They and the redemptioners were used for much of the unskilled labor; but at a number of forges—Pine Forge, Valley Forge, Charming Forge, Green Lane, Durham Furnace, and others—Negroes, most of them free, were employed at such highly skilled labor as refining and drawing the iron into bars.

At the iron plantations an attempt at prohibition promoted sobriety by keeping liquor at a distance. By an act of 1726 no public house or tavern could be licensed within two miles of a forge. That this was ineffective is shown by a similar act of ten years later that increased the distance to three miles.

The iron plantations were small communities in themselves. In addition to the forge and furnace and charcoal house there were the ironmaster's mansion, the office, the workers' houses, the blacksmith shop, a barn, a store, sometimes a gristmill and a sawmill. Usually part of the plantation would be farmed to provide food for the workers. The houses for the furnace men, miners, colliers, farmhands, and other workers were usually either small stone houses, often whitewashed, or log cabins. Sometimes men would be born on one of these iron planta-tions and work there all their lives, and their children and grand-children after them.

The ironmasters were of various strains. Many of the early ones, such as Thomas Rutter and Samuel Nutt, were English. Some were Welsh—Thomas Potts and David Jenkins; and some were Irish—Robert Cole-man and Robert Grace. General Udree of Oley Furnace was French Huguenot. Naturally some were German—Baron Stiegel and Valentine Eckert. Whatever their blood, the ironmasters supported the American cause in the Revolution with energy and enthusiasm. Without the Pennsylvania forges and furnaces the Continental Army could hardly have fought a war, let alone won it. Throughout the war the iron-works in the Dutch country remained in American hands, the furnaces running full blast to keep the armies supplied with guns and ammuni-tion. The Council of Safety thought the work of the forges and furnaces of such importance that no laborer was permitted to leave his job or enlist without express permission of the council. A number of prisoners, especially Hessians, were sent to Elizabeth Furnace, Mary Ann Furnace, and Durham Iron Works to supplement the ordinary labor. At Charm-ing Forge Hessian prisoners cut a mill race 100 yards long, 20 feet wide, and from 12 to 20 feet deep through solid rock. One curious contribution to the war effort was the saltpans made at Cornwall for saltworks on the Jersey coast, where an attempt was made to obtain salt from the waters of the Atlantic to take the place of the salt cut off by the war. The shortage of salt was one of the most severe of the war. In 1776 the Reverend Henry M. Mühlenberg recorded in his diary: "The people push and jostle each other wherever there is the smallest quantity of salt to be found. The country people complain bitterly because they suppose there are hidden stores in Philadelphia."

With ironmasters with the extravagant tastes of Stiegel, and many of them living in a style the country people regarded as magnificent, it is only natural that legends grew up about them. One of the more fantastic of these tales, the one about Colebrook Furnace in Lebanon County, was put into verse about the middle of last century and has been attributed to the Philadelphia dramatist, George H. Boker. The ironmaster of this furnace (hardly a literal portrait) was a man of violent temper and cruel disposition as well as a drunkard and a lecher. Fond of hunting, he liked to brag about his pack of hounds. One day, however, when he was particularly eager to show off his hounds, the whole pack acted like so many whipped curs. Furious and cursing, the ironmaster drove the pack down the road to the furnace, where he forced his workmen to throw the hounds, one by one, into the furnace flames until only one hound, his favorite Flora, was left. Flora, in the true style of melodrama, had saved her master's life when he had been lost in a snowstorm. Now she bared her teeth and snapped at the workmen so that they were afraid to go near her. Damning the workmen as cowards, the ironmaster picked up Flora, who licked his face; yet so hardened was his heart that he resisted this show of devotion and hurled the dog into the flames. There was a low moan from Flora, and then the words, "God! God! God!," were heard from the furnace. After that day the ironmaster never hunted again. Losing all interest in life, he shut himself up in his mansion and so besotted himself with drink that he was out of his mind a good deal of the time. For weeks and months he was confined to his bed. Then one day he sat up and, gazing out of his window at the furnace fire that lighted up the skies, he shouted:

> "Here they all come, the hellish pack
> Pouring from Colebrook Furnace, back
> Into the world!"

And with a look of terror on his face he fell back on his pillow and died.

There the poem ends, but there has been added to it a further legend. On stormy nights during the fall and winter the dread baying of a pack of hounds is heard in that countryside. Any man brave enough to stay will see fleeing across the hills the ghost of the terror-stricken ironmaster with the hounds at his heels.

Although many new furnaces and forges were built in the Schuylkill Valley after the Revolution, the industry began its move to the westward part of the state. The great iron center of Bethlehem, of course, was still in the future. During the course of the nineteenth century almost all the old forges and furnaces were abandoned, although a few were transformed into modern mills. Only one improvement was made before the middle of the nineteenth century: the lining of the furnaces with slate. The ore deposit at Cornwall, which turned out to be the richest in the East, is still mined today; indeed, it has been worked continuously for more than two centuries. By 1907 more than 20,000,000 tons of ore had been taken from it. Today it has an annual ore production of nearly a million gross tons.

From time to time other metals have been mined in Pennsylvania: zinc in the Saucon Valley, chromite and nickel in Lancaster County. Copper, silver, and gold have all been found at Cornwall. There is even a romantic legend of a lost copper mine, the old Perkiomen mine in the Stone Hills. To call it a legend is less than fair, since there actually was such a mine, which was worked as early as 1740. Back in those days the ore was sent to Bristol in England to be smelted. Just before the Revolution a particularly rich vein of ore was discovered and some cargoes of it sent to England. When war broke out the entrance to this rich vein was sealed to prevent its falling into the hands of the British. Unluckily, with the war the secret of its entrance was lost, never to be rediscovered to this day.

Although no other industry was comparable to iron and steel in colonial Pennsylvania, the manufacture of wagons was vital to the well-being of Pennsylvania all through the eighteenth century and well into the nineteenth. The absence of navigable rivers forced the Pennsylvania Dutch to turn to wagons. It was not until their country was covered by a network of canals that they came to depend on other forms of transportation. The early four-wheeled wagons with tops of canvas were crude and heavy. Nothing light could withstand the rocks and sloughs of the first roads. For a crude world that was just on the point of being cut out of the forest, crude wagons were good enough. In those days babies in the back country cut their teeth on strings of wolf's teeth. Yet these lumbering farm wagons were the prototypes of the greatest of all American wagons, the Conestoga. Here was the beginning of a national institution, the covered wagon. But whether the awkward early models or the graceful Conestoga, all were designed and built by local workmen. Many smiths and wheelwrights in the Dutch country were occupied in their manufacture.

Another important product of Pennsylvania manufacture in colonial times was the Kentucky rifle. This was as superb an example of Pennsylvania Dutch industry as the fine glass made by Baron Stiegel. This rifle was known as the Kentucky rifle not because it was made there but because it was so highly prized on the frontier, in Kentucky as well as elsewhere. Only by an accident of fate was the name of Kentucky wished upon this Pennsylvania Dutch rifle. This was the rifle of the frontier; the older settlements on the coast knew it only by reputation. The shot fired at Lexington was not from a Kentucky rifle but from the brown Bess, a crude, heavy musket with a kick almost as deadly as its bullet. The brown Bess had neither the range nor the accuracy of the Kentucky rifle. The enemy to their acute discomfort soon came to know the rifle of the Dutch country. Howe spoke feelingly of the "terrible guns of the rebels," as well he might, for the deadly fire of these rifles was something new. The sharpshooter picked out one particular man instead of shooting at random and trusting to luck that his bullet would hit the enemy. In excusing all gunsmiths from combat service during the Revolution, as did the Committee for Safety in Northampton County, the authorities were merely showing proper appreciation of this remarkable gun.

The enemy, too, had rifles; that is, the Hessians did but not the British, which was one reason why the British hired the Hessian mercenaries. The rifle, invented by Gaspard Kollner in Vienna about 1500, was widely used through much of Central Europe and had early been brought to Pennsylvania by the German immigrants. But the rifle made by the Pennsylvania gunsmiths was a great improvement on the European model. Instead of a bore of .50 to 1.00 it had one of .45—the same bore adopted by the United States Army for its rifle in 1873. The Pennsylvania Dutch had beaten the army to it by more than a hundred years. The Pennsylvania rifle also had a longer barrel and better rifling than the European gun. This refinement had been made by the early gunsmiths to give the rifle greater accuracy and a longer range, to make it a more effective weapon for hunting—whether the game was a squirrel high in a hickory tree, a deer, or an unfriendly Indian.

Many of the Kentucky rifles were decorated so lovingly and with such taste that in a sense they became works of art. Usually the stocks were of black walnut, though sometimes curly maple was used. The mountings were of brass, often intricately engraved. On the right side of the stock was a brass patch box. Later on, some of the very finest rifles had inlays of silver.

Possibly the best known of all the Pennsylvania Dutch manufacturing plants before the Revolution was Baron Stiegel's glass furnace at Manheim, where the finest flint glass in the colonies was made. The glass house there was so large that it is reported that a coach and four could turn around in the brick dome of the melting house.

Much more important, however, were the flour and grist mills, of which there were a large number scattered through southeastern Pennsylvania, often only a few miles apart. Most of the year these mills were busy places. Only in the worst droughts did the streams go dry. In

January and February, however, the millrace often froze over and the miller was forced to take life easy—to try the flip at the Black Horse Tavern at the crossroads or to hug the fire at home. Today most of these mills are deserted; only a few are still in operation. It is not as in colonial days, when the flour was hauled to the wharves of Philadelphia and shipped to Boston and the South, even to New Orleans.

Colonial Pennsylvania took great pride in the quality of its flour. There was even a standard system for grading flour, with "superfine" as the top grade. Each barrel was tested by boring before it was shipped out. This is much the same standard system of grading that in our own time has been so denounced by manufacturer and distributor alike when any consumer has had the temerity to suggest it; but back in the 1700's people apparently wanted to know what they were buying— they wished to have a better guide than the claims the manufacturer chose to put on the label.

Naturally there were numerous sawmills too, since Pennsylvania was heavily wooded. Even today there are many forests in southeastern Pennsylvania, although there are no longer any stands of virgin timber. But for a long time virtually all sawmills, particularly in the thickly populated sections of the Dutch country, have disappeared from the scene.

Stone quarries and brickyards became common toward the end of the colonial period. So readily did the stone lend itself to building purposes and so suitable was the clay for making bricks, that stone buildings and brick ones both became far commoner in southeastern Pennsylvania than anywhere else in the country. As limestone when burned provided lime to enrich the soil, little quarries and limekilns are found on many of the Dutch farms. These are but relics of the past, for few are still in use. Most of them have long given way to the great commercial quarries and rock-crushing plants. Pottery, too, was a thriving industry, particularly in upper Bucks, where Nockamixon Swamp provided fine clay. Pennsylvania stoneware was exported to Connecticut and tiles to Charleston.

Many industries fitted easily into the pattern of country living. The shop in the back yard became a familiar feature of Pennsylvania Dutch life. Cigar makers, carpet weavers, broom makers, tinsmiths, cheesemen, and today florists, radio repairmen, electricians: all of them busy in the little shops in the back yards. One man will paint automobiles, another will stencil designs on old furniture. Along with the farm laborers, the factory workers, the storekeeper, and the hotel-keeper, these are the people who make up the population of the villages and small towns.

Although colonial manufacturers were scattered through much of the Dutch country, Lancaster, Reading, and York were the leading industrial and trading towns. Lancaster in the years just before the Revolution was the largest inland town in America. In addition to the more usual trades, it could boast of brass founders, gunsmiths, coppersmiths, silversmiths, printers, clockmakers and watchmakers, tobacconists, rope-makers, and skin dressers. Even the little town of Lititz near-by had a tilemaker, a bookbinder, and a gunsmith as well as the more ordinary trades. Lancaster was not merely a manufacturing town but was also a financial center in a small way. After 1763 some of its wealthier men put their money in the fur trade of the Ohio country and the Wabash. Reading and York, though both smaller than Lancaster, were also busy places. The manufacture of felt hats was Reading's chief industry in the eighteenth century. In 1795 there were 38 hatters in Berks County who produced that year about 2,200 fur hats and 54,000 wool ones. Reading's most surprising industry was shipbuilding—if the building of quite sizable boats comes under that term. Actually it was more sensible than it sounds. Much iron was used in the construction of the boats, and Reading was close to the source of supply. There was also plenty of timber available. Beer, too, was made in early Reading, even as it is today. In the eighteenth century Pennsylvania beer was sold throughout the South and in Canada as well. York, too, was a thriving town. Though there were no factories of any consequence, its smaller work-shops brought York a growing trade. Tanners, distillers, gunsmiths, and hatters were especially prosperous, but all the crafts were represented, down to breeches maker and sugar baker.

Bethlehem and Ephrata were two settlements in which manufacturing was undertaken as part of the community life. In Bethlehem most of the crafts of the day flourished: there were blacksmiths, nailsmiths, carpenters, masons, wheelwrights, wagonmakers, coopers, potters, weavers, dyers, tailors, tanners, saddlers, hatters, millers; there were turners to make spinning wheels for Bethlehem and the surrounding country; there was even Matthias Tommerup, the bell founder. In the cellar of the Brethren's House, Tommerup cast a prayer bell and refectory bell for that building, a bell for the Widow's House, another for Bethabara, the first Moravian settlement in North Carolina, one of

236 pounds for the courthouse at Easton, one for Zion's Reformed Church in Allentown, and one of 228 pounds for the Bell House in Bethlehem that is still hanging there. Bethlehem was an amazing place. Probably no other American town of so small a size had so many and such ambitious industries. There were no idle hands. The girls and women in the Sisters' House plaited straw that they fashioned into hats. As early as 1752 an attempt to raise silkworms was made. There was another cocoonery at Nazareth and a third at Christiansbrunn. For several years there was a considerable yield of silk.

Ephrata was famous for its printing house. This and Christopher Sauer's press in Germantown were the two most important of the Pennsylvania Dutch presses. In the eighteenth century the Pennsylvania Dutch presses turned out more books, and for the most part better books, than those of Boston.

Almost every town was a small hive of industry. The Berks County village of Kutztown in 1794 had the usual assortment of carpenters, turners, joiners, bakers, and shoemakers and in addition two hat-makers, a jeweler, a potter, a gingerbread vender, a tobacco factory, five taverns, and a place where five women spun. Some towns had outstanding specialties. Such a one was Lititz, where David Tannen-berger built the finest church organs in America. Lancaster County was famous for organs, spinets, and pianos; Bucks in its turn was noted for zithers. Reading and Lebanon were both known for their clock-makers, although there were clockmakers here and there through much of the Dutch country.

All during this early period Philadelphia was the banking center for the Dutch towns, though during the first half of the eighteenth century, when barter was common, few Pennsylvania Dutchmen had much need of banks. The little money a man got his hands on could easily be stowed away in an apple butter crock, and a small one at that. A handful of the money hidden away in those old crocks would reveal a strange mixture of coins. Money was money; and a coin of almost any nation passed current in Lancaster, Reading, or York: Dutch and Guinea ducats, German carlins, French pistoles, Arabian chequeens, Spanish and Portuguese coins, and of course English shillings as well.

With the nineteenth century the Industrial Revolution arrived in Pennsylvania, and almost at once there was a rapid growth in population. Many of the older towns changed into cities, while new settle-ments sprang up along the railroads. Manufacturing on an impressive scale became one of the features of the Dutch country. Though many new industries were established, a goodly number of those founded in colonial times have persisted to the present. The country of the Pennsylvania Dutch is still a land of iron and textiles. Though most of the old forges have vanished, iron and steel are made at Bethlehem, Lebanon, and Steelton. Yet in all three cities the great furnaces are of comparatively recent date. The first blast furnace at Bethlehem was lighted in 1863. In the same year the first rolling mill there was put into operation, the first iron was puddled, and the first rails rolled. This is a far cry from the small eighteenth century forges making firebacks and stoves with quaint biblical designs.

In the late nineteenth century Reading not only had one of the largest wagon works in the state but was an early center of the automobile industry. The early Duryea, with its patent-leather dashboard and its whipsocket, some models with four wheels and some with three, was made in Reading from 1892 to about 1902. When the industry was running at top speed, as many as three cars were turned out every week. The Duryea was followed by the Acme, a six-cylinder car with a custom-made body and brass fittings. The Acme, which was produced from 1902 to 1909, was a famous racing car, three times victor in the annual cross-country race from Savannah to Seattle against a field of all other cars made in America. In 1911 the Acme gave way to the S.G.V., which was manufactured until 1914. S.G.V. were the initials of the officers of the company: Herbert M. Sternbergh, Robert E. Graham, and Fred Van Tine. Selling from $2,500 to $12,000, the S.G.V. was a luxury car for royalty and the four hundred. The king of England, the kaiser, and the czar, not to mention the Vanderbilts and Astors and Drexels, all owned models of this car. Only by blessed chance did Reading escape the fate of Detroit.

Textiles, too, have retained their importance in the Dutch country. Reading, with the largest hosiery mill in the world, is the textile center. One Dutch city after another has both iron and textiles. Very often it is the wives and daughters of the steelworkers who furnish the labor for the textile plants. Bethlehem, of course, has factories manufacturing textiles; and even Reading, for all its emphasis on textiles, had mills turning out metal products. By and large, however, textiles have become even more important than iron and steel. There is scarcely a city or town without its textile mills.

Other old industries have lived on into this century. Paper is made at Easton and York, and printing is important in both these cities and in Lancaster and Harrisburg as well. The manufacture of church organs has been shifted from Lititz to Hagerstown. Bethlehem's great guns have replaced the Pennsylvania rifle, and Allentown's trucks the Conestoga wagon. There is no glass furnace, however, to succeed Baron Stiegel's. Stone is still quarried, some of it for building stone, some to provide material for highway construction, and some for the great cement mills north of Allentown. Large deposits of slate in the northern side of the Great Valley in Lehigh and Northampton counties and also along the Susquehanna near Peach Bottom have been worked for many years. Bricks are still made, especially at Reading, but also in various other places in the Dutch country.

Thus it goes with one industry after another. Few clocks are made today in the Dutch towns. The watchmaker—if the great watch factory in Lancaster can be adequately described by so modest an appellation —has edged out the clockmaker. Tobacco has remained important from the old days of the stogies on down. Back in the early part of the nineteenth century, when the Conestoga cigar, better known as stogie, was in its heyday, Pennsylvania made more cigars than any other state. Today Lancaster, York, Red Lion, and numerous other Dutch towns have flourishing cigar factories. The gingerbread baker, however, has given way to the pretzel baker.

There are, to be sure, a number of industries in the Dutch towns and cities that have come into existence in modern times. Not everything Pennsylvania Dutch is old. The large factory in Lancaster manufacturing linoleum is but one of these; the chemical plant in Pottstown, the chocolate factory in Hershey, and the shoe factory in Hanover are others. Possibly the oddest of all the industries in the Dutch country, one which was forced on them almost by necessity, is that of dredging for coal in the rivers. On the Susquehanna and the Lehigh are coal dredges—the only mining fleet of its sort in the world—at work reclaiming the fine coal washed down into the river from the coal mines beyond the mountains.

Wagon Road, Canal, and Railroad

Transportation was a serious problem to the early settlers of the Dutch country, inasmuch as this was a land without seaports and with rivers navigable only for short distances. As no ship could sail up the Delaware, the Schuylkill, or the Susquehanna to the Dutch settlements, the early pioneers were forced either to ascend the rivers and creeks in small boats or to make their way along the Indian trails in the woods. At first most of the settlements were along the streams: the Skippack, the Perkiomen, the Schuylkill, the Pequea, the Tulpehocken, the Manatawny, the Conestoga, the Cocalico, the Lehigh, the Quittapahilla, and the Swatara. Despite the occasional rapids or shallows the streams became highways. Even most of the old Indian trails followed the streams. Since navigation on all these streams is non-existent today except for a few rowboats and canoes, it is only with difficulty that it is possible to think of them as highways. Yet on September 2, 1736, Conrad Weiser saw eighteen canoes, filled with the chiefs of the Onondaga Council, sweep down the Susquehanna between the wooded mountains above Sunbury.

The migration of the fifteen families of the Schoharie pioneers from upper New York to the Tulpehocken region is a good illustration of the use to which the streams were put by the early settlers as well as by the Indians. This migration, one of the great feats in the annals of American travel, occurred in the spring of 1723, probably as soon as the rivers were navigable, since they wanted to reach the Tulpehocken country as early as possible to begin spring planting. From the Schoharie villages north of the Catskills these pioneers cut a path through the forest to the Charlotte Creek, which flows into the Susquehanna. Reaching the creek halfway along its course, they felled trees and made dugouts from them. Then began their descent of the Susquehanna down to the Swatara. Dangerous rapids confronted them at Wyoming and again at Nescopeck, halfway between Wyoming and Shamokin (now Sunbury), and extremely bad rapids below Shamokin. These they passed safely. But the journey was a long one: from the point of embarkation on Charlotte Creek, down the Susquehanna, and up the Swatara to the Tulpehocken region is almost four hundred miles. Their horses they drove overland, roughly by way of the Delaware and the Great Valley. But after they reached the new settlement at Tulpehocken, twelve of their horses ran away. Eighteen months later ten of the twelve turned up at Schoharie.

With the growth of the settlements came roads, at first fanning out from Philadelphia, striking north and west into the Dutch country to link the isolated pioneers in the wilderness with civilization. The earliest roads were little more than wretched lanes through the forests. At many places the heavy wagons sank axle-deep in the mud. And these were the best roads; many of the others were so bad that they served only for riders on horseback and trains of pack horses and mules. Yet before the eighteenth century was half over many of the roads within a hundred miles of Philadelphia were good enough for wagons.

One of the earliest of the roads was the one up along the Schuylkill to the little colony of Swedes at Molatton and the Quakers near-by at Exeter Meeting. As this road was built during the reign of Queen Anne, about 1710, it became known as the Queen's Highway. A road built when a king was on the throne was inevitably called the King's Highway. Neither title meant much more than State Road would mean today and consequently was usually dropped in favor of a more specific name. The Queen's Highway to Molatton was later extended to Tulpehocken, but when Reading was founded where the road forded the Schuylkill it became known as the Reading Road. Still later the road was extended farther, north from Tulpehocken to Sunbury on the Susquehanna and also west to Harris's Ferry. From the start this road to Reading has been one of the more important of Pennsylvania roads. During the Revolution Mühlenberg at his church in the village of Trappe described in his diary the hordes of refugees fleeing north on this road in the face of the British invasion of Pennsylvania: "During the whole day wagons have been passing with goods, and men, women and children flying from Philadelphia." And again, after the defeat at Brandywine: "A distracted Sunday. Coaches, chaises, and wagons loaded with fugitives passing without interruption."

Even more important was the road to Lancaster, built about 1733. This was the main road to the West even in the days when the West lay just across the Susquehanna. This road was soon extended west from Lancaster, crossing the Susquehanna at Wright's Ferry and connecting Lancaster with York. In those days before the Alleghenies had been penetrated the road struck south to the Shenandoah Valley. Later, when vast numbers of Conestoga wagons traveled this road, it became known as the Great Philadelphia Wagon Road. It was over this road that Daniel Hollenbach made his monthly trip from Winchester to Philadelphia, carrying flour and wheat north and bringing back city merchandise. Before the French and Indian War a road ran west from Frederick, Maryland, to Fort Cumberland on the Potomac, but even then there was no road over the Pennsylvania mountains. At a time when the mountains hampered western expansion the Great Philadelphia Wagon Road led directly to the fertile Valley of Virginia and even to the Carolina Piedmont. During the early years of the Republic it became the highway to Kentucky, for in southern Virginia it joined the Wilderness Road, which Daniel Boone had blazed in 1774–1775. Crossing the mountains at Cumberland Gap, the Wilderness Road led across Kentucky to the falls of the Ohio, where Louisville now stands. In the decades when Braddock's Road across the Alleghenies was growing up in brush and when the Indians on the plains of western New York barred the way across that state, the road down the Shenandoah to Cumberland Gap was the most practicable route to the West. Used at first by pioneers on horseback eager to cross the passes into Kentucky, it was soon crowded with covered wagons, almost by the thousand. Many settlers heading west visited Lancaster, York, or Carlisle first to acquire a Conestoga wagon, a Kentucky rifle, or other equipment. From 1775 to 1800 more than three hundred thousand settlers traveled this road to the West. It was the use of this route rather than the one across the Pennsylvania mountains that accounted for the settlement of Kentucky at a time when Ohio was still Indian territory.

The third important road of the Dutch country was the one following the Great Valley. The section from Easton to Reading, laid out in 1755, was but one link in a road that ran through the valley from the Delaware in the north through Pennsylvania and Maryland south to the Shenandoah Valley. The southern part of the Great Philadelphia Wagon Road was really a section of this road. In lower Virginia it met a road from Salem in North Carolina, thus linking the Moravian center of Salem in the South with Lititz and Bethlehem in the North. The Lititz church diary for March 26, 1756, mentions "the North Carolina wagon" that passed through Lititz regularly every few months on its way between North Carolina and Bethlehem: "We had bread baked from the flour made in the North Carolina mill, brought here by the two returning wagons." During the Revolution the Pennsylvania section of the road through the Great Valley from Easton to Bethlehem and then through Reading and Harris's Ferry to Carlisle and so on to the South was of great strategic importance. When Philadelphia was in the hands of the British, it was this road that connected New England, New York, and New Jersey with the colonies in the South. It was then the most heavily traveled highway in America. Later, during the Civil War, the southern section of this road through the valley was a natural route of invasion of the South by the North and the North by the South. The very excellence of the road, which was covered with crushed limestone when most roads were sloughs of mud, invited the invading armies. In the South one skirmish in the valley followed another. In the North the road led to Antietam and Gettysburg.

West of Carlisle there were for a time only packers' paths through the mountains. At Carlisle, which was the eastern terminus of the pack-horse trains, there were sometimes as many as five hundred pack horses assembled at one time, ready to start their trek west with loads of iron, salt, sugar, and other necessities. Iron shaped in the form of a U to fit the horses' backs was made in the Pennsylvania forges for the western trade. In the pack trains there were from ten to twenty horses in a string and several strings of horses in a train. All traveled in single file, with a rider on the lead horse and another rider at the end; or very often there was but a single rider, who rode either in front or behind.

A skillful driver was able to manage a train of ten or more horses merely by his voice. Each horse had a bell because at night the horses were hobbled with withes and turned loose. As a rule every horse carried a pack of about two hundred pounds, the train making about fifteen miles a day. Even as late as the last decade of the eighteenth century such trains carried iron from the Juniata forges west to the Monongahela and Ohio.

The first great road across the Alleghenies was Forbes Road, later known as the Pennsylvania Road. Built in 1758 to enable the British and American forces to capture Fort Duquesne, it ran west from Bedford to the forks of the Ohio. At Bedford it joined a road running east through Chambersburg and Shippensburg to Carlisle. Forbes Road was a military road guarded by forts at strategic points to protect it from the French and Indians. Built not by a single colony but by the military forces defending all the colonies, it was one of the first national roads in America. As the shortest way west it soon became the most important route to the Ohio country. During the Revolution it was of particular importance because it led directly from the West to Carlisle, the main depot of ammunition and the supply center of troops for the West. In the early nineteenth century the Erie Canal in New York and the Portage Railroad in Pennsylvania supplanted it. Almost forgotten, it lost its proud title of the Pennsylvania Road and was known simply as the Chambersburg and Pittsburgh Turnpike.

There were many lesser roads in the Dutch country. One of the more important of these was the road from Philadelphia to Doylestown and Easton, completed in 1722, when the second link in the road, the section from Doylestown to Easton, was finished. The road from Philadelphia to Bethlehem was built about twenty years later, soon after the founding of the Moravian settlement. Even earlier was the Skippack Road, built in 1713. The Monocacy Road, surveyed in 1739 and soon an important trading route, ran west from Wright's Ferry on the Susquehanna to York and then on to the Monocacy River and south to the Potomac. The horses and wagons Franklin collected for Braddock were started on their way to Fort Cumberland over this road. The Paxtang Road connected Downingtown with Harris's Ferry. Later this road was replaced by the Horseshoe Turnpike. The New Castle and Conestoga Whisky Road, though never a main highway, had a name to make it linger in men's memories. By the time of the French and Indian War most of the settlements south of the mountains were connected by roads. Goshenhoppen, Oley, Shaefferstown, Lititz, Emmaus, Falckner's Swamp, and dozens of other villages all had roads linking them to the outside world.

As soon as passable roads were constructed, a postal route of sorts was set up. The weekly post from Bethlehem to Philadelphia by way of Falckner's Swamp and Germantown began on July 15, 1742, with four postilions. Another amenity was the inns and taverns for the ease and refreshment of the traveler. On the busier roads there was sometimes an inn every mile along the highway.

The cost of transportation on these early roads was high. In Pennsylvania it cost a shilling to carry a bushel of wheat a hundred miles, while in New York a boat could carry the same amount of wheat down the Hudson for twopence. Farmers in the other colonies who were able to ship their grain by water were able to undersell the Pennsylvania Dutch farmers. Instead of depending on agriculture alone, the Dutch turned to manufacturing, where they were less handicapped by the sheer bulk of their products. Transportation was a less considerable item in shipping fine glass or hats or even stoves than it was with wheat and corn. It was the high cost of transportation that made it profitable to make things at home instead of bringing them in from the outside. Before the Revolution the cost of freight by wagon for fifty miles was more than that by boat for the three thousand miles across the Atlantic.

Whenever possible, boats instead of wagons were employed for moving freight. On the Delaware the Durham boats, 60 feet long, 8 feet wide, and drawing only 2 feet of water, were used to take the ore down the river to Philadelphia. Each boat held as much as fifteen Conestoga wagons. After 1750 much of the freight on the Delaware between the Forks and Philadelphia was carried in these boats. Charges were twenty-five cents a barrel downstream and fifty cents per hundred pounds for the tedious journey upstream. These were the boats that made it possible for Washington to cross the Delaware and attack the Hessians at Trenton on the Christmas Eve of 1776.

No other river in southeastern Pennsylvania was as navigable as the Delaware. The Susquehanna was shallow and full of rocks and rapids; yet even so, a river boat known as an ark, triangular in front and back, was constructed for traffic on that river. From twenty to thirty feet long and fifteen to twenty wide, it could float when loaded with three hundred barrels of flour in only three feet of water. By 1790 about 150,000 bushels of wheat was being brought down the Susquehanna each year, much of it from the Juniata Valley. On the Schuylkill about fifty boats, each sixty feet by eight, were used in the spring when the river was high to take wheat from Reading down to Philadelphia.

Oddly enough, it was a Reading Dutchman, Jacob Yoder, who was the first man ever to float a flatboat down the Mississippi. Embarking from Redstone on the Monongahela in May of 1782, he floated down the Ohio and thence down the Mississippi. Apparently the Dutch country had boats on the brain: both John Fitch and Robert Fulton were born in the thoroughly inland county of Lancaster.

Despite the use made of the rivers, attention had to be paid to roads. The great triumph of eighteenth century road building was the Philadelphia-Lancaster Turnpike, the first paved road in America. Capital to build it was raised by subscription from six hundred stockholders. David Rittenhouse, the noted astronomer, made the preliminary surveys. Begun in February, 1790, the road was completed in December, 1795. This turnpike was a macadam road twenty-four feet wide and sixty-two miles long. Then as now this was the main road to the West. Even in this century there was a signpost at the corner of Broad and Walnut streets in Philadelphia with the simple words, *To Lancaster and San Francisco.*

The success of the Philadelphia-Lancaster Turnpike led to the construction of other turnpikes: the Lancaster, Elizabethtown, Middletown, and Harrisburg Turnpike; the Chestnut Hill and Springhouse Turnpike; the Perkiomen and Reading Turnpike; the Little Conestoga Turnpike; and so on and on. One turnpike company after another sprang up. By 1832 Pennsylvania had chartered two hundred and twenty of them, and about three thousand miles of road had been built. Some of the turnpikes were only a few miles long, but until the First World War their tollhouses and tollgates were a familiar sight in the Dutch country.

In the eighteenth century the roads crossed creeks and rivers at fords and by ferry, but after the Revolution bridges replaced most of the fords and ferries. The first bridges were handsome arched structures of fieldstone, simple in line and graceful, like the bridge across the Perkiomen at Collegeville, or the bridge across "the Branch" near Black Rock, or Jug Bridge across the Monocacy near Frederick. Jug Bridge got its name because a demijohn of whisky was sealed up in the eastern end by the trowelmaster—or at least, so legend has it. The nineteenth century brought the covered bridge, far cheaper to build than the arched stone bridge. With the planked floors protected from the rain and snow by roofs and boarded sides, the covered bridges lasted for many years. Leisz's Bridge, which crossed the stripling Schuylkill north of Reading by a single span, was an unusually graceful example of the covered bridge. The old "camel-back" bridge across the Susquehanna was a great lumbering affair. This is probably the bridge Dickens crossed on his way from York to Harrisburg and of which he spoke as being nearly a mile long and "profoundly dark." The covered bridge over the Susquehanna farther south at Wrightsville was burned during the Civil War to check the rebels' invasion of the North. Even the bridge north of Harrisburg at Northumberland, a mile and a quarter long and with twenty-three piers, was destroyed when the Confederate forces advanced on Harrisburg. But as stone gave way to wood, wood was replaced by iron and concrete. Few of the old covered bridges are left. Even on forgotten back roads, where only three cars a morning rattled across them, they had to give way to concrete structures.

During the late eighteenth and the early nineteenth centuries the stagecoach was an important part of the life on the Dutch roads. Stagecoaches arrived and departed regularly in all the leading towns and cities. There was a great bustle and stir at the Sun Inn in Bethlehem when the stagecoach from Philadelphia drew up at its door. Then life was as heart-warming and romantic as a Christmas card. Most thrilling of all the stagecoaches that ever traveled the Pennsylvania turnpikes was the one at the end of the War of 1812 that, in large letters on a white banner bound round the top, carried the news of peace to a cheering countryside. Yet it was both an expensive mode of travel and a slow one. In the early years of the service, the stage left Reading for Philadelphia at five on Monday morning and got to Philadelphia Tuesday noon. The fare was £2. For your £2, though, you sometimes got full value in excitement. On a Sunday morning in December, 1809, highwaymen held up the Reading mail, robbed the passengers and tied them to trees before the stagecoach had left the limits of Philadelphia, an episode that was later dramatized and put on the stage of the Walnut Street Theater.

By 1796 the journey from Philadelphia to Lancaster was made in one day. The stage left the Spread Eagle in Market Street at five in the morning and got to the Swan in Lancaster on the evening of the same day. This became the line of the Great Western Mail to York,

Carlisle, Shippensburg, and Frederick. By 1804 the stage called "The Good Intent" was awarded the contract to carry the mail from Philadelphia to Pittsburgh in four and a half days. By 1831 two lines were running from Philadelphia to Pittsburgh: the Good Intent and the United States Mail. Both made the trip in three days. As late as 1842 Dickens traveled from York to Harrisburg by stagecoach. He described the coach as "a kind of barge on wheels" that "carried 12 passengers inside; the baggage, including a rocking-chair and a good-sized dining-table on the roof; and the driver and 2 passengers on the box—not to speak of the intoxicated gentleman among the baggage on the roof, later replaced by a small boy in a snuff-colored coat."

The outstanding vehicle of the early roads in the Dutch country was not the stagecoach but the Conestoga wagon. By 1775 more than ten thousand Conestoga wagons made the trip to Philadelphia annually. Sometimes there were one hundred wagons in a single train. Fifty to a hundred such wagons bound for Philadelphia were to be found practically any day in the year on the Lancaster or Reading road. These vast vehicles, crawling along at the rate of twelve to fifteen miles a day, hauled glass, pottery, linen, sugar, salt, tobacco, grain, flour, flaxseed, whisky, cider, fruit, charcoal, iron ore, and pig iron. The larger part of the scanty supplies that reached Washington at Valley Forge was hauled in these wagons. In the spring of 1778 one of them, guarded by a company of Continental soldiers, brought $600,000 in silver, a loan from the French government, all the way from Portsmouth, New Hampshire, to York, Pennsylvania. Year by year the number of Conestoga wagons increased until by 1830 there were three thousand each day on the road from Philadelphia to Pittsburgh, for these carried the land freight to the West.

This greatest of all American wagons was an astonishing vehicle. The wagon itself was boat-shaped with slanted ends and a sag in the center of the wagon bed, both crosswise and lengthwise, to make certain that the load would settle toward the middle when it shifted. The heavy back wheels were five and one-half or six feet across. The hickory bows, from eight to twelve in number, slanted upward and outward to form great arches for the homespun canvas. In the canvas top as well as in the wagon body there was a graceful curve, the hallmark of the true Conestoga wagon. The overhang of the cover, in both the front and the rear, to keep the rain out was another characteristic of this wagon. The wagon frame, sturdily made by Pennsylvania Dutch workmen to meet hard use, was of seasoned white oak with axle trees and single trees of hickory. None of these wagons was drawn by fewer than four horses, while some had as many as eight; but six was the usual number. These horses were mighty draft animals, many of them bred in the Conestoga valley. Though their exact lineage is unknown, they are believed to be of the strain of the magnificent stallion, Tamerlane, and the three brood mares brought over by Penn. They stood from 16 to 17½ hands high and weighed about 1,600 pounds. Since the largest of the Conestoga wagons was able to carry eight tons, powerful animals were needed to draw them. The Conestogas were one of the most notable and one of the few breeds of horses this continent has produced. It is a great pity that with the passing of the Conestoga wagon this breed of horse was permitted to become extinct.

A Conestoga wagon in all its glory was a brave sight. The wagon body was that color so dearly loved by the Pennsylvania Dutch, a light but brilliant blue verging on peacock blue; the great wheels and all the running gear as well as the sideboards were vermilion; the iron-work was black and the hempen homespun top white. The horses were often black or bays, although later dappled grays became popular. Over the horses were bows of bells in the Russian manner. From each flat iron hoop hung three to eight bells—four was the usual number—carefully selected to chime. These were small open bells of brass or bronze or sometimes of iron. Usually there was no bow of bells on the saddle horse, the left wheel horse, on which the wagoner rode when he was not walking by the side of the wagon or sitting on the lazy board, a picturesque name for a sliding board that could be pulled out on the left-hand side of the wagon. The harness on the horses was black, and almost black were the bearskins that half covered the horses in winter. The wagoner himself wore high boots, a broad-brimmed hat, a great-coat in winter with a gay home-knit scarf and mittens. Every small detail enhanced the picturesque quality of the spectacle: the toolbox on the left side of the wagons, a box eagerly sought by museums today because of its strikingly beautiful wrought iron; the red bucket hanging beneath the wagon; the black tar-box, the blue feedbox, and the red wagon jack. It was a sight by no means merely picturesque; it was noble and stirring as well. This great wagon with its huge horses, covering a distance sixty feet in length when pulling a heavy load, left the beholder with an increased respect for both horse and man. A train of a hundred or even fifty Conestoga wagons traveling the Great Philadelphia Wagon Road or the Reading Pike was one of the more impressive sights of the early days of the Republic.

The bells especially were highly prized by the wagoners, not so much for their beauty, though they took great pride in their tone; nor for their usefulness, though they warned other travelers on the road of the approach of a Conestoga wagon; but because they were proof of a wagoner's ability to take care of himself. If a wagon got stuck in a ditch or a mudhole and the driver was forced to appeal to another wagoner to help him to get out, his bells were the price he paid to the man who came to his rescue. To anyone as tough and two-fisted as the Conestoga wagoners this was a humiliating experience. These wagoners prided themselves on their manhood, on their ability to slug it out with other wagoners, to down drink after drink of Monongahela whisky. They were a hard, tough lot, though one of them, Joseph Ritner, rose to be governor of the state. In summer they slept out of doors, in winter on a tavern floor before the fire. They patronized only certain taverns that catered to them alone. No namby-pamby genteel inns for them! To their horses and wagons they gave the best of care. In winter the wagons were driven on planks at night to keep the wheels from freezing to the ground.

One of the most interesting features of the Conestoga wagon was the lazy board. This was a board of white oak strong enough to bear the wagoner's weight. Sitting on it, the driver could operate the brake. This sliding board extended from the left-hand side of the wagon; and it was on the rear horse on the left that the wagoner rode, for sitting on the left wheel horse he could reach all the horses with his whip, held in his right hand. In passing other wagons or coaches he kept to the right of the road to make sure that he did not sideswipe them. As John Omwake has pointed out in his invaluable book *The Conestoga Six-Horse Bell Teams of Eastern Pennsylvania*, to which I am greatly indebted for most of this information on the Conestoga wagon, it was the Conestoga wagoner who decided that America was going to drive on the right-hand side of the road. Not that he thought it out in quite so arrogant a fashion, but when he met a coach or wagon he pulled over to the right—if he pulled over at all. To this gigantic wagon all lesser vehicles were forced to give way. When the Conestoga wagoner chose to drive on the right, he decided for everybody else as well as himself: all they could do was follow suit. And as the roads became more and more crowded with Conestoga wagons, all other conveyances

—gigs, phaetons, chaises, 'Sopus wagons, *blutzwagons* [1]—and men on horseback, too, did follow suit until all America was driving on the right side of the road. Rather an odd contribution of the Pennsylvania Dutch to the American way!

The Conestoga wagoner did not depart from the scene without adding a word to the American language. I am not referring to the Conestoga wagon itself, which most Americans would call a covered wagon, but to the *stogie,* the long, strong, pencil-like cigar smoked by the wagoners and obviously a corruption of the word *Conestoga.* Even in those days Lancaster County produced tobacco and made cigars. The stogie was hardly a choice cigar—quite otherwise. It was long and rank and it sold four for a penny. It made up in size and cheapness what it lacked in quality.

With the coming of the canals the heyday of the Conestoga wagon passed. By the end of the 1830's there were so many canals in southeastern Pennsylvania that, to use only a slight exaggeration, the land was honeycombed with them. Canals lined the banks of the rivers: the Delaware to Easton, and then the Lehigh; the Schuylkill to Pottsville; the length of the Susquehanna with a canal connecting Bellefonte with the West Branch and another linking Pittston on the North Branch with Sunbury; a canal along the Juniata to Hollidaysburg; one along the Cordorus to York; and still another along the Conestoga to Lancaster. Furthermore, the Union Canal joined the Susquehanna at Middletown with the Schuylkill at Reading. Near Lebanon this canal passed through a tunnel, dug in 1823, the oldest in the country. By 1835 there were 601 miles of canals in the state and only 108 miles of railroads; by 1840 there were 954 miles of canals in operation, more than in any other state.

A number of the canals were built with money raised in lotteries. Lotteries were a common feature of the life of that time, not only in Pennsylvania but elsewhere in America. There were lotteries to build churches and schools. There was a lottery to help build the Lutheran church in Germantown in 1754, one for the Lutheran church in Lebanon in 1762; one for the Reformed church in York in 1769, and another for the Reformed church in Easton in 1774. Scores of other churches were paid for in this way. In 1761 there was a lottery for the payment of the "Tulpehaucken Rangers" for their services in the French and Indian War. There was a lottery to build the stone bridge

[1] Light farm wagons without springs.

across the Perkiomen at Collegeville. There was even a lottery to pay for the Washington Monument, with a top prize of $50,000. Most ambitious of all were the lotteries for the Union Canal. Between 1811 and 1833, when the state legislature finally abolished lotteries by law, there were about fifty lotteries for the Union Canal. Rivaling the Irish sweepstakes of this century, they offered prizes from $10,000 to $100,000. Tickets were sold throughout the United States. All told $33,000,000 were awarded in prizes; for the single year of 1832 the prizes amounted to $5,216,240.

Some of the projects in canal building were badly bungled, the Union Canal in particular. Far shallower and narrower than the canals along the Susquehanna and the Schuylkill, which it connected, its boats were of only twenty-five tons burden instead of the usual sixty tons of the Schuylkill and the Pennsylvania canals. Freight had to be moved from the larger Susquehanna and Schuylkill boats in order to pass through the Union Canal. To avoid so expensive an operation the Union Canal was enlarged. It was not reopened to traffic, however, until 1856, too late to profit the company, which promptly went into bankruptcy.

The most ambitious of all these projects was the construction of the Portage Railroad to link the canals of eastern Pennsylvania with those of the western part of the state. By this railroad passengers crossed the Appalachian Divide at a point nearly 2,500 feet above sea level. Once on the western side they could proceed by canal to Pittsburgh, and from Pittsburgh the Ohio and Mississippi would take them all the way to New Orleans, if they so desired. At first the passengers had to leave the canalboats at Hollidaysburg to make the ascent of 1,398 feet from that town in railroad coaches. Later the boats were loaded on flatcars and taken across the mountains to Johnstown, where they were placed in the canal once again. Dickens's description in his *American Notes* of his journey on the Portage Railroad in 1842 is justly famous:

It was very pretty travelling thus, at a rapid pace along the heights of the mountain in a keen wind, to look down into a valley full of light and softness; catching glimpses, through the tree-tops, of scattered cabins; children running to the doors; dogs bursting out to bark, whom we could see without hearing; terrified pigs scampering homewards; families sitting out in their gardens; cows gazing upward with a stupid indifference; men in their shirt-sleeves looking on at their unfinished houses, planning out to-morrow's work; and we riding onward, high above them, like a whirlwind. It was amusing, too, when we had dined and rattled down a steep pass, having no other moving power than the weight of the carriages themselves, to see the engine released, long after us, come buzzing down alone, like a great insect, its back of green and gold so shining in the sun, that if it had spread a pair of wings and soared away, no one would have had occasion, as I fancied, for the least surprise. But it stopped short of us in a very business-like manner when we reached the canal; and before we left the wharf, went panting up this hill again, with the passengers who had awaited our arrival for the means of traversing the road by which we had come.

Dickens's account in the same book of life on board a canalboat is amusing and vivid. The boat, which he called "a barge with a little house in it," was drawn by three horses. There were thirty passengers, with a red curtain separating the ladies' quarters from the gentlemen's. Three tiers of narrow shelflike bunks on either side of the cabin formed the sleeping quarters. The bathing facilities consisted of a tin basin on the deck and a dipper on a chain with which to scoop water out of the canal. There was a barber on board to shave the gentlemen and to wait on table at mealtime. The food served was sufficient: shad, salmon, steaks, chops, ham, sausages, liver, black puddings, potatoes, pickles, bread and butter, tea and coffee for supper and the same for breakfast. Furthermore, there was a bar selling whisky, brandy, gin, and rum. As though this were not enough, some of the canals had taverns with bars at canal level. The Black Bass at Lumberville along the Delaware was such a tavern.

The canalboatmen, like the drivers of the Conestoga wagons, were a hearty, virile lot—hard-swearing, hard-drinking, hard-living. In some of the sleepy villages lining the canals there is still a blue haze from the profanity uttered a century ago. Some canalboatmen, however, took their wives along and were half domesticated. A canalboat with a line of washing fluttering in the breeze was a sorry spectacle. And even the worst of the men did not sink into a sinner's grave without an effort to save them. The Philadelphia Sabbath Association, with the backing of the Moravian Church, sent out a missionary to work among them.

Today the canals are abandoned. Cat-o'-nine-tails, joe-pye weed, and wild asters grow head-high in some of them; others are filled with brackish water. The sound of the boatman's horn no longer disturbs the quiet of the sleepy afternoon. The brave packet, the *Swan,* which started its run on the Lehigh Canal in 1829, has left behind it no brood of cygnets. It is a long time since there were boating parties on the canal. The Old Froshun, a singing club made up of the young bloods of Bethlehem, had an annual outing on the canal. A piano was hoisted on board boat; and to its music they raised their voices, filling the summer night with melody, drowning out the tinkling of the bells on the mules drawing the boat, and startling into silence the fat bullfrogs on the lily pads and the whippoorwills in the woods. But all that was a century ago.

The Philadelphia & Columbia was the earliest railroad of any consequence in Pennsylvania. In 1834, when the railroad was opened, the management had so little faith in the locomotive that an empty horsecar was attached to the train, with relays of horses here and there along the line, in case the engine broke down. Sometimes it was necessary for the passengers to get out and push to get the locomotive started—and this on the Pennsylvania Railroad, for that is the name later adopted by the Philadelphia & Columbia Railroad.

The first trip of the Black Hawk—the name of the locomotive—was on April 15, 1834, from Columbia to Lancaster, where the passengers rested overnight before proceeding on their journey to Philadelphia. An early advertisement catches the spirit of this perilous experiment far better than I can: "The locomotive engine built by M. W. Baldwin of this city will depart daily when the weather is fair, with a train of passengers' cars. On rainy days horses will be attached." Ironically enough, this was the first railroad anywhere to be government built. Its construction had been authorized by the state legislature in 1828. Such an example of state socialism should be a warning to us all.

It was not until 1846 that the Pennsylvania Railroad Company was incorporated. Then it was given the authority to construct a railroad from Harrisburg to Pittsburgh. The first section, the 60⅔ miles from Harrisburg to Lewistown, was opened in 1849. The whole route to Pittsburgh was finished in 1852, although the Portage Railroad was used to get the passengers over the moutnains until 1854, when the railroad across the Alleghenies was completed.

The railroads were the doom of the canals. By 1839 the Reading completed its line between the city of that name and Philadelphia. The Lehigh Valley connected Allentown, Bethlehem, and Easton with New Jersey and New York in 1855. When the first passenger train passed through Bethlehem, the whole town turned out to cheer. These two lines, the Reading and the Lehigh Valley, along with the Pennsylvania, are the railroads most familiar to the Pennsylvania Dutch; but in the past they knew others less ambitious. The Cumberland Valley

Railroad from Chambersburg to the Susquehanna opposite Harrisburg, a distance of forty-nine miles, was opened in December, 1837. Later a bridge was built across the Susquehanna to extend the railroad to Harrisburg and the Pennsylvania Canal. It was the Cumberland Valley's proud boast that it was the first railroad in the country—possibly in the world—to use a sleeping car. The Portsmouth, Mount Joy & Lancaster Railroad was opened for its full thirty-six miles in 1838. One railroad line followed another, some of them only a few miles long. The Strasburg Railroad was only four and one half miles, while the Catasauqua & Fogelsville, the Cornwall & Lebanon, the Middletown & Hummelstown, the Bellefonte Central, and the Quakertown & Eastern were all less than thirty miles.

Most of the small railroad lines have long since been swallowed up by the larger systems. A few still provide service so meager that they have become a standing joke to the countryside they pretend to serve. Farmers along the line of the Berks and Lehigh remark dryly, "Every Saturday night a train goes down to Reading, and every Monday morning it comes back again."

The Philadelphia & Reading Railroad, better known as the Reading, became one of the leading railroads of Pennsylvania. In 1842 its line was extended to Pottsville and Mount Carmel. This was of the utmost importance because it connected the coal mines with Philadelphia. Furthermore, it drew on the rich agricultural regions around Reading. By 1847 the Reading Railroad was the great freight road of the United States. In that year it carried more freight than the Erie Canal and at a much lower rate. Before the completion of the railroad anthracite coal had sold at $14.00 a ton; a few years afterward it was down to $5.50 to $6.00 a ton. The Reading also became an important passenger road. By 1846 it was carrying over 88,000 passengers each year. Its express train, the Queen of the Valley, is regarded with particular pride and affection. Clocks are set and life is ordered by this train speeding down the Great Valley each evening. Elsewhere in America the Queen of the Valley might not be a crack train, but to many a Pennsylvania Dutchman she is almost as dear as Mom. What do you want to go so fast for anyway, when the country is so pretty to look at?

Some of the smaller stagecoaches carrying mail and passengers to outlying villages lingered until the day before yesterday, but they are all gone now. They have been replaced by busses, as have the trolley cars that rocked and bounced along the roads and through the fields of the Dutch country. The sleighs are gone, too, except where the Amish and Mennonites dwell. On snowy days sleighs still go dashing through the streets of Bird in Hand and Intercourse or tie up at the hitching posts before the general store. But the automobile is king even in Amish villages, as it is everywhere else in the United States. The modern concrete highways and the black pinchot roads crisscrossing the Dutch country are filled with cars. This part of America has more miles of good roads than any other, even California. There are all kinds of roads, from mud lanes with grass growing down the middle to the Pennsylvania Turnpike, which cuts through a part of the Dutch country. And in the skies above the roads on which Amish wagons jog, airplanes soar. Reading and Allentown and several other Dutch cities have become regular stops for flights of transcontinental airlines. The twentieth century has caught up with the Pennsylvania Dutch, whether they like it or not.

Part Four

THE COUNTRY AND
THE PEOPLE

The Dutch Country

The country in which the forefathers of the Pennsylvania Dutch settled is one of the most fertile and beautiful sections of the United States. Generally speaking, it is the arc in southeastern Pennnsylvania south of the Blue Mountains and north of the Quaker corner hemming in Philadelphia. But the Dutch country cannot be confined to Pennsylvania, nor even to the East; it has spilled over its original borders east, west, north, and south. It is almost impossible to say precisely where it ends. Parts of Jersey across the Delaware have taken on a Dutch coloring. Frederick County, Maryland, is so Dutch that the Mason-Dixon Line counts for little in setting it apart from Pennsylvania. The heart of the Shenandoah Valley and the northern part of Loudoun County, Virginia, are Dutch, too, but with a difference: here the Pennsylvania Dutch have gone Southern. Somerset County in western Pennsylvania is so Dutch that it seems to have strayed on the wrong side of the Alleghenies. The streams that drain its meadows flow into the Mississippi, and by that criterion this should be the Middle West and not the East. And what is a town so thoroughly Dutch as Kitchener doing up in Canada? All this is not to mention the less obvious Pennsylvania

237

Dutch flavor of many communities in Ohio, Indiana, Illinois, Iowa, and even in the Carolina Piedmont. The paradox is more apparent than real. As a Berks County Dutchman, I feel that all proper Pennsylvanian Dutchmen must be Americans at heart, even if they happen to be living in Canada, just as I feel that they must be Northerners and Easterners even if they make their homes in Frederick County, Maryland, or the Shenandoah Valley, or on the west side of the Appalachians.

Even in Pennsylvania the Dutch country forms no geographical unit, although it can be loosely described as spreading itself over three different sections. The first of these is what geographers sometimes call the Pennsylvania piedmont. If the literal meaning of the word *piedmont,* "at the foot of the mountains," is kept in mind, the geographers' use of this word to describe the southeastern corner of Pennsylvania becomes immediately clear, for this is the country south and east of the first range of mountains. At the very bottom of the corner is Philadelphia, and surrounding Philadelphia are the home counties of the Quakers, once fat, productive farms but now largely suburban estates and towns. In the lower piedmont there was but one Dutch oasis, Germantown; elsewhere all was Quaker with an occasional dash of Anglican and Presbyterian. But the upper piedmont—that is, upper Bucks and Montgomery counties, the northern tip of Chester County, and Lancaster, York, and Adams—is pretty solidly Dutch. Much of this section is gently rolling, sometimes with little valleys and sometimes with broad valleys rising to hills. Only rarely, as in the Lancaster Plain, is it almost flat. At least part of it is limestone soil and exceedingly rich. This is a country of prosperous farms and two of the finest Dutch cities, Lancaster and York.

The second section is the country between the first and second ranges of mountains. This is the Pennsylvania portion of the Great Valley, which cuts across the state from Easton on the Delaware west to Reading and Harrisburg and then bearing south to the Mason-Dixon Line below Chambersburg. The Great Valley is the outstanding geographical feature of the Dutch country and possibly of the eastern United States. With its thousand miles of length the valley is so vast that most Americans have been hardly aware of its existence—a perfect example of failing to see the woods because of the trees. Sweeping across Pennsylvania and Maryland through Virginia into Tennessee and Georgia, it finally peters out in Alabama. Its inhabitants by and large call it simply "the Valley"; almost no one refers to it as the Great Valley. Or some local name may be given to it: the Lebanon Valley, the Cumberland Valley, the Shenandoah Valley, or the Valley of Virginia. Seldom more than twenty-five miles wide, it is walled in sharply by mountains, except in parts of Pennsylvania where the southern range dwindles into foothills. Farther south this same range, known in Pennsylvania as the South Mountains, rises into the Blue Ridge Mountains and the Great Smokies. But it is the range to the north, the Blue Mountains, that the Pennsylvania Dutchman regards as peculiarly his own. When he speaks of "the mountains," he means the Blue Mountains nine times out of ten. The South Mountains he is apt to look on merely as "considerable protuberances," to use Dr. Johnson's phrase, rather than mountains. A Westerner might deny even the Blue Mountains the right to be called mountains, for they are not at all like the tormented Rockies; there are no sharp, angular peaks. Instead they are gentle and rounded and sensibly aged and worn off. Much of the floor of the valley itself is astonishingly uneven. So many little hills rise and fall that sometimes only the sight of the higher mountains on either side makes one aware that this is a valley. Often the limestone pokes its way through the earth in outcropping knolls. Water dripping through the limestone has formed numerous caves, underground passages, and sinkholes. There are fewer streams in the valley than in the piedmont, and most of the larger of these force their way through the mountains instead of following the course of the valley. In Pennsylvania the Delaware, the Lehigh, the Schuylkill, and the Susquehanna and in Maryland the Potomac have all cut gaps in the mountains to cross the valley. All through Pennsylvania and Maryland and Virginia the valley is filled with one fine farm after another, for the soil of the valley is almost as fertile as that of the famed Lancaster Plain. Yet in Pennsylvania, in the northern portion of the valley particularly, there is a string of towns and cities that makes this one of the most thickly populated parts of the Dutch country. From the Delaware to the Susquehanna, Easton, Bethlehem, Allentown, Reading, Lebanon, and Harrisburg follow one another in rapid succession.

The third section of the Dutch country lies beyond the Blue Mountains. Much more indefinite than the upper piedmont and the Great Valley, it is made up of scattered settlements in valleys, large and small, tucked in among the Appalachians. In general the pattern is of one mountain ridge after another, with long, narrow valleys in between.

Much of this country is wild and lonely, but east of the Susquehanna, where the rich seams of anthracite lie, the towns jostle one another for miles on end. The Coal Regions are hardly Pennsylvania Dutch: they are a melting pot of Irish, Welsh, Hungarian, Slav, Pole, and half the other races on earth. Neither Pottsville nor Tamaqua nor Hazleton nor Mauch Chunk are Pennsylvania Dutch, though there are Pennsylvania Dutchmen living in all these cities. The onion spires of Shenandoah are unlike anything in Lancaster and York. But even in the Coal Regions, particularly in the upper Schuylkill and Lehigh valleys, many of the farms are in the hands of the Dutch. A few of the Dutch too, though not many, have gone into the mines; they are more likely to be found running the general store in the village or handling the Ford agency. West of the Susquehanna most of the country is sparsely settled. Much of this section is still wooded, with the forest stretching on as far as the eye can see. Often the land is poor, the soil largely shale; but in a few of the valleys there is limestone, and where there is limestone there are Pennsylvania Dutch. The Kishacoquillas Valley in Mifflin County, where there is a large Amish settlement, is such a place. North of the Blue Mountains there are only a few small cities that can be called Pennsylvania Dutch: Stroudsburg and East Stroudsburg in the Delaware Valley, Sunbury on the Susquehanna, and Lewistown on the Juniata. None of these is as thoroughly Dutch as the cities of the Great Valley and the upper Pennsylvania piedmont, nor are they comparable in size to them. Some of the Dutch counties beyond the Blue Mountains—Union, Snyder, Juniata, Perry, Fulton, and Bedford—have no town with as many as 5,000 inhabitants. In 1940 New Bloomfield, the county seat of Perry County, had only 858 people, and McConnellsburg, the county seat of Fulton, only 1,055. Fulton County is the only county in the commonwealth without a railroad. Though these counties are sparsely settled, all are beautiful and in many ways finer places in which to live than more populous areas.

Many of the Pennsylvania Dutch are extremely county conscious. A man from Joanna Furnace or New Jerusalem or Maiden Creek Township almost invariably refers to himself as a Berks County Dutchman. Even a man from Reading generally uses the same term for himself, possibly from a conscious or unconscious objection to that uncouth word, *Readingite*. Inhabitants of Lancaster and York counties are quite as proud of their counties as are the citizens of Berks, and the same is true of several other Dutch counties. County pride is most acute where the counties are natural units instead of hit-or-miss squares on a gigantic checkerboard and where one large city in the center serves as county seat and market town for the surrounding farms and towns. Berks, Lancaster, and York are all counties of precisely this sort. Furthermore, each of these counties has a character of its own that sets it off from its neighbors and each is an old county rich in history.

Some of the counties are more intensely Dutch than others. Of the more populous counties, York, Lancaster, Lebanon, Berks, and Lehigh are rightly considered particularly Dutch. Dauphin and Northampton are less so, possibly because of the number of "foreigners" who have come in with the steel plants at Steelton and Bethlehem—a "foreigner" being a Yankee from Boston, a York State Dutchman from Albany, a Middle Westerner from Pittsburgh, or a laborer from Budapest or Cracow. Although the cities have a high proportion of native Pennsylvania Dutch, they are never as Dutch as the country around them. And such a thinly populated county as Snyder is "Dutcher" than the Dutchest of the thickly settled counties.

In spite of its extent and its variety, the Pennsylvania Dutch country possesses a unity that distinguishes it from other regions of the United States. It is a country of stone and brick—stone barns, stone farmhouses, brick towns. There are, to be sure, many brick farmhouses and a number of frame ones; there are brick barns and a few wooden ones; but the general rule holds true. The neat towns are as spotless and trim and homely as an old-maid schoolteacher. Among the well tilled fields of the farmlands the fat barns huddle over broods of farm buildings. A hillside slopes gently to a sluggard stream. Fields clamber over rounded hills. Against the horizon is the long, level line of the mountains.

The landscape has an English quality on which many visitors remark. Probably it is the soft haze that hangs over southeastern Pennsylvania that makes it seem so like England—a haze that tones down the red of barn and the green of wheat, that turns the mountains smoky blue. The gentle hills and the field-checkered valleys intensify the English character of the country. England, of course, does not have Pennsylvania's great bank barns, and very often England's farmhouses are older and almost always the villages are lovelier to look upon. Pennsylvania's trees are larger and more varied; a Pennsylvania Dutchman would feel poor with only one kind of oak. Yet the countryside, the fields and the roll of the hills, are very like those of England. The scale is larger in

Pennsylvania: England has no valley to sweep through the land for a thousand miles; the Thames and the Severn would seem small beside the Delaware and Susquehanna; the Blue Mountains and the Alleghenies dwarf the Chiltern Hills and the Cotswolds and even the Pennine range just as the tulip trees tower over England's tallest oaks. England is part of an island, Pennsylvania part of a continent.

The Pennsylvania Dutch country has a quiet, unspectacular beauty of which one never tires. It may be a view of far distant hills on the other side of the Great Valley or a smaller, simpler landscape that by its very littleness becomes more intimate, more human, more completely one's own: a plowed field crowned by a woods against the sky, a cluster of willow pollards along a brook, a gnarled buttonwood rising above a springhouse. All these are repeated over and over again in the Dutch countryside.

Below, a fertile Valley spaced with barns and the orchards of summer.

Here in Walt Whitman's line is the full flavor of the Dutch country. There is seldom anything breathtaking in its beauty, there is none of the grandeur of the Rockies. Nor is there much of the wild, rugged beauty of New England, with its higher mountains and its many lakes. This is a farming country, gentle, peaceful, serene. It is a country in which man is in harmony with nature. It was not necessary to overcome nature, as it was in New England, where the long, hard winters and the boulder-strewn fields convinced man that nature was hostile to him. Nor was nature the seductive creature she was in the South, so rich and soft that the very land seemed to be waiting to be ravished—and ravished it was. In Pennsylvania the soil was richer and the winters less harsh than in New England, yet nature was not as easy nor as languorous as in the South. In Pennsylvania man had to labor, but his labors were rewarded.

"It's a kindly, softly country there, back of Philadelphia among the German towns, Lancaster way," Kipling wrote of it. "Little houses and bursting big barns, fat cattle, fat women, and all as peaceful as Heaven might be if they farmed there." *

"As peaceful as Heaven might be if they farmed there." One repeats the words to taste them on the tongue; in them Kipling has caught the very essence of the Dutch country.

* From *Rewards and Fairies* by Rudyard Kipling. Copyright, 1910, by Rudyard Kipling. Reprinted by permission of Mrs. George Bambridge and Doubleday & Co., Inc.

This is a land of milk and honey, of wheat and corn, of apple and peach and cherry, of bloodroot and bluebottle, of cardinal and wood thrush. This is a lush land with more than a hint of the tropics, not only in the steaming heat of summertime but in the jungle growth of meadow and woods. This is a Paul Bunyan land where a single box-huckleberry bush can cover ten acres more or less, and mostly more than less. The tall tales of the early settlers were not so tall after all, though Daniel Falckner drew on his imagination when he wrote of bullfrogs as "a very lárge kind, that emit an abominable bark, so that when one has one of these for a neighbor in the summer, there is no need of any night watch with his horn, as he keeps diligently on until day, with a bellowing and roaring like a young bull." Gabriel Thomas's account of Pennsylvania back in 1698 must likewise be taken with a grain or two of salt, particularly when he writes: "Jealousie among Men is here very rare, and Barrenness among Women hardly to be heard of, nor are Old Maids to be met with; for all commonly Marry before they are Twenty Years of Age, and seldom any young Married Woman but hath a Child in her Belly, or one upon her Lap."

The poet Wollenweber wrote the amusing though chauvinistic lines:

> Ich bin e Pennsylvanier,
> Druff bin ich stolz un froh.
> Das Land is schö, die Leut sin nett.
> Bei Tschinks! ich mach schier en'ge Wett
> 'S biets ke Land in der Welt.

Translated, this is:

> I am a Pennsylvanian,
> Of that am I proud and glad.
> The country is beautiful, the people are nice.
> By jinks! I'll make almost any bet
> There's no better country in the world.

Certainly it is a rich country, this land of Penn's woods; and to a surprising degree the woods remain. There are towns and there are farms, but where the houses and the wheat stop the trees begin: handsome, great-shouldering oaks; tulip trees with trunks like masts of clipper ships; tough, shaggy hickories; rounded maples; dark, slender hemlocks; and dogwoods whiter than morning milk. Over the streams bend ancient buttonwoods and willows straight out of Corot. Blight has killed off the chestnut, but the black walnut is still the tree of the meadowland. In the fence row to mark field from field are cherries and toylike junipers. Locusts line country lanes, and the mitten-leafed sassafras sprawls over the banks of the roadside. Catalpa, ash, elm, beech, horse chestnut, linden, pine, persimmon, sour gum, shadbush, Judas tree: the Dutch country is rich in trees.

It is a land that has kindled the imagination of men. But why shouldn't it? It is in the latitude in which history is made. Get out the atlas and look at the galaxy of names that stud the 40th parallel: Toledo, Salerno, Olympus, Troy, Mount Ararat, Bokhara, Samarkand, Peking. There is magic in this girdle of the globe. And to these Pennsylvania can add two more—Valley Forge and Gettysburg. Pennsylvania, as well as Troy and Samarkand, has been able to stir men's minds. From the days of Penn with his "holy experiment" to the declaration of independence in the Statehouse at Philadelphia—an even more successful "holy experiment"—one attempt after another has been made to found an ideal state in Pennsylvania. No wonder that Coleridge dreamed of establishing a utopia on the banks of the Susquehanna.

Whatever it may be, there has been something in this part of the world that went to men's heads. Was it the green fire of the winter wheat in April or the drifts of dogwood in May? From time to time otherwise sober Dutchmen have suddenly turned romantic. Thus Caspar Wistar, in a deed dated December 10, 1745, gave land to Trinity Reformed Church at Tulpehocken, asking but one red rose as rent. The idea appealed to Baron Stiegel, and twenty-five years later he too asked a red rose for land he gave the Lutheran Church at Manheim. In 1747, at the Corner Church near Robesonia, the two donors of land, Johann Artz and Michael Schauer, each asked a handful of wheat brimming over. And in 1764 George Fisher sold land to St. Peter's Church in Middletown for seven and six and the annual rent of a grain of wheat. Rather nice, these old romantic notions; but from the start Pennsylvania has been a curious mixture of the utopian and the practical, the dreamer living among visions and the hardheaded realist hacking away at the oaks to make a clearing in the forest.

Added to all the other blessings of the Pennsylvania Dutch country is the weather. Not for it the endless sunny days with which God cursed southern California. Nothing as montonous as that! Rain, sleet, drought, flood, hail, sunshine, fog, haze, thunder and lightning, snow, drizzle—name it, and the Dutch country has it. Only a woman can be as changeable as Pennsylvania weather. One strange fit of weather, good, bad, or indifferent, follows another right around the calendar year after year. In Pennsylvania only abnormal weather is normal. Yet of the four seasons spring and fall are best. The summers are almost as sweltering as those of Washington, which put them among the world's worst; the winters are often chill and penetrating, with not enough snow but with some bright, sunshiny days to make them endurable. The springs, though undependable, are the best America has to offer. The mild and sunny weather, the call of the cardinal, the fields of bluebottles gaudy as a jay, the pinxter and dogwood in flower in the woodland: these are what spring means to a Pennsylvania Dutchman. Yet fall is even better. Hunt as you will the world over, you will not find an autumn to match that of the Dutch country. Always there is some fine weather, for autumn never lets you down: crisp days in October when the air is as heady as wine; sleepy, lotuslike days in Indian summer, when God is most certainly in His heaven. With sumac, sour gum, dogwood, sassafras, hickory, maple, tulip tree, and oak, fall in Pennsylvania has as extravagant color as fall in New England and Canada. Yet in its prolonged Indian summers Pennsylvania is one up on its northern neighbors. In many parts of the world November is one of the most detestable months in the year; even in Pennsylvania it is occasionally as completely foul as it usually is elsewhere. But not often. Most years it is a month of warmth and mellowness and soft blue haze and a blessing to man.

Yet there are serpents in this Eden—copperheads through much of the country and rattlesnakes in the Blue Mountains. There are mosquitoes, too, though not in the vast swarms of Jersey. There is poison ivy, and there are sundry "varmints," both four-legged and two-legged. As a Pennsylvanian I hate to admit all this, but the truth will out.

FK.

"A Local Habitation and a Name"

One of the paradoxes of the Dutch country is that it sports so many English names. Take the names of the counties, Lancaster, York, Northampton, Berks, Cumberland, Northumberland—not to mention Bucks, Montgomery, and Chester, all three part Quaker and part Dutch; or the cities, beginning again with Lancaster and York and adding to them Reading and Carlisle. Isn't it a beautiful English sound bringing up visions of the War of the Roses, of cathedrals and hedgerows and crumpets? Many of the towns, too, bear English names: Northampton, Northumberland, Cornwall, Bath, Hatfield, Fleetwood, Hereford, Portland, Middlesex, Halifax, Huntingdon, Chalfont. York Haven, York Furnace, and Little Britain are three more names with an English flavor. When the contrast between the English name and the Pennsylvania Dutch village is too great, the name becomes ludicrous, as in the case of the Berks County crossroads village of a church, a hotel, and eight or ten houses with the royal name of Windsor Castle.

It was the English and not the settlers from the Rhineland who gave the land these English names. It was Penn and the early Quakers who decided to honor the homeland by creating, on paper at least, a second

England. The names of the townships deepen the English coloring. In Berks County alone the townships bear such fine English names as Richmond, Albany, Greenwich, Ruscombmanor, Exeter, Hereford, and Windsor.

Singularly few of the place names are German. Manheim, Hamburg, Hamlin, and Bingen are all named after old German cities; Strasburg, after the old Alsatian capital. There are townships honoring Heidelberg and Franconia; and there is a fine Dutch flavor to such names as Eshbach, Womelsdorf, Klappenthall, Litzenberg, Appenzell, and Schoeneck. To anyone with a knowledge of German, Hosensack, meaning "pants pocket," is the most wonderful of all the Dutch names. Far more usual is the combination of a German family name with the French *ville*. Kleinfeltersville, Wenksville,. Sassamansville, and Schnecksville all betray their bastard origin. The addition of the English *town* to a German family name, as in Kutztown, Hellertown, and Hecktown, is almost as bad. The use of *burg* is much rarer but far more suitable. Fredericksburg, Gettysburg, and even Ickesburg sound much more natural. Sometimes the German family name added to an English noun is picturesque. Landis's Store, Reinhold's Station, and Hummel's Wharf are so obviously country cousins that they fill us with delight. One of the oddest formations is the use of the possessive form of the family name with the common noun omitted, as in Rahn's, Wanamaker's, Ronk's, Collbaugh's, and Neff's. Sometimes the possessive *s* is dropped, as in Hoffman, Kistler, and Minnich.

In addition to the English and German names there are a few bestowed by settlers of other nations. The Holland Dutch named the Schuylkill and the Northkill. Lititz is a Bohemian name that keeps green the memory of the Moravians' first sanctuary. Boyertown, Bonneauville, and Alsace suggest the French strain in the Pennsylvania Dutch. Bangor, Brecknock, Pen Argyl, Penryn, Caernarvon, and even Morgantown, Pricetown, and Jonestown betray the presence of the Welsh. Dublin, Limerick, Bally, and Kelly Crossroads all make one wonder if somewhere or other in the Dutch family tree there may not be an Irish great-great-grandfather. Belfast, Scotland, Campbelltown, McMichael's, and McKnightstown show the presence of the Scotch-Irish. But what about New Tripoli? Was it an early marine who named that town? And surely Monterey and Vera Cruz were named not by Dutchmen with a Spanish or Mexican grandmother but by veterans of the war with Mexico.

Religious names among a people so transported by religion are to be expected. The Moravian settlements of Bethlehem, Nazareth, and Emmaus are the best known of the towns with such names. To them may be added Goshen, Bethel, Lebanon, Hebron, New Jerusalem, Old Zionsville, Eden, and even Smyrna and Palmyra.

Though the Indian names are the most beautiful of all the Pennsylvania place names, they were seldom given to towns. Wyomissing, Catasaqua, Perkasie, Macungie, Moselem, Skippack, and Paxtang and that delightful foursome of Oley, Little Oley, Oley Furnace, and Oley Line are among the few towns and villages honoring the ancient inhabitants of the land. Fortunately a great many of the streams have Indian names: Susquehanna, Juniata, Lehigh, Perkiomen, Tulpehocken, Swatara, Ontelaunee, Quitapahilla, Cocalico, Wyomissing, Pequea, Manatawny, Mingo, Tohickon, Cocorus, Conestoga, Tuscarora, Cacoosing, Towamencin, Skippack, Conewago—half of them, at least, music to the ear. And if we cross the Mason-Dixon Line to the Dutch country to the south: Monocacy, Conococheaque, Potomac, Opequon, and Shenandoah. Some of the streams have English names, often with a distinct eighteenth century flavor: Sixpenny Creek, Gallow's Run, Molasses Creek, Yellow Breeches Creek, Indian Corn Creek, Plum Creek, and Maiden Creek. There are Indian names, too, for some of the mountain ranges; Tuscarora, Kittanning, and Shochary are three, and Allegheny still another. A few individual peaks have Dutch names —Hexenkopf and Spitzenberg. English names, however, are far more usual. Some are simple and plain—the Blue Mountains and the South Mountains are such; others show a touch of imagination—the Flying Hills, Owl Head, Fancy Hill, and Devil's Hump.

It is the names of the towns, though, that betray a flight of fancy surprising in a people as solid and stable as the Pennsylvania Dutch. The names that the Amish gave to their villages are unsurpassed even in the mining towns of the West: Gap, Intercourse, Paradise, Fertility, Bird in Hand, and Blue Ball. Then there are the two Berks County villages almost side by side, Virginville and Molltown. What do they show, a sense of humor or a complete lack of it? With some of the names there spring up visions of the country at its loveliest: Peach Bottom, Highspire, Fawn Grove, Charming Forge, Seven Valleys, Honey Brook, Cherry Ford, and Green Lane—to which might well be added Red Well School in Lancaster County and Green Tree School in Berks. Milford Square and Bedminster Center have a strong English flavor; Bunker Hill and Line Lexington are staunchly American. Other names delight because they are so "country": Smoketown, Yellow House, Plowville, Woodchoppertown, and Bandana. In some there are echoes of a more exciting past: Warrior's Mark, Indiantown Gap, Powder Valley, Burnt Cabins, and Rough and Ready. There are villages that preserve the names of old inns and taverns: Red Lion, White Bear, Unicorn, Cross Keys, and Seven Stars. But what whim or fancy inspired such names as Spry, Effort, Fairplay, Donation, Anise, Mascot, and Leather Corner Post? And how did Ono get its name?

The street names are the same throughout the Dutch country, for the Dutch towns, like the rest of the nation, followed the fashion set by Philadelphia, where half the streets were numbered and the other half named after trees. Chestnut, Walnut, Spruce, Pine, Buttonwood, Willow, Elm, and Locust appear in town after town. With Orange, Lemon, and Lime, Lancaster has given the tree names an exotic twist. Names of statesmen provide a third pattern, for in the flush of patriotism after the Revolution, Washington and Franklin were honored in practically every Dutch town by having streets named after them, and so was Penn. Other street names are a heterogeneous lot. Except for a few old towns such as Womelsdorf and Pottstown, High Street has given way to the more modern Main Street. Most of the names are obvious enough: Broad Street, Green Street, Church Street, Water Street. Only rarely is there a name with distinction, such as Cowpath Road in Souderton. Most street names are so depressingly dull that one comes to the conclusion that for the past century there has not been an ounce of imagination in all the town councils of the Dutch country. There is nothing to match the full-flavored names of the West, nothing to put beside Tombstone Canyon, OK Street, and Brewery Gulch—all three from a single Western town, Bisbee, Arizona.

Town and City

The towns of the Dutch country are red towns of brick. House after house and street after street are of red brick: that is the obvious feature that strikes every stranger. In the center of the town, houses flush on the sidewalk are built up against houses on either side. Even on the edges of the town, houses are often built so close together that there is room for only a tiny grassplot between them. In the older sections of the towns and cities the houses, although much alike, differ slightly. Along straight streets they huddle together in the hit-or-miss fashion of hens on a roost. But where the houses were built within the last seventy-five years, any tincture of individuality all too often gives way to rows of identical houses, one tight against another. Few of the houses have much architectural merit, though some of the older ones from the eighteenth century or the early part of the nineteenth have sturdiness and simplicity of line. In most towns, unfortunately, there are few houses so old; the great majority were built after the close of the Civil War and therefore have the vices of that period.

The villages have been more blessed than the towns in preserving a larger number of old houses; and because more of their houses are old, more of them are of stone. An occasional village even dares to be beautiful. Spangsville, with its dirt road, a meadow in which cows are forever browsing, and the placid Manatawny near by, is even idyllic; and Churchtown, with its air of age and quiet, a long and sleepy main street with old trees, is one of the pleasanter Dutch villages. Lititz, with the old Moravian buildings and the squat old houses of stone facing them, has character and charm. The springs at Lititz help to give the town individuality. Used for watering cattle in the eighteenth century, they were fitted up as a *Lushtplatz* [1] more than a hundred years ago. Trees were planted, arbors built, and walks made along the stream: an ideal place for Lititz swains to go a-sweeting on June nights. The old stone church on the hill above the town gives Womelsdorf character. Strasburg, with its old brick houses, has a pleasing, old-fashioned appearance. Myerstown has a church spire so graceful and Sellersville a church that is so perfectly what a Pennsylvania Dutch country church should be that both towns linger in your memory. Cornwall is proof that a mining town need not be unattractive. The old brownstone houses make it almost quaint, and the earth disemboweled on so vast a scale is impressive. Hershey, with its grand Italian Renaissance buildings, is so grotesque that one marvels at the chance or caprice that placed this town in the peaceful Pennsylvania Dutch countryside. These are only a few of the Dutch towns with character and some slight measure of beauty.

The number of the Dutch towns is legion. As this is one of the most thickly populated areas in the Western Hemisphere, the towns and villages are separated one from another by only a few miles. Of all of them Gettysburg is easily the most famous. Today it is a pleasant, quiet country town with a thriving tourist trade. The Stroudsburgs, close to the Poconos, are tourist towns too. Nazareth is an old Moravian settlement with some fine old buildings, but the gray pall of the cement mills impairs much of the town's attractiveness. Bangor is a slate town with a distinct Welsh flavor; Birdsboro owes its prosperity to iron; Souderton has a large Mennonite population, and Quakerown a Quaker past; Red Lion makes cigars; and New Holland has a main street three miles long, with corn and tobacco fields behind the stores and houses. No two towns are alike, though many are first cousins. Set

[1] Literally "pleasure place."

any of them down on the plains of Kansas and it would be recognized at once for what it is—a Dutch town from Pennsylvania.

The plan of the towns is a heritage from Philadelphia: straight streets crossing one another at right angles to form a gridiron. Occasionally there is a small square in the center of the town, as in Orwigsburg, Bethel, and Morgantown. At Womelsdorf the square is so diminutive as to be only the suggestion of a square. The large green with old elms, so beautiful a feature of many New England villages, is never found in Dutch towns.

Almost all of the towns are well governed. The corruption so typical of large American cities has not taken hold in the towns. The borough system of government, with its chief burgess and borough council, operates efficiently. The townships, too, taking in the farms and smaller villages, have a system of government that in the main is honest and successful. The police force of the boroughs, sometimes consisting of one man, is more for show than for use. After all, any self-respecting town has to have at least one policeman.

The name *borough* in use in Pennsylvania often puzzles people from other states. The charter granted to Penn by Charles II gave him the authority to "divide the country into Townes, Hundreds and Counties, and to erect and incorporate Townes into Boroughs, and Borroughs into Cities, and to make and constitute ffaires and markets therein, with all convenient privileges and munities." The old word *hundred* as applied to divisions of land is still used only in Delaware; in Pennsylvania even such terms as *town* and *village,* though in common use, have no standing in the eyes of the law. In the whole state there is but one town, Bloomsburg; otherwise Pennsylvania is divided into counties, townships, boroughs, and cities. When a village considers itself of sufficient size to be incorporated, it becomes a borough. Only the thickly settled section is included in the borough limits; farms and woods and crossroad villages are left to the township. When a borough has at least ten thousand inhabitants, it is eligible to become a city. There are a good many cities, small and middle-sized, in the Dutch country, but no large ones.

All Pennsylvania Dutch cities have a strong family resemblance. They are so unlike other American cities that people from other parts of the country sometimes speak of their foreign appearance—a phrase that is an enigma to their Dutch inhabitants, who think of their cities as ordinary, normal American cities.

Once upon a time Germantown would have led the list of the Pennsylvania Dutch cities. In 1700, when many of its double-hipped roofs were covered with red tiles and when people strolled out on spring evenings to admire the mile of peach trees in blossom along its main street, it was the only Pennsylvania Dutch town. As early as 1692 the settlement was large enough to be celebrated by Richard Frame in his poem, *A Short Description of Pennsylvania*:

> The GERMANTOWN, of which I spoke before,
> Which is, at least, in length one Mile and More,
> Where lives HIGH-GERMAN People and Low-DUTCH,
> Whose Trade in weaving Linnin Cloth is much.

Dutch it was when the town was the scene of a battle, though Pennsylvania Dutch and not low Dutch; and Dutch it remained until the yellow fever epidemic of 1793, when Philadelphians driven from their city flocked to Germantown to escape the plague and, seeing the goodness of the place, stayed on. It has been many a year since it was swallowed up by Philadelphia to become an old and pleasant residential section of the city.

Philadelphia itself might be numbered among the Dutch cities; in many ways it is as Dutch as it is Quaker. Such Philadelphia names as Rittenhouse, Pepper, Wanamaker, Leidy, Widener, and Wister with an *e* and Wistar with an *a* are evidence of the city's Dutch heritage. And so are scrapple, cinnamon buns, and pepperpot, all Pennsylvania Dutch and all of the very essence of Philadelphia. In the eighteenth century many Germans and Swiss settled in the city, and since that time large numbers of upcountry Dutch have drifted down to Philadelphia. Though Baltimore by its proximity attracted the Dutch from York County and Adams, the rest of the Dutch inhabitants of Pennsylvania looked upon Philadelphia as peculiarly their own. Nevertheless, Philadelphia can hardly be counted a Pennsylvania Dutch city. In a sense it is that, but it is also Quaker and to a lesser degree Scotch-Irish; and today it is Polish, Italian, Negro, and Jewish as well. It is one of America's melting pots.

Much more thoroughly Dutch is Lancaster. In Lancaster the eighteenth century is just around the corner. The old town hall in the center square, the beautiful old Lutheran church with its fine spire, and the many old red-brick houses with graceful doorways all show that Lancaster has roots deep in the past. They speak of the stirring times of the

Revolution and the hopeful days of the early Republic, when Lancaster was America's largest inland city. Here is the country's oldest tobacco shop and oldest hardware store; and to dive into a much later period, here even the country's first five-and-ten. The archaic dress of the large number of Mennonites and Amish and other "plain people" on the street strengthens the feeling that in Lancaster, at least, the eighteenth century is not altogether dead. Even the street names bespeak a royalist past: King, Queen, Prince, and Duke. Yet the city is thoroughly alive; it is no museum piece to show what the dead past was like. The Lancaster of today suffers from no inferiority complex. It had enough self-assurance to invite the United Nations to make its permanent home there.

In 1818 William Cobbett called it "a very clean and good town." "No beggarly houses," he added. "All looks like *ease* and *plenty*." A dozen years earlier another English traveler, Priscilla Wakefield, spoke of the two-story houses, "chiefly of brick or stone, with a broad stone pavement, and pumps placed at small distances before them." But it is Cobbett who is most enthusiastic in his praise:

> Lancaster is a pretty place. No *fine* buildings; but no *mean* ones. Nothing *splendid* and nothing *beggarly*. The people of the town seem to have had the prayer of HAGAR granted them: "Give me, O Lord, neither *poverty* nor *riches*." Here are none of those poor, wretched habitations, which sicken the sight at the *outskirts* of cities and towns in England; those abodes of the poor creatures, who have been reduced to beggary by the cruel extortions of the rich and powerful.

Fortunately this is still largely true of modern Lancaster. It is one of the pleasantest and most interesting of American cities, and one of the most fortunate as well. It has never had a period of mushroom growth but has developed slowly and steadily. Lancaster is a county seat, the market town of a farming country rich almost beyond belief. Few cities in the world have been so blessed.

York is Lancaster all over again with a flavor less distinct. The two cities are twins—not identical twins, but twins nevertheless. Of very much the same size as Lancaster, it has less of the atmosphere of the eighteenth century. York is one of the two Pennsylvania Dutch towns that once served as the nation's capital; but York was the capital for the nine months from September 30, 1777, to June 27, 1778, and not, as in the case of Lancaster, for a day only. Despite its brave past York has fewer old buildings than Lancaster to show for it; yet many of the streets, lined with red-brick houses, have an air of colonial days. York, too, has Mennonites and other "plain people" on its streets, though not as many as Lancaster. And York's streets still bear the old royalist names: George, King, Duke, and Princess. Like Lancaster, York is thoroughly alive today. It is a busy manufacturing city and yet a pleasant place. Again like Lancaster, it may be called blessed.

The largest of the Pennsylvania Dutch cities is Reading, which lies in a somewhat cramped position between the Schuylkill River and the wooded hills of Mount Penn and Neversink. Its old Anglo-Saxon name, meaning "red settlement," fits it to a T. Seen from the drive on top of Mount Penn, Reading is a city of red-brick houses with red roofs of tin. Though many of its houses suggest the eighteenth century, the dominant impression is that of the nineteenth. The administrations from Grant to McKinley left a heavy imprint on the architecture of the city. Though Reading does not lack handsome buildings, they are often far from the center of the city, like the Reading Hospital. Two conspicuous buildings, on the other hand, give the city a somewhat bizarre appearance: the Chinese pagoda on Mount Penn overlooking the city; and the Outer Depot, the principal railroad station and a museum piece straight out of the Victorian Age. In 1795 La Rouchefoucauld described the inhabitants of Reading as "temperate, industrious, and prudent." They are still all three. The city as a whole is prosperous, yet down by the river and in the little alleyways there are slums or the beginnings of slums. Like Lancaster and York, Reading is a county seat and the shopping center for a rich farming section and numerous small towns. Penn Street, the main thoroughfare, is crowded every day of the week with people from the country. The rise and fall of the Dutch dialect is a familiar sound on the streets of Reading, though few people born in the city are able to speak Dutch. Despite the many Italians and Poles who have moved into the city in this century, Reading is still one of the most intensely Dutch cities in Pennsylvania.

Bethlehem is the most dramatic of the Pennsylvania Dutch cities and the most paradoxical—dramatic because the great steel mills along the river are such a vivid contrast to the sleepy old Moravian city, paradoxical because this city, named for the birthplace of the Prince of Peace, became one of the world's greatest munition centers. In Lancaster and York and in most of the other Pennsylvania Dutch cities it is sometimes possible to forget that they are manufacturing cities; in

Bethlehem, never. The giant stacks of Bethlehem Steel, with their clouds of smoke by day and their pillars of fire by night, are a constant reminder that steel is the very essence of modern Bethlehem.

It seems a very long time since the first century of Bethlehem's existence, when it was a quiet religious community disturbed only by the Revolution. Market Street was then Cow Lane, and the square at Main and Church streets was the Platz. The road to the West, then the Ohio Road, crossed the Monocacy by the old log bridge at the tannery. *Die Biene* (The Bee) was the name of its newspaper. The little town with its orchards on the hillside and its old-fashioned gardens is in that name. But all that came to an end a century ago when the town was opened up and steel moved in, when Lehigh University was founded, and the modern city took shape.

Today Bethlehem is a city pulsing with life. Like its mammoth star on South Mountain shining forth at Christmas, Bethlehem stands out from the rank of American cities; it is in no danger of being lost in the shuffle. Its Moravian heritage alone would be enough to give it individuality, or the sprawling steel plant lining the Lehigh for miles, or its great Bach Choir. The three combined make Bethlehem more than a mere huddle of houses, stores, and mills; it is a city with genuine character.

Among the Pennsylvania Dutch cities Allentown is pretty much of a newcomer. It was only a small village in colonial days and hardly comparable to such thriving settlements as Lancaster, York, and Reading or even Bethlehem. Until 1803 the inhabitants of Allentown were forced to go to Bethlehem to get their mail. Today Allentown is a bright, substantial modern city, neat and clean and well turned out. The town has an air of well-being, of prosperity and civic pride. Large metal bowls filled with flowers adorn the lampposts of the main street. Many of the stores and offices are new; others are Victorian structures that have had their faces lifted. Above these soars the city's one skyscraper, as bright and handsome as the buildings below. In amusing contrast to these is the usual hideous Civil War monument in the central square, as far a departure from a work of art as it is possible for a monument to be.

Allentown is a busy place, for it is the center of a thickly populated area. Bethlehem is its next-door neighbor, and within a few miles are an unusually large number of towns, many of them of respectable size. It is no wonder that Allentown merchants are prosperous. There are rich farmlands and orchards near-by as well as towns. Furthermore, Allentown is important for its manufactures as well as its trade.

Though many of Allentown's inhabitants are foreign-born, with those of Austrian, Czech, Hungarian, German, Polish, and Italian origin making up a quarter of the population, the city has a strong Dutch flavor. Even among the Dutch, Allentown is noted for its Dutchness. As in Reading, the dialect is frequently heard on the street, and English is often spoken with a Dutch accent. Like Reading, too, it is a stronghold of the Lutheran and Reformed churches. Few "plain people" are seen on its streets.

As Harrisburg is the state capital it belongs to the state rather than to the Dutch country alone; yet it, too, must be included among the Dutch cities. With a Scotch-Irish past and a somewhat more cosmopolitan present, it is less thoroughly Dutch than Lancaster, Reading, or Allentown. It is an impressive city finely situated on the banks of one of America's most beautiful rivers. The imposing government buildings are grouped around a state capitol that, with its inevitable dome, is the very archetype of state capitols. The handsomest feature of Harrisburg is the long drive along the Susquehanna, one of the most beautiful river fronts in the country. Although the city is a manufacturing center, its iron and steel mills are kept at a distance, most of them down the river at Steelton. Yet within sight of the capitol dome are slums housing the large Negro population, slums that show almost as extreme a degree of squalor as those of Philadelphia or Washington. In colonial days, when the settlement was known as Harris's Ferry, Harrisburg was only a trading post on Pennsylvania's frontier. Selection of the town as the capital of Pennsylvania made it the city it is today. On the national scene Harrisburg has been important enough politically to play host to a Republican national convention. Here William Henry Harrison was nominated for the Presidency, with John Tyler as his running mate.

On the easternmost edge of the Dutch country, at "the forks" of the Lehigh and the Delaware, is the river city of Easton. This is one of the smaller Pennsylvania Dutch cities and less Dutch than most. More than a third of its population is of foreign stock. Yet it is one of the few Dutch cities where the old-fashioned curb market is still held regularly in the square. Easton is a city of much variety. An old church, an old schoolhouse, and a number of old houses show its colonial origin, and a jewelry store is the oldest in the country. Among the buildings from the nineteenth century the courthouse and the jail are particularly conspicuous; and there are numerous buildings of the present century. Though the center of town is flat, Easton is strikingly hilly, with steps cut into some of the steeper slopes. It is a busy manufacturing city, a county seat, and a college town.

In the Great Valley, halfway between Reading and Harrisburg, is Lebanon, another small Pennsylvania Dutch city. It, too, is a county seat and a market town; but above all Lebanon is a steel town. Though its bologna is of so superior a quality that more than one Pennsylvania Dutchman has been tempted to remember Lebanon in his prayers, it is iron and steel that make the city dirty and iron and steel that make the city hum. Against the dirt and grime of the steel mills the Dutch housewives of Lebanon wage a vehement but losing battle. Despite the steel mills Lebanon has rather a quiet, old-fashioned air. Two old stone churches and a handful of old houses have come down from the early days of the Republic. A graceful courthouse, destroyed by fire early in the century, was wisely rebuilt on the old lines. Yet Lebanon is hardly a beautiful city; it is too unplanned, with mills, factories, churches, and houses cheek by jowl. A peculiarity of the city is a summer colony, Mount Gretna, that it has built for itself in the woods a few miles out of town.

Carlisle is one of the smallest of the Pennsylvania Dutch cities and one of the most attractive. In the beginning it was a Scotch-Irish town, but a century and a half ago it turned Dutch. It is the second oldest army post in the country, a fact that calls up memories of the French and Indian War. From Carlisle, Colonel John Armstrong with 280 men set out to destroy the Indian village of Kittanning, and in Carlisle Colonel Henri Bouquet equipped the expedition that ended the Pontiac conspiracy. Two signers of the Declaration of Independence were from the town, and a third practiced law in Carlisle. Here Molly Pitcher lived and was buried, and Washington reviewed the troops assembled to suppress the Whisky Rebellion. With the coming of the nineteenth century Carlisle quieted down. In September, 1818, when the English traveler James Flint passed through, he remarked on its antiquated appearance. "With so much grass growing in the streets, a suspicion arises that there is not much traffic here." The Civil War, however, brought excitement enough. Then the town was shelled by rebel troops under the command of General Fitzhugh Lee and the United States Army barracks burned. Probably only the outbreak of the battle of Gettysburg saved Carlisle from the fate of Chambersburg. In 1783 a grammar school established ten years earlier was transformed into Dickinson College; and from 1879 until the First World War the town also housed the Indian school renowned in gridiron history. American football has never been the same since the Carlisle Indians gave up the ghost; with them went as much life and color as the game has ever seen. In this century the old army post became the United States Army Medical Field Service School. During the Second World War thousands of army doctors were trained in Carlisle.

There are a number of other small cities in the Dutch country. Pottstown and Phoenixville are two Schuylkill Valley iron towns between Philadelphia and Reading. Pottstown, with a plant manufacturing airplane engines, was a boom town during the Second World War. It is the site of Hill School, a fashionable preparatory school for boys. Phoenixville, on the edge of Chester County, is another thriving manufacturing town, but it is less certainly Dutch than Pottstown. Two other Schuylkill Valley towns are Pottsville and Norristown. Both are on the borders of the Dutch country and both have Dutch blood, but Pottsville belongs to the Coal Regions and Norristown is practically suburban Philadelphia. In the Susquehanna Valley are half a dozen small cities. Columbia and Sunbury are two of the older towns on the river. In the early days tens of thousands of logs floating down the Susquehanna put money into Columbia's pockets. Today it is a quiet town overshadowed by its neighbors, Lancaster and York. Farther up the Susquehanna, on the site of the old Indian town of Shamokin, is Sunbury, a pleasant, quiet town, a county seat and in a minor way an industrial center. Here, in 1883, Edison built an electric power plant, the first of its kind in the world. Between Columbia and Sunbury is Steelton, the workshop of Harrisburg. Great mills pour their smoke and grime over the workers' houses. Dirty, shabby, raw, and hideous, this is the modern industrial city very near its nadir. Yet in Steelton once a year, on Epiphany, there takes place a truly beautiful religious ceremony. As a priest of the Greek Orthodox Church throws a cross into the waters of the Susquehanna, a flight of doves is set free, whereupon several young men of the congregation dive into the icy river to retrieve the cross, a great honor for the youth who succeeds. When the cross has been recovered, water is taken from the river and blessed by the priest and then distributed to the congregation. On the Juniata, which flows into the Susquehanna above Harrisburg, is yet another small industrial city, Lewistown. The main factory here is across the river from the city. Like so many of the Pennsylvania Dutch cities, Lewistown is both a county seat and a shopping center. Near the Maryland line are several other small cities. Hanover is a prosperous York County manufacturing town famous for shoes and horses. To those who follow the races American style—and that, of course, means trotting races—Hanover is as magical a name as Goshen. Two Great Valley towns not far north of Mason and Dixon's line are Waynesboro and Chambersburg. Both are small market towns in the apple country. Chambersburg has the dubious distinction of being the only Northern town to be sacked and burned by the Confederate armies; today it seems to be as far removed from war as any American town can be. It is the site of Wilson College, a women's college of high standing.

With these Pennsylvania towns the Maryland cities of Frederick and Hagerstown might be included. Though south of the Mason-Dixon Line, they are almost as Dutch as Lancaster and York. Both are fine cities. In Civil War days Frederick moved Oliver Wendell Holmes to write, "How gracefully, how charmingly, its group of steeples nestles among the Maryland hills!" Earlier, in 1818, William Faux wrote of Hagerstown: "This town is highly delightful, and almost surrounded by small mountains; the scenery is beautiful, and both in and around an air of grandeur prevails." I am even tempted to go farther south and add such Virginia towns as Winchester and Staunton to my list of Dutch cities. If blood counts, both are Dutch towns; if not Pennsylvania Dutch, then Valley Dutch—which is very much the same thing. Even Winston-Salem in North Carolina might be included as an outpost of Pennsylvania Dutchland; next to Bethlehem it is the leading Moravian city in the country. But to go on in this way is to invite a second War Between the States. I refrain.

Rich Man, Poor Man, Beggarman, Thief

More than by its towns and cities, a people is judged by its great men. It is through them that ideals and ambitions are revealed. Most Pennsylvania Dutchmen, of course, were either farmers or artisans, occupations which were taken pretty much for granted. A good farmer and a good mechanic were proper, solid citizens with important places in the fabric of society; but these were not occupations to capture men's imaginations, nor ones by which greatness is achieved. It was not of such stuff that heroes were made. Who, then, were the men the Dutch admired?

Probably the most highly respected man in the community day in and day out was the preacher. It is no accident that the Pennsylvania Dutch have produced a long line of preachers, some learned clergymen, some sawdust-trail evangelists. From Zinzendorf and Mühlenberg to Billy Sunday and Frank Buchman there have been many Pennsylvania Dutch names famous in the religious history of America. The preacher in his pulpit, the words rolling smoothly from his tongue, moved men to admiration. There was even respect for his learning. No other churches in America have insisted so vigorously on an educated clergy as the Lutheran and Reformed churches.

Even in men other than clergymen learning was worth respect. Pastorious was but the first of many Pennsylvania Dutch scholars. Educated at the universities of Altdorf, Strasbourg, Basel, and Jena, he knew law, theology, science, medicine, history, poetry, and agriculture. His tastes were simple—not riches but leisure enough for his reading and writing and for his garden and his bees.

Another scholarly Pennsylvania Dutchman, one who lived almost a century later, was David Rittenhouse. His observation of the transit of Venus in 1769, which won the approbation of the scientific world, enabled him to make for the first time in history an approximately accurate calculation of the distance between the earth and the sun. His orrery was the forerunner of the modern planetarium and like it in representing the planetary system by machinery. Ivory or brass planets revolved around a brass sun with varying velocities. Jupiter and its satellites, Saturn and its rings, the moon in all its phases, and the eclipse of the sun: all were shown. The solar system at any period of time from five thousand years ago to five thousand years hence could be instantly displayed. Nothing like this orrery could be found in all of Europe. Jefferson was so moved with admiration as to call it "a machine far surpassing in ingenuity of contrivance, accuracy and utility anything of the kind ever before constructed." "He has not indeed made a world," Jefferson went on to say, "but he has by imitation approached nearer its maker than any man who lived from the creation to this day."

Moreover, Rittenhouse was a versatile man. He performed experiments upon the compressibility of water. He made a thermometer based upon the expansion and contraction of metals. He was a surveyor of such note that he was called in to help determine the boundaries between Pennsylvania and Delaware, New York and New Jersey, Pennsylvania and Virginia, Pennsylvania and New York, and New York and Massachusetts. He was the first director of the Mint. He succeeded Franklin as president of the American Philosophical Society, and in 1795 he was made a foreign member of the Royal Society. After the death of Franklin he stood first among the scientists of this country.

Since Rittenhouse's day there have been other eminent Pennsylvania Dutch scientists, possibly none as great as Rittenhouse but some not far behind him. Arthur Holly Compton, winner of the Nobel Prize for his achievements in physics, might be named here, for he is half

Dutch. His mother was Otelia Augspurger, of Mennonite parentage.

Another type of learned man is the doctor, and among the Pennsylvania Dutch the doctor has stood second only to the preacher. The doctor, however, was honored not so much for his learning as for his devotion to the sick. The man who traveled long miles to a lonely farmhouse to pull a small child through diphtheria or who saved a man's wife in childbirth was paid with esteem as well as with coin. Wistar, Gerhard, Gross, and Pepper are names attesting to the greatness of the Pennsylvania Dutch in medicine. These were the men who made Philadelphia a great medical center in the nineteenth century.

One of the most brilliant of Philadelphia physicians was Caspar Wistar, whose service in the yellow fever epidemic of 1793 helped to establish the heroic tradition in American medicine. Wistar's *System of Anatomy,* published in 1811, was the earliest American textbook in the field of medicine. Succeeding Thomas Jefferson as president of the American Philosophical Society, he not only presided over the meetings of that learned body but he also kept open house every Saturday night for all members of the society and visiting scientists as well. These were the famous "Wistar parties"—the most noteworthy intellectual gatherings of the early years of the Republic. It was to honor Caspar Wistar that the name *wistaria* was given to the beautiful vine brought from China.

Of lesser fame, but hardly of lesser ability, was William Wood Gerhard, the first man to distinguish typhus from typhoid fever. But the greatest of all these men, and possibly the greatest of all American physicians, was Samuel D. Gross. His *System of Surgery, Pathological, Diagnostic, Therapeutic, and Operative,* which won for him a D.C.L. from Oxford and LL.D.'s from Cambridge and Edinburgh, was the great surgical treatise of the century. Ironically enough, it is Thomas Eakins's masterpiece, *The Gross Clinic,* that has best succeeded in keeping his fame alive among the public at large. Another great physician was William Pepper, who as provost of the University of Pennsylvania paved the way for drastic reforms in American medical education. And still another eminent doctor of Dutch blood was William C. Gorgas, surgeon-general, whose victory over "yellow jack" made him one of the great men of American medicine. This is a list of names hard to match in the annals of medicine. These men added as much luster to medicine as the Concord group of writers did to literature.

During the early years of the colony the Dutch gave scant attention to politics. By the time of the French and Indian War their only political leader of note was Conrad Weiser, the able backwoods diplomat. The Revolution made the Dutch more aware of the central role played by politics. Even so, there were few Dutchmen among the Founding Fathers. Frederick Muhlenberg, speaker of the first House of Representatives, and Michael Hillegas, treasurer of the United States from 1775 to 1789, were exceptions rather than the rule. Perhaps to these should be added the Revolutionary patriot, John Henry Miller. It was in his paper, the *Pennsylvanische Staatsbote,* that the Declaration of Independence first appeared in print. Earlier Miller had denounced the Stamp Act as "the most unconstitutional law which the colonies could ever have imagined."

Once the nineteenth century got under way there was no dearth of Pennsylvania Dutch political figures, good, bad, and indifferent. By this time the Fourth of July orator who could make the eagle scream had won the admiration of the Dutch. The sober statesman who governed wisely got some measure of honor, too; but oh, to hold men in the hollow of your hand! Some men of Dutch blood became Supreme Court justices and some members of the cabinet, but whether statesmen or rabble rousers most of them are pretty well forgotten today. Possibly better remembered are the Pennsylvania Camerons, Simon, Secretary of War under Lincoln, and James, son of Simon and Secretary of War under Grant, who were Dutch on the distaff side, and John Hay, Secretary of State under McKinley and the first Roosevelt, who was Virginia Dutch. There was a long line of Pennsylvania Dutch governors too, a number of them able men and several even better than that. George Wolf, Francis R. Shunk, and Samuel W. Pennypacker are in the top flight of Pennsylvania governors. Of the lesser men, Joseph Ritner's forthright condemnation of slavery in 1836 made him notable among the statesmen of his day, while Simon Snyder's memory is kept green largely through an anecdote dating from his election in 1808. His children, greatly excited that their father had been elected governor, asked their mother, "Mommy, are we all governors now?" "No," was her prompt reply; "just me and Pop."

In recent years there have been numerous men of Pennsylvania Dutch blood in politics (and curious bedfellows they make!): Herbert Hoover, William E. Borah, George W. Norris, Huey Long, Harold Ickes, Alfred M. Landon, Henry Wallace, and John W. Bricker.

Norris and Wallace are the only ones whose names are not Pennsylvania Dutch. Both these men are sons of Pennsylvania Dutch mothers. But Ickes and Landon are the only Pennsylvanians on the list.

Another Dutch hero is the soldier. Possibly Battalion Day, with the marching militia and the colonel on a white horse, led many a Dutch boy to dream of glory on the battlefield. Certainly before Battalion Day became a feature of the life in the Dutch towns, there had been but few Dutch military leaders. General Peter Muhlenberg was the only Pennsylvania Dutch general of the Revolution, unless we include General Anthony Wayne, who was Dutch on his mother's side. There was General Nicholas Herkimer, too; but he was one of those stubborn Germans who stayed on in upper New York instead of coming south to Pennsylvania. During the Civil War the pickings are just as lean or even worse. There was General John D. Imboden, of Pennsylvania Dutch descent, who had the temerity to fight on the side of the Confederacy; and to keep him company was General Josiah Gorgas, born in Dauphin County, chief of ordnance for the Confederate Army. To make up for this dearth of Dutch military heroes were two Dutch women who, so to speak, won their spurs, one in each war—Molly Pitcher in the Revolution and Barbara Frietchie in the Civil War. In the present century, however, you can't beat the Dutch. And quite literally that is true. Not with General John J. Pershing of Dutch descent, and his second in command, General Hunter Liggett, a Berks County Dutchman; not with General Dwight D. Eisenhower, of a family that had lived in Dauphin and York counties for generations, and General Jacob Loucks Devers of York County, and General Henry Hartley Arnold of Montgomery, and General Carl Spaatz of Berks to back him up. It is ironic that the Pennsylvania Dutch, who include such ardent pacifists as the Mennonites and the Amish, should in this century produce such a wealth of military leaders.

Still another Dutch hero is the rich man, the man with a coach and four or a Rolls Royce, the man with money in the bank. In the America of yesterday and today, in the Dutch country and in every one of the forty-eight states, the millionaire has received a full measure —brimming over—of men's admiration. Like the rest of the world, the Dutch have remained convinced that riches are happiness—all except the "plain people," who in this respect have shown greater wisdom than the generality of mankind. Of rich men the Dutch have produced more than their share. Widener, Wanamaker, Yerkes, Frick, Schwab,

Studebaker, Cramp, Seiberling, Cunard, not to mention Rockefeller and Astor: have not these names a golden sound? Every one is Dutch, and all but Rockefeller and Astor Pennsylvania Dutch. Even Johann Peter Rockefeller and Johann Jacob Astor were of the same eighteenth century Rhineland stock as the Pennsylvania colonists. In fact, the Astors so loved the sound of their native village that they made all America ring with it: Waldorf—a luxury hotel, a salad, and a little village in Baden.

Some of the millionaires of Dutch blood conformed rather closely to the robber-baron type. Such a one was Charles T. Yerkes, immortalized in Theodore Dreiser's trilogy, *The Financier, The Titan,* and *The Stoic.* Having gained control of the streetcar lines of Philadelphia, Yerkes was on the verge of becoming the financial dictator of the city when a panic on the stock exchange caught him short, with the result that he was charged with technical embezzlement and later convicted. Sentenced to two years and nine months in jail, he served only seven months when he was pardoned. Though he was able to recoup much of what he had lost, Philadelphia gave him a frigid reception. Seeking greater opportunities both in finance and in society, he moved west to Chicago. There with the help of two Philadelphia friends, Peter A. B. Widener and William L. Elkins, he won control of the Chicago streetcar lines. His method of making money was simple: "to buy old junk, fix it up a little, and unload it upon other fellows." His methods were so flagrant that eventually his rapacity was checked by mounting public indignation. In his love of magnificence and splendor he also ran true to the robber-baron type. He filled his office windows with stained glass; he slept in a gold bed that had once been owned by the king of Belgium; he had two—not one, but two—huge art galleries in the mansion he built for himself; and he became a patron of learning and gave to the University of Chicago the observatory that bears his name.

Greed and rapacity on almost as large a scale might possibly be encountered in the lives of one or two of the other Pennsylvania Dutch millionaires, though Henry Ford, son of a Pennsylvania Dutch mother, was closer to the rule than was Yerkes. Still farther removed was Milton Snavely Hershey, the chocolate manufacturer, who was even more interested in giving his money away than he was in making it. At the opposite pole from Yerkes was a fellow Chicagoan, one of Pennsylvania Dutch descent, whose whole life was devoted to improving the lot of her fellowmen. This was Jane Addams, who very appropriately was descended from Abraham op den Graeff, one of the signers of the first American protest against slavery and one of the first settlers of Germantown. The ancestors of Jane Addams lived for generations not far from the village of Adamstown, where Lancaster County joins Berks. Also in marked contrast to Yerkes is the Pepper family of Philadelphia. Both George Seckel Pepper and his son, William Pepper, left the larger part of their fortunes in wise public benefactions. Few families in America or elsewhere can match the Peppers in generosity and intelligence.

What does it all add up to? Preacher, doctor, politician, soldier, and millionaire: are these the Pennsylvania Dutch heroes? To a large degree, yes. The poet, the painter, the musician, and the philosopher are pretty much ignored. It is somewhat paradoxical that a region so rich in folk art should have produced so few good artists. In the past there were the two sculptors, Charles Grafly and William Henry Rhinehart. Just yesterday there was Charles Demuth of Lancaster, one of the more gifted painters of this century. By virtue of his Dutch blood Benjamin Latrobe, architect of the capitol, may also be included. And by virtue of his long residence in the Dutch country and his choice of subject, I would claim William Swallow of Allentown, whose work in ceramics is on the level of fine art. But this is only a handful of names where they should be as many as bluebottles in a meadow in early April. Of course the Pennsylvania Dutch can acquire art, as Widener and Frick have proved, even though few can create it.

On a lower plane is the great glassmaker, Baron Stiegel, a figure so romantic that he has captured the popular imagination. The life of this self-styled baron was pure theater. That, as well as the antique hunter's desire for his glass, has kept his memory alive. Stiegel was a man with a taste for the grand manner, one who believed in living life high, wide, and handsome. On a wooded hill near Schaefferstown he built an enormous tower where he could break his journey to Charming Forge or entertain guests in the banquet hall with which it was fitted out. The tower, painted bright vermilion, had a square base fifty feet across and was seventy-five feet in height. Cannons on top of the tower—and also on his house at Manheim—were fired to announce his approach. Preceded by a pair of outriders in livery and followed by a pack of hounds, he rode into town, trumpets blaring, in a coach drawn by four black horses decked with black plumes. Such a sight was never seen before in the Dutch country, nor has it been seen since. On summer nights musicians played on the roof of his house at Manheim to help him while away the hours. No wonder that his money was soon "all." But like Chaucer's Wife of Bath he might have said,

". . . it dooth myn herte boote
That I have had my world as in my tyme!"

Although the Pennsylvania Assembly came to his aid by granting him £150 in recognition of service to the colony in establishing his great glassworks and although a lottery was held for his benefit, he sank deeper and deeper into debt. When he was arrested for debt, the Assembly once more came to his assistance and by a special act set him free. Perhaps it was dramatically right that he should have lost every penny and been forced to spend his last years earning his bread by teaching in a little one-room school in Womelsdorf and working as a clerk at Charming Forge, which he had once owned. Even his burial in an unmarked grave, perhaps on the hill at Womelsdorf but quite possibly somewhere else, was a fitting part of the drama. Yet the man was not mere gesture; he had real ability. At the very least he proved to the colonies that America could make glass, clear flint and colored, as fine as any imported from abroad.

Oddly enough, the Pennsylvania Dutch have done more in the field of literature than in the fine arts or in music, this despite the handicap of language. Among the older writers was Sally Wister, whose sprightly journal is one of the livelier human documents of the Revolutionary period. Luther Long, whose tale "Madame Butterfly," was set to music by Puccini, was Dutch. Bayard Taylor was partly Dutch, with both Swiss and German strains in his blood. Even William Dean Howells had a Pennsylvania Dutch grandmother. Owen Wister is a writer of Dutch descent, and so is Joseph Hergesheimer, as his name clearly shows. Pearl Buck, whose maiden name was Sydenstricker, has Pennsylvania Dutch blood. Willa Sibert Cather, who was born near Winchester, was partly Dutch—Valley Dutch from Virginia. Thomas Wolfe was the son of a Pennsylvania Dutchman from Gettysburg. Elsie Singmaster, whose quiet tales of Pennsylvania Dutch life combine understanding with art, is Dutch through and through. So is Conrad Richter. Wallace Stevens, the poet, is Berks County born and bred. Stephen Vincent Benét and H. D. were born in Bethlehem; James Boyd was born in Dauphin County. And this does not take into account the writers who choose the dialect in preference to English.

Some of the Dutch heroes have been forgotten by the Dutch and by the rest of America as well. Such a one is Christopher Ludwick. It is interesting to speculate on the accident of fate that gave fame to Paul Revere and not to Christopher Ludwick. Was it chance, or was it Longfellow? Why was the man whom Washington affectionately called "old gentleman" forgotten? Surely Ludwick was one of the Revolutionary patriots who richly deserved the grateful remembrance of his fellow countrymen.

Arriving first in Philadelphia in 1753, Christopher Ludwick had an adventurous life behind him. Born at Giessen in Hesse on October 17, 1720, he was taught the trade of a baker by his father. This proving too tame for him, he enlisted at seventeen as a soldier to fight against the Turks. After four years of army life, in which he saw quite enough fighting to lose any romantic notions he had about the life of a soldier, he was discharged, whereupon he went to London and there signed on an East Indiaman as a baker. There followed three and a half years at sea, most of them in Asiatic waters. In 1745 he was back in London; but hearing that his father had died and left him an estate of 500 guilders, he crossed to Hesse to collect the money. Then back in London again, he lived high on his inheritance till every penny was gone; whereupon he shipped to sea once more, this time as a common sailor. After seven years at sea, mostly in West Indian and European waters, he accumulated £25, which he invested in ready-made clothes and sailed for Philadelphia. There he sold the clothes for four times as much as he had paid for them. Pleased with the money in his pocket and liking the looks of the town, he decided to settle there. He looked over the city to see what opening there might be for him. What Philadelphia needed, he decided, was a gingerbread baker. Once more he crossed the Atlantic and spent the next nine months in London mastering this art. The following year he returned to Philadelphia and set up business in Letitia Court as a gingerbread baker. That his judgment was sound was proved by the way Philadelphians thronged to his shop and bought his gingerbread. Soon he was so prosperous and in such good repute with his neighbors and customers that he was called "the Governor of Letitia Court."

With the coming of the Revolution Ludwick became an ardent supporter of the American cause. When in 1776 Governor Mifflin proposed that arms should be purchased for the American rebels by a public subscription, most Philadelphians looked askance at an action that seemed to them heedlessly rash and that hit them in their pocketbooks as well. But when Ludwick stepped forward and declared, "I am but a poor gingerbread baker, but put my name down for £200," many of his fellow townsmen forgot their caution and thrift and boldly staked their money on the rebel cause.

To give money to his country was not enough for Ludwick; only direct action could make him feel that he was of real service to America. Enlisting as a volunteer in the Flying Camp, he refused to draw either pay or rations for his services. When a group of mutineers, dissatisfied with their beggarly rations, threatened to desert, he was so moved that he got down on his knees and begged them not to leave. He promised them good bread and plenty of it if they would only stay, though this was the army's province and not his. Nor did he appeal to them in vain. The British use of Hessian mercenaries particularly saddened him. That fellow Hessians should be fighting against the country he loved so well filled him with shame. When eight Hessian prisoners were taken and brought into camp, he joined in the debate of what should be done with them. "Let us take them to Philadelphia," he proposed, "and there show them our fine German churches. Let them see how our tradesmen eat good beef, drink out of silver cups every day, and ride out in chairs every afternoon; and then let us send them back to their countrymen, and they will all soon run away, and come and settle in our city and be as good whigs as any of us."

Seeing clearly that the Hessians were not fighting of their own free will but had been forced into the war, he believed that if they could be made to realize what a fine country America was and the opportunities it afforded a man they could be won for the American cause. He was so convinced that he was right that he was willing to venture his life on it. He approached several members of Congress and proposed that he pass himself off as a deserter and get into the Hessian camps on Staten Island, where he would persuade the Hessians to desert to the Americans! That he would have been hanged as a spy by the British if he were detected did not daunt him. Nor did it matter that he was nearing sixty. This daring plan he actually put into operation, and it worked out as he foresaw. A Hessian by birth, he was able to hoodwink the British authorities and get into the Hessian camps. To the Hessian mercenaries he sold the American dream. He told them of the wonders of Philadelphia, of the mile-long market in the High Street with counters laden with plump chickens and sausages, with crisp fresh bread and buns fragrant with cinnamon, with cherries and sparrowgrass and peas and other vegetables in season; of the snug inns were a man could sit at ease before the fire and down his pot of liquor or turn in between fresh, lavender-scented sheets. He told them of the Pennsylvania farms with sleek cattle in the meadow, of the springhouses where crocks of cream stood in cold water. It was a land where men who had come as indentured servants only a few years before now wore broadcloth to church on Sunday and cast their vote for assemblyman. No one pressed their sons into the army and sold them to a foreign king to fight across the sea. This was America, a land that gave a man a chance to make something of himself. They were fools to fight for King George, who meant nothing to them. Why not desert? The Americans wouldn't be too hard on them. Into all this Ludwick poured his heart and soul. Why shouldn't the Hessians believe him? He meant every word he said. And desert they did, by the dozen and the score. According to Benjamin Rush, hundreds of Hessian soldiers took Ludwick's advice and deserted to the American side.

On May 3, 1777, Ludwick became baker general to the Continental Army. When a committee from Congress in all innocence proposed that he deliver 100 pounds of bread for every hundred pounds of flour, he refused indignantly:

"No, gentlemen, I will not accept your commission upon any such terms; Christopher Ludwick does not want to get rich by the war; he has money enough. I will furnish 135 pounds of bread for every hundredweight of flour you put into my hands!"

At Yorktown he baked 6,000 pounds of bread for Cornwallis's men. "Let it be good, old gentleman," warned Washington, seeing the starved British soldiers; "and let there be enough of it; if I should want myself."

Ludwick was honest, blunt, and outspoken, yet never offensive. Of an open, frank, and forthgiving nature, he loved people, talking freely with everyone he met; and to everyone he was the same—himself, Christopher Ludwick. His voice was strong; all the neighborhood knew when he was around. Regarded by his fellow officers as something of a character, he had a privileged position in the camp. Though they smiled at him, they looked on him with affection and admiration as well. His good humor and his fund of amusing anecdotes brought life wherever he went. His patriotism, his honesty, and his generosity were beyond question. And to these qualities he added common sense—rare in any army.

At the close of the war he settled down on his farm in Germantown. His house had been plundered by the British; he had no household goods and no money. Friends and neighbors offered to lend him money to refurnish his house, but he disliked the idea of going into debt. Instead he sold part of his property to replace the stolen clothing and furniture.

In 1795, upon the death of his wife, he moved to Philadelphia, where he made his home with one of his former journeymen. During the yellow-fever epidemic in 1797 he volunteered his services to bake bread for distribution to the poor. He was then seventy-seven years old. This act was characteristic of the man, for toward those less fortunate than himself he was all kindness and consideration. Dr. Benjamin Rush declared that there was hardly an institution in Philadelphia that Ludwick had not helped. For many years Ludwick had sought out those in distress "with a delicacy and secrecy that conferred double pleasure and obligation," as Rush so happily put it. Only drunkards filled him with scorn; to them he refused to give a penny. He had not carried bags of flour on his back for twenty years, he declared bluntly, "to help people destroy themselves by strong drink."

In 1798 he married for the second time. A woman pricked up her courage to tell him she felt sorry for his loneliness. She was concerned for his happiness—and for her own, too—and therefore proposed that he make her his second wife. Thinking it over, he liked the straightforwardness and the good sense of her proposal and he married her. The marriage turned out well: she made him a good wife and he made her a good husband.

Three years later, on June 17, 1801, he died. He was buried in Germantown in the graveyard of the Lutheran church. Among the many mourners at his grave were three Negro slaves he had freed. Most of his money he left to charity. To the Pennsylvania Hospital he bequeathed £100 for the relief of poor patients. To the German Reformed Church of Philadelphia, to the German Society of the University of Pennsylvania, and to the Lutheran Church at Beggarstown he left £500 in equal shares, "to be employed in educating poor children." To the Guardians of the Poor he gave £200 to buy firewood for the poor of Philadelphia. All these were minor bequests; the bulk of his estate was left to establish free schools "for the education of poor children of all denominations without any exception to country, extraction or religious principles of their friends or parents." The money was directed to be turned over to a school with these aims, or if none was established within five years the money was to be divided among the German Lutheran, German Reformed, English Episcopalian, the First and Second Presbyterian, the Roman Catholic, and the African churches and the University of Pennsylvania to be used exclusively to educate poor children. Here was complete freedom from prejudice, both religous and racial. He included the Roman Catholic Church to express his gratitude for the kindness shown him more than sixty years before by some Catholic peasants when he was a young soldier fighting against the Turks. They had befriended him when he was half naked and starving.

Surely there cannot have been many finer or even greater men in the America of his day. Yet this is one of the Founding Fathers America has forgotten. Not one man in a thousand knows his name. Except for the tombstone marking his grave, there is no memorial to him. At the very least the bakers of America owe it to themselves to do honor to this man, who might almost be regarded as their patron saint.

So far I have resisted the temptation to include the people born in the Dutch country who are not of Dutch blood. There is that famous son of Berks County, Daniel Boone. Though he may have been able to speak a few words of Dutch in his youth, he is not Dutch. And there is that native of Germantown, Louisa May Alcott; by no stretch of the imagination can she be called Pennsylvania Dutch. Nor can the loyalist, Lindley Murray, whose English grammar was the bane of generations of schoolboys. Though he was born on the banks of the Swatara, I lay no claim to him.

Some of the sojourners in the Dutch country I would very much like to include. Priestley, the metaphysician, and Audubon, who lived in Montgomery County, where Pennsylvania Dutchman meets Quaker, are but two of the most famous. Another was Sutter, who was so callously dispossessed of his lands in the Sacramento Valley when gold was discovered there. Sutter is buried in Lititz, where he spent the last years of his life; and there in the quiet Moravian graveyard he still lies, though California has tried to persuade Lititz to part with his body.

One of the most curious of all the ertswhile Dutchmen is Lorenzo Da Ponte, who wrote the librettos for *Figaro, Don Giovanni,* and *Cosi fan tutte.* Born in Venice, Da Ponte was a converted Jew who became an abbé for a time. When he was denounced by the Inquisition, he fled to Vienna, where he wrote librettos for Mozart. He was a friend of Casanova, to whom he introduced his wife as his mistress so as not to lose face with that notorious amorist. Finally, in 1811, he turned up in Sunbury and was so delighted with "the amenity of the spot" and so filled with "a yearning for repose" that he decided to stay on. He tutored some of his neighbors' children in languages and he set up as a grocer and distiller. A born speculator, he was soon trafficking in country produce, which he sent to Philadelphia by Conestoga wagon. On the return trip the wagons brought city wares north to Sunbury. But Da Ponte's lack of business acumen kept him in hot water. Shrewdness alternated with gullibility. Other traders, far sharper, found him a lamb ready for the shearing. Once, in Reading, he was showered with credit when he was mistaken for Monsieur Dupont, the Wilmington powder maker, only to suffer bitterly when his Reading creditors learned their mistake. In Sunbury he failed spectacularly. Arrested for debt, he even spent a night in the old Sunbury jail. After seven years he had enough of country quiet and retired to New York. Later, in his *Memoirs,* he told the world in great detail of the rascally businessmen he had encountered in Sunbury, Reading, and Philadelphia.

Part Five

FOLKWAYS

Dialect

That many Pennsylvania Dutchmen still prefer their native dialect to English is one of the most startling facts about them. To many a Dutchman English is a language that he shares with the rest of America, but Dutch is peculiarly his own. It was the language of his forefathers, and it is his language, too. The way these people cling to this dialect even though the vast majority came to this country before the French and Indian War indicates a deep-rooted conservativeness and stubbornness. The average Pennsylvania Dutchman may be a nice enough fellow, but more likely than not his grandmother was a mule. In contrast, those later Germans who came to America in the nineteenth century abandoned their native tongue with almost indecent celerity; no other immigrants became Americanized with such speed. Not so the Germans who settled in Pennsylvania in the first half of the eighteenth century; along with their folk customs and their ways of cooking they preserved their speech. Cut off from the rest of colonial America by the difference in language, the Pennsylvania Dutch formed a language island in a sea of English. Pennsylvania was the only one of the thirteen colonies that was truly bilingual; and bilingual it has remained to this day. So common was Dutch in

Philadelphia in pre-Revolutionary times that, according to Franklin, many of the street signs were in both English and German and some in German alone. Although English has become the dominant language, there are probably more than three hundred thousand Pennsylvania Dutch who are more at home in Dutch than in English, and four hundred thousand more who habitually speak English but have little difficulty making themselves understood in Dutch if the necessity arises. Radio programs in the dialect presented by Allentown and Reading stations bear witness to the continued popularity of Dutch. The dialect is always called Dutch. As Holland Dutch is not spoken in Pennsylvania, there is no confusion with that language. And not even the most learned Pennsylvania Dutchmen, of which there are not a few, call it German, since that is a name reserved for High German.

There are, of course, a large number of Pennsylvania Dutch who cannot speak the dialect, a full half or more of the population; yet it is not safe to talk Dutch in front of them, as they have inconvenient moments of understanding what is being said. Most of the Pennsylvania Dutch have at least a slight knowledge of the dialect, though the city dwellers speak English instead of Dutch. Yet Dutch is heard so often on the streets of Allentown and Reading that it attracts no particular attention. Many of the clerks in the stores are able to speak Dutch; indeed, in some stores the ability to speak the dialect is an essential part of a clerk's qualifications. In the small towns, especially in Berks, Lehigh, and upper Montgomery counties, Dutch is heard fully as often as English, while in the country in those counties it is the preferred language. Some of the old people living in the country speak only Pennsylvania Dutch. And to this day many of the children who come to the little country schoolhouses for the first time know only Dutch. The instruction in the schools is in English; but during recess the children revert to Dutch. The parents at home talk Dutch to each other and frequently only Dutch to the children. No wonder that little Leroy Himmelberger at the Christmas entertainment wishes you a Christmas filled "mit choy."

Until recent years German was the language of both the Lutheran and the Reformed churches. This was not Pennsylvania Dutch nor even contemporary German but the archaic High German of the eighteenth century. This seemed to the Pennsylvania Dutch the only language right and fitting for a church service, just as most English-speaking Americans considered the archaic English of the King James version of the Bible more appropriate than modern English. Towards the end of the nineteenth century most Lutheran and Reformed churches changed over to English, provoking a minor war and feelings highly unchristian—this not for one year but literally for decades. Many of the old conservative members felt that the old-time religion and High German were inseparable. In the country churches especially German held its own. In some of the more recalcitrant churches it continued to be used until the 1930's.

Dutch is spoken not only by the descendants of the original Germans but also by their fellow citizens and neighbors of English, Scotch-Irish, Welsh, and French Huguenot descent. An Italian immigrant in Reading apologized for his poor English with this explanation: "When I come to America I think I learn speak English. I get job digging ditch. I listen to what man working on one side of me say to man working on other side. Every little while I learn a word. 'Dunnerwetter,' he says; 'dunnerwetter,' I say. Ha, I thought, now I learn English; I real American. But no, I no learn English. I learn Pennsylvania Dutch!" Strangest of all is to hear the dialect from the lips of a Negro or a gypsy. A few of the old Negro families who settled in the Dutch country shortly before or after the Civil War adopted the speech and customs of their Dutch neighbors a long time ago; while to the gypsies, many of whom came from the Rhineland, Dutch is as much their mother tongue as Romany.

In the Cumberland Valley less Dutch is spoken than in the Great Valley east of the Susquehanna. South of the Maryland line Dutch becomes increasingly rare; in the Shenandoah Valley it has virtually disappeared, although it was common enough half a century ago. But in Dutch Canada the dialect is as vital and lush as in Dutchest Pennsylvania.

Up to 1900 Pennsylvania Dutch was very much alive. Most of the weekly newspapers in the small towns of Lehigh, Berks, and Lebanon counties were German. Allentown, too, was Dutch—and proud of it. Under the militant leadership of the Reverend S. K. Brobst, Allentown put up a last-ditch fight to keep Dutch the language of the Dutch country. The attempt was successful enough to make Allentown in its speech and accent the Dutchest of the Dutch cities. Yet after 1900 more and more people spoke English in preference to the dialect. Today it is clear that Pennsylvania Dutch is doomed as a language. Another century, and it will be gone. Even now Franklin and Marshall College and Penn State each offer a course in Pennsylvania Dutch—as they do in those dead languages, Greek and Latin. The writing on the wall is plain to read. One of the chief obstacles to the spread of the dialect is the lack of standard spelling. Each person spells each word at will. Consequently people perfectly at ease in speaking the dialect often have difficulty in reading some of the versions of it. Despite the literature in the dialect Dutch is a spoken language rather than a written one.

Many Americans with only a superficial knowledge of the dialect believe it to be a humorous mixture of English and German. It is that, but that is only a small part of the story. The number of English words is relatively small, probably about 5 per cent. Yet even commonplace English words and phrases become strange and wonderful when they go Dutch; *of course* turns into *uf kors, politics* changes to *balledicks*, and *life insurance* is reborn as *leifinschurings*. The sound is much the same, but how weird the words look! Among those people more at home in English than in Dutch the borrowings are particularly numerous, for when their Dutch fails they fall back on English words and phrases. The English words that have been borrowed by the dialect generally lack Dutch equivalents; often they are the names of things that the early settlers came upon in America for the first time.

To this day Pennsylvania Dutch is virtually the same language as the one spoken in Heidelberg or Mannheim. After the First World War the Pennsylvania Dutchmen who formed part of the American Army of Occupation along the Rhine, especially in the Palatinate or Württemberg, had no difficulty in making themselves understood. Listening to the conversations in the markets or in the beer gardens, they might have thought themselves back home in Reinholds Station or Hellertown. In the Second World War a group of Pennsylvania Dutchmen out on a skirmishing party at night were mistaken for Germans by a group of Nazis who overheard them talking Dutch to one another. This is not so strange as it may seem, for Pennsylvania Dutch is merely the eighteenth century dialect of the Palatinate, especially the eastern half, with some borrowings from Württemberg and Switzerland. If the particular brand of Pennsylvania Dutch is that of Lancaster County or upper Montgomery or Bucks, there are more Swiss additions, since the early settlers of these places were frequently from

Switzerland; but if the Pennsylvania Dutch is that of Berks County or Lehigh, it is almost pure Pfalz. Pennsylvania Dutch differs slightly from county to county according to the origin of the original settlers. Yet there is a remarkable degree of standardization: the differences from one county to another are not many—more in vocabulary than anything else. A Lehigh County Dutchman would have no difficulty in making himself understood even to a Dunkard from Somerset—that is, if the Dunkard knew Dutch.

Many of the Dutch words have been adopted into the English of southeastern Pennsylvania. I was nearly twenty before I discovered that *spritz* (meaning *to squirt,* as in "the grapefruit spritzes") and *strubbly* (meaning *disheveled,* as in "the boy with the strubbly hair") were not perfectly good English words. Most of the words so borrowed are extremely expressive and fill a lack in English. *Wunnerfitsich,* meaning *inquisitive,* is such a word. To tell a child not to be so *wunnerfitsich* is far more emphatic than to tell him not to be so curious. And to tell a small boy not to *rutsch* around so is more expressive than the English equivalent; compared to *rutsch, squirm* has little life or color. And *putz,* the Bethlehem name for the crèche or Christmas crib under the tree, has no exact English counterpart. A number of these words are used by most English-speaking Pennsylvania Dutchmen as a matter of course. *Klook* and *peep* are universally used in the Dutch country for a broody hen and a baby chicken. *Hex,* the noun for *witch* or verb for *to bewitch,* is in common usage, while *spook* for *ghost* has been adopted by the United States as a whole except in the South, where *ha'nt* holds its own. Some of these words are so humorous or picturesque as to appeal to the fancy of their users. *Blutz-wagon,* a farm wagon without springs, is one of these; *toot,* a small paper bag ("Shall I put it in a toot, or will you take it so?"), is another. Especially conspicuous are the attempts at English by the country Dutch that give birth to sentences overly rich in adverbs. "I've known her long already," and "Don't let her run off now yet," will suffice to illustrate this tendency. The dialect also has many expressive interjections, of which *Ach!, Ei! ei!, Ei-yi-yi!,* and *Ei-yi-yi-yi-yi!* are the most important. These two last lose much of their vigor in print; they must be set to music—for they are always sung to a little tune—for the hearer to get their full beauty.

Not all of the Pennsylvania Dutch words are Teutonic. *Powwow* is a verb borrowed from the Indians. To powwow is to cure sickness or even to scare away a cross dog by the use of magic spells. *Herschel,* introduced by the almanacs, is a noun used in Lebanon and Lancaster counties to denote a sharp change in the weather. Herschel is the name once proposed for the planet Uranus in honor of its discoverer, Sir William Herschel. Though the Pennsylvania Dutch call Uranus by its proper name they have bestowed the old name for the planet on the sort of weather they expect Uranus to bring. *Butterbread* and *jellybread* and *applebutterbread* are descriptive compounds. *Beet* always has the adjective *red* added to it. *Red beet* brings up visions of Sunday-school picnics in summer groves, while *beet* by itself is too cold and naked a word for human use. The Pennsylvania Dutch have even a few nicknames of their own—Euge, rhyming with *huge,* for Eugene instead of the usual Gene; Pass for Percy or Percival; and Yonnie for Jonathan.

The Pennsylvania Dutch have long realized that in their dialect lay an inexhaustible mine of humor, a fact that does much to endear the dialect to them. It is not a language possessing dignity or grandeur; it is not a speech fit for tragedy. But it is one in which humor and homely sentiment can be well expressed. Of course, it is the broken English of the more ignorant Dutch that much of America finds most humorous. Some of the specimens of slaughtered English often cited as typical of Pennsylvania Dutch English are altogether too good to be true. Of these the most celebrated is the note that is supposed to have been pinned to a door where the bell was out of order: "Bell don't make; bump." It is a wonderful sentence; and so is "My off is all," meaning "My vacation is over." I should like to believe that the Pennsylvania Dutch were capable of murdering the English language with such verve and style; but it takes a city slicker to swallow sentences like these. Funny only in a mild way is the use of the adjective for the noun, as in the sentence, "Did you have the electric put in the house?" Amusing, too, is the reference to the husband and head of the house as *the mister.* This is the shibboleth of the true country Dutchwoman.

Humor in the dialect is even richer and more extravagant than it is in the familiar broken English. On August 28, 1869, there was printed in a Bethlehem paper an advertisement with so fantastic a mixture of Dutch and English that its writer's tongue was obviously in his cheek. For the edification and pleasure of readers with a knowledge of German I append it here:

GOOK YUSHT AMOHL DOH!
Monsleit un Weibsleit!!
Buwa un Maed — Yungy un Olty.
Attention!
DER EAGLE DRUG SHTORE!
Der Besht un der Wholfealsht!

WM. S. SEAGER, OBBADEAKER.
In der Dritt Shtrose, Sued Bethlehem.

Olsfort uf hond, olly sorta fun de beshty Drugs un Meditziena, un on de wholfealshty prices. Also, Paint, Oehl, Glaws, Varnish, &c. Mer hen aw an neier article dos gor net gebutta konn waerra; es is de bareemt
"SALTED SODA"
un waerd g'used for seaf kocha. Prowiers amohl—de directions we mers braucht geana mit. Om Eagle Drug Shtore is aw der plotz for
PATENT MEDITZIENA, BITTERS, &c., &c., &c.
Fun olly ort, un on de wholfealshty prices.
Also, Coal-Oehl, Lompa, Waugha-Schmeer, &c., &c.
Now mind was mer sawya; mer hen olles uf hond was mer denka konn in unser line of bisness. We g'sawt, unser prices sin wholfealer dos in ennichem onnera Drug Shtore im County. Ferges't net der platz,

IN DER DRITT SHTROSE UNNICH DER LOCUST
SUED BETHLEHEM
Now is de tseit; macht eich bei, un judg'd for eich selwer; kummt in foor weasa, uf horseback, uf em Railroad odder tsu foos—mer sin gor net particular wie, yusht so dos der kummt on
DER EAGLE OBBADEAK IN SUED BETHLEHEM.
Un bringt eier greenbacks mit. Wholfeal for Cash—sell is unser style.

WILLIAM S. SEAGER
August 28, 1869   Obbadeaker

The question the village girl put to the young swain, "Do you want to go for steady, or for so?" is as funny to the average Pennsylvania Dutchmen as it is to anyone, because of its phrasing and its naïveté. "She came to the city to be went with, but the boys weren't so very for her," is funny largely because of its grotesque use of the English language. Such simple constructions as "The paper wants rain," "The butter won't reach," and "The bread is all" are so common as to cause only a flicker of amusement. If the sentence is picturesque enough it may circulate through all the Dutch country, as did the question the little boy watching a freight train go by is supposed to have put to his father, "Say, Pop, when it gives a little red house, then it makes all?" Almost as good is the explanation of the Walnuttown boy who failed to pass in school, "They didn't try things at me any more; they just said, 'You keep here another year'." Occasionally there is magic in the phraseology, as in the case of the Amish girl who was expelled from meeting because she married a Reformed youth and "went gay." For me there is poetry, almost a philosophy of life, in that phrase, "went gay."

The Dutch tell many amusing stories on themselves. Possibly the best known is the one about the old farmer in from a hard day's work in the fields who was told by his wife that a man who spoke only English was coming to see him that evening. "Ei-yi-yi!" the farmer growled. "Such a dog's life! Work hard all day you must, and then in the evening talk English yet."

Often the humor is of a rather genial sort, as in the tale of the fat Dutchman who was asked what he would choose if he could have three wishes granted.

"Ach, that's easy!" he said. "As much beer as I could drink."

"And then?"

"As much fried sausage as I could eat."

"And third?"

"Third?" he repeated, frowning and scratching his head. "Ach well, if everything went all right, I guess I'd have some more beer."

Sometimes the humor is distinctly dry, as in the story of the four pallbearers who were driving back from the cemetery to the center of Reading. One was very old, and a younger member of the group asked him, "How old are you anyway, Charlie?"

"Seventy-nine," the old man replied.

"Seventy-nine! H'm, hardly worth while carrying you home."

Earthiness is a characteristic quality of the dialect, which was little influenced by Victorian prudishness. There is nothing timid about this language. It is notable, too, for highly colored oaths, which are more florid and vehement than those in English. Even such tepid cusswords as "Heilich dunnerwetter!" and "Verdammte dunnerwetter!" sound well, though they are as harmless as "Jack Robinson!" and "Jumping Jehoshaphat!" when translated.

Once at least Dutch was heard on the floors of Congress, more than a century ago when George Kremer, the representative from the Union-Northumberland district, replied with a torrent of Dutch to a high-falutin speech of John Randolph of Roanoke studded with Latin and Greek quotations.

The bilingual speech of the Pennsylvania Dutch has resulted in a local intonation that is one of the least lovely of American accents. The rising inflection and the singsong quality characteristic of the English speech of many of the country people adds even more to its comic effect than the choice of words or the word order. This is most noticeable in questions, for there the voice is raised in the middle of the sentence and lowered at the end. By this means any simple question is converted into a melody. Yet it is a friendly, homely speech with a rich folk flavor, completely natural and unaffected, as unlike the speech of a radio announcer as it is possible for English to be—no small virtue in itself.

Among the better educated people there is little trace of the characteristic Dutch intonation. Their English is the English of southeastern Pennsylvania, less nasal than that of Philadelphia and therefore more pleasant to the ear. They are not quite so determined as the Philadelphians to turn every diphthong into two vowels. This accent is a full-flavored Eastern and Northern accent, hearty and unashamed. *Rather* is always the good, plain American *răth-er*—there is no *ah* sound; and *either* and *neither* are the ordinary *è-ther* and *nè-ther*. An Alabaman once described it to me as "deep North." Whether or not it is deep, I don't know; but most assuredly it is North. There is no suggestion of magnolia and moonlight in this accent. If anything, it calls up visions of bank barns and shoofly pies, of blossoming cherries and red brick pavements—and all in bright sunlight.

The Three R's

In education the record of the Pennsylvania Dutch has not been notable. This is so touchy a matter with most Pennsylvania Dutchmen that it is easy to see that they are suffering from an inferiority complex. Few subjects put them so surely on the defensive. Let the discussion turn to education, and at once and with unnecessary violence the Pennsylvania Dutch record will be defended. Any criticism from the outside is resented. Yet it must be admitted that the record is rather middling. Compared to much of the South, the Pennsylvania Dutch have done fairly well. It is only in comparison with New England or their neighbors, the Quakers, that the lack of distinction comes to light.

Today their public schools are fairly representative of the country as a whole—better than those of the South but much on a level with those of New England, the rest of the Middle Atlantic area, the Middle West, and the Pacific coast. The schools vary from city to city and township to township, but the average is respectable. In the country the consolidated township schools have tended to replace the one-room schoolhouse; but the state sees to it that even in the one-room schools the teachers are kept on their toes.

There are very few private schools in the Dutch country. Hill School at Pottstown and Mercersburg Academy are the two outstanding exceptions. Although a few of the wealthier of the Dutch families send their sons to Hill, it is not a Pennsylvania Dutch institution. Mercersburg is more representative of the Pennsylvania Dutch, but it, too, attracts many students from outside the region. Linden Hall, a Moravian school at Lititz, and Penn Hall at Chambersburg are the two best known schools for girls in the Dutch country. It is not the custom of the Pennsylvania Dutch to send their children to private schools; they believe thoroughly in the democracy of the public school.

There are a number of small colleges and even a university or two in the Dutch counties. Lehigh is an engineering school with a national reputation. The University of Pennsylvania in Philadelphia and Penn State in Centre County are partly Dutch; many Pennsylvania Dutchmen have gone to these universities as students and served there as teachers, but neither institution is dominantly Dutch. None of the colleges in the Dutch country is so well endowed as such New England colleges as Williams, Amherst, and Bowdoin or such Pennsylvania colleges of Quaker foundation as Swarthmore, Haverford, and Bryn Mawr. Lehigh and Lafayette have the highest endowments, yet neither is truly Dutch despite a large number of Dutch students and despite their location in Dutch cities. Nor is Bucknell, a Baptist institution, truly Dutch; nor Dickinson, which is Methodist; nor Wilson College, which is Presbyterian. None of these colleges was founded by a denomination with many Dutch adherents.

Of the more purely Pennsylvania Dutch churches, the Reformed Church has four colleges in the Dutch country, and the Lutheran three; the Evangelical United Brethren two, and the Moravians and the Church of the Brethren one each. The Reformed Church has one college for men, Franklin and Marshall; one coeducational college, Ursinus; and two colleges for women, Cedar Crest and Hood. The Lutheran colleges are Muhlenberg, Gettysburg, and Susquehanna. It may be that both the Reformed and Lutheran churches spread themselves too much in the number of colleges they founded in Pennsylvania; for, like many religious foundations, these colleges are inadequately endowed. It might have been wiser if each church had concentrated its efforts on a single college in Pennsylvania and done its very best by that one institution. This was the policy pursued by the Moravians in founding Moravian College, the United Brethren in Lebanon Valley

College, the Evangelical Church in Albright, and the Brethren in Juniata; but these churches, without the numbers and the wealth of the Lutheran and Reformed churches, did not have the same opportunity to establish a truly superior college. Furthermore, it was only in fairly recent years that the Dunkards became convinced of the need of education. Juniata College was founded only in 1876.

In spite of this plethora of colleges in their own country, many Pennsylvania Dutchmen go away to college, particularly those in the top income group. Princeton, Yale, Harvard, Dartmouth, Wesleyan, Amherst, Swarthmore, Haverford, Vassar, Smith, and many other institutions of note have students from Pennsylvania Dutch families.

In the past there was a cultural lag among the Pennsylvania Dutch because of the language difference. Their use of Dutch instead of English cut them off from the main stream of American culture. Nevertheless, the Dutch as a whole are not an ignorant people and never have been. By and large they are like the rest of the American people, neither ignorant nor learned. A few of them, at least, have been to school. Even when they landed at Philadelphia in the old days they were not illiterate. The ships' lists preserving the signatures of the German and Swiss immigrants from 1727 to 1808 prove that three-quarters of them, at least, were able to sign their names. Benjamin Rush, writing in 1789, declared, "There is scarcely an instance of a German, of either sex, in Pennsylvania, that cannot *read*; but many of the wives and daughters of the German farmers cannot *write*." Some of the early immigrants had degrees from German universities. Indeed, this was the rule among the Lutheran and Reformed preachers, since both these churches and the Moravians as well insisted on an educated ministry. A few of these immigrants were highly learned men. Pastorius, for instance, was the most learned man of his day in America. Massachusetts, Connecticut, Virginia, and South Carolina could not produce his equal.

Undoubtedly the Dutch schools of the eighteenth century were inadequate. This was but natural since most of the immigrants from the Rhineland did not come as organized groups but as families or even individuals. Often they were wretchedly poor—with four or more years of the hard life of the redemptioner to pay for their passage. Even without this handicap there were trees to be cut down and houses to be built. Once a start was made on such primary tasks, a church was built and then a schoolhouse. Practically all of the colonial Reformed and Lutheran churches had their own schools. Where the two denominations occupied the same church, as was often the case in the country, the school too was a union one. Very often the schoolmaster led the singing in church; and if the church was fortunate enough to have an organ, he played the organ. Naturally the children were taught their catechism along with the three R's. According to the rules and regulations adopted February 27, 1744, the school at Tulpehocken taught the three R's, Luther's catechism, and the Bible. Scripture texts and hymns were memorized. The primer and reader studied were the ones issued by the University of Jena. With this start a man was expected to go ahead and educate himself, and many did. Books from abroad were imported: witness the advertisements of Lessing, Wieland, and Goethe in the Dutch newspapers of the early nineteenth century.

All the schools were parochial schools, as were the Quaker schools of the time and the Roman Catholic schools of today. The Mennonites, the Amish, and the Brethren had their schools too; they all wished their children to be able to read the Bible. The Schwenkfelders, also, set up schools. At the Schwenkfelder academy opened at Hosensack in 1790 German, English, Latin, and Greek were taught. It was the Moravians, however, that really took education to heart. The Moravians, of course, came as a community. There was wealth behind them. Consequently, they were able to build up a completely equipped settlement in a few years. Furthermore, the influence of the great Moravian bishop and educator, John Amos Comenius, was at work on them. Comenius was known throughout the world for his works on education, *Didactica Magna* and *Methodus Linguarum Novissima,* and also for his book for children, *Orbis Sensalium Pictus*—an early example of teaching by object lessons. Sweden, England, and America all sought his services. He received an invitation to "come over into New England and Illuminate this Colledge [Harvard] and Country in the Quality of President." Unfortunately for American education, he declined Harvard's invitation. The Moravian concern for education was so great that schools were set up not only in Bethlehem, Nazareth, Lititz, and Emmaus but also in Germantown and Lancaster and even in such small places as Muddy Creek, Oley, Mill Creek, Warwick, and Heidelberg.

What most surprised people of the day was the Moravian insistence that girls as well as boys should be educated. This advanced point of view was thought singular in London as well as in Boston and Philadelphia. In the eighteenth century the serious consideration that Bethlehem and Lititz in Pennsylvania and Salem in North Carolina gave to the education of girls was exceptional. The school at Bethlehem was the first boarding school for girls in America. Opened at Germantown on May 4, 1742, by the Countess Benigna, daughter of Count Zinzendorf, it was moved to Bethlehem on June 25 of the following year. A school for boys was established at Nazareth on July 18, 1743. In 1764 it had one hundred and six pupils and sixteen masters. The boarding school for girls at Nazareth was opened on the 28th of March, 1745, with eighteen pupils. There little Indian girls studied side by side with the Moravian maidens. In one of the early years five out of twenty-eight pupils were Indians: Quatsch'l, Martha, Little Dove, Beata, alias Chicken, and Sarah, alias Little Worm. During the early years most of the pupils at these schools were Moravian, for the schools had been designed by the Moravians for the education of their children. All went quietly until the Revolution, when Bethlehem became a military center for the American armies. Then an extremely large number of American officers and statesmen had occasion to visit Bethlehem and thus become acquainted with the school for girls. They were so favorably impressed by it that they asked the Moravians to open the school to other faiths and to accept their daughters as scholars. The Moravians assented, and opened it to Protestants of all faiths and to Catholics and Jews as well. Within a few years girls from all over the new republic were in residence. George Washington sent his niece, Eleanor Lee; Ethan Allen his niece, Anna Allen; Chancellor Livingston his daughter, Cornelia, who later became the wife of Robert Fulton; and Nathanael Greene and John Jay their daughters. The Roosevelts, Vanderheydens, Lansings, and other old Dutch families of New York sent their daughters. There were Sumters and Alstons and Hugers from the South. Even some of the planters in the West Indies sent their daughters north to school at Bethlehem. Girls from Quaker and Pennsylvania Dutch families shared their secrets with girls from tidewater Virginia or Charleston.

What did these girls study? Reading, writing, and arithmetic; French and German, grammar, geography, history, and astronomy; and, since it was the eighteenth century, sewing; and, since it was Bethlehem, music. Care was taken to suit the subjects to the age groups. This was very much what the boys in the Moravian schools studied—

with sewing omitted, of course. At the boys' school in Nazareth the curriculum in 1785 consisted of reading, writing, and arithmetic; English, German, French, Latin, and Greek; history, geography, mathematics, music, and drawing. On the whole this was a program eminently sound.

The most ambitious scheme for the education of the Pennsylvania Dutch that the eighteenth century witnessed was William Smith's proposal to establish schools to Americanize the Germans. Funds were to be raised, largely among the adherents of the Church of England, to found and support free schools to teach the Palatine immigrants the English language, mathematics, geography, history, ethics, and most important of all, "the Constitution and interest of the Colonies." Even German was to be taught—probably as bait. Among the trustees chosen in 1753 to administer the funds were Benjamin Franklin, Governor James Hamilton, William Allen, Conrad Weiser, and Richard Peters. At first the proposal had the support of the Reformed and Lutheran churches, particularly of the foremost Reformed clergyman of the colony, Michael Schlatter. No effort was made to include the "plain people" in the administration of the scheme. This was unwise. In no time at all Christopher Sauer, the great Dunkard printer, began to smell a rat. It was the politics and the religion of the Dutch that Smith and two or three others at the head of the scheme really disliked, declared Sauer. The main idea, he charged, was to win the Germans over to the Anglican point of view, to make them desert the pacifist policies of the Quakers. Sauer was right, at least in part. Some of the trustees were sincere in their effort to educate the Germans; but Smith and Peters particularly were far more interested in increasing the influence of the Church of England. Schools were set up in Lancaster, York, Reading, Easton, New Hanover, Skippack, Tulpehocken, and Vincent Township, Chester County—all Pennsylvania Dutch settlements. In 1759 there were eight schools with four hundred and forty pupils; but the opposition to them was so strong that five years later they all were closed.

The Dutch on the whole resented this Machiavellian attempt. Schlatter, because of his part in the scheme, found himself suspect even among members of the Reformed Church. In the end the stratagem had the opposite effect of the one intended. The Dutch, now deeply suspicious of the English, redoubled their efforts to set up schools of their own to preserve their religion and culture and clung more stubbornly than ever to their language. It is impossible to say to what degree this abortive scheme kept the use of the dialect alive in Pennsylvania; certainly more than a little.

There were various other experiments in education among the Pennsylvania Dutch during the eighteenth century. There was even a nursery school in Germantown, begun by Christian Leman. There were night schools in Philadelphia—one run by Godfreyd Richter, and another by Lazarus Pine, to teach English to the Palatines. One of the best of the secondary schools was the German Seminary of Philadelphia under the direction of Johann Christian Lips of the University of Halle and Johann Christopher Kunze of the University of Leipzig. With the purpose of preparing Pennsylvania Dutch boys for college, instruction in this school was offered in history, geography, letter writing and oratory in German, nature study, mathematics, commerce, colonial industry, Latin, and elementary Greek.

For a time in the late eighteenth century the University of Pennsylvania tried teaching German-speaking students in German instead of English. In the preparatory classes in 1785 the German division was twice as large as the English. When the university returned to all-English instruction, the new German school in Lancaster (later Franklin and Marshall) took up the idea.

By far the most interesting of all the early Pennsylvania Dutch schoolmasters was the gentle Mennonite, Christopher Dock, whose long career as a teacher covered the years from 1714 to 1778. One of the mildest and most pious of men, Dock spared the rod yet did not spoil the child. He substituted sympathy and understanding for the caning so commonly practiced in his day. Instead of beating a child for being naughty, he tried to discover the reason behind the deed. He dealt with quarreling, swearing, lying, and stealing by making the culprit feel the social disapproval of his fellows. Sloth and disobedience were dealt with in the same fashion.

"If anyone comes up again and fails as many as three times," he wrote, "it is shown with a word to the scholars that he has failed three times, and all shout out at him 'Lazy' and then his name is written down. Now whether a child naturally fears the rod or does not fear it, this I know from experience that this shaming cry of the children gives them more pain and drives them more to study than if I should hold the rod before them and use it all the time."

He believed, too, in rewarding a child for good work. "When it gets this far [the mastery of the ABC's] its father must give it a penny and its mother must cook for it two eggs, because of its industry; and a similar reward is due to it when it goes further into words, and so forth. But when it begins to read I owe it a token, if it has learned industriously and in the time fixed, and on the next day when this child comes to school it receives a ticket, on which is written the line 'industrious'—one penny."

At times the reward took the form of a card on which Dock had painted a bird or a flower. Some of these cards were so highly prized that they have been preserved to this day. Despite the air of quaintness that clings to Dock's school at Skippack it was extraordinarily advanced in its educational techniques. He instituted an exchange of letters between pupils of different schools. And he introduced the blackboard into the American schoolroom. There never was a more conscientious schoolmaster: every night he prayed that whatever injustice or neglect had been his might be forgiven him, and that he might do his best for each and all on the morrow. Many of his practices are set forth in *A Hundred Necessary Rules of Conduct for Children*. Dock's place in American pedagogy is sure: his *Schulordnung*, completed August 8, 1750, is the first treatise in America on education.

During the early nineteenth century the Pennsylvania Dutch clung to their parochial schools. In 1834 the Reformed Church had about one hundred and sixty schools in Pennsylvania and the Lutherans about two hundred and fifty. Along with the Quakers, the Lutheran and Reformed churches opposed the establishment of state schools. These church groups had few poor among their members. Practically all their people were able to pay for the schooling of their children; and all desired their education to be under the supervision of the church. The Quaker part in this quarrel has been largely forgotten, possibly because the Quakers are so quiet; but the hot words the Dutch spoke are still remembered. Actually, some Quakers and Dutchmen favored the establishment of schools by the state. As a matter of fact, it was under one Dutch governor, Wolf, that the public school system in Pennsylvania was inaugurated and under another, Ritner, that it became firmly established. After the passage of the public school law in 1834 parochial schools were gradually given up—far more rapidly among the Dutch than among the Quakers. Yet the Dutch opposition to state schools was so strong that the change had to be gradual. By 1870 the last of the Dutch parochial schools had been closed; but for a long time the instruction in many of the state schools had to be in Dutch because the children knew no English. By 1890 practically all the schools had changed to English, although it was not until 1911 that instruction in English was made compulsory.

Today as yesterday most of the Mennonites and all the Amish oppose higher education for their children. "Die Weisheit dieser Weld ist ein Greil vor Gott," declare the Amish. "The wisdom of the world is foolishness before God." It is the Amish desire to keep their young people on the farm that leads them to oppose all education beyond the three R's. And it may be that the Mennonites and Amish are right, at least in part; for those who have been most successful in resisting higher education have likewise been most successful in keeping their farms. Doesn't this fact lay the schools open to suspicion? May there not be a serious defect in a system that makes young Americans unfit for a life on the farm? Much of the schooling of the nineteenth century was, possibly subconsciously, part of a campaign to get people off the farm. The city dweller with his smug belief that the simple fact of living in the city made him superior to the farmer was a product of nineteenth century education. This mentality led him to refer to farmers as "hicks" and to the country as "the sticks." Bankers, lawyers, and above all businessmen were idolized; it was money that counted. Sensible men looked down on the farmer, who seldom had an opportunity to make a big fortune. It was no more a disgrace to be born on a farm than it was to be born in a log cabin; the disgrace was in staying there. This was the lesson taught in the schools between the lines of the textbooks.

Second in importance to the schools in educating the Dutch were the newspapers. Franklin's *Philadelphische Zeitung,* published in 1732, was the first foreign language newspaper in America. Probably it was the failure of the Pennsylvania Dutch to support this paper that led Franklin to call them stupid. Far more influential was *Der Wöchentliche Philadelphische Staatsbode,* established by Henry Miller in 1762. Within two years this paper was circulating as far as the Mohawk settlements and Nova Scotia in the north and Georgia and the West Indies in the south. Its enthusiasm for the patriot cause helped to make the Pennsylvania Dutch the fervent rebels they were. Two other powerful newspapers were the Reading *Adler,* "the Democratic Bible of Berks," and the Lancaster *Volksfreund,* "the Whig Bible of Lancaster," which attained their maximum influence about the middle of the next century. There were many other newspapers, both English and German, in the Dutch country. Contrasted to the comparatively few newspapers of today, their number seems fantastic. *The Plough Boy, The Magician, The Log Cabin Rifle, The Yeoman, The Watchman, The Signal, The Argus, The Commonwealth, The Penny Advocate,* and *The Champion,* all were published in Harrisburg in the six years between 1838 and 1844.

In 1835 Charles Joseph Latrobe noted that the Pennsylvanians read the Bible, the almanac, and one newspaper. Some of them, however, read books as well, though books were not as effective in educating the mass of the people as schools and even newspapers. Yet Bethlehem had a bookstore in the Crown Inn by November, 1745, when it was only four years old; and the Pennsylvania Dutch presses were among the busiest and best of colonial America, especially Christopher Sauer's at Germantown and the one in the Cloisters at Ephrata. At one time before the Revolution thirty presses in Pennsylvania were printing books in German, more than were turning out books in English. Prior to the Revolution the Pennsylvania Dutch presses printed more books than all the presses of New York and New England combined. Books from these early presses still turn up at country auctions in upstate Pennsylvania. Furthermore, Franklin printed more books in German for the Dutch trade than in English for Philadelphia and the home counties. The books from Franklin's press, however, failed to sell as well as those from Sauer's, possibly because Roman type was used instead of German.

Sauer's great achievement was the printing of the Bible in 1743. Except for a Bible in Latin printed in Mexico in 1620 and John Eliot's translation into the Indian tongue, Sauer's German Bible in 1,272 quarto pages was the first in the western hemisphere, preceding the Bible in English by thirty-nine years. Oddly enough, the Pennsylvania Dutch printed the Bible, Old Testament and New, three times and the New Testament seven more times before the first English Bible was printed by Robert Aiken in Philadelphia in 1782.

The great monument of colonial printing in Pennsylvania—and, indeed, in all the colonies—was the extraordinary story of the persecution of the Mennonites, *The Martyr Book,* 1,514 pages in length. This was printed by the Ephrata press in 1748.

Most of the books printed by the Dutch presses found their way into private hands. There were almost no libraries in pre-Revolutionary days, and there are few today. Only the cities had libraries. Even today a public library in a Dutch town is rare. There may be a small lending library in the local drugstore, a small, old-fashioned library in the Sunday school, and a few shelves of books in the high school: that is all. Compared with the average small town in New England, the provision is woefully inadequate. Therefore it comes as a surprise to discover that eighteenth century Lancaster had one of the best subscription libraries in the colonies. Founded in 1759, this was the oldest Pennsylvania Dutch library except the one founded in Germantown in 1745. Its full name was "The Juliana Library Company in Lancaster"—bestowed in honor of Juliana Penn, daughter of the Earl of Pomfret and wife of William Penn, Jr. On its shelves were books representative of the best thought and literature of the time. Locke's *Essay Concerning Human Understanding* and his two treatises on government were there; so were *Tom Jones* and *Sir Charles Grandison*, Milton's *Paradise Lost* and *Paradise Regained,* Pope's translations of the *Iliad* and the *Odyssey,* Theobald's edition of Shakespeare, and Dr. Johnson's dictionary. *Campanalogia Improved, or, The Art of Ringing Made Easy* and *Select Trials at the Sessions House, in the Old Bailey* were there, too, as were the *Tatler* and the *Spectator,* the works of Swift, Gay's *Fables,* and Young's *Night Thoughts.* There also were Hooker's *Laws of Ecclesiastical Polity,* Newton's *Optics,* and Anson's *Voyage Round the World,* and even Glanvill's *Sadducismus Triumphatus, or, A full and plain Evidence concerning Witches and Apparitions.* Urquhart's translation of Rabelais and Voltaire's *Candide* were balanced by Barclay's *Apology* and Longinus *On the Sublime.* The inquiring, catholic mind of the eighteenth century gentleman is well represented by this library. Nor was it the only library in the Dutch towns in the days before the Revolution. Reading had a subscription library as early as 1763, not as notable as the Juliana Library or the one at Germantown but still a library of sorts.

In this century the Washington County Free Library at Hagerstown, Maryland, has been one of the most progressive libraries in the country. In an effort to make books accessible to people in the rural areas, it placed them in country stores, schools, and here and there in the homes of public-spirited citizens—wherever country people could get to them. A few years later a two-horse wagon with open shelves traveled to even the most remote outposts of the county. Today the library has several branches in small towns as well as several trucks on the road. Its example has been widely copied in America. Probably the best known and one of the most rewarding of its experiences was the request of a country boy who had dug into a play of Shakespeare's. "Give me another by that same man," he asked. "I think he's a right good writer."

Powwowing, Hexerei, and Other
Pennsylvania Knowledge

The Pennsylvania Dutch are among the most superstitious people
in America, yet they are not so superstitious as they are reputed to
be. So many of their superstitions are so picturesque that they have
been distorted and puffed up. Few Pennsylvania Dutchmen are more
than superstitious enough to add a touch of color to their lives. A
hundred or a hundred and fifty years ago, with the dying down of the
religious enthusiasm of the seventeenth and eighteenth centuries, superstition was intense; but during the past hundred years this superstition
has been gradually but surely reduced by education. Among an infinitesimal number of the most ignorant of the Pennsylvania Dutch a
belief in witchcraft lingers on. The trial in York County earlier in this
century in which the poor deluded murderer honestly believed he had
been bewitched took us hurtling back through the centuries to the days
of James I, Sir Thomas Browne, and Cotton Mather. It is odd that
such beliefs should persist in Pennsylvania, for Pennsylvania was never

so excited about witchcraft as New England. Witches were never hanged in Pennsylvania. I can account for the longevity of the belief in witchcraft only by the far commoner acceptance of powwowing. Powwowing is a minor form of sorcery that attempts to cure disease or repel evil through magic. Like the Roman Catholic Church it makes use of amulets; like Christian Science it heals through faith. It is, in fact, a kind of white magic that stems straight from the Middle Ages. When spells are used for evil ends, which occurs but rarely, it becomes black magic and savors of witchcraft.

Most of powwowing today is based on John George Hohman's *Lang Verborgne Freund* (Long Lost Friend), which was published in Reading in 1820. This is a collection of spells for all possible occasions, many of which can be traced back to Albertus Magnus, who died in Cologne in 1280, while some are even more ancient. The number of editions of Hohman's book shows that it was a favorite with powwow doctors. Only less popular were the last four books of Moses, especially the 6th and 7th. Powwow doctors regarded Moses less as a Hebrew prophet than as a magician.

Many charms employed by the powwow doctors are fantastic and even verge on the quaint. This is a spell to stop a hemorrhage:

"This is the day the wound was made. O blood! thou shalt stop and be still until the Virgin Mary bears another son."

This is one for snake bites:

"God has created all things and they are good. Thou only, serpent, art damned. Cursed be thou and thy sting. Zing, zing, zing."

And this a charm to turn away the wrath of a cross dog:

"Dog, hold thy nose to the ground. God made me and thee, hound."

Sometimes the powwow doctor gave the patient an amulet in the form of a small muslin bag with an inscription in German on a piece of paper inside. The writing was often inverted—to be read only in a mirror; or sometimes only every other line was written backwards. Such an amulet was believed to be most potent when it was prepared at midnight on St. John's Eve or Christmas Eve. The amulet was either attached to a string and worn around the neck or pinned to the underclothes. Printed on the bag in red ink were the letters INRI, the well known abbreviation of Iesus Nazarenus, Rex Iudaeorum (Jesus of Nazareth, King of the Jews); below them was a row of four Latin crosses; below the crosses was printed the Christian name of the patient, and below that the surname. The charm inside the bag varied with the disease to be cured or the evil to be guarded against. A charm against evil spirits had an intensity and poetry lacking in many of the others:

Jesus of Nazareth, King of the Jews: the triumphant name of Jesus be between me [name of the patient], and all my enemies, visible or invisible, that they may neither approach nor harm my body or soul: Amen. Thou mysterious evil spirit, thou hast attacked this man [or woman, or child], and it shall now go away from him [or her], thus to be paid back to thee again. By the five wounds of Jesus I order thee to permit him [or her] to get well again at this hour. In the name of God the Father, God the Son, and God the Holy Ghost: Amen. In the name of God the Holy Trinity, I forbid thee my house and garden, my flesh and my blood, my body and my soul. I forbid thee every nail hole in my house until thou climb every little tree, until thou wade through every little creek, until thou count every tiny star in the sky, until the beautiful day bring forth her seasons. In the name of God the Father, God the Son, and God the Holy Ghost: Amen.

The names of Christ and the Trinity were used in many of the charms since they were believed to be particularly efficacious in warding off evil. Sometimes the charm was simpler but more mysterious, as in this one for malaria and other sicknesses:

```
A  b  a  x  a  C  a  t  a  b  a  x
A  b  a  x  a  C  a  t  a  b  a  x
A  b  a  x  a  C  a  t  a  b  a
A  b  a  x  a  C  a  t  a  b   .
A  b  a  x  a  C  a  t  a
A  b  a  x  a  C  a  t
A  b  a  x  a  C  a
A  b  a  x  a  C
A  b  a  x  a
A  b  a  x
A  b  a
A  b
A
```

A particularly interesting charm is the palindrome below, apparently an ancient one since the British Archaeological Association in excavations made near Cirencester in 1868 found it carved on an old wall:

```
S   A   T   O   R
A   R   E   P   O
T   E   N   E   T
O   P   E   R   A
R   O   T   A   S
```

It has been suggested that it is a rearrangement of the word *pater-noster* with the addition of the Greek alpha and omega, the N at the center doing double duty, as in the charm below:

```
                            A
                            ‾
                            P
                            A
                            T
                            E
                            R
    A | P A T E R N O S T E R | O
                            O
                            S
                            T
                            E
                            R
                            ‾
                            O
```

Incantations and amulets by no means exhausted the resources of the powwow doctor. In cases of erysipelas, called wildfire by the country people, three strands of red silk or wool were wound around the body of the patient, or three shovelfuls of live coals were carried three times around him. Each disease had its own treatment—rheumatism, goiter, warts, marasmus, consumption, and all the others. Powwowing was also used to stop bleeding and to ease the pain of burns, sprains, cuts, and bruises. Powwow doctors, like physicians today, specialized. One man was known far and wide for his success with goiters, another for his luck with marasmus.

To effect a cure the powwow doctor always insisted on the good faith of the patient. "If you don't believe, I can do nothing," he would tell the patient at the start. Powwowing was not an art to be joked about or to be examined too inquisitively. Always behind it was the shadow of the supernatural. No fee might be charged by the doctor; yet it was commonly believed that the charm would not work unless the doctor was adequately paid, and several powwow doctors accumulated sizable fortunes. Powwowing could be taught only "crossways," as the country people put it; that is to say, a man could impart the secrets only to a woman, and a woman only to a man—another indication of the supernatural. At least a part of powwowing is a remnant of the ancient medical lore that was so closely identified with magic as to be almost inseparable from it. The old practice of the kings of England touching for scrofula is possibly the best known example of this mixture of medicine and magic.

There is no doubt that powwowing effected many cures. Where mind could cure matter, powwowing was often useful. Where the illness lay beyond the reach of faith, however, the result was often tragic. A good deal of the belief in powwowing was based on the human instinct of self-preservation, on the belief of the sick that somewhere there existed a cure for his illness. The sick man turned to the powwow doctor as a drowning man clutches at a straw, very often after the regular doctor had failed to cure him. Sometimes he resorted to powwow doctor and medical doctor simultaneously, although he would do his best to keep the regular physician in ignorance of this.

In George Washington's account book is the following entry under the date October 18, 1797: "Gave my servant, Christopher, to bear the expenses to a person at Lebanon in Pennsylvania celebrated for curing persons bit by wild animals—$25.00." This may have been a powwow doctor, but it is more likely that it was William Story, an herb doctor famed for his cures with "Rage Herb," or scarlet pimpernel.

Many of the powwow doctors were skilled in herbs and simples. They, and many a good housewife, grew herbs in their gardens, such as wormwood, rosemary, rue, sage, thyme, blue mint, woolly mint, horehound, feverfew, southernwood, and lemon balm. The herb doctors gathered herbs from the woods and fields as well. Boneset, tansy, celandine, camomile, herb-all, elder flower, mullein, yarrow, pennyroyal, beebalm, mandrake, shinleaf, rattlesnake weed, ginseng, sweet flag, slippery elm, witch hazel, wild cherry bark, and sassafras root were all prized for their healing powers. Hanging from the rafters in many a farmhouse attic were half a dozen or more bunches of these herbs from garden, woods, and field. Tea made from the bark, roots, flowers, and ripe berries of the dogwood was used as a tonic for fever and ague, an early substitute for quinine. Bitters made from buds of balm of Gilead steeped in whisky were thought excellent for pain in belly or bowels. Strong sage tea provided a gargle for sore throats. Tea from the bark of wild cherry lowered the pulse and helped to quiet the nerves. This was a lore handed down for generations in Europe or sometimes borrowed from the Indians.

During much of the nineteenth century powwowing was common in the Pennsylvania Dutch country. It was not so common that regular physicians had to give up their practice, but neither did a man have to seek far for a powwow doctor. It was even carried by the Pennsylvania Dutch to North Carolina, where it was known as "using." So common was powwowing in Pennsylvania that when a little child skinned a knee the mother, or more likely the grandmother, would say as she dried the child's tears: "Come, I'll powwow for it, and that will take away the hurt." Then uttering a bit of gibberish in imitation of the powwow doctor's spell, she would kiss the child and send him back to his play. Sometimes the child tried his hand at spells. The quaintest of all powwowing took place when a child lost one of his baby teeth. Carefully placing the tooth in a mouse hole, the child addressed the mouse in these words:

> Meisel, Meisel, do is en Zah;
> Geb mir nau en neuer drah.

> (Mousie, mousie, here is a tooth;
> Now give me a new one there.)

Powwowing was even practiced in a debased form by housewives to turn balky cider into vinegar. Putting their lips to the bunghole of the vinegar keg, they shouted the names of the three sourest and most evil-tempered women in the neighborhood: this is still said to be a sure recipe to turn the mildest cider into vinegar.

Powwowing could also be used to get back anything that had been stolen. Let a man who had had chickens stolen take three splinters from the doorsill over which the thief had passed and fasten them in the hub of a wagon wheel, and then, placing his lips to the hub, say: "I pray thee, Holy Trinity, to constrain the thief who has stolen my chickens to be stung by remorse and return them to me." After that he had only to put the wheel on the wagon and when the wheel had made three revolutions the thief would come running with the chickens.

It was not always necessary to resort to powwowing to effect a cure. Turning a somersault upon first hearing the whippoorwill in the spring was a way to be free from backache. A "liver-grown" child was persuaded to crawl through a horse collar. And in many a Dutch village a woman who did not change her name in marriage—for example, an Allebach who married an Allebach—was asked to give a child with whooping cough a piece of bread or cake of her own baking. There was a choice of ways of getting rid of a toothache—to pick the tooth with a splinter from the east side of a tree struck by lightning or with a nail from a coffin or with a needle used in sewing a shroud or with the nail of the middle toe of an owl. Most revolting of all was the remedy for reducing a goiter—to rub it with the hand of a corpse.

A few of the old medical beliefs have been slow in dying out. Bloodletting still exists in the form of cupping. Tea made from sassafras root is used to thin the blood. Dandelion salad in early spring is a most delicious substitute for sulphur and molasses. Goose fat is rubbed on the chest to break up a cold. These are a far cry from powwowing or magic of any sort. Compare them with the directions for casting a bullet certain to hit your enemy, no matter where he may be: go to a lonely crossroad between eleven and twelve on Christmas night and, in utter silence, cast a bullet, using bones from a grave, a nail from a coffin, and human hair. This is pure hexerei—black magic or witchcraft.

Though belief in witchcraft is extremely rare in the Dutch country today, it still exists. When I was a boy early in this century the grandmother of some of my playmates told us tales of witchcraft. They were old wives' tales, to be sure; yet the fact that they began not "Once upon a time," but "This happened to me," doubled their mystery and horror. There is no doubt in my mind that the teller believed every word of them; and though at home I was assured that there were no witches, I was not altogether certain. Was there not an old woman a short way out of town on the Cowpath who was known as the Witch of the Cowpath? I can't recall anything she ever did to deserve the name of witch, but the children of the neighborhood let her strictly alone. Here and there in pockets of darkness the very simplest of the country people, upon finding a horse enfeebled and sick and its mane tangled, might declare that a witch had been riding it; or, if a cow went dry, a witch was robbing it by milking the corner of the towel in her kitchen. If a baby had fits, if a hunter had no luck, a witch was to blame: so said the simple-minded and benighted. Children were taught never to accept anything whatsoever from a woman who was suspected of being a witch, lest they be put in her power. As it was well known that witches hated water, dogs often were given the name *Wasser*. It is evident that these people thought a witch easy to deceive. Again, let me repeat that the belief in witches was never common. The great majority had nothing but scorn for such foolish notions; yet here and there, often in remote spots, a few simple or ignorant people persisted—and to this day persist—in believing in witches.

Relics of a belief in witchcraft are found in children's games. In the Dutch country children almost always try to "hex" one another in marbles or hopscotch. A St. Andrew's cross is drawn on the ground while the words, "Hex, hex," are uttered. If a child is really up on his magic spells, this longer incantation may be used, though such a charm probably will be saved until his opponent produces his prize aggie:

> Hexefuss,
> Hexefuss,
> Grottefuss,
> Grottefuss,
> Long sam naus,
> Long sam naus,
> Nix kum raus.

Children never take such spells seriously. They are part of the game; if anything, compliments to the player's skill.

A very few people accepted magic so fully as to mark their tools with the toad foot, swastika, or some other form of the cross—all hex marks to prevent the tools from being stolen.

Far better known are the decorations that brighten so many barns in Berks and Lehigh and other near-by counties. These have often been mistaken for "hex signs" to ward off evil; on the contrary, their purpose is a decorative one and for a long time has been only that. In the words of an Oley Valley farmer, they are "for fancy." A barn without them looks too plain, too naked. Pennsylvania Dutch farmers are proud of their barns and show their pride by adorning them with decorations. Centuries ago, long before these symbols were painted on Pennsylvania barns, they may have had some religious significance. August

Mahr traces the star or lily pattern back to Crete, where it symbolized the sun as early as 1300 B.C., and to Mycenae, where it existed about 1550 B.C. Much later it was regarded as a symbol of fertility in horses and cattle and was carved on barn doors or used on harness ornaments in central Europe. The six-petaled flower that appears so frequently in barn signs Mahr takes as a pre-Christian symbol of immortality; while the spinning whorl, quite a usual decoration on Lehigh County barns, was used not only in Crete but in ancient Troy. At one time the sort of symbols later painted on barns may have been intended to ensure fertility in the stock, to guard against lightning, and to keep out witches; but I have never come across a farmer who believes that barn symbols are anything but decoration. He thinks they look nice, and that is all. Whatever they may have been centuries ago, today they are only one more instance of the Pennsylvania Dutchman's love of the gaudy. Oddly enough, these signs were never painted on barns in Europe; that use was a Pennsylvania inspiration. Very similar decorations, however, appear on houses in the canton of Bern in Switzerland.

Another curious feature of some Pennsylvania Dutch barns in Dauphin County is carved gable posts. According to August Mahr, the posts are a remnant of the worship of Thor and at one time were intended to protect the barns against lightning and promote fertility in the stock.

Tales of the supernatural are common among Pennsylvania Dutch children, especially on a winter evening when the wind roars round the house. Many are the sort known the world over—of mysterious footsteps in the garret, clanking chains on the staircase at midnight, clocks striking thirteen, strange lights and headless horsemen. Often there are tales of haunted houses; but I have never known of such tales being taken seriously enough to prevent the renting or sale of a house.

Rarer than the spook stories are those of dragons living in one or another limestone cave in the Dutch country. Most of these are vaguely remembered versions of ancient legends of the Rhineland. Another such story is that of the *Ewige Jaeger,* the eternal hunter who, with his wild phantom pack baying at his heels, rides through the night down into the valleys and up into the hills. Possibly it was a variation of this tale that was told only a decade or two ago by an old man from Oley Furnace. One night in the narrow gap above Oley Furnace he saw a herd of horses leap magnificently through the air from the top of the cliff guarding the gap to the hill on the opposite side, their hoofs striking fire on the rocks.

One of the most moving legends is of the drummer boy at Valley Forge who wandered away from his regiment in one of the worst snowstorms of that bitter winter and was frozen to death. On winter nights when a blizzard sweeps across the fields and hills of Valley Forge a lone traveler, if his ear is keen enough, may hear the muffled drumming in the snow of that boy lost so long ago.

Other tales are of an early immigrant from the Rhineland never entered on the ships' lists, a rascal by the name of Tyl Eulenspiegel. In Pennsylvania his name became corrupted like so many other German names. Eulenspiegel, after all, is not too easy a name to spell, so it became Eileschpijjel or at times Eileschpickel. No matter how the name is spelled—and the change in spelling is evidence that the man became an American—Eulenspiegel or Eileschpijjel, call him what you will, is a good Pennsylvania Dutchman. Although the rogue's pranks were played a good many years ago, they still live on on the lips of men. Sitting on the bench at the back of the country store or lined up along the porch of the Black Horse Tavern, men talk about the tricks Eileschpijjel played on the devil. A large number of these tales have been collected by Thomas Brendle and William Troxell.

Once the devil was boasting to Eileschpijjel how far he could swim. "You come down to the Susquehanna tomorrow and I'll show you," said the devil, for in those days he lived—at least part of the year—in Pennsylvania. He was good at talking Dutch too. The next morning the devil was down by the river bright and early, and after a time Eileschpijjel showed up, dragging a calf by a rope.

"What do you want with that calf?" asked the devil. "I thought we were going swimming."

"We are," replied Eileschpijjel; "but first we'll butcher this calf. I can't swim for fourteen days without eating first."

At that the devil turned on his heels without even wetting a foot in the Susquehanna.

Another time the devil and Eileschpijjel were bragging about how much heat they could stand.

"We'll settle this right now," said the devil. "We'll build a fire under a bake oven, and we'll both crawl in. Then we'll see who can stand the most heat." So they built a roaring fire under a bake oven with some nice dry oak, and they both crawled into the oven. After a minute or two Eileschpijjel had had all he could take. He started to inch toward the door.

"Hey, where are you going?" asked the devil.

"Just outside to put some more wood on the fire," answered Eileschpijjel. "I think it's kind of chilly in here."

"Heilich Dunnerwetter; let me out of here!" yelled the devil, diving for the door. "I'm burned to a crisp!"

Still another time, away back during the French and Indian War, Eileschpijjel had a fine new Pennsylvania rifle he had just bought from a gunsmith over Lancaster County way.

"What's that?" asked the devil, seeing it.

"That? Oh, that's my smoke-pipe," answered Eileschpijjel. "Want to try it?"

No sooner had the devil put the end of the barrel into his mouth than Eileschpijjel pulled the trigger. Off went the rifle, and the devil's mouth was full of smoke. He coughed and coughed, and finally he spat out the bullet.

"Pretty strong tobacco you smoke," he said.

Not all the Eileschpijjel tales have to do with the devil. One is about the time Eileschpijjel hired out to a farmer. The farmer sent him to a field on a hill to pick peas.

"Here, put them in this bag," said the farmer. "And you might as well hull them up there while you're about it. We want a good many for dinner."

Eileschpijjel picked the peas and hulled them and put them into the bag just as the farmer had told him to do; but the bag had a tiny hole in it, and as he was walking down the hill a pea fell out and began to roll down the road.

"Well, if that's the way you want it that's the way you shall have it," said Eileschpijjel, and he dumped all the peas out of the bag into the road.

"Where are the peas?" asked the farmer when Eileschpijjel got back to the house.

"Oh, they're coming after. A little slowly, but they're coming."

One of the more curious examples of magic is the *Himmelsbrief,* or letter from heaven, said to have been written by Christ or the Archangel Michael. It is supposed to have been found originally in a surprising number of places—Magdeburg, Mecklenburg, Cologne, Holstein and Neuruppin, among others. Those of Magdeburg and Mecklenburg were printed as early as 1725. All are essentially the same. The reader is warned to believe the letter. "Whoever disregards it will be forsaken by the Lord," threatens the Magdeburg version. "Who does not believe this may copy it and tie it to the neck of a dog and shoot at him; he will see this is true," proclaims the Holstein letter. There are warnings to sinful man to repent, to keep the Sabbath holy, to honor his father and mother, to avoid blasphemy, not to bear false witness; and in the St. Germain version is the further proscription, "Ye shall not curl your hair nor practice the vanities of the world." All versions promise divine protection to the bearer. "Whosoever has this letter shall not be taken prisoner nor wounded by the enemy," declares the Holstein letter. He cannot be hurt by gun, pistol, sword, or musket. Among them they promise protection from lightning, fire, and flood, while the St. Germain letter goes so far as to assert that a married woman who carries the letter with her shall bear happy and handsome children. The letters are still circulated and still taken seriously by a few of the more credulous Pennsylvania Dutch. Even in the last war an occasional youth tucked a himmelsbrief in his pocket as he left home to face the dangers of the battlefield. "It can't do any harm," he may have reasoned, "and anyway a little piece of paper doesn't take up much room." However, it is as much of a curiosity to the average Pennsylvania Dutchman as it is to a Texan, say, or a man from Maine.

A book that was believed to protect its owner against fire and flood was the *Paradies Gärtlein* (Garden of Paradise). This was one of the books, along with Luther's catechism and the Heidelberg catechism, that were burnt at Tulpehocken by Conrad Weiser and John Peter Miller in an orgy of abjuration when they left the Reformed Church to join the Order of the Solitary at Ephrata. Tradition has it that when the flames died down the copy of *Paradies Gärtlein* was found with its edges charred but the print untouched. This incident greatly strengthened people's belief in the book's magic power.

Almanacs have long been important in the lives of Dutch farmers. The first to be published in German was *Der Teutsche Pilgrim*, printed by Andrew Bradford in the 1730's. Far more popular was the *Hoch-Deutsch Americanische Calender*, published by Christopher Sauer in 1738 and for forty years more, after which it was taken over by other firms. Almanacs have been published at one time or another in most of the Pennsylvania Dutch cities. One of the most famous is the *Hagerstown Town and Country Almanac,* first printed by John Gruber in 1797. It is still flourishing and is sold in country grocery stores all through the Dutch section of Maryland and the Shenandoah Valley. One Maryland governor, William T. Hamilton, even consulted it to make sure of good weather before he set the date for a hanging. In Pennsylvania it is generally replaced by Baer's almanac, published in Lancaster. These are the favorite Pennsylvania Dutch almanacs of today.

The almanacs contained a good deal of folklore about the weather. Signs of a hard winter were innumerable: long, shaggy hair on horses and cattle; a bountiful crop of nuts; a large store of honey; a heavy crop of hay. The belief that God would provide was the basis for most of these predictions. The early departure of the birds foretold an early winter, as did the early molting of chickens. A caterpillar in November was a sign of a mild winter. The number of snows for the winter was indicated by the number of days between the first snowfall and Christmas; the depth of the snow, by the length of the icicles on the kitchen ell between Christmas and New Year. If the geese waddled in the mud between Christmas and New Year they would do so every month in the year. If the cat sunned itself in February, it would hug the stove in March. Of St. Matthias's Day it was said, "When he [Matthias] finds ice, he breaks it; when he finds none, he makes it." Another bit of weather lore was summed up in the saying, "Before Easter winter is not to be trusted." Wild geese, too, foretold the weather: if they flew high, it would be warm; if they flew low, cold. Good Friday always brought rain, a symbol of tears for Christ's death. Ascension Day was always fine: on that day Christ kissed the clouds that received Him. The most widely current of Dutch weather lore is that about July 2, the day on which "Mary goes over the mountain." If it is fair on that day, there will be no rain until she comes back, on August 15. If it rains on the day Mary goes over the mountain, there will be a great deal of rain until she comes back. This is a superstition the Dutch newspapers play up much as they exploit the folklore about Ground-Hog Day and St. Swithin's Day. The coming of rain is foretold in many ways. When the old women air their nightcaps—that is, when there are cobwebs on the grass—then you may expect rain. When all the food on the table is eaten you may look for dry weather.

Morning rain, of course, is short, or in the words of the proverb, "Morning showers and old women's dancing do not last long."

Naturally there are many superstitions about the proper time to plant. The right time to plant corn is when the oak leaves are as large as squirrels' ears—a lesson learned from the Indians and good common sense. Flowers should be planted in the sign of the Posy Woman (Virgo). Grain should be planted in the waxing of the moon and, if possible, in the sign of the Twins for a more abundant yield. All root crops—onions, potatoes, beets, carrots, turnips—should be planted when the horns of the moon point down. Fence posts, too, should be put in only when the horns of the moon point down to have them stay in the ground, and shingles laid on roofs to keep them from curling. The early Moravians at Bethlehem ordered the spring to be cleaned in the light of the moon as this was declared to be the best time by men who possessed "Pennsylvania knowledge." I like this phrase, "Pennsylvania knowledge," to describe the early folklore of the colony. Without it a man is very likely to go wrong. How else would he know that Gallusday, the 16th of October, is the proper day to pick apples? Or how would he know that iron—say, an old horseshoe—must be hung on fruit trees so that they, like man, may have a burden to bear? Otherwise they will produce no fruit.

As Fogel's painstaking collection of Pennsylvania Dutch proverbs and superstitions so richly shows, the Pennsylvania Dutch have a vast store of folk sayings. One of my favorites is, "A fat wife and a fat barn don't hurt any man." Almost as good is, "A girl should not think of marriage until she can make a man's shirt and roll out a round pie-crust." Good, too, are, "The first wife through love, the second a gift from God, and the third from the devil," and the advice to take a young wife: "A cradle may be in the way, but an old woman more so."

Pennsylvania Dutch lullabies are still sung to Pennsylvania Dutch babies. Most of them are of a very simple sort, like the following:

> Hei-yo, bubli, schlof.
> Der dawdy hüt die schof;
> Die mammi hüt die rote küh,
> Un kommt net heem bis morge frieh.
>
> (Hei-yo, little boy, sleep.
> Daddy tends the sheep;

> Mommy tends the red cows,
> And won't come home till morning early.)

All of which makes no more sense than many a Mother Goose rhyme.

A child's prayer of the guardian angels is not unlike the English one of the four angels, even though the Pennsylvania Dutch version increases the number to fourteen:

> Oweds wann ich schlofe geh
> Vierzeh engel mit mir geh:
> Zwee zu kopp,
> Zwee zu fuss,
> Zwee zu links,
> Zwee zu recht;
> Zwee die mich decke,
> Zwee die mich wecke;
> Zwee die mich weise
> In das himmlische paradies. Amen.

> (In the evening when to sleep I go,
> Fourteen angels with me go:
> Two at the head,
> Two at the foot,
> Two at the left,
> Two at the right;
> Two to cover me,
> Two to wake me;
> Two to guide me
> Into the heavenly paradise. Amen.)

Pennsylvania Dutch folklore is at its worst in riddles. These have a smart-alecky twist that sinks them to a lower level than most bad puns. Here are three of the worst ones:

What kind of stones are found in water? Wet stones.

On which side does a dog have most hair? The outside.

Why do farmers build pigsties between the house and the barn? For the pigs.

Somewhat better is this one:

What uses the largest handkerchief in the world? A hen. It wipes its nose anywhere on earth.

And in this there is a touch of poetry:

What is as white as snow, as green as grass, as red as blood, and as black as a hat? A black cherry.

Upcountry Dutch

To Philadelphia the Pennsylvania Dutch are the "country" Dutch or sometimes the "upcountry" Dutch—seldom "upstate," which is a favorite word with New Yorkers for their hinterland. "Upcountry" is well chosen; it has direction and flavor. Furthermore, it captures the essential truth about the Pennsylvania Dutch, for Pennsylvania Dutch life has had from the very start a country quality. Before the Revolution few Pennsylvania Dutchmen lived in the cities. Then Germantown, Lancaster, York, and Reading were the largest Dutch towns. Because all four figured so prominently in the early history we are apt to think of them as larger than they were. Yet in 1800 Lancaster, then the largest of the four, had only 4,292 inhabitants. York and Reading were smaller, and Germantown and Bethlehem only little towns. Easton, Allentown, Lebanon, and Harrisburg were country villages, pretty much the same size as Womelsdorf, Ephrata, Kutztown, and Lititz. Although all of the better land and even much of the hill country in southeastern Pennsylvania were occupied by the time of the Revolution, Philadelphia was the only true city in the province. In spite of a rapid growth in population, it was not until the latter half of the nineteenth century that there were more people living in the Dutch cities and towns than in the country. With the growth of the cities and with large-scale immigration this country culture was necessarily modified. Today in many of the counties a great majority of the people live in towns and cities. Yet in all the counties there are still farmers—a great many of them; and the farmers are vigorously Dutch. Even in the cities the life is often rural in spirit rather than urban. As the cities grow and our lives are surrounded by concrete and steel we turn to the country more and more for the repose of the spirit and the restoration of the body. Quite literally we lift up our eyes to the hills—and to the valleys and the mountains. To almost every Pennsylvania Dutchman the country counts for more than the city. And this is not strange: we have been city dwellers for one or two generations only. For centuries our forefathers lived on farms or in small country villages.

Philadelphia's description of the Pennsylvania Dutch includes the word *Dutch* as well as *upcountry;* and that word too is well chosen. Although the Pennsylvania Dutch have been in America two hundred years, more or less, Dutch they remain. The Dutchmen who move down to Philadelphia or who go West may soon lose their Dutch character and become indistinguishable from the rest of America; but those who stay put in the Dutch country remain Dutch. One of the essential differences between the Pennsylvania Dutchman and the average American is that he has roots. He actually likes old ways of doing things. He wants to stay as he is. Back in 1794 Cazenove was astonished when at a Lutheran church near Myerstown he saw the congregation coming out in the costumes of their ancestors—coats of green and light blue, large Westphalian hats, and boots extending above the knees. The good people of Myerstown may no longer dress in an antique fashion; but in so far as the modern world permits they govern their lives much as their forefathers did before them.

Among the Pennsylvania Dutch there was never the break between the first and second generations that there was among the later immigrants. Their culture was not sloughed off in any violent effort to prove themselves Americans. Old habits die hard in all the Dutch country, and memories are long. People still living remember Black Dan, the chimney sweep, perched on a chimney top in the hills of Ruscombmanor, singing his heart out in a spring long past.

In the Dutch country old ways are good ways. A man who walks in the footsteps of his forefathers is heartened by the assurance that he is following a tried and true path. He knows that where he is at one with his fathers he will not easily go wrong. At least subconsciously he is aware of a sense of continuity, of belonging to the past as well as to the present and the future. He will paint the old barn built by his great-grandfather to preserve its timbers; and in his old age he will poke a hole in the red earth with his cane and drop in a hickory nut so that his great-grandchildren may go nutting some frosty morning after he has been in his grave many years.

Though the Dutch country is no museum, and though in recent years much sophistication has been creeping into the country districts, tradition nourishes the lives of its people. Only rarely does it hamper or bind them. In the early part of this century five sisters and a lone brother were living on a fine, fat farm in the Oley Valley. They had been born and bred and had grown old in the big stone farmhouse built by their ancestors in the eighteenth century. Once or twice a year one of them would venture into Reading to do some necessary shopping; but for the most part they stayed at home. They were what the Dutch call "crowd-shy." The front gate was kept locked; anybody who wanted to see them had to stand out in the road and call. Then one of the sisters would go out front. Hiding behind an enormous box bush, she would part the branches and peer through to see who was calling. If it was someone she knew she might unlock the gate; but no "Yankee" ever got inside that house. All the cooking was done over an open fire in the great fireplace in the kitchen; and the baking in the stone bakehouse. On winter nights five spinning wheels were hauled out, and the five sisters spun the flax and wool with which their clothes were made. The rise and fall of the whirring of the wheels filled the room. The brother sat by the hearth and cracked black walnuts or read the Bible. In this way they lived their lives until a year or two before the First World War, when the last one died. Nearly a hundred thousand dollars in gold and silver coins was found hidden away in crocks in the bottom of the woodbox and in other unexpected places. There was no will and there were no sons and daughters to inherit the estate; but many kinsfolk—second cousins, third cousins, and so on, some of them very proud people in Reading or down Philadelphia way—came in for a goodish bit of money. Everything was put up for sale; and the house was filled with the accumulation of the better part of two centuries. It was a big house, too; there were fourteen beds alone.

As far as I know, this case was unique. I have heard of no other Pennsylvania Dutch family that did its cooking over an open hearth and wove the cloth for its own clothes well into this century, though in the little log cabins and stone huts in the coves of the mountain ranges are people living in a past century: a basketmaker or even a gunsmith, an old woman who makes a scanty living picking berries, a father and son who run a still. Though of Pennsylvania Dutch blood they are not unlike the Southern mountaineers. They force you to remember that the Pennsylvania hills and mountains are part of the same ranges that farther south become the Blue Ridge and the Great Smokies.

Ironically enough, the other principal group living in the past prides itself on family and manners. This is a feminine society, usually widows and spinsters, that is to be found in all the older Pennsylvania Dutch cities and in many of the towns as well. In this group of gentlewomen, all of whom have ancestors and some of whom have money, the niceties of Cranford are still preserved. A very few are bluestockings and write novels under pseudonyms; some hold literary meetings and read papers on Shakespeare or Browning; some merely gather for tea and gossip and exchange recipes for sandtarts or wine jelly. About this antiquated society there is the fragrance of lavender even if the old lace is wrapped in tissue paper and packed away in bureau drawers and dower chests. Among the old china and polished mahogany the graces of the past are cherished and preserved. This, too, is a part of Pennsylvania Dutch life.

Family often assumes a particular importance in the Dutch country because very often one family name prevails throughout a neighborhood, though only a few miles away none of that name is to be found. A village may be filled with Rothermels, or a graveyard be lush with Lichtenwalners; yet in the next village there will be no Rothermels, and in the neighboring graveyards nary a Lichtenwalner. Lancaster County is the county of the Herrs; Lebanon, the city of the Lights. Look for Moyers down Souderton way, for de Schweinitzes in Bethlehem. Since their voyage across the Atlantic two or more centuries ago most Pennsylvania Dutchmen have stayed put. With Charles Lamb they can say, "Nature, where she does not mean us for mariners and vagabonds, bids us stay at home."

The Pennsylvania Dutchman seldom has any desire to live anywhere else. He was born in Pennsylvania, and he likes it. Even during the hot summers the Pennsylvania Dutch stay at home. They may visit the Jersey shore for a fortnight; but not even the richest of the rich close their houses for the whole summer and flee to the Adirondacks, the White Mountains, or the Maine coast. They may drive up to Canada or out to California. But why close a perfectly good, comfortable house just because the summers are hot? Most of them are even immune to the Circean spell of New York. Impossible as it may be for New Yorkers to believe, the Pennsylvania Dutch can stay away from New York for years at a stretch and scarcely give the sacrifice a second thought. "When I was at home, I was in a better place." To this sentiment of Touchstone's most Dutchmen will say "Amen!"

This can be carried too far. A lack of interest in the outside world is apt to result in too intense an interest in little things at home. If a man builds an expensive house, one or two of his neighbors may be so curious, so *wunnerfitsich,* as to go to the courthouse to see whether or not there is a mortgage on it. Clearly they would be better off minding their own business—even squandering their money in New York.

Yet many Pennsylvania Dutchmen have left home. All through the nineteenth century they went West to take up lands, though the farms back home were never abandoned as in New England. It was only the younger sons without a patrimony that joined the trek to the West; men provided with farms stayed in Pennsylvania. The family farm was never lightly abandoned. Even today it is not impossible to find a farm that has been handed down from father to son from the time the land was first cleared. Eight or nine generations of a single family will have tilled the same fields. The houses and barns, solidly constructed, were built to last. In many parts of the Dutch country most of the houses and barns are at least a century old, many of them far older. With a deep attachment to his farm the Pennsylvania Dutchman never for a moment considered that he, his sons, or his sons' sons might ever leave the farm. His mind was not stirred by visions of land that lay beyond the horizon. To him the here and now was good. What did it matter that there was black loam in the Ohio country, that the prairies of Iowa stretched on farther than the eye could see, or that the mountains of California were mountains of gold? His own world was made after his heart's desire.

That he did not get about did not trouble him. There is a story about a Berks County farmer that may throw light on this attitude: "I've been about in my time," this farmer boasted. "Yes, sir, I've been places. I've been to New Jerusalem and Dryville and Kutztown. I've been to Kempton and Hamburg. I've been to Myerstown and Ephrata; I've been to Pottstown and to Schwenkville. I even went to Philadelphia one time—on the steamcars—to the Centennial. Yes, sir, I've been around."

In a way he was right. He felt his life was rich, and it may have been at that. For his day he had traveled quite as much as most Berks County farmers. Not all of them got to the Centennial. Before automobiles became common, country people seldom went far from home. When the trolley lines were built out into the country, the farmers and their wives acquired the habit of going into the Dutch cities to do their shopping; but before that day a woman could live her life through at Landis's Store or Plow Church and never once get into Reading. Her clothes she made herself from some yard goods she bought at the country store or from some homespun she or her mother had made.

Beyond a doubt the Pennsylvania Dutch are provincial—maybe no more so than the Philadelphians, the New Yorkers, or the Bostonians; but that is enough. The rest of the world hardly exists for these people. All that matters is what happens within the county. Cut off at first from the rest of America by language, the Pennsylvania Dutch had some doubts about their fellow countrymen. The Quakers they respected as a hardheaded, thrifty people, perhaps too joyless in their lives, yet good, honest people on whose word you could depend. The Scotch-Irish, they thought, had delusions about the high value of education; too many became lawyers. They were an unsteady people with a perpetual itch to move on. Though the Scotch-Irish were not the stuff of which good farmers were made, they respected them for their manliness and independence. As for the New Englanders, the Yankee peddlers had given them a bad name throughout the Dutch country. Before the Civil War the Southerners were known only slightly; they were viewed with distrust as a proud people who owned slaves.

Nor does any other country mean anything to them. There is not the slightest attachment to Germany, and never has been. No Pennsylvania Dutchman ever spoke of Germany as the "mother country." The passionate loyalty of the Irish-Americans to Ireland has no counterpart among the Pennsylvania Dutch. No umbilical cord bound them to Europe. Whether they were Lancaster County Dutch in Pennsylvania or Frederick County Dutch in Maryland or Valley Dutch in Virginia, they were all Americans deeply attached to the part of the country they inhabited. There were no divided loyalties. They never flirted with the idea of setting up a separate German nation among the English colonies. Even if such an ambition had entered their heads it would have been difficult to bring about because, if for no other reason, so many of them had come as separate groups—Mennonites, Brethren, Moravians—with little interest in others than themselves. Though the Reformed and the Lutherans never had this sense of separateness, neither did they have much of a sense of unity with the "plain people" and the Moravians. The Rhineland Lutherans and Reformed of the frontier had more in common with the Scotch-Irish Presbyterians than they had with the Swiss Mennonites.

One of the most absurd incidents in the history of the Pennsylvania Dutch occurred in 1917 when Provost General Crowder asked Governor Brumbaugh if he thought it would be necessary to send federal troops to Pennsylvania to keep the Pennsylvania Dutch in order! This was a supreme example of gross ignorance. Nowhere in the country, not even in Texas, are there more loyal Americans. As Carl Schurz long ago pointed out, the Pennsylvania Dutch are "brimful of that sort of patriotism which swears by one's country and is ready to fight and die for it."

Many of the old ways live on because the Dutch have seen no reason to change. They believe in keeping their lives and their houses in order. They like to do things on schedule. On Monday the women wash; on Tuesday they iron; on Wednesday they clean the upstairs, and on Thursday the downstairs; on Friday they bake, and on Saturday they scrub the front porch and go to market—or they may go to market on Friday and bake on Saturday morning; and on Sunday they go to church. The schedule varies somewhat from one family to another. Saturday evening is reserved for courting. If anything throws them off schedule—say, a rainy Monday—it troubles them all through the week. They are so insistent on keeping to schedule that many women wash on Monday come hell or high water. If Noah's wife had been Pennsylvania Dutch she would have washed Monday morning, forty days' rain or no forty days' rain.

The Pennsylvania Dutch are deliberate as well as orderly. Not many like to do things on the spur of the moment; they like to plan their days in advance. They have an unfashionable belief in punctuality. If a Pennsylvania Dutchman promises to meet you at a certain time, there's a fifty-fifty chance that he will be at least five minutes ahead of time. In many Dutch homes clocks are kept ten to thirty minutes fast— so that no one will ever be late. And very few of them are late. The Pennsylvania Dutch are not a people who miss trains.

On Monday morning there is keen competition among neighbors to see who can first hang wash out on the line. Desperation has led some to hang out perfectly clean sheets and pillowcases so as to best the next fellow. The desire to get ahead, not of the Joneses but of the Hinterleiters and the Dutts, has led housewives to start the spring housecleaning in February and the fall housecleaning in July.

Some of them believe in getting to market at the crack of dawn so as to have first pick of the choicest products. One Dutchman from Reading whose habit it was to get to market early went to bed as soon as it got dark so as to get up at four or five. One night he was awakened by his wife coming to bed late, whereupon he proceeded to get up and dress.

"What are you doing?" the wife asked.

"I'm getting up to go to market."

"Come back to bed, you fool!" she said. "It's not midnight yet."

But he had made up his mind it was time to go to market, and he continued with his dressing. He clumped down the stairs and to the markethouse, where he sat on the curb on Penn Street all night long waiting for it to open.

The philosophy of abundance is another Dutch heritage. John Reesor of Markham, who was known for miles around as Drei-mohl-dreizeh (Three times thirteen), took this idea all too literally: his first wife bore him thirteen children; so did his second wife; and so did his third. Most Pennsylvania Dutch think of abundance in terms of food rather than children. All through the summer and fall the housewife prepares for winter, proof of a generous strain of squirrel blood in the Dutch. Though she does not fill the cupboards she did before the corner grocery and the supermarket became so ubiquitous, yet November finds them loaded with homemade jellies, canned tomatoes and string beans, sour cherries for pies, chowchow and piccalilli and ketchup, spiced pears, and especially peaches—the sickeningly sweet peaches of commercial canneries are rightly rejected by Dutch housewives. In the cellar are a crock or two of sauerkraut and some jugs of homemade wine, while in the attic bags of apple snitz and dried corn hang from the rafters. Most of the Pennsylvania Dutch believe in savoring the good things of the earth. While most of them are as moral as the next man, there is little of the denial of the senses that was so characteristic of Puritanism. To live in a land that flowed with milk and honey without partaking of them would be ungrateful to God. "May your house be warm, your friends be many, and your sausages long," is a typically Dutch blessing. In the fat countryside of Pennsylvania it is easy to believe that God means man's life to be rich. God is to be worshiped for the well filled barn, the bounteously laden table, and a buxom wife as well.

In the men at least there is an earthy inclination to the pleasures of the flesh. The women here as elsewhere in America felt the effects of Victorian prudery, and as late as our own century country doctors were compelled to rely on touch alone in delivering women who insisted that even in childbirth their bodies be covered by a sheet. However, the majority of the Dutch look upon man as the son of Adam and therefore prone to sin. Though children born out of wedlock are no more common among them than among other Americans, their lot is often easier. They are usually brought up by the mother's family and treated as one of their own. In most instances the sin of the erring mother is soon forgotten; but now and then one looks upon herself as a pariah and hides behind drawn blinds for the rest of her life.

Many of the Dutch are friendly and hospitable, and anyone dropping in at mealtime is likely to be asked to eat with the family. The spare room was an essential part of the nineteenth century house, and was much more common than the guest room today. Yet the good life includes thrift. Waste is sinful, and to leave food on the plate is bad manners. Children's clothes are bought one size too large, and tucks are put in the sleeves or skirts. You live within your income; you pay your debts, and pay them promptly. Most of the Dutch pay cash, or do without. At the same time they feed a tramp who comes to the door and they help a family that has been burnt out. The well-to-do couple who divide a single egg between them at breakfast moves them to laughter. For the *schnupperich* (prying) young man who before popping the question went to the courthouse to make certain that the girl's father had no mortgage on the farm, they feel only scorn. For the old woman whose stocks brought in more money than she knew what to do with, yet who had the firebox in her kitchen range divided by bricks so that she could have a fire on one side only, and that the only heat in her house all winter through, they feel more pity than scorn. But the *geitzich* (stingy) old woman who baked her pies a fortnight in advance, so that they would always be stale and the boarders would not eat so many of them, arouses only contempt. Stories of the greedy and the *geitzich* circulate throughout the Dutch country, for stinginess and

sloth are despised. In Lehigh County they tell of old Mommy Mum-
bauer, well-to-do but *geitzich,* who begrudged her horse the oats she
fed him. Day by day she gave the horse fewer and fewer oats until she
got down to a single handful; and then the horse died. "Ei-yi-yi!" she
complained. "It spites me to have him die on me just when I was getting him trained. One day more, and he wouldn't have been eating
anything at all." If the Dutch put their minds to it, they can be as
mean and miserly as anybody. Fortunately, there are not many such.

The love of cleanliness among the Pennsylvania Dutch is so marked
that sometimes one feels that in their minds it is not next to godliness
but *is* godliness. Many of them have been overcome by so immoderate
a passion for scrubbing that cleanliness has become a vice. Women get
down on their hands and knees and scrub the kitchen floor as though
it were a religious rite. Everything must be neat and clean. Even the
cellar stairs are scrubbed. No one is going to call them *schlappich*
(untidy). A dust mouse under a chair or bureau sends them into fits.
Tell a Dutch housewife that her kitchen floor is clean enough "to eat
off," and you have paid her the supreme compliment. That no one ever
does eat off a kitchen floor doesn't matter. The walks in the yard and
the front pavement must be immaculate, too; every Saturday morning
they are swept and washed. In some towns—Fleetwood is one—the gut-
ter and the street at the front of the house are swept and washed.
Porches are often swept two or three times a day and washed off at
least once a week. Some front porches are completely bare; not a chair
mars their spotless surface. Potted plants on the doorsill show that the
front door is never used except for funerals. Only a person unversed in
the ways of the Pennsylvania Dutch would think of knocking at the
front door. In the Dutch country you go to the side door or the back
door. The whole front of the house—the parlor as well as the front
porch—is sacrosanct. The mania for cleanliness reaches its apex every
spring and fall at housecleaning time when rugs are taken up and
beaten, the cellar walls whitewashed, and the whole house from the
garret down thoroughly cleaned.

The desire to be clean and neat is by no means wholly admirable.
Many a time it makes a house unlivable, though few carry it to the
extreme of an old couple in eastern Berks. Owning one of the largest
houses in town, they kept everything "just so." Nothing was out of
place; nowhere was there a fleck of dust. To do this they lived in a room
in the cellar where a bed had been set up and an oil-stove enabled

them to do a little cooking. In the summer when the cellar became too damp the couple moved out to the threshing floor of the barn. None of the rooms in the big house was lived in; all were kept "for nice."

The zeal for cleanliness reaches its worst form in the attitude of some of the Dutch toward trees. Though in part this may be a relic of the pioneer time when trees by the hundred had to be felled to make room for crops, it is more a belief that trees are untidy: they drop their leaves, they are impossible to housebreak. The Dutch do what they can to subdue them, lopping off limbs until only mangled stumps remain; or if the desire for order is ardent enough, the whole tree comes down. Pennsylvania Dutch towns are not distinguished for the beauty of their trees; often the streets are naked and sun-baked. Even many farmhouses face the relentless summer sun without the solace of a single tree; bleak and bare and tidy, they sit in closely shaven grassplots unmarred by a single fallen leaf.

Closely related to the love of cleanliness and the love of the gaudy is the passion for fresh paint. Come to southeastern Pennsylvania from Jersey or up from the Eastern Shore, or cross the Alleghenies from Pittsburgh, or come down through the mountain passes from the Coal Regions, and you will realize that the Dutch country is a country of fresh paint. This is the paint salesman's paradise. House, barn, shed—all are painted, and most of them freshly painted. Even brick and stone in an excess of enthusiasm have coats of paint. Nor are the Dutch satisfied with the white and green of the New England towns. Red above all is the color they love; but they like blue, too, and yellow —any color so it be gay. Porch furniture is painted an orange as loud as the twelve o'clock whistle. The house gets a sulphur-yellow trim around the base to set off the scarlet brick above. Nothing is too gaudy, nothing too perverse.

One of the most attractive qualities of the Pennsylvania Dutch is naturalness. They are the least snobbish of Easterners. That all men are created equal is taken literally by most of them. A man is given a chance to prove his worth. In the country sections there is virtually no class distinction. The village doctor may be given the respect and admiration his skill seems to warrant; but if he is a local boy he will be addressed by his Christian name all his life. And so will the principal of the high school. The president of the bank is Jake to everyone, the mechanic in the garage is Harry. Almost none of these people think of themselves as belonging to any particular social class. They are just ordinary men and women, natural, unassuming, and often good-natured and friendly and ready to meet strangers halfway and more.

Though there is genuine respect for their forefathers, there is little ancestor worship in the Dutch country. People take satisfaction in being descended from good, solid stock, and there is a keen interest in the family and all its connections—the *freindschaft,* as it is called. People can usually tell you who their great-grandparents were and even the name of their grandmother's sister's first husband. There are almost no chapters of the D.A.R. in the Dutch towns; in the cities, yes, but not in the towns. There is little kudos to be gained from a great-great-great-grandfather who fought at Brandywine when every Tom, Dick, and Harry in town can produce five or six Revolutionary ancestors. A stranger might be taken aback to hear himself praised as "nice and common"; but no insult is intended or even implied. It means that he puts on no airs.

The cities are less democratic. There wealth has persuaded some people that they are superior to others. They join the country club; they send their sons to Princeton or Harvard; their daughters join the Junior League; and they begin to think of themselves as Society. Such exclusiveness is founded almost entirely on money. Some families have distinguished ancestors—a colonial bishop, an early governor, or a noted ironmaster; but money is the important criterion. A brewer's son or a butcher's daughter may be excluded, yet if there is enough money their children and most certainly their grandchildren will be accepted.

Society with a capital S is taken seriously by relatively few. The great mass of people go on believing that one man is as good as another. Like most Americans the Pennsylvania Dutch are dominantly middle-class. Those who have coats of arms unearthed by genealogists regard them as curiosities and make no attempt to engrave them on stationery or silver. Only a handful have family portraits to hang above their fireplaces; and silver that antedates the Revolution is rare. Yet many houses are well stocked with simpler antiques—luster pitchers, *tauf-scheins,* Staffordshire plates, woven coverlets, maybe even a grand-father's clock or dower chest. With the recent growth of historical societies the Dutch have become more conscious of their past and the part their own culture has played in the life of the country.

There is not much race prejudice. With strong respect for individual worth the Dutch are likely to judge each man on his own merits rather than by the color of his skin. Negroes do not often settle in the country among the Dutch farmers, but those who do are apt to discover that their darker skins make little difference to their neighbors. In the cities, however, Negroes are confined to the worst slums. Race prejudice appears at its ugliest among people who worry about their social standing. A few years before the last war a Reading suburb became greatly exercised because a Negro physician purchased a lot within its borders. The borough suddenly decided it needed a playground in the very part of town in which the physician had bought his lot. The right of eminent domain was employed, and it was saved from the contamination of a cultured Negro.

There are virtually no Jews on farms in the Dutch country, though many of the towns and small cities have one or more families, usually engaged in trade. The prejudice against them is negligible. As a boy I lived for a time in the city of Lebanon, where our neighbors on either side and directly across the street were all Jews. I played with their children, I watched the lighting of the candelabras in their homes at dusk, I even ate matzoth at Passover time without ever becoming aware of any prejudice against them as Jews, without ever hearing any slighting reference to them. But in the larger cities Jews tend to form social groups of their own, largely because of prejudice in many of the Gentiles.

An adjective often applied to the Pennsylvania Dutch at which most of them take umbrage is *stolid*; and a phrase widely current and even more insulting is *the dumb Dutch*. These are fighting words in the Dutch country. The Dutch themselves use this phrase, but almost always ironically. Never do they admit its truth, although they often joke about it. They like to tell the story of the Irishman and the Dutchman who were out trapping and caught a possum and a skunk. Said the Irishman to the Dutchman: "You take the skunk and I'll take the possum, or I'll take the possum and you take the skunk."

The Dutchman looking a little puzzled, took off his hat and scratched his head. "There's something wrong here somewheres," he said finally. "The stinker always falls to me."

Even better is the tale that made the rounds during the Second World War. It was the winter of the attack on Pearl Harbor, and there was much talk of the Germans bombing American cities.

"Do you think the Germans will attack Reading?" one Dutch woman asked another.

"Ach, no! Of course not," the other reassured her. "Why should they? The battlefield's at Gettysburg."

Apparently this charge of stupidity—for that is what it amounts to—started back in the eighteenth century in Philadelphia, a mark of the superiority the city commonly feels for the country. That many of the country Dutch knew no English made them seem even more stupid to the Philadelphians. It was self-evident that a man who spoke German but not English was more stupid than a man who spoke English but not German. Even Benjamin Franklin joined in scolding them, possibly because of his chagrin at the failure of the German newspaper he had started.

Another word used by Philadelphia to damn the Dutch was *peasant*. And over and over American historians have spoken of the Pennsylvania Dutch as coming from peasant stock. This is a snide remark, an intangible insult difficult to disprove. In so far as it means that the immigrants from the Rhineland were country people, rustics, farmers, it is true in part. Some of them did come from the country; and some came from Mainz, Speyer, Worms, Mannheim, and Heidelberg. But those who came from the country were not so different from the immigrants whom, when of English blood, historians love to describe as "sturdy yeoman." The immigrants to Dutch Pennsylvania were not more unlike the settlers at Jamestown, the Pilgrim fathers at Plymouth, the traders along the Hudson, the converts of George Fox, and the French Huguenots than these people were unlike one another. On the whole the small farmers who came to the Dutch country were poorer than the small farmers who went to New England. England had not been bled white from recurring wars as had the Rhineland. There were not many aristocrats among the Dutch, although there was a higher percentage of noble blood at Bethlehem than at Williamsburg, Charleston, or along the Hudson. Although most of the Pennsylvania Dutch were plain, simple people, and many were refugees, they did not come from a backward part of Europe. Their descendants, however, have not been impelled to turn the red blood of the pioneers into blue. Some of the immigrants to the Dutch country were of innate refinement; some were rough and boorish. To pretend otherwise is silly. Probably fewer among the Pennsylvania Dutch were from the criminal classes, were professional rogues and vagabonds, than among the English settlers.

For the most part they brought bitter memories of oppression. Wherever they encountered great landlords on this side of the Atlantic

—the Penns in Pennsylvania, Lord Baltimore in Maryland, Lord Fairfax in Virginia, and Lord Granville in North Carolina—they steadily set to work to undermine their position. In Lord Fairfax, whose domain included five million or more acres between the Rappahannock and the Potomac, they had to struggle against the greatest of Virginia landlords. Oddly enough, Lord Fairfax, the only British peer who was a permanent resident of the American colonies, had his seat of Greenway Court near Winchester, in a section peopled by the Pennsylvania Dutch. Primogeniture and entail the Dutch regarded with suspicion. The Pennsylvania law of 1776 against entails was largely their work.

The fact that so many of the Pennsylvania Dutch settled on the frontier strengthened their democratic spirit. There in the old West each man was expected to stand on his own feet and to work with his own hands. There were ironmasters and well-to-do farmers among them, but no idle gentlemen. Everybody worked; it was the normal, natural, and honorable thing to do.

It is hard to generalize about the temperament of so large a group of people as the Pennsylvania Dutch. Some are stolid, but as a whole I would say that *deliberate* is a better word—deliberate and thorough and placid. Compared to the Italians, they do seem stolid; but compared to the English or New Englanders or Middle Westerners they have life and animation. *Stolid* implies a want of sensibility and intelligence and is not only insulting but also incorrect when used of the average Pennsylvania Dutchman. They are unemotional and placid rather than stolid. They are sparing of praise. They will content themselves with saying a thing is all right when they mean it is perfect. *Super* has no place in their vocabulary. There are not the stuff of which blurb writers and advertisers are made. But of course there are exceptions. I remember a young workman, a stranger, who stopped to watch me one day when I was out painting, trying to put the copper of the wheat and the blue of the Oley hills on canvas. He began to speak of the beauty of that particular countryside. "Have you ever seen the view from the hill just south of Shanesville?" he asked. I had to admit I hadn't. "Well, it's a bad road—you can hardly get up in a car," he went on; "but sometimes on a Sunday afternoon I climb up there— and *just gloat*."

There are all kinds of people among the Pennsylvania Dutch— stolid, lively, sober, gay, placid, tempestuous, sluggish, brisk, serene, spirited, gentle, wild, dumpish, lighthearted, ponderous, intense, staid,

impetuous, sedate, headlong, unruffled, gusty, lifeless, vivacious, apa-
thetic, animated, grave, jolly, leaden, sunny, dull, merry, slow, quick,
boorish, sprightly, heavy, buoyant, tranquil, violent, static, volatile,
penny-minded, ne'er-do-well, chimerical, literal, quixotic, phlegmatic,
mercurial, saturnine, jovial, solemn, stormy, calm, sweet, sour, some
three-fourths vegetable, some all air, some veering like a weathercock,
some steady as a wooden Indian. Whatever you are looking for, it's
there: sober citizen or tag rag and bobtail. By and large they are a
good solid people, hard-working and law-abiding. It is not often that
life is baroque among them; but it is at times: witness Baron Stiegel, or
the country girl from Lyons Station who woke up one morning in a
seat on the New York Stock Exchange.

Even to describe the physical characteristics of the Pennsylvania
Dutch is difficult. When it is pointed out that there are more fat people
among them than anywhere else in America and quite possibly in the
world, almost everything has been said. The Pennsylvania Dutch
country could supply all the circuses in the world with fat men and fat
ladies and have thousands left over. Probably it is the superabundance
of pork and pie the Dutch have been eating for generations that turns
so many of them into walking mountains of flesh. In height they are like
most Americans—not so tall as the cowboys of the Southwest but taller
than any Europeans. Their skin is commonly a light olive, their hair
brown, and their eyes hazel. Blue eyes are rare; china-blue ones almost
unknown. Brown eyes, some as light as topazes and some almost black,
are not unusual. Fair hair, sometimes as light as tow, sometimes pure
gold, but more often ash-blond, is common, especially in children. Black
hair, too, is often seen; red hair, but seldom.

The Pennsylvania Dutch are neither handsome people nor homely;
like most of mankind they are middling. If you are in the dumps the
homely ones will seem to outnumber all others, and the average man
will be not the average man at all but only a caricature. Actually the
proportion of good-looking people is about what it is in the rest of the
country, with good looks evenly divided between the sexes. Strikingly
handsome people are few, but there are some. There are some, too, with
an air of distinction and breeding; there are some who are merely
pretty; and there are more who are neither. Many of those who fall
in the middle group have faces full of character. And there are those
with weak and foolish faces. There's God's plenty here, enough for any
casting bureau, choose whatever it may.

High Jinks and Divers Capers

The way a people take their pleasures tells much about them. The most popular sources of pleasure among the Pennsylvania Dutch are eating, drinking beer, making love, talking, listening to the radio, and going to the movies—possibly in that order and possibly not. In this they resemble the rest of America. Though there may be a difference of emphasis in different sections of the country, these ways of passing the time are popular from the Atlantic to the Pacific. In their liking for certain sports, baseball, hunting, and fishing especially, the Dutch are like much of the rest of America, too. Contract bridge flourishes at the country club, haasenpeffer at the firehouse. A drive into the country on Sunday is regarded as a pleasant relaxation. On a hot summer day boys go swimming in the abandoned quarry hole, in winter they skate on the ice.

In the towns and cities the firehouse is the social center for the men. Every village has its volunteer fire company with hundreds of members paying the nominal dues. The cities have half a dozen volunteer fire companies—and they are real fire companies with up-to-date equipment and an excellent record in fighting fires. They survive even in as big a city as Reading, which boasts of having the largest and oldest volunteer system in the United States. The Reading volunteer fire department, which dates from St. Patrick's Day of 1773, now has more than seven thousand volunteer firemen. For many years there was great rivalry between the several companies of the city when they set out to show that they could throw a stream of water over a church spire or with what dexterity they could erect their ladders. In the villages and small towns many of the fire companies have large halls built on to the firehouse. There the countryside gathers to dance and drink beer. The fire companies have the advantage over the country hotels of being able to sell beer on Sundays—to members only, to be sure; but since everyone in the town or township belongs to the fire company this limitation does little to cramp their style. The carnivals, or "picnics," fill the nights with noise and drunks for miles around.

Quite often the dances at the firehouse or country hotel are the old square dances or hoedowns as opposed to the "city dances." Everybody joins in, from the children just beginning school to the great-grand-fathers. The people who dance *Kiss Your Honey* or *Throw Your Chain Behind You* are the ordinary country people, and they dance these dances because they like them. In the Dutch villages there has been no group of intellectuals to foster the hoedowns as a dying art.

The big dance of the year used to be the dance on Battalion Day; but Battalion Day vanished with the nineteenth century. This was the day, usually Whitmonday, when the local militia was mustered out and put through its paces. As the law required all men between the ages of eighteen and forty-five, except those in important government positions, to do military duty once a year or pay a fine, almost every township and village had its company of militia, most of them in gaudy uniforms. In some of the poorer townships, where few could afford to buy uniforms, men turned up in corduroys and linsey-woolseys, carrying pistols or sticks instead of guns. Even so it was a big day in Bernville or Rehrersburg or Kutztown. There were enough men in uniform to make the review of the troops a brave sight to the country people thronging into town, especially if one of the companies was made up of light horse cavalry. It was a gala day, from the morning salute of the cannon on the hill behind the town to the dance at the tavern, ending sometimes only with dawn. Mardi gras, the Fourth of July, and Fair Week all rolled into one would have something of the flavor of the old-time Battalion Day. The big feature of the day was the drill with the field maneuvers, the manual of arms, and dress parade; and finally, with the fife and drum corps leading the way, the parade through the town. Venders sold peanuts and small beer. Children waved flags and narrowly escaped death under the hoofs of the prancing horses. After the parade the officers, resplendent in uniform, dined in state at the tavern. It was as magnificent a dinner as local cooks could make it, and with much ceremony and many toasts: "To Old Hickory, deeply rooted in the hearts of American freemen!"; "May the thunder of British cannon or the points of their bayonets never daunt the sons of liberty!"; "The fair sex of America—may they blossom as a rose, with sweet smiles for the welfare of our country!". After ten or twelve such toasts the officers unbent; many were in as fine fettle as the privates at the bar. Outside music filled the air. Hired by the town was a band of musicians on a wagon. Children crowded the merry-go-round, where a horse going round and round provided the power and a fiddler on a perch the music. There were side shows, and some years there was even a company of Negro minstrels. The dance that night was the climax to the day's festivities. It was a lively dance if not always genteel. It's a great pity that the old Battalion Days are gone. The little country towns have never seen so much life since then.

Public executions, too, belong to the past. No longer do wagons loaded with people jam the roads leading to town on the day of a hanging. Indeed, hanging has given way to electrocution; and now only the newspapers make holiday. But back in 1809 on June 10th more than twenty thousand people crowded into the little town of Reading to see Susanna Cox hanged for the murder of her infant child.

A much happier diversion, Fair Week, is still with us. In many of the Dutch towns the fairs have a long history. They began as market fairs. In Reading, for instance, a spring fair and an autumn fair were held in the market square in the center of the town, and cattle and horses were offered for sale. The spring fair was known in Reading, and in Lebanon too, as the "cherry fair" because it was held when the cherries were ripe. At Lancaster there was racing on the green in colonial days, but elsewhere horse racing was of a purely informal sort as when a man put his horse through its paces before a prospective buyer. Even more exciting was the cockfighting—at Reading usually in the back yard of one of the inns on the square, the Golden Swan or the Plough and Harrow. There was a good deal of dancing, too, in these taverns, and more than a little drinking. Cazenove in the journal of his tour through Pennsylvania in 1794 gave a vivid description of fair time in Lancaster:

During the Fair, which lasts for three days in June, and while Court is held (which is once every three months) all the County farmers and their children always come to Lancaster and then everything is good cheer. All the young farmers, men and women, must have pleasure, as they have none the rest of the year: people say that nothing is more interesting than their loud joys and the big kisses exchanged everywhere by the sweet-hearts who fill the streets. So, young people have an opportunity to see each other, and marriages follow, while the fathers get drunk in the taverns.

This is a far cry from the sobriety of the Quakers. In 1705 the Provincial Assembly passed an act against "Riotous Sports, Plays and Games" that forbade stage plays, masks, and revels; bullbaiting, bearbaiting, cockfighting, throwing at cocks, cudgels, and backsword; cards and dice; and even "ninepins, quoits, bowles, rowley-powley, and shove-groat." Happily this act was annulled by Queen Anne because it restrained "her Majesty's subjects from innocent sports and diversions."

Further testimony on the fairs comes from William Faux, an Englishman traveling in America in 1818: "In October, at the fairs in Pennsylvania all is fine, mighty fine, and dashy flashy."

Precisely what "dashy flashy" means, I do not know, though I can give a pretty good guess. Compared to this, fair week today is rather tame. Yet York, Allentown, and Reading in particular pride themselves on their fairs. There is a keen rivalry between the three sister cities, each claiming to have the best and biggest fair in the state. In addition, there are a dozen or more smaller fairs in the Dutch country. The pattern is that of fairs the country over. Elsewhere the fancywork may be just as fancy and the midway louder and gaudier, but in the Dutch fairs the displays of fruit and vegetables and often of livestock, too, are unsurpassed. While the trotting horses at Goshen may put on a better show, Reading Fair is able to boast of its Grand Circuit races. The great stock farms at Hanover are proof of the devotion of many Pennsylvania Dutchmen to this sport.

Horse racing in other forms is rare in the Dutch country. The more fashionable steeplechase and racing on the flat have never taken hold. There is no polo, and there are few fox hunts. In earlier days fox hunts were more common, though even then it was a sport enjoyed by rustics on stout farm horses galumphing after the fox rather than by gentlemen in pink coats spurring thoroughbreds over fence and hedge. An uncle of mine, now long dead, delighted to tell of a fox hunt in his boyhood at Womelsdorf. That the boys had neither horse nor fox did not discourage them. They had dogs, and they had a salt mackerel on a string, a perfectly adequate substitute for a fox. Trailing the mackerel in the dust, one of the boys was given a five minutes' start before the dogs were let loose. Down the High Street he went, and pellmell, *holler-boller,* helter-skelter, *hobbertibobberti*—in other words, hell for leather, lickety-split—behind him came the dogs and the other boys. Looking for a means of escape, he darted in the front door of the general store on the square and out the back door with dogs and boys at his heels. The good women of Womelsdorf and the Lutheran preacher, there on innocent errands—such as a jug of molasses or two or three yards of calico—were scattered right and left by the invading hunt, to pick themselves out of the keg of dill pickles and the basket of eggs as the hullabaloo subsided. The boys of Womelsdorf sat down very gingerly for a fortnight after that.

Many of the old amusements have died out. No longer does the man with the dancing bear wander from village to village, though up until the time of the First World War he did so. Even organ grinders with monkeys are rarely seen. Hurdy-gurdies, too, are growing scarce. A camel "from the wilderness of Arabia," like the one shown in Reading on October 19, 1791, would attract few spectators today. The puppet shows traveling the Dutch roads with those captivating dolls, "der alt Waffelbach un' sei Fraw, die alt Waffelbachsy," no longer delight the children as they did in the forties and fifties of last century; and no longer do Faust and the devil send chills down their spines. Even Punch and Judy, who replaced the old Dutch dolls, have danced and squeaked for the last time. And it is a century since the roads of Berks and Lehigh saw old man Zeisler with his cart, piled high with second-hand books, drawn by four Newfoundland dogs.

The theater has had better fortune. Although it never had much life in the Pennsylvania Dutch towns, there were strolling players in Lancaster in early days who put on scenes from Shakespeare; and during the Revolution British prisoners and their wives, confined there, amused themselves in a similar fashion. The first theater in Lancaster was built in 1791. Reading, too, had occasional snatches of drama, usually enacted in a local tavern. In the late eighteenth century Vanbrugh's *Provok'd Husband* was played in Reading. Today the theater is moribund in Reading and Lancaster; even so, they and the other larger Dutch cities are luckier than most cities of their size in that road companies, sometimes fresh from Broadway, play there half a dozen times a year. The stock companies, once the pride of the local opera houses, have long since taken their bow. Only an occasional group of amateurs or a summer theater supplements the road companies. Movies, of course, are the universal entertainment. Several of the larger cities also have symphony orchestras or choral societies, often of surprisingly high caliber. Once or twice a year there are concerts by one or another of the great orchestras, usually the Philadelphia Orchestra. There are concerts, too, by leading pianists and violinists, by string quartets and singers of world renown. The musical life of many of the Dutch cities is vigorous and healthy.

On a different level are the annual family reunions, often so ambitious in scale as to take in all cousins to the eighth and ninth degree of kinship. They are usually held on a summer day in a grove in a part of the county in which the family is especially prolific. The main feature of the reunion is a speech glorifying the family. The Rothermels are told what fine, sturdy stock the Rothermels are; the Schaeffers are told what fine, sturdy stock the Schaeffers are. In addition there are "exercises," a piano duet or a violin solo or both, a recitation or a series of them, and a cakewalk with prizes for the oldest person present and the person from the greatest distance. Family reunions afford a perfect opportunity to renew acquaintance with the whole *freindschaft*, to inspect Cousin Mattie's new baby, to meet Great-Uncle Harvey's third wife. It's pleasant, too, to sit in the shady woods on a nice summer day and have a good talk with the cousins of one's youth.

Auctions, or vendues, have long been popular. If you are a collector of antiques and the great ambition of your life is to have a three-day sale when you die, why, naturally you go to auctions every blessed Saturday in the year; but if, like most people, you can take antiques or leave them you will be more moderate in your attendance. You may go to bid on an apple-butter kettle or a painted settee, or to visit with old friends and neighbors. Church suppers are popular for much the same reason. Of course, better food and more of it is served there than could be obtained for the same money elsewhere, all of which counts. Quilting parties are still held on winter afternoons in country villages, but snitzing bees and apple-butter cookings are few and far between. Among the more sophisticated "church people" the old-time "frolics" have disappeared; among the more innocent "plain people" a barn-raising is still the occasion for a frolic. Archaic as much of this sounds, it still persists as a way of life in Pennsylvania. Not all the old country ways are dead.

Going to market, another feature of colonial life that has lasted in the Pennsylvania Dutch cities to the present day, is as much a diversion as it is a necessity. The old markets, built in 1766, that stood in Penn Square in the heart of Reading were torn down in 1871. The old markets in Lancaster and York have also vanished. In all the Dutch cities except Easton, where a curb market is held in the central square, large brick market houses, most of them dating from the Victorian period, have replaced the more primitive market houses of colonial times. To these the farmers bring their produce, and the whole city comes to buy—streams of people, all carrying baskets. This, too, is a social occasion. Friends gather in the aisles and chat with one another. It is not mere buying and selling. There is life in the step and triumph in the eye as the heaping basket is borne home. Going to market never wears anyone out as shopping does; it is a pleasure and not a chore.

One look at a Pennsylvania Dutch market is enough to account for its effect on man's spirit. Each market is a harvest festival. Mounds of food everywhere pleasure the eye: here a spick-and-span Mennonite with baskets piled high with brown and white eggs, fat loaves of bread fresh from the old bake oven behind the house, and a row of paradisiacal shoofly pies; here a portly butcher with great slabs of pork and beef, ropes of smoked sausage, and pans of scrapple; here an Italian with pyramids of oranges and grapefruit, boxes of kumquats, French artichokes, Malaga grapes, pomegranates—fruits from Florida, the Rio Grande, Arizona, and California; here an Amish girl with nothing but Lancaster County Swiss cheese; there an apple-cheeked man with only celery, hundreds and hundreds of stalks and each as tender as a mother's heart; here an Amishman, complete with broadbrim and bushy beard, standing in a tremendous nosegay of zinnias, marigold, gladioli, asters, cockscomb, and ageratum—scarlet, gold, violet, blue, rose, and every other color on the painter's palette; here a Ruscombmanor farmer with peaches rosy, round, fragrant, juicy, perfect, and far above life size; there a farmer's wife from out Joanna way with a crock of apple butter and the first sauerkraut of the season. At stand after stand there are chickens, ducks, turkeys, and guinea hens. Sometimes the chickens are cut up and sold by the piece—breasts, necks, drumsticks, livers, whatever you will; but usually the chickens are whole, with liver, heart, and gizzard on a bed of parsley resting on the breast of the fowl, as though posing for a portrait by Dali. Each chicken is a chicken of distinction with nary a pinfeather to mar the beauty of its flesh. At one stand there is fuchsia in pots; at another, piles of gourds; and at still another, cups of shellbark meats. Here is a basket of light, toothsome doughnuts; and here are rows of tumblers of jelly, currant, blackberry, quince. There is pungent horseradish newly ground; and at one stand after another there are potatoes, each one freshly scrubbed and washed behind the ears. What is it you want? Dandelion, poke sprouts, honey-in-the-comb, Lebanon bologna, country-cured ham, an angel-food cake? They're here and more too—lilies in tubs, pots of white geraniums, bunches of pennyroyal; pigs' feet jelly, blood pudding, mush: if not at this market then at the next. Springerles, sandtarts, gingerbread men, mince pies, toy candy, striped shepherds' crooks, wreaths of holly, garlands of ground pine, and moss from the woods at the Christmas market; hyacinths, daffodils, Easter lilies, tulips, chocolate rabbits, and dyed eggs at the Good Friday market. Each market is different, each an adventure, each a gala occasion. Like the old-time fair, all is dashy flashy.

In the country villages the general store even now is a social center in a small way, in spite of the fact that shopping in the five-and-tens is one of the favorite pastimes of the country people. Shopping in a country store has a personal element that is lacking in the supermarkets with their metal go-carts and empyrean cashiers. At the very least you pass the time of day or venture an opinion on the state of the crops with the country storekeeper, though more likely than not you go farther afield and speak of Jake Landis, back from the hospital and looking real good, too. Back in the last century the country store was a lively place twice a year when the new stock arrived in the spring and in the late fall in time for Christmas. That was the time the women came in to get some calico or gingham for a new dress or a bit of ribbon to smarten up last year's hat, and some lemon sticks and pink and white hearts on which were printed words of love—these for the children. But the country store is the province of the older men rather than the women. In the Dutch villages there is often a bench at the back of the store just as there is in the country stores in the Palatinate. There many of the older men of the neighborhood, and sometimes a few of the younger ones, gather each evening to talk over the state of the nation and the price of eggs. If a young man sufficiently guileless turns up, he'll be set to catching an *elbedritsche,* a mythical animal now extinct. This is one of the most ancient of practical jokes. The difficulties of catching an elbedritsche are dwelt upon in loving detail. Almost grudgingly the old men consent to the young man joining the hunt. The greenhorn is given a bag in which to catch one and taken far off, up on Haycock Mountain, say, or Spitzenberg, and stationed behind a rock or tree while the old men separate—or so he is given to understand—to drive the elbedritsches toward him. There he is left literally holding the bag while the older, wiser hunters steal home.

Far commoner than catching elbedritsches is the hunting of deer and such lesser game as rabbits, squirrels, pheasants, quail, and grouse. Ever since the days when Daniel Boone dwelt among them the Pennsylvania Dutch have been enthusiastic hunters. Although a surprising number of deer are shot even in the thickly settled Dutch counties—for Pennsylvania has far more deer than any other Eastern state—many of the hunters go to the counties farther north. And many of them come back with deer. Occasionally one appears with a bear and carves out bear steaks for his friends. Those who have to do their hunting close to home usually concentrate on rabbits and pheasants, yet there are those who find the meat of the groundhog palatable and those who think possum mighty tasty. The number of hunters is large. Indeed, the day the hunting season opens, almost every man and boy is out scouring the woods and fields for game. Nearly every town has its gun club, still another mark of the widespread enthusiasm for hunting.

There seem to be as many fishermen as hunters. As you see them on the banks of every pond and creek you feel that never have so many fished so long for so little—an impression as erroneous as it is unfair. The streams are well stocked. Trout streams exist even in some of the more heavily settled counties. Most of the fishermen, however, are not attempting to hook a trout; bass, white carp, yellow perch, chubs, suckers, fallfish, catfish, eels, and even sunfish are what they are after. Even so, fishing is not what it was in 1763, when the settlers along the Conestoga complained that the dams were ruining their catch of shad, salmon, and rockfish, all of which they had caught before in great abundance. Sometimes a group of Dutch fishermen journey down to Cape May for a day or two of deep-sea fishing, or try their luck on the Chesapeake. These scores of men sitting quietly on the banks of Ontelaunee, or two or three of them wandering along the Branch by Black Rock on the trail made long ago by the Lenni Lenapes, are an essential part of the landscape, as much so as the slowly moving streams and the gentle hills. Sitting under the willows or an old buttonwood weighed down with wild grapes, they are as much in their element as the snow-white heron wading a hundred yards downstream or the snake-doctor skimming over the water. The placid Pennsylvania Dutch countryside demands fishermen. It is exactly right for them, and these wise men have tumbled to the fact. It was inevitable that so tranquil a land as the Dutch country should breed fishermen.

Festivities of sorts accompany birth, death, and marriage. Birth can be included only by making baptism count as part of birth. All through the colonial period, and for a long time afterward, baptism followed birth among the "church people" only by a fortnight or so. Each child, of course, had his sponsors; he was not permitted to go through life minus godfather and godmother as most of us do today. The godparents, the preacher, often the grandparents of the child, maybe some uncles and aunts, and possibly a few close friends of the family were all asked to dinner after the ceremony. Such a dinner would be a fairly elaborate meal, a "preacher's dinner"—a name still used here and there in the Dutch country for a sumptuous meal. Sometimes a bowl of the water with which the child was baptized was carried home and poured over a red rose bush so as to give the child red cheeks.

Weddings among the Dutch are often relatively simple. A couple slips away and is quietly married by a popular preacher of the neighborhood. Or a few friends may be asked to the wedding and the dinner afterward. Elaborate weddings are popular with few except the Amish and the fashionable city people. Occasionally a family of wealth, deciding that nothing is too good for its daughter, sets out to do a wedding up brown. Charles of the Ritz is brought over from New York to dress the bride's hair, pots of daffodils by the thousand are sunk into the garden in front of the house, a large marquee is erected for the wedding reception, and champagne flows.

Out in the country a newly married couple is serenaded on its first night back home by a Dutch band—sometimes known as a bull band, a callithumpian band, or a shivaree—made up of all the young men and boys in the neighborhood and very often many of the older men as well. Anything that makes noise serves as an instrument: cowbells, sleigh bells, horns, dishpans, kettles, or what have you. Best of all is a *sei-geik* or "pig fiddle." This is made by stretching wires across the trough for scalding hogs. The bow, a piece of two by four covered with rosin, is drawn across the fiddle by two men so as to produce the greatest possible discord. The din is earsplitting. It is stopped only by the police or the couple appearing to be greeted in person. Usually the bridegroom has been foresighted enough to lay in a supply of cigars, which he now passes out; or cider and cookies may placate the serenaders. A serenade of this sort is generally a compliment to the bridegroom, even a sign of affection. The more popular the groom the larger the shivaree. A man who is disliked may marry three times without a single serenade, though if his choice is sufficiently bizarre—a homely old maid or a shrew—a bull band may turn up to make merry over the wedding.

Death is treated with greater ceremony by the Pennsylvania Dutch than either birth or marriage. Today, of course, funerals have sadly degenerated. Most of them are held in funeral parlors with a public viewing of the corpse the night before. Only the Amish and the Mennonites keep up the fine old burial customs of a century ago. With them a funeral is simpler, more dignified, and eminently more human than it is with the rest of us. Yesterday death was invariably marked by the tolling of the church bell, even the death of a derelict tramp in a farmer's barn. In the very early days when someone died out in the country, sons of friends and neighbors rode from farm to farm to invite people to the funeral. Neighbors came in to help, some to redd up the house, and some to cook and bake for the funeral dinner. Four men dug the grave—married men if the one dead was married, single men if he was single. The same men served as pallbearers and later filled in the grave. As there were no hearses in the country in early times, the plain coffin, made by a carpenter of the neighborhood, was placed in a Conestoga wagon or in a farm wagon with straw spread on the bottom. While the long procession, headed by the pastor, moved along the country roads, the bell in the church tolled continuously. In the journal of his trip through Pennsylvania in 1794, Cazenove described a funeral procession he met near Annville, with a hundred and fifty on horseback and in carriages, headed by a man on horseback carrying a small coffin in his arms.

Perhaps it was the funeral "baked meats" that most distinguished the old-fashioned funeral from the modern one. In the old days all the mourners were invited to return to the house for dinner. If the weather was mild tables were set up out of doors under the trees or on the threshing floor of the barn as well as in the house. In the Lebanon of

my boyhood there was a man—not quite right in his head, I think—
known as Eddie Süssekuche, whose invariable practice it was to attend
every funeral for miles around for the sake of the dinner. A funeral
was not quite a funeral without the corpse and Eddie Süssekuche. The
funeral dinner was always a hearty meal: stewed chicken, often baked
ham, and sometimes cold meats; mashed potatoes, applesauce, cole
slaw, red beets, a half-dozen other sours and sweets, cheese, pie, and
coffee. Invariably there was raisin pie, commonly known as funeral pie
because it was always served at funerals. Often when someone was
dangerously ill, people would shake their heads and say, "Yes, well,
there will be raisin pie yet." After the funeral dinner neighbors washed
the dishes and tidied up the house before leaving. Such was the old
way, and a good way it was.

Sometimes burial was in the small family graveyard on the farm.
Then the funeral was at the house instead of the church. There are
many small family graveyards in the Dutch country. Some on farms
far distant from the church are a matter of necessity rather than choice.
A hundred or more years ago it was often difficult to take the body to
the churchyard for burial in the bad winter months. In other cases,
and these not a few, the small family graveyards were a matter of
choice. Some of them are little more than a stone's throw from the
graveyard by the church. It is clear that these home-loving Dutch chose
to be buried on the farms on which they spent their lives. To them it
must have seemed the best possible place to spend eternity. Usually
these small graveyards are surrounded by a stout stone wall with a box
bush or a cedar or two growing within the enclosure.

In the country most people still bury their dead in the graveyard
by the church. In the towns and cities cemeteries long ago replaced
the old graveyards by the church, and now "memorial parks" are coming into fashion. The old graveyard has an intimacy lacking in the
larger cemeteries; it was no little thing to be buried among one's
friends and neighbors. Tombstones, too, have lost much of their old
charm. Those of colonial days with cherubs, hearts, and tulips are the
most attractive; yet the weeping-willow tombstones of the early nineteenth century with full-bosomed females weeping upon a monument
have a quaintness quite unmatched today. The heavy, stately table-
tombstones of governors, generals, bishops, and wealthy ironmasters
have a solid dignity that even now is impressive. In those days a
tombstone was a biography in little. And the epitaphs, trite as many of

them were, lent interest to every graveyard. An old walled graveyard with tombstones askew, two or three old box bushes, thyme growing wild over the graves, and a small flock of sheep nibbling the grass between the tombstones, has a poignant beauty and a touch of poetry that no modern cemetery or "memorial park" ever succeeds in capturing.

One curious early burial custom was that of placing the *taufschein* (decorated baptismal certificate) in the coffin. In Lehigh County it was sometimes put under the tombstone. From the large number of old baptismal certificates still in existence, I doubt if this practice could ever have been widespread. Underlying it, no doubt, was the suspicion that the taufschein was a valuable document to have in one's possession when appearing before the Judgment Seat, a sort of passport to heaven. Here was proof in black and white that a man was a Christian, that at the very least he had been properly baptized.

Holiday

Christmas and Easter are the two principal holidays among the Pennsylvania Dutch. Thanksgiving, New Year's Day, and the Fourth of July all pale beside them. Many other holidays are little more than dates on the calendar. On Labor Day women go ahead with their washing just as they do on every other Monday. Groundhog Day differs from other days only because of the weather lore connected with it, although in Allentown and Souderton there are societies that seize upon this day as an excuse for a dinner. St. Valentine's Day, April Fool, and Halloween are all children's holidays, with the Dutch version pretty much that of the country over. The Fourth of July was once a day of firecrackers and picnics but now is much more sober. The Lancaster County town of Lititz still celebrates the Fourth with gusto. Down at the Springs the waters reflect the flickering lights of seven thousand beeswax candles fixed on arches spanning the stream or whirling about on paddlewheels. Decoration Day, with its parade of Civil War veterans, was another gala day for the children. Among the grown-ups it was taken more seriously, for almost everyone went to the cemetery to decorate the graves with flowers. The peony, which comes into bloom toward the end of May in the Dutch country, is the flower most widely used to honor the dead. Thanksgiving is celebrated largely because it gives the Dutch the opportunity of having a big dinner, but it is not the important holiday it is in New England. It never became the substitute for Christmas that it did among the New Englanders.

The spirit of thankfulness sometimes connected with Thanksgiving is more apparent among the Dutch at the Harvest Home festival. Harvest Home is usually held in late September, though the date varies from one church to another. In the old days members of the congregation brought vegetables and fruit they had grown themselves, usually the very finest of the harvest: apples, pears, quinces, grapes, pumpkins, corn, potatoes, eggplants, peppers—all the fruits and vegetables of the Pennsylvania earth. The show in church was almost as good as that at the fair. Banked around the pulpit and rising tier on tier before the altar, the finest yield of garden, field, and orchard filled the front of the church. In the past everything was given to the minister, and badly he needed it. Almost all clergymen were woefully underpaid. Today Harvest Home is less poetic. There are still some fruits and vegetables and even a shock or two of corn and some sheaves of wheat and, as a symbol of the harvest, a loaf of home-made bread; but rows and rows of canned fruit and vegetables and even bags of sugar and boxes of cornflakes have replaced most of the garden produce. It is a harvest removed by several degrees. And in a world in which ministers are slightly better paid than they were in our grandfathers' time, orphan asylums and old people's homes divide the harvest offering.

Although Battalion Day no longer makes Whitmonday one of the gala days of the year, many country people still crowd to the cities on that day. There is a feeling among the more old-fashioned people that Whitsuntide is different from the other times of the year; it is not an ordinary end of the week. The Reformed and Lutheran churches commonly hold Communion on Whitsunday. Those who distrusted the fickleness of Easter weather appear now in new straw hats and summer dresses. And among the Amish, too, Whitsunday is carefully observed.

Ascension Day is another religious festival kept by the Amish, as it is by many people of other faiths. Throughout the Dutch country it is believed that it is bad luck to do any work, especially sewing, on Ascension Day. The more superstitious are convinced that to use a needle on this day is to invite the vengeance of the Lord. Stories like the one of the two girls from Jacobus caught in a thunderstorm on Ascension Day are widely told. Hurrying along a country road just outside of town, the girls were terrified by the cataclysmic bolts of lightning striking all around them.

"You're not wearing anything you sewed today, are you?" the one girl anxiously asked the other.

"Why, yes; a new petticoat I just finished this morning."

"Well, for goodness sakes! You take that petticoat right off. No wonder it's lightning!"

The girl took off the petticoat at once and put it under an old hickory beside the road. She had hardly turned her back before a blinding flash of lightning struck the hickory, splitting it from top to bottom and tearing the petticoat into shreds.

Old Michaelmas, which comes on the 11th of October, is an Amish fast day, as is Good Friday. The rest of the Pennsylvania Dutch pay no attention to Michaelmas, new or old. Fasnacht Day is another matter. Fasnacht, or Shrove Tuesday, is celebrated by practically all the Dutch, who gorge themselves on the delicious doughnuts dedicated to this day. All the chores of the household are assigned to the one who gets up last. To be *die alt Fasnacht,* as the last person up is called, is looked upon by the children as a disgrace. It isn't so much taking out the ashes and bringing up the coal and feeding the chickens or even shoveling the walk if there is any snow to shovel; it's going to school and being forced to admit that you are "the fasnacht" at your house. The taunting cries of your schoolmates, "Fritz is a fasnacht! Fritz is a fasnacht!" are bitter to the ears. On other mornings Pennsylvania Dutch children may be slowpokes, but on Fasnacht Day they rise at the crack of dawn. Fasnacht is not a religious holiday; quite the contrary. Fifty years ago it was still a favorite day for dances. These were the last remnants of the Mardi gras spirit with which this day was celebrated in the Rhineland as well as in France. Now the dancing and the carnival high jinks are left to New Orleans. The food alone is remembered, the merrymaking forgotten—which may mean that the Pennsylvania Dutchman's idea of a good time is eating.

New Year is celebrated in several ways. The more pious of the "church people" hold watch-night services. The Moravians usher in the new year with a blast of trumpets from the belfry, while inside the church the organist with a tremendous crescendo breaks into the strains of "Now Let Us Praise the Lord," the congregation rising in a body and singing. The more pagan of the Dutch shoot the New Year in—quite literally. The night is filled with the sound of gunfire.

Good Friday and Easter Sunday are the principal religious holidays of the year. Christmas is important too, but with Christmas the religious element is outweighed by the merriment. Even with Easter the festive side has become pronounced, though as yet it is not as prominent as the religious aspect. Good Friday is a legal holiday in Pennsylvania. The Lutheran and Reformed churches and many of the other faiths as well observe this day as one of the most sacred in the calendar. Yet Easter market is held on Good Friday. It is then that farmers bring bowls of gayly dyed eggs for city folk to buy.

With the sole exception of Christmas, Easter is the great holiday of the year. With Lutheran and Reformed and Moravian it is a religious festival of the utmost importance. All three churches hold dawn services on Easter morning. The trombone choirs of the Moravians, playing Bach's cantata, "Sleepers, Wake," start their circuit of the town long before daylight. From the belfry of the church and from the street below they summon their people to worship the risen Christ. The beginning of the service is held in the church, but shortly before dawn the whole congregation, headed by the pastor and the trombone choir, moves to the graveyard, there forming a semicircle facing the east. As the first rays of the rising sun break through the sky, the pastor reads, "Glory be to Him who is the Resurrection and the Life!"

The dawn services of the Reformed and Lutheran churches are not unlike those held in many Protestant churches. The churches are almost literally filled with flowers; the altar and the pulpit and the whole front of the church are banked with them. There are hundreds of pots of spring bulbs, for in many of the Dutch churches there is at least one pot, and often four or five, for every family in the congregation. For the most part the flowers are white—towering Easter lilies and fat white hyacinths, with the gold of daffodils, the rose-red of tulips, and the purple of still more hyacinths for accent. The church is filled with their fragrance. Throughout the Dutch country Easter is a holiday of flowers. There are flowers at the front window of every house in village, town, and city. Pots of spring bulbs are as much a part of Easter as wreaths are of Christmas.

The folklore of Easter is one of the happiest heritages the Dutch brought with them from the Rhineland. The Easter rabbit and the Easter egg made the voyage across the Atlantic with the early German immigrants. Although they are still rare in England, despite the Hanoverian monarchs that country has had for more than two centuries, and still comparatively unknown in New England, most of the United States has adopted the Easter rabbit and Easter egg with enthusiasm. According to the old Teutonic legend, the goddess Ostara transformed the rabbit—at that time a bird—into an animal. Ever since then the rabbit in grateful remembrance lays eggs on the feast of Ostara every spring. This was the belief the early Christian priests encountered when they introduced Christianity into pagan Germany. Instead of dying out, the legend was transferred to the Christian festival of Easter, and the egg became the symbol of the regeneration of life in the spring. Most of the Pennsylvania Dutch, to be sure, are not acquainted with the details of this legend; yet every child, except among the "plain people," grows up believing in the Easter bunny just as he believes in Santa Claus. It is true that the Easter bunny's habits vary slightly from one section to another. In one town every child knows that he must set out caps and hats under tables and chairs for nests for the Easter bunny to lay his eggs in. In another town, not so many miles away, the Easter bunny comes well provided with baskets for the eggs. And in the town beyond that the Easter bunny lays his eggs in hidden spots in the garden and orchard.

The eggs are usually colored with dyes bought at the store, yet some families still adhere to the country way of dying eggs with onion skins. All through the winter the onion skins are religiously saved so that the eggs will have the proper color—a deep, glowing red like a horse chestnut freshly spilled from its hull. The week after Easter bits of colored eggshell litter the sidewalks all through the town. The older boys have been busy "picking for keeps"—matching eggs to see which has the harder shell, with the winner getting the loser's egg. A boy with low instincts has been known to use a guinea hen's egg and thus, with the aid of fraud and a hard shell, end up with half the eggs in town. "Picking for keeps" was the origin of the famous egg roll on the White House lawn.

Easter is so popular with the Pennsylvania Dutch that they try to make it last as long as possible. It may begin on Maundy Thursday (*Grienerdunnerschdaak* to the Dutch), when every Pennsylvania Dutchman, if he knows what is good for him, eats dandelion salad to make sure that he will have good health all through the year. Then comes Good Friday, then Easter itself, and finally Easter Monday. This too is a holiday; no work is done except what is absolutely necessary. This is a favorite day for calling and visiting.

Christmas, though, is the principal holiday of the year. The Christmas customs, like the Easter ones, came from the Rhineland. Some of these have been adopted by the rest of the country; some remain peculiar to the Pennsylvania Dutch. It seems highly likely, though no historical proof can be offered, that the Christmas tree is a Pennsylvania Dutch contribution to the American way of life. And even Santa Claus is partly Pennsylvania Dutch. The first Christmas tree in the world's history was one at Strasbourg in the year 1608—or at least this is the earliest of which there is any record. Almost at once this happy inspiration spread to the Protestant sections of the upper Rhineland, where it continued as a local custom for two hundred years before it was taken up by the rest of Germany. Since Alsace and the upper Rhineland were the very parts of Europe from which so many of the forefathers of the Pennsylvania Dutch came, I cannot believe that they failed to bring with them so well beloved a custom as the Christmas tree. Not until the middle of the nineteenth century was the Christmas tree introduced into England and the rest of the Christian world. The man who first conceived this blessed idea that has added so much joy to life deserves canonization; instead he remains one of the humble unknown.

Except among the "plain people" Christmas trees are universal in the Dutch country. Even houses without children have their Christmas trees. Last century it was the pointed juniper of the rocky hill land, the tree growing along the fence rows, that was the Christmas tree of the Dutch. Even now some grocery stores in Dutch towns offer junipers for sale each year, though they are no longer common. The balsam fir from Maine has nearly driven them from the market, but an increasing number of evergreens are grown on Pennsylvania hillsides for the Christmas trade. These are cut only a few days before Christmas and carted into the cities and towns by truck. Nowhere else have I seen trees of such beauty, so fresh and so full of needles, as those offered for sale in Berks County.

Today the Christmas trees are hung with the conventional glass balls. Apples and cookies, especially the animal cookies decorated with red sugar, were hung on many of the trees until the latter part of last century. Candles have given way to electric lights, but children still make long strings of popcorn and cranberries and chains of brightly colored paper and cover nuts with tinfoil. Yet store-bought ornaments are the order of the day. Some choose only red balls, some silver, some blue; but most people trim their trees in a haphazard fashion with a medley of ornaments, some descending unbroken from former generations, some fresh out of boxes from the five-and-ten. Ancient angels of wax, a stuffed turnip with green feathers for leaves, a parti-colored *distelfink* [1] with horsehair for tail, a Santa Claus in glass, a bell that tinkles faintly, a star of Bethlehem for the top of the tree, festoons of small glass balls, giant balls of solid colors, icicles of tinfoil or glass, and tinsel galore: these make a fir or spruce or juniper a cheerful sight. And on the evergreen branches are hung shepherds' crooks of red and white peppermint and little baskets and even pretzels of the same candy.

The outdoor trees arrayed with electric lights adorn the streets of the Dutch towns as they do those elsewhere in America, but these are always in addition to the trees within the houses. In the cities there is a large municipal tree, and the center of town is decked with garlands of laurel and lights.

Inseparable from the Christmas trees are the "yards" or "gardens" beneath them. These are elaborate landscapes, usually with jagged rocks in the background and hummocks of green moss for fields and at least a house or two and sometimes a whole village. On the ponds made of mirrors swim swans and ducks; in the fields sheep and deer and sometimes camels and elephants graze side by side; and down the mountainside over the glistening snow dashes Santa Claus in a sleigh drawn by reindeer, while the latest model streamliner shoots madly over bridge and through tunnel. In almost every village there are one or two yards on which the father of the family has labored every evening for a fortnight or two before Christmas. Some of these may have a running stream or a waterfall or a windmill that works. All the children in the neighborhood and a good many of the grown-ups flock to this house to see the yard under the tree. Even more ambitious are the yards in the local firehouses, where the men to while away the time between fires construct marvels of ingenuity: trains burrowing under mountains down which waterfalls leap, lakes with aircraft carriers, and towns with fire engines rushing through the streets.

In the Moravian towns and cities—Lititz, Emmaus, Nazareth, and Bethlehem—the *putz* replaces the yards. Putz, although literally mean-

[1] Literally goldfinch, but used loosely for any small gay bird.

ing a decoration, is used by the Moravians as a noun to designate the Christmas crib, the nativity scene with Mary and the Christ child, Joseph, the shepherds, the three kings, and all the animals. A century or more ago, Benigna Ettwein, who lived in the Sisters' House in Bethlehem, was famous for the sheep and chickens she made for the putzes: the sheep of clay wrapped with cotton, four matchsticks for legs and a splash of Chinese vermilion for the nose; and the chickens of tow, a bit of glue, and real chicken feathers. The putzes are quite as elaborate as the yards. Indeed, Bethlehem has a municipal putz that rivals the ambitious yards of the fire companies in Allentown, Reading, and York. There is something delightfully naïve and childlike about many of the Moravian putzes with their combination of Alpine scene, a barnyard with the nativity, and right in front of the startled Virgin and Christ child an electric train whizzing by.

During the Christmas season people in the Moravian settlements go putzing—that is, make a round of the houses boasting of the better putzes of the town. It was on these putz parties that the two sexes were first permitted to mingle when the old order was abolished and Bethlehem "opened up" in 1844. Of course, in the old days in Bethlehem everybody knew everybody else. Today you can take your chance, knock on someone's door, and ask to see the putz; but it is better if at least one person in the group has some acquaintance with the family. This is also true in the other Dutch communities where people sometimes make up parties to see the finest yards in town. Though your host recognizes the fact that you come to see the yard and not the family, this is no cause for offense; quite otherwise. It is thought a compliment that their yard is chosen as one worth seeing. All the social amenities are preserved. You are a guest in the house, and as this is the Christmas season wine and Christmas cookies are usually forthcoming. In Bethlehem, however, the hordes of strangers that descended on the town at Christmas have forced the Moravians to choose between serving the traditional wine and cookies and going bankrupt. Today you may still see the putzes, but unless you are a friend of the family you get none of the marzipan hearts and the brown and white Moravian cookies.

Santa Claus is descended from the *Sinterklaas,* or the St. Nicholas of the Netherlands, and the Kriss Kringle of Germany. In Holland on December 6th, St. Nicholas's Day, the saint visited each family, coming down the chimney by night to bring gifts to all good little boys and girls. In Germany, not on December 6th but on Christmas Eve, the Kriss Kringle, or *Christkindlein,* in the guise of an angel brought gifts to the children who had said their prayers and obeyed their mothers and fathers. When the Holland Dutch settled along the Hudson, they brought their good saint with them; and when the Palatines crossed the Atlantic to Pennsylvania, their Kriss Kringle made the voyage too. Even in Europe the two legends were tending to coalesce, while in America the Dutch St. Nicholas and the German Kriss Kringle soon became one. To this figure the name Santa Claus was given, and Christmas Eve became the proper time for him to climb down the chimneys with his bag of toys.

In the Dutch country of Pennsylvania, as well as in Holland and along the Rhine, Santa Claus had his direct opposite, a Mr. Hyde to his Dr. Jekyll, in a creature who punished the naughty children. This was the *Belsnickel,* who visited the house on Christmas Eve or possibly a few days before. He was usually a wag of the neighborhood dressed in a shaggy bearskin coat, if he had one, or a skunkskin cap—a vestige of the original meaning of Belsnickel, St. Nicholas in furs. Otherwise there was little of the kindly St. Nicholas in this fearful creature. Over his shoulder he carried a bag from which protruded a bundle of switches, and with a switch he hit the windowpane—a sound to chill the blood—before he opened the kitchen door. It was an even more dreadful moment for the children when in his gruff voice the Belsnickel asked if Mahlon and Kate and little Johnny had been good boys and girls during the year. The next moment fear was forgotten with the floor strewn with candies and nuts from the Belsnickel's bag, but when the children scampered to pick up the nuts and candy a crack from the Belsnickel's switch on their knuckles or little round bottoms sent them scurrying back to their parents. The Belsnickel had counterparts in at least several of the European countries. Sometimes very appropriately he was called *Teufel,* or devil. In Luxembourg he was known as Père Fouettard; in Holland, as Black Pieter, a slave to *Sinterklaas* who carried the bag full of presents as well as a light birch stick with which he switched the bad children, though in a halfhearted fashion. In parts of Germany *der Nicolaus* was both Santa Claus and the Belsnickel rolled into one.

The Belsnickel no longer visits the Dutch country—and a good riddance, say I. The fear with which his appearance filled so many children led to his banishment. The agony the children suffered was not in keeping with the Christmas spirit.

Many other old folk superstitions about Christmas have died out, some picturesque and a few poetic. The belief that cattle speak on Christmas Eve was current in many parts of the Christian world, and it is the subject of one of Thomas Hardy's most beautiful poems. Very like it is the belief that the water in the wells turns into wine for three minutes on Christmas Eve. Still another is that the Christmas rose bursts into bloom between eleven and twelve on Christmas Eve, no matter how cold the weather. It is on Christmas Eve, too, that bees lose their numbness and crawl outside the hive. One old custom was to make sure of a bountiful crop of fruit. Old cloth or straw was tied around the trunk of the tree while this rhyme was repeated:

> In dare nacht is Christus geboren.
> Du bischt noch nee verfroren.
> Ich wickle dich mit lumpe;
> Nau henkscht du dich mit glumpe.

Roughly translated, this is:

> On this night Christ was born.
> You have not yet frozen.
> I wrap you with rags;
> Now hang thick with fruit.

To make doubly sure of a good crop the tree was later wished a happy New Year, and sometimes a health was drunk to the tree. These customs, too, have their English counterparts. In the villages of the New Forest spiced ale was poured out to the orchards and meadows on Christmas Eve, and in the west of England the orchards were greeted in song.

Although burning candles on Christmas Eve is an old Moravian custom dating back to 1752 in Bethlehem, it has been only in recent years that the Pennsylvania Dutch have followed the example of Beacon Hill and placed candles in their windows. The Christmas Eve candlelight service of the Moravians is well worth lingering over for a moment. The Christmas Eve service is a children's service in honor of the Christ child. The story of the birth of the Christ child is read from the Scriptures, but chiefly this is a night of music. The cherished Moravian carol, F. F. Hagen's "Morning Star the Darkness Breaks," is sung alternately by the choir and by the children, always to the delight of the congregation. The other traditional music of Christmas Eve is Handel's "Lift up Your Heads, O Ye Gates" and "For unto Us a Child Is Born," Haydn's "Sey Wilkommen," the Gloria from Mozart's Twelfth Mass, and the Benedictus from Haydn's Sixth Mass. A part of the service is the "love feast" when coffee and Moravian buns dusted with sugar are served by specially chosen young women and men, the *dieners,* or servers. During the singing of the last hymns the dieners enter bearing trays of lighted candles, fifty to a tray. These are passed out to the congregation, the music rising at this point and filling the church with a thrilling crescendo. Each lighted candle is a symbol of the Light that came into the world many centuries ago in another Bethlehem. Slowly the candles are blown out here and there throughout the church and the service ends. Everyone takes home the precious beeswax candle with him, for more than anything else this candle is the essence of Christmas to the Moravian. During the Second World War every Moravian boy in the service was sent two beeswax candles for Christmas Eve, one for himself and one to give to a friend. From the earliest days of the settlement the beeswax candles have been made in Bethlehem. After the candlelight service the children go home to see the tree and the putz; it is then that everyone unwraps his presents.

As one thinks back over the history of the Moravian settlement of Bethlehem to that first Christmas Eve that gave the town its name, one feels that the people of Bethlehem have done well to make Christmas Eve the chief festival of the year. That Christmas Eve of 1741 was the first in the settlement. Ordered off the barony of Nazareth, the Moravians had made a clearing in the woods ten miles away and there built a log structure, part house, part stable. As they held their Christmas Eve services in the part of the building that served as a house, they could hear the cattle in the stalls on the other side of the wall that divided the log cabin in two. The story of the nativity must have come home to them in a way that it does to few of us. The three kings and even the shepherds watching their flocks by night may have seemed strange and remote to the devout Moravians in the lonely Pennsylvania forests, but the Child lying in a manger must have seemed almost in their midst. Possibly it was this that struck Count Zinzendorf as he picked up a candle and led the way into the stable, singing all the while the ancient carol in honor of Christ's birthplace:

"Nicht Jerusalem
Sondern Bethlehem
Aus der kommt,
Was mir frommet."

"Not from Jerusalem
But from Bethlehem
There cometh that
Which blesseth me."

We can well believe the words of the old Moravian diary: ". . . and in memory of the Birth of our dear Saviour, we went into the stable in the tenth hour and sang with feeling, so that our hearts melted." Thus with song on their lips they found the name for their new settlement. Bethlehem was born in a Christmas carol.

The Christmas dinner among the Pennsylvania Dutch—once more the "plain people" must be excepted—is the most elaborate of the year. As elsewhere in America, it is usually a turkey dinner ending with mince pie. Two traditional vegetables, dried corn and stewed onions, invariably accompany the turkey. It would be a heathen act to substitute other vegetables—green peas or broccoli, say—for these two. If such Johnny-come-latelys are served, they must be in addition to the dried corn and stewed onions. The fowl is almost always stuffed with that favorite Pennsylvania Dutch stuffing, potato filling; and very good it is.

Still another ancient holiday custom, *Christkindling,* was brought over from the Rhineland and Switzerland. Though it has died out in Pennsylvania, it persists among the distant kinsmen of the Pennsylvania Dutch in North Carolina, and therefore I give it its North Carolina name. Almost every night during the Christmas holidays a group of young people gathered at a country crossroads to make the rounds of near-by houses and farms. Often they wore disguises—blackened faces or masks and old clothes resurrected from the garret, thus proving their descent from the Swiss Knecht Ruprecht of hideous aspect and the Alsatian Hans Trapp with his string of bells. At each house or farm visited, the leader of the band, who back in Pennsylvania was known as the *wünscher,* stepped forward and, if the Christkindling were done in proper fashion, wished the master of the house and all his family and sometimes even his horses and cattle a merry Christmas, a happy New Year, and good health and wealth for the coming year, all this in a set singsong style. Often these wishes, which were in verse or at least doggerel, were astonishingly long. After the *wünscher* had done his part, the whole company burst into song, in Pennsylvania usually the hymn, "Hilf, Herr Jesu! loss gelingen." Thereupon several youths shot off guns, while others beat on drums or pans or blew a horn or conch shell. In the old days in Pennsylvania the masqueraders were treated at every farm to cider, apples, and Christmas cookies, for each family considered the visit of the Christkindlers a compliment. Sometimes rum or applejack or whisky was forced upon the serenaders in a desire to make them drunk. At the last house or two a farm breakfast, almost always including smoked sausage and raw fried potatoes, would be offered them, for the party broke up only at dawn.

During the nineteenth century *Christkindling* in Pennsylvania tended to center upon New Year rather than Christmas. "Shooting in the New Year" is one of the most firmly entrenched of New Year customs in the Dutch country. Oddly enough, it is Philadelphia rather than any of the Pennsylvania Dutch cities that keeps alive the old tradition of *Christkindling,* though in its elaborate Mummers' Parade and fantastic "shooters" the country masqueraders are altered almost beyond recognition.

Second Christmas, the day after Christmas, is often celebrated as a holiday. Long ago this was a rowdy festival filled with horseplay, fun, and frolic. Mühlenberg once thought it necessary to preach a sermon against the excesses of Second Christmas. Today it has become much more decorous and is largely given over to visiting and receiving visits. Probably more wine and cookies are consumed on this day than any other in the year. Since visiting back and forth is a favorite Amish diversion, Second Christmas is especially popular with them. The Pennsylvania Dutch try to prolong Christmas as much as possible. With them it is a fortnight rather than a day; it is the favorite time of the year for calls and parties and dances. Not until New Year has come and gone do they settle down to sober, normal life. Only when the Christmas tree is taken down and the needles swept up from the floor is the workaday world accepted once more.

One old Christmas custom that has vanished this many a year is the barring out of the schoolmaster a day or two before the Christmas holidays. The pupils used to shut themselves up in the schoolhouse and refuse to let the schoolmaster in until he bought his way with Christmas cookies, hard candies, and nuts. Sometimes they made him promise to give them shorter lessons, more holidays, and fewer birchings. The barring out of the schoolmaster occurred largely at the old subscription schools. When the state schools came in and the subscription schools went out, the custom died with them.

Part Six

THE ARTS

Music

The history of music among the Pennsylvania Dutch is largely that of three religious groups, the Society of the Woman in the Wilderness, the Ephrata cloisters, and the Moravians. The rest of the Pennsylvania Dutch, like settlers in New England, New York, and the South, took music in their stride. To be sure, there was Dr. Adams of Lancaster, who confessed that in his youth he had been "a consummate rake, but soon after he had married he turned himself to a sober and religious life and praised his Maker several hours in a day by playing on and singing to his organ"; but I feel that Dr. Adams must have been unique. There cannot have been very many like him among the Pennsylvania Dutch. True, the Pennsylvania Dutchman liked music: it was fine to have an organ in church; it was good fun to sing out an old tune on a sleighing party, especially if he had had a couple of swigs of rum. Otherwise he could take music or leave it. None of the religious groups, however, foreswore music as the Quakers did. The Mennonites, the Dunkards, and the Schwenkfelders all sang lustily, in church at least. The Amish prided themselves on their ancient hymnbook, the

Ausbund. And though the hymns celebrate the sufferings of the early
Amish martyrs, some of them were set to music of a worldly nature.
"There Went a Maiden with a Jug" is a surprising tune for the solemn,
tragic words of an Amish hymn. If anything, it is strange that there
was not more music among the early Pennsylvania Dutch, for in the
Germany from which they came music was in a flourishing state and
played a large part in the life of the people. This was a part of the
culture the Pennsylvania Dutch brought with them but which was
for the most part lost except at Ephrata and in the Moravian
towns.

The first of the Pennsylvania Dutch groups to show a marked interest in music was that curious nest of pietists on the Wissahickon known
as the Society of the Woman in the Wilderness. Almost as old as the
community itself is Kelpius's manuscript songbook of twelve hymns
written in German with metrical translations in English. Some of
these are of extraordinary length: one has 32 stanzas; one, 43; and one,
136! These were probably sung to the accompaniment of a virginal,
which the monastery is known to have possessed; or with the virginal
there may have been viols, hautboys, trumpets, and kettledrums, for
all of these instruments were used in their concerts. Furthermore,
Christopher Witt built an organ for them, probably the first organ in
the colony. The titles of the hymns are strange and wonderful: "Colloquium of the Soul With Its Self over her Long during Purification. Set
in a pensive Longing in the Wilderness. Anno 1698 ye 30th Jan.";
"The Power of Love which conquers The World, Sin & Death, in a
Pensive Poem Composed 1705"; and "A Loving Moan of the Discon-
solate Soul in the Morning Dawn. Or, from the Will's Rising, falling,
& still stand. As I lay in Christian Warmers House very weak, in a
small Bed, not unlike a Coffin, in May 1706." And still another, "A
Comfortable & Incouraging Song; Made intentionally for two lone-
some Widows: But here, for common good, something altered: By
occasion of a great Cold which seized me in July 1706."

The words of the hymns came close to living up to the titles, which
is saying a good deal for them. There is a certain vigor in the sixth
verse of the "Colloquium":

> I Dye indeed Daily
>   from Earthly degree,
> And crucify freely
>   Old Adam in me:

> Yet when I am thinking, now is he quite dead;
> He has but a little aside laid his head;
> So deep in the Heart is the Old lying hid!

In the seventeenth stanza of the hymn "Of the Wilderness" (not its full title!) there are lines not unlike some of Blake's:

> Consider the Sunflower, in Dark and Cloudy weather,
> How faithfully she turns her face to her dear Lover;
> Untill She's Pregnant grown, and bears like him a Seed;
> Then Rests She, and does bow in gratitude her hed.

In a number of the hymns there is a good deal of erotic imagery. More than once Kelpius tries the ice to see how much weight it will bear, drawing back only when it begins to crack. "The Power of Love," a long hymn with 136 stanzas, sets to music a story of seduction and repentance. In a few of the hymns the imagery is very like that of the metaphysical school of the early seventeenth century. They sound very much as though Kelpius had been reading John Donne, which I think highly unlikely. As Kelpius was a man of some education, a graduate of the University of Altdorf, his mind may have been attracted by some of the same sort of imagery that fascinated Donne.

Other members of the Society of the Woman in the Wilderness, or the Contented of the God-Loving Soul, as they preferred to call themselves, likewise wrote hymns. Justus Falckner, educated at the universities of Leipzig and Halle, wrote a number of hymns, one of which is still included in hymnals in Germany. This is "Auf, ihr Christen, Christi glieder," or "Rise, ye children of Salvation," to give it its English title. When Justus Falckner was ordained as a Lutheran minister at Old Swedes' in Philadelphia, there was music not only on the organ, but his Wissahickon brethren came with viol, hautboy, trumpet, and kettledrum to gladden the occasion.

At Ephrata the enthusiasm for hymns was more intense than it was at Germantown. Beissel, who had a gift for music, was able to pursue this passion to his heart's desire since his autocratic position at Ephrata enabled him to mold the community to his will. The production of hymns was astounding: if the chronicle is to be believed, more than 1,200 in the five years between 1741 and 1746. Christopher Sauer printed Beissel's *Zionistischer Weyrauch-Hügel* in 1739, probably the earliest American hymnbook. Dedicated to "all solitary turtle-doves cooing in the wilderness as a spiritual harp-playing in the many tunes of divine visitation," it presented to the world in its 792 pages 692 hymns, 441 of them by Beissel. The manuscript from which was printed the *Turtel-Taube,* or *The Song of the Solitary and Deserted Turtle-Dove, namely the Christian Church,* was a compilation of all the Ephrata hymns in existence before 1746. There were 763 titles of hymns, of which 310 were set to music twice, 69 three times, and 4 four times. The printed form of the *Turtel-Taube,* with 495 quarto pages, was first published at Ephrata in 1747, with later editions in 1755 and 1762. The *Paradisisches Wunder-Spiel,* or *Paradisiacal Wonder Music,* was a volume appearing in 1754, partly in manuscript and partly printed, with a second edition in 1766. The edition of 1754 was a book of choruses and anthems; the edition of 1766 was quite different. It contained 725 hymns, most of which had already appeared in the *Turtel-Taube.* In the 1766 edition 441 hymns were by Beissel, 72 including "Das Bruder-Lied" of 215 stanzas by the Brethren, and 99 including "Das Schwester-Lied" of 250 stanzas by the Spiritual Virgins.

This volume Ludwig Lewisohn praises for the variety of meter and stanzaic form as well as the fluidity and ease with which both were used. Lewisohn points out one of the most interesting characteristics of these hymns, the omission of all references to Hell and hate. In spite of the severe asceticism of their lives, it was the God of love these people worshiped and not the God of vengeance.

The music at Ephrata had its origin in the German chorales of the early Reformation. More like chants than hymns, these anthems were usually written in five, six, or seven parts, though sometimes only two or four. All parts except the bass, divided into high and low bass, were for women's voices. On occasion there was elaborate antiphonal singing. Beissel for all his absurd notions had an ear for music; and so had two of the brethren, John Peter Miller and Ludwig Blum, the latter a trained musician. The choir was ruled by Beissel with an iron hand. With rehearsals lasting four hours, nerves were so on edge by the end of the evening that the session seldom ended without tears. The diet of the singers was carefully regulated by Beissel. All meat was ruled out, as was milk, which caused "heaviness and uneasiness." Cheese, "which produced heat," was banned; and so was butter, "which makes indolent and dull and satiates to such an extent that one no longer feels the need of singing or praying." Eggs, too, were proscribed, since they "arouse numerous capricious cravings"; and even honey, "which brings bright eyes and a cheerful spirit but not a clear voice," was forbidden. Beans were too heavy. As Beissel considered that fruit, too, had a harmful effect on the voice, the diet on which the singers lived was one of wheat, buckwheat, potatoes, beets, turnips, parsnips, and carrots—with water to drink. Thus, Beissel believed, the voice "may become angelic, heavenly, pure, and clear." Great pains were also taken to learn to break the voice in the proper way, to acquire the right falsetto tones.

Only the Spiritual Virgins and the Solitary Brethren, all of whom had taken vows of chastity, were permitted to sing in the choir, for Beissel maintained that sexual intercourse was injurious to the voice. These ideas Beissel set forth in the preface to the *Turtel-Taube*, but on second thought he decided to omit the declaration that sexual intercourse harms the voice. When the brethren objected to this deletion, he consented to keep it in, for in the words of the *Chronicon Ephratense*: "This was but fair, for who does not know that carnal intercourse not only stains the soul, but also enfeebles the body and renders the voice coarse and rough, so that the senses of him must be very blunt who cannot distinguish a virgin from a married woman by her voice."

The best contemporary description of the singing at Ephrata occurs in a letter written to Governor John Penn by the Reverend Jacob Duché, the fashionable Tory clergyman ensconced at Christ Church in Philadelphia when the Revolution was gathering head:

The music had little or no air of melody; but consisted of simple, long notes, combined in the richest harmony. The counter, treble, tenor and bass were all sung by women, with sweet, shrill and small voices; but with a truth and exactness in the time and intonation that was admirable. It is impossible to describe to your Lordship my feelings upon this occasion. The performers sat with their heads reclined, their countenances solemn and dejected, their faces pale and emaciated from their manner of living, their cloathing exceeding white and quite picturesque, and their music such as thrilled to the very soul.—I almost began to think myself in the world of spirits, and that the objects before me were ethereal.

Legend had it that shortly after the French and Indian War some English visitors to Ephrata asked that a copy of the music be sent to the king. This was done, and some time later a gift was received in return; but the gift so shocked Beissel that it was buried secretly, and to this day no one knows what it was. Since the king was a sound Protestant, it could hardly have been a crucifix or an image of the Virgin. That it was a bust of the king, and maybe one of the queen as well, which

Beissel would consider to be forbidden by the First Commandment, is one of the better guesses.

But it was Bethlehem, born in song—the Christmas carol of Adam Drese of Bohemia—that was the center of music. No other settlement of the Pennsylvania Dutch could hold a candle to Bethlehem in this respect; no other town among the American colonies, not Philadelphia, not Boston, not Charleston, could surpass it. From the very start music was the heart and soul of Bethlehem. To a large degree it was the life of the people. Just as the *Mayflower* was loaded mast-high with fine furniture—or so we are given to understand—the Moravian ships had musical instruments as part of their cargo. At the Christmas festival in 1743 there was an orchestra of violins, viola da braccioes, viola da gambas, flutes, and French horns. In 1744 a spinet was brought from London; two years later a small portable organ, made by the Moravian organ builder, John Gottlob Klemm of Philadelphia, was added to it; and in 1751 a large organ was built for the chapel. In 1742 the first *Singstunde,* a service devoted entirely to the singing of hymns, was held. Although the Moravians were extremely fond of hymns, their love of music did not stop with hymns, as did that of so many other religious groups; yet the Moravian Church was rich in hymns. Its first hymn-book, published at Jungbunzlau in 1501, was largely made up of para-phrases and translations of old Latin hymns to which were added some original hymns, mostly by John Hus, Bishop Luke of Prague, and Bishop Matthias of Kunwald. A later hymnbook, *Ein Neu Gesang-büchlen,* was published at Jungbunzlau in 1531. Zinzendorf was a most enthusiastic composer of hymns, surpassing even Beissel. He was the author of more than two thousand hymns, many of them filled with minute references to the Pennsylvania of his day. Some of these hymns, translated by Wesley and other Methodists, are still included in Metho-dist hymnals. About seventy are to be found in Moravian hymnbooks and a few in the Episcopal. His daughter, the Countess Benigna, also wrote hymns, as did Bishop Nitschmann and Bishop Cammerhof; in fact, almost all of the leading Moravians tried their hand at hymns at one time or another.

In 1744 the Collegium Musicum was organized, and one hour each evening was devoted by the orchestra to practice. At this early date the symphony orchestra was small; there were only fourteen players: two first violins, two second violins, two violas, one cello, one double bass, two flutes, two trumpets, and two French horns. In Europe, also, orchestras at this time were small. By 1771 the orchestra at Bethlehem had added six more players: two bassoons, two oboes, one clarinet, and one kettledrum. By this time they had the full complement of instruments used in the European orchestras of that day. There were even such ancient instruments as serpents and zinkes, but these were not dignified by use in the symphony orchestra.

By the time of the French and Indian War, Bethlehem was noted for its music. Benjamin Franklin, who had gone north to Bethlehem to direct the defenses of the frontier, wrote to his wife in January, 1756: "We listened to very fine music in the Church, close by. Flutes, oboes, French horns, and trumpets do accompany the organ for our Bethlehem brethren." This was nothing out of the ordinary, as such musical instruments were regularly used in church to accompany the anthems.

From the first *Singstunde,* formed in 1742, choirs developed to take their place by the orchestra. Music at Bethlehem was never confined to a small group. There was nothing exclusive about it; it was a common possession belonging to everyone. Everybody sang and played some instrument or, more likely, several instruments. Children were taught music as a matter of course. In 1759, when the boys' school was transferred from Bethlehem to Nazareth, an orchestra of boys played at the head of the procession. From 1768 to 1795 there were two separate choruses, male and female. Yet some of these Moravians were not satisfied with playing in an orchestra or singing in a chorus; they attempted to compose music. Even before 1760 whole concerts were given over to music they themselves had written. In 1761 the Reverend Immanuel Nitschmann became the director of the Collegium Musicum, bringing with him a rich store of manuscript copies of quartets and symphonies. With Moravians going back and forth to Europe, Bethlehem musicians were kept well abreast of music abroad. Moravians America-bound brought scores of the newest music to Bethlehem with them. These old scores, many of which are still in existence, are so well thumbed that it is plain that they were put to good use.

The most noted of the early Bethlehem composers was John Frederick Peter, born in 1746 at Herrndyck in Holland. The organist of the church at Bethlehem, he succeeded Immanuel Nitschmann as director of the Collegium Musicum, serving from 1770, the year of his arrival in Bethlehem, to 1786 and again from 1793 to 1813. His "Partitur einen Freuden Music zum Friedens Dank Feste," dated 1763, is scored for a four-part chorus, strings, two flutes, two trumpets, and "fondamento."

His six quintets were written for two violins, two violas, and a cello. In addition to these works he wrote thirty-eight anthems for chorus, solo, and orchestra. Though by no means a genius, John Frederick Peter was an accomplished musician, a trained violinist and organist, and the first composer of serious music in this country. There was no other musician in the American colonies who was his equal. His closest rivals were the other Bethlehem musicians, John Antes and David Moritz Michael. All three were clearly superior to the other American musicians of their day.

Under the direction of Nitschmann and Peter, works by Bach and Handel were rehearsed and performed by the chorus and some of the chamber music and symphonies of Haydn and Mozart by the orchestra. Three of Mozart's earlier symphonies as well as some of Haydn's string quartets and other chamber music and nine of his symphonies all had a hearing at Bethlehem before 1790, some of them within a few years of their composition. The copies of Haydn's and Mozart's quartets and symphonies were the first of their works to reach this country. In the library at Bethlehem are manuscript copies of six trios and three symphonies for which the latest possible date is 1785. Finally, in 1811, Peter's career as director at Bethlehem reached its climax when Haydn's *Creation* was given its first complete performance in America.

The first of the important Bethlehem musicians of American birth was John Antes, who was born in Frederick Township, Montgomery County, in 1740. Antes composed a number of string quartets and also some anthems. Some of his music was performed by Haydn, with whom Antes was acquainted.

Another of the early composers was David Moritz Michael (1751–1823), who wrote a "parthie" and suite, both of which were scored for two clarinets, two horns, and a bassoon, and even a symphony for a full orchestra. Michael was particularly noted for his compositions of wind music, then called *Parthien,* or "harmony music," played at the summer evening concerts by the little orchestra on the belvedere of the Single Brethren's House. Yet his best known work by far was "Die Wasserfahrt" (The Boat Ride), a suite for two clarinets, two horns, and two bassoons. For many years "Die Wasserfahrt" was played each Whitmonday, when all of the little town of Bethlehem took a holiday on the river. Musicians on a flatboat propelled by four men with poles headed the procession to Calypso Island, with the rest of the town following in boats or walking along the banks. The music of "Die

Wasserfahrt" was suited to the journey. A mile from town was Deep Hole, where the men were unable to touch bottom with their poles. Here where the boat was whirled in a small eddy the music was wild and tempestuous; then when the boat moved into quiet water the music in turn was filled with joy at their escape. Whitmonday was celebrated at Bethlehem in this fashion through much of the nineteenth century, though in 1874 the flatboat was replaced by the *Calypso,* run by steam, which was later followed by another boat, the *Lotta.* But when the *Lotta* fell into disrepair, no boat succeeded her.

With the Moravians' love of music it is only natural that their towns should have attracted builders of organs. John Gottlob Klemm and David Tanneberger, associated together in business, were two of the most skillful builders of organs in the colonies. Between 1757 and 1762, the year of Klemm's death, the two men built organs for the churches at Bethlehem, Nazareth, and Lititz. In 1765 Tanneberger moved to Lititz, where he had his workshop until his death in 1804. Tanneberger built organs for many churches in the Dutch country: Maxatawny, Goshenhoppen, Hebron, Easton, Hanover, Macungie, Tohickon, New Holland, York, and for four different churches in Lancaster. But his fame was not confined to the Pennsylvania Dutch: he built organs for churches in Albany, New York; White Plains, New York; Baltimore; Madison, Virginia; Salem, North Carolina; and Philadelphia. The organ for Zion's Lutheran Church in Philadelphia was the largest in the country. When it was dedicated on January 8, 1791, George and Martha Washington and many members of Congress attended the service. Tanneberger also manufactured pianos in his shop, selling them for £20 each. In North Carolina there was another famous Moravian builder of organs, Joseph Bullitschek. Apparently there was an affinity between the Moravian faith and organbuilding.

Of the music at Bethlehem the children had their full share. A girl of twelve in school at Bethlehem wrote to her brother in Connecticut on August 16, 1787:

"There are about thirty little girls of my age. Here I am taught music both vocal and instrumental. I play the guitar twice a day; am taught the spinet and forte-piano, and sometimes I play the piano."

Of the church service she wrote:

"They sing enchantingly, in which they are joined with bass viols, violins, and an organ. To call the people into the chapel four French horns are blown, with which you would be delighted."

A final touch makes the school life sound idyllic, "After we are in bed, one of the young ladies, with her guitar and voice, serenades us to sleep."

Music at all times was a "must" at Bethlehem. There were a number of formal concerts, too, especially after the building of the new church in 1806, one of the largest structures in the country. Between 1807 and 1819 there were 241 concerts in all, sometimes as many as 36 in a single year. All of these were free, although near the door was a box labeled "For the Support of Music" into which people could drop money. The largest receipts were for the year 1809, when 36 concerts were given. That year the take was $42.86. The average per concert over a period of thirteen years was $1.25. This money was used to buy strings for the violins or cellos, or even to purchase new instruments, or to pay for copying music, or to buy candles for the music stands, each of which had a folding candlestick on an arm to the left. It is clear that these people played for the love of it.

In 1819 the Collegium Musicum was permitted to lapse, but the following year the Philharmonic Society, with both an orchestra and a chorus, was organized. In 1834 and 1835 Haydn's *Seasons* had its first American production at Bethlehem. "Spring" and "Summer" were sung in 1834, and "Autumn" and "Winter" in 1835. Some of these concerts were extremely ambitious: the program for the third performance of Haydn's *Creation,* given on May 20, 1839, shows that there were 125 participants.

In the early 1880's the Philharmonic Society went out of existence, to be replaced by the Bethlehem Choral Union under the direction of John Frederick Wolle. With the Choral Union began the enthusiasm at Bethlehem for Bach. On June 5, 1888, Bach's *Passion According to St. John* was sung, its first complete performance in America; and four years later, on April 8, 1892, *The St. Matthew Passion.* When, however, Dr. Wolle proposed to go on with the more difficult *Mass in B Minor,* he was faced with revolt and the chorus was broken up. In the season of 1892–1893 the Bethlehem Oratorial Society took the place of the Choral Union. Then for five years there was no organized music in Bethlehem, although the choir of the Moravian Church sang parts of Bach's *Christmas Oratorio* on December 18, 1894. In 1898 a group of singers got together to form a chorus that was formally organized as the Bach Choir after the first Bach festival in 1900.

The performance of the *Mass in B Minor* at the first Bach festival on March 27, 1900, by a chorus of eighty and an orchestra of thirty under the direction of Dr. Wolle, was its first complete production in America. At the second Bach festival, in 1901, the *Christmas Oratorio* was sung on May 23, the *St. Matthew Passion* on May 24, and the *Mass in B Minor* on May 25. This was the first complete American production of the *Christmas Oratorio*. The Bach festivals were off to a brilliant start. The whole town took a holiday for the festivals, and visitors came from far and near. In 1905, with the departure of Dr. Wolle for California, the choir was disbanded, to be reorganized in 1911 when Dr. Wolle was persuaded to return. With his return the Bach festival became a national institution. Since 1912 the orchestra has been strengthened by the addition of players from the Philadelphia Orchestra, but the choir continues to be made up of people of the neighborhood. The festival each May is devoted entirely to Bach, his oratorios and masses, with the *Mass in B Minor* given on the second day of the festival. The music is presented, not as a concert, but as a religious service with the congregation joining in the chorales. There is no applause. The beginning of the service is announced each day from the belfry of the church by the trombone choir playing the ancient Moravian chorales. Incidentally, the Moravian Trombone Choir, founded in 1754, has the longest continuous existence of any musical organization in this country. The Bach Choir, of course, is not exclusively Moravian, but certainly it is the flowering of the Moravian enthusiasm for music. Its roots strike deep into Moravian history and into American history.

All through this chapter I have grossly neglected Nazareth and Lititz, both overshadowed by Bethlehem but both with considerable music. At Nazareth in the eighteenth century the concerts often concluded with Haydn's "Farewell" Symphony. As each player finished his part, he blew out his candle, the music dying down as one by one the candles were blown out until only a lone violinist was carrying the soft melody of the andante; and then, reaching the finale, he too blew out his candle to provide a close unusually quiet yet striking too.

In 1938 a number of old manuscripts were unearthed in the music loft of the Moravian church at Lititz—294 pieces all told, most of them hymns but among them some chamber music and several symphonies. All the more usual musical instruments were in use at Lititz as well as such antiquated instruments as the ophicleide and the serpent. The first church orchestra at Lititz was organized in 1765. Between 1815 and 1845 there was quite a respectable orchestra, the Philharmonic Society, which in 1838 was so ambitious as to present *The Creation*. One of the Lititz musicians, Tobias Hirte, was an eccentric whom Kipling pictured in "Brother Square-Toes" and "A Priest in Spite of Himself," two stories in his volume, *Rewards and Fairies*. In this century monthly concerts at Lititz have been given by the Symphony Club, organized in 1890.

A Mennonite contribution to music were the "shape-notes," usually associated with the Southern mountains but which were widely used by the Mennonites and probably devised by them. This was a system by which musical notes were represented by diamonds, squares, triangles, and circles.

A further contribution was made by Joseph Funk, a Mennonite who settled in the Shenandoah Valley at the base of the Alleghenies and set up a music school. This proved such a success that the region in which he lived was dubbed Singers' Glen. Not satisfied with the pupils who came to his door, he sought out singers all through the Valley of Virginia. He wrote many songbooks, of which one, *Harmonia Sacra*, went through seventeen editions. After the Civil War his grandson, Aldine S. Kieffer, published two songbooks, *The Christian Harp* and *The Temple Star*, both very popular.

The folk ballads of the Pennsylvania Dutch went unnoticed until yesterday. Only in very recent years has there been an attempt to collect them. Scouring the hills and valleys of Pennsylvania, Thomas R. Brendle and William S. Troxell have recorded more than two hundred folk songs, many of which might have been lost had it not been for their efforts. A goodly number of the ballads were brought to America two or more centuries ago by the earliest settlers. "Der Tod von Basel" (Death from Basel) is an old European ballad, while "Des Buchlich Mennli" (The Little Hunchback) is a ballad about a house sprite from pre-Christian times. The accumulative ballad "Jockeli will net biere schittele" (Jakie Will Not Shake the Pears) is likewise of ancient origin; and "Wie Ich von Frankreich komm" (As I Came from France) goes back, at the very least, to the flight of the Huguenots from France. "Tru die li," though made their own by the canal men of Lehigh and Northampton counties, is undoubtedly much older. Many of the other ballads, too, may be old: "Shpinn, shpinn, meine liewe Dochder" (Spin, Spin, My Dear Daughter), the most popular of them all; "Was kann Ich so zwitzerich danze" (I Can Dance So

Flashily), in which the tempo of the dance accompanying the ballad builds up to a frantic climax; "M'r schlochta 'n alder Hawna" (We'll Kill an Old Rooster), outstanding for its humor; and "Maedel, widd du Heiere?" (Maiden, Will You Marry?), begun by a young man and taken up by a maiden, supposedly lovesick. In a different category is Philip Gombert's "Ein Trauerlied der Susanna Cox" (A Dirge of Susanna Cox), which in the manner of the Elizabethan broadsides celebrated the hanging of Susanna Cox in Reading on June 10, 1809, for the murder of her infant child. Few of the old ballads and folk songs are heard today, which is a real loss to us, for along with their simplicity and naïveté many of them have the freshness and charm of an earlier age. Such a one is "Hawwer Reche" (Raking Oats). It has a fine country flavor and a touch of poetry, two qualities seldom encountered in the songs of tin-pan alley.

> Es rejjert un schneejet,
> 'Sis kalt schtaermich Wedder:
> Glei kummt d'r Bauer rei
> Un holt e wennich Cider.
>
> Wer will d'r Hawwer reche?
> Wer will en binde?
> Ich hab emol en Schetzelkatt,
> Kann's nimmi finde.

In English this is:

> It rains and it snows,
> It's cold, stormy weather;
> In comes the farmer
> And gets a little cider.
>
> Who will rake the oats?
> Who will bind them?
> Once I had a true love,
> Now I cannot find her.

"For Fancy"

Another side of the Pennsylvania Dutch, as naïve and gaudy as their belief in powwowing and their tales of Tyl E[i]leschpijjel, is to be found in their folk art. Nowhere in America except in the early art of the Spanish Southwest was there folk art comparable to that of the Pennsylvania Dutch. The folk art of New England and the South is feeble and pallid in contrast to the rich vigor of the barn signs, taufscheins, and dower chests of Pennsylvania. This folk art was born of the Pennsylvania Dutch love of the gay and the beautiful. It was a part of their desire to add color to life. It put no dollars and cents in the pockets of these practical people. A chest or barn without designs was just as useful as an elaborately painted one; the folk art was only "for fancy."

This Pennsylvania Dutch love of color and decoration expressed itself in many ways. Barns, dower chests and bride boxes, chairs and settees, stoves and firebacks, tombstones, Kentucky rifles, the tool chests of the Conestoga wagons, Bibles and hymnbooks, *geburtsscheins* [1] and taufscheins, *trauscheins* [2] and *haus-segens,* [3] towels and quilts, hooked rugs, pie plates, crocks and jugs, pitchers and sugar bowls, trays and platters, coffeepots and tea caddies, cooky cutters and cake molds: these show the range and wealth of Pennsylvania Dutch folk art. The familiar things of life, things used day after day: on these were sprinkled the tulips and hearts, the distelfinks and peacocks, and the other motifs so dearly loved by the Pennsylvania Dutch. Of these designs the tulip

[1] Birth certificates.
[2] Marriage certificates.
[3] Literally "house blessings"—wall mottoes.

was the most popular, and second to the tulip was the heart. There are pinks, too, and an occasional fuchsia or rose, but unless some of the conventional barn signs are intended to represent the lily other flowers are largely ignored. The tulip is everywhere. Very often it appears in clusters of three. These may be a symbol of the Trinity, especially when they adorn tombstones; or they may be merely a particularly graceful design. Another theory is that the tulip is a symbol of fertility—though why a tombstone should be decorated with symbols of fertility I do not know. As I tend to shy away from symbolism, I think that the tulip was used so widely because it lent itself so readily to decorative effects and not because of any symbolism, either holy or profane. The tulip appears on dower chests and bride boxes (could it have been intended as a symbol of fertility here!), on stove plates and firebacks, on tauf-scheins, on quilts—indeed on everything the Pennsylvania Dutch decorated. It is used so often on slipware that this pottery is sometimes called tulipware. As I said before, the tulip is decorative; and it is one of the easiest of all designs to draw. I think this goes a long way, too, to explain the popularity of the heart—or does the heart always stand for true love? Fertility and true love: a curious people, these Pennsylvania Dutch! Or perhaps not so curious; perhaps just full of common sense.

Birds, too, appear frequently in Dutch folk art, though not to decorate barns. The distelfink, a sprightly little bird that is probably an imaginative Pennsylvania Dutch version of the goldfinch, embellishes dower chests, chairs, and settees, taufscheins and hymnbooks and other illuminated writings, and even towels. I have no idea what it is a symbol of. It's gay and it's saucy. Does it need to be anything else? The pea-cock, with its exotic beauty, early took the fancy of the Pennsylvania Dutch. It is encountered most frequently on china and pottery or in fraktur. The dove, the pelican, and the parrot were also used in decoration, especially in the illuminated manuscripts. The symbolism of the dove may be peace, but it may also be wedded bliss: pay your money and take your choice. The pelican all through the Middle Ages was believed to feed its young by feeding on itself; it is the symbol of self-sacrifice. As for the parrot, I think the Pennsylvania Dutch were enchanted by its gaudy plumage. I doubt if the parrot was meant to symbolize anything. Most other birds the Dutch ignored. Apparently they never saw a robin, a blue jay, or a cardinal. Even that fantastic bird, the turkey, made no impression on them—which goes to show

how thoroughly the Pennsylvania Dutch designs were ruled by convention. The rooster appears as a weather vane, particularly those on churches. After the Revolution the American eagle was used widely but rarely with imagination. It never became a Pennsylvania Dutch bird like the distelfink and the peacock.

As for animals, Berks County chests sported unicorns and men on horseback. There are men on horseback, too, on some of the finest of the sgrafitto pie plates. Both horses and cows appear as weather vanes, rabbits as cooky cutters. A deer very occasionally crops up, too; and a fish—just any fish—may appear as a cake mold or cooky cutter. Dogs and cats, sheep and pigs, bears and foxes went pretty much unnoticed.

Among the other motifs are angels, largely confined to taufscheins and other forms of illuminated writing, and also to tombstones, although it may be that some of the cooky cutters were intended to represent angels. Either they are angels or women with tremendous leg-of-mutton sleeves; my guess is angels. Fruit in the form of peaches, plums, grapes, and cherries prettifies the backs of chairs and settees, while pomegranates enliven fraktur. Perhaps I had better explain again that *fraktur* is the Pennsylvania Dutch word for illuminated writing as it survived in the Dutch country, particularly at Ephrata, during the eighteenth and early nineteenth centuries. Fraktur is especially notable for its stylized foliage and its dramatic use of scrolled letters. Countless other motifs adorn fraktur, among them the human figure clothed and unclothed, mermaids and sea horses, lions and bobcats straight out of Edward Hicks's "Peaceable Kingdom," hummingbirds, quails, and the tree of life from the midst of Eden.

The Persian origin of much of Pennsylvania Dutch design is one of the most extraordinary things about it. Compare the tulips, pinks, and pomegranates of Persian prints with those in Pennsylvania Dutch fraktur or the decorations on dower chests and the close resemblance is indisputable. Not only is there similarity in detail but often the general treatment is very much alike. Nor is such Persian influence as fantastic as it seems at first sight. There was a certain infiltration of Eastern culture into western Europe with the Crusades; there was more with the Ottoman conquest of the Balkans: but probably it was the traders of Venice who did most to introduce Persian art into Europe. During the Middle Ages Venice built up a rich trade with the Levant. From Venice the luxuries of the East were carried to Padua, Verona,

Bolzano, and other northern Italian cities; thence to South Germany and down the Rhine. In this way the Rhineland came into contact with the art of Persia. Why the Rhineland was so strongly influenced by Persian art is more difficult to explain. It may have delighted in the tulip so lavishly used by the Persians, yet tulipomania never seized the Rhineland as it did Holland. But examine some of the fraktur painting, particularly that of the Ephrata Cloisters, and see how amazingly like Persian art it is.

In the fraktur of the Pennsylvania Dutch, the medieval ages made their last stand. Even after illuminated writing died out in Europe it lived on in Pennsylvania. The finest examples of fraktur are those from Ephrata. Usually it graces the title pages of books or the chapter headings; sometimes it is found all through the book. Much fraktur is crude and most of it is naïve, but it has a liveliness and gaiety that make it art—on one of the lower levels, at least. Henry S. Borneman, the notable collector of fraktur and the chief authority on the subject, has reminded us that it fits to perfection William Morris's definition of folk art as "art made by the people and for the people as a joy to the maker and the user."

Although the monks and nuns of Ephrata, who were able to devote endless hours to their work, created the most elaborate specimens, fraktur was produced in many other parts of the Dutch country as well. Taufscheins were in great demand. A child was not properly baptized of there was no taufschein to show for it. Because little was needed in the way of materials for fraktur, the local schoolmaster or even the preacher often set up as a practitioner of the art. Quill pens were used for the lettering. The ink, home-made, has long since faded to a reddish brown. Paints were mixed with the white of egg and cherry-tree gum according to a recipe centuries old. In the eighteenth century the schoolmaster or preacher made the whole taufschein, but later, when the printing presses began to turn out taufscheins, he merely colored the angels and distelfinks and filled in the names. Johann Philip Gombert, schoolmaster of Bern Township, Berks County, and the author of the "Trauerlied of Susanna Cox," was such a filler-in of taufscheins. In this he was ably assisted by his wife, Catharina, who made her living after her husband's death in 1822 by painting baptismal angels and distelfinks by the thousand. The schoolmaster's careful printing also appears in marriage certificates and in the birth, death, and marriage records in family Bibles. This printing was done with goose quills or

376   *The Pennsylvania Dutch*

sometimes with pen and brush. It is not fraktur at its height; rather it is its dying gasp.

The barn symbols or "witch signs" are so diverse and gay that they are one of the brightest glories of Pennsylvania Dutch folk art. Though there are hundreds of patterns, they are largely variations on a few designs: the star, the lily or tulip in full flower, the sun, the sunburst, the spinning whorl, and the inverted teardrop. There is the star with four points, with five, with six, and with eight; the star within circles; the star combined with the lily, the spinning whorl, the inverted teardrops, or hearts. Almost every possible variation has been used. Some of the barn signs are so simple, a five-pointed star in white within a circle in white, that the most mechanical painter could turn them out. Others are so intricate that they are obviously the work of skilled craftsmen. In the country west of the village of Virginville the barns have witch signs twice life-size and of unusual intricacy. It must have been a painter with a touch of genius who decorated the barns in that neighborhood. Usually there are three witch signs on the front of a barn, but if the barn is large enough there may be five. If there are three signs, the one in the center usually differs in design from the other two. If there are five there may be three separate patterns. If a farmer has set his heart on making his barn really gay, there may be a witch sign on each of the gable ends of the barn as well, these of still another design, thus bringing the total number of witch signs to the mystic seven; and there may even be smaller stars or lilies or spinning whorls on the hood above the barn door, quarter witch signs in the lower corners of the front, and scallops in white along the edge of the overhang. A barn so lovingly decorated is a warming sight.

Toward the end of the nineteenth century paintings of horses and cows began to replace the geometrical witch signs on the front of the barns, or sometimes they appear in addition to two or three witch signs. Seldom naïve enough to be amusing, the paintings of horses and cows nevertheless contribute to the total decorative effect. They, too, are "for pretty" and not to scare away witches or ward off lightning. Other decorative devices used are the broad white bands of paint along the bottom and the sides of the forebay, and outlining the great north doors, and sometimes marking other structural lines of the barn. Or there may be huge false arches of white over the doors and windows. These, too, are purely decoration.

Pennsylvania Dutch pottery, like fraktur, is of ancient origin. The sgrafitto type, in which the designs are etched in the clay with a quill, dates from the thirteenth century; while slipware, in which the design is formed by a light liquid clay trickling through a tube over the darker surface of the pottery, was made by the Romans. The designs in slipware are of the crudest sort—a few wiggle-waggles to represent a snake, if your mind runs to snakes; or if your imagination soars, a simple tulip or distelfink. In sgrafitto something more ambitious could be tried—an eagle with a flag that was just as hideous as that on the butcher's wagon. Luckily most of the designs used were traditional and vastly superior to the eagle with the flag. The tulips, peacocks, and pelicans were especially good, although even better was the galloping dragoon by David Spinner, the noted Bucks County potter; most delightful of all were the dancing figures of the Meschianza, the famous Tory ball given in Philadelphia during the winter of its captivity. It was usually on the pie plates that the finest decorations were lavished. The pie plates, decorated or undecorated, are rather flat, with an unbroken curve so that a cut piece of pie will slip out easily. Without either rim or base the Pennsylvania Dutch pie plate is unique; there is no plate like it anywhere. Sometimes there was a motto or bit of verse around the edge:

> Alle schoene Junfern hat Gott erschaffen.
> Die sein vör die Heffner
> Awer nicht vür die Pfaffen.

Translated this is:

> God has created all the pretty girls.
> They are for the potters
> But not for the priests.

Occasionally the verse was poetic instead of merely jocular:

> Juferlein und rosen bleder
> Vergehen wie regen weder.

Which means:

> Youth and rose petals
> Fade away like a rainy day.

Much of the pottery was devoid of decoration. The apple-butter crocks and milk pans, of warm redware or shining black, were perfectly plain. Simple, too, were the Turk's head molds in redware for sponge cakes. Very often the gray stone jugs and crocks had a tulip design in blue. The flowerpots were almost invariably plain. Yet the shapes of all these were so frequently graceful and the color of the glaze so beautiful that one does not regret the absence of decoration. Warm shades of brown, red, orange, yellow, and even green, in almost every possible hue, appear in this pottery. In many respects the plain pottery is very like that of North Carolina, which is to be expected since the Carolina pottery is Pennsylvania Dutch in origin. Occasionally a potter to please a child or give expression to a holiday mood would make a water whistle in the form of a bird, a toy both good to look at and pretty to hear. Though only yesterday the Stahl brothers were still making pottery in Powder Valley, it looked for a time as though Pennsylvania Dutch pottery was a lost art. Then suddenly making pottery became a fad and amateurs took to it with gusto. You could hardly throw a stone without hitting a potter. In quite a different class from these amateurs is Mrs. Naaman Keyser of Plymouth Meeting, whose spirited designs are traditional in feeling yet fully alive and vigorous.

The china of the Pennsylvania Dutch was imported from England. Strangely enough, two types were made specifically for the Pennsylvania Dutch market, gaudy Dutch and spatterware. Gaudy Dutch had a bold design of flowers splashed over it—to my mind often ugly. Spatterware is another matter; it has a gay, childlike quality that gives it charm. Usually there is a band of color, not solid but a fine spatter of dots, blue, rose, yellow, green, or purple, and then an oasis of white with a crude design of a rose or possibly a peacock or a little house. Other china, too, was popular, especially Staffordshire in multifold patterns and Adams ware with the chaste and lovely rose. These, however, were not typically Dutch. And then there were luster pitchers, which sold well in the Dutch counties as they did elsewhere.

The Dutch made their own glass, of which that made by Stiegel is by far the best known. Its perfect shades of blue, violet, amber, rose, and green have made Stiegel glass highly prized among American antiques. Less beautiful but attractive nevertheless is the clear flint glass enameled with crude but sprightly Dutch designs.

Much fine work was done in iron, both by Stiegel and other iron-masters. The stove plates with biblical scenes or primitive designs in which tulips and the ironmaster's name share prominence are justly celebrated. Oddly enough, the earlier stove plates are the best. Though a few of the biblical plates have grace and elegance, the vigor and naïveté of the work of the lesser designers make many of the cruder stove plates more delightful than the more sophisticated patterns. Besides the stove plates there were some other good pieces of cast iron—trivets for pots and sadirons, many of them with intricate, lacy designs very like the barn signs; and andirons representing Hessian mercenaries. There was much good work in wrought iron, too, especially in locks and latches and hinges. There were some interesting weather vanes, such as the one of the paschal lamb of St. John on the cupola of the Bell House in Bethlehem and the elegant one on the old church at Trappe. Some of the best wrought iron of the time is that of the tool boxes of the Conestoga wagons. In these elaborate decorations the smiths vied with one another to show what they could do.

There was an abundance of other forms of folk art. Nowhere were patchwork quilts more beautiful in design, more exquisitely sewn. One extraordinarily fine quilt, now at Morrisienna, near the village of Chatham in Chester County, has a border of cherry trees. Some of the old quilts had names as gay as the patchwork: Cherry Spray, Seven Stars, Tree of Paradise, Turkey Tracks, Four Doves in a Window, Philadelphia Pavement, The Drunkard's Path, and Forty Times Around the World. Even now in country villages there are quilting parties on winter afternoons. Woven coverlets of wool, frequently in blue and white but also in other colors, were made by the Pennsylvania Dutch, though oftener by professional weavers than at home. Finest of all the fancywork, and a treasured part of the *Haus-steier*,[4] were the show towels that were hung over the everyday towel when company was expected. These were long homespun panels embroidered in cross-stitch with tulips, hearts, stars, peacocks, roosters, distelfinks, and always with the maker's initials and usually the initials of her true love as well. The Dutch made hooked rugs, too, usually rather crude and primitive; yet these were never as common as the braided rugs or the long strips of brightly striped rag carpet woven to order by a carpet weaver in the village.

Baskets of willow, of oak splints, or of coils of rye straw were made in the neighborhood. To this very day a traveler in the Dutch country comes upon polled willows in the meadows, the twigs sold to a near-by basketmaker. In a number of the country stores baskets of willow or oak splint, made by local artisans, are offered for sale. The straw baskets, however, turn up only at country auctions. The commonest

[4] The linen and household equipment that a bride brings to her husband.

type of straw basket was the bread basket. These were floured and the dough set to raise in them; then the baskets were turned upside down, usually on the bake-oven shovel. There were also large hampers of straw, commonly used for storing snitz, and even cradles of ropes of straw on a framework of hickory strips.

The old gaudy toleware coffeepots, tea caddies, bread trays, and waiters can be purchased today only in antique shops. In spite of their gay splashes of color, the toleware was not Pennsylvania Dutch in origin. The tin coffeepots made by Dutch craftsmen were not painted but had intricate designs of the usual peacocks, tulips, and hearts in punched work. The spoons and ladles with handles of iron fastened to bowls of hammered copper and brass have not been made for a hundred years or more. The cooky cutters used for the animal cookies at Christmas were made by local tinsmiths. Today the only cooky cutters available are ones of anemic pattern offered by five-and-tens and department stores. Your great-grandmother, if she was Pennsylvania Dutch, had cooky cutters correctly classified as art. There were even Pennsylvania Dutch pewterers, notably Wilhelm Will of Philadelphia and Johann Christopher Heyne of Lancaster. Some of the early pieces of pewter, especially the flagons owned by Trinity Lutheran Church in Lancaster, show distinct Teutonic influence. The Rhineland and not London inspired the cherub heads that form the feet of these flagons. Sometimes wood took the place of glass, china, silver, or tin. Sugar bowls and snuffboxes were made of apple-wood and mahogany; these, however, were never common. The most elaborate of the small wooden pieces are the spoon racks, some of them so beautifully carved as to be museum pieces. Some of the salt boxes, too, are of pleasing design, though these are more likely to be painted than carved. Much commoner are the butter molds of walnut or apple-wood, many of them with vigorous designs of tulips or eagles.

The folk art of the Pennsylvania Dutch extended even to their tombstones. Many old graveyards have tombstones decorated with crude attempts at cherubs or angels, with clusters of tulips, and with the six-lobed flower that may be a full-blown tulip or a lily of the field. Many of the tombstones are decorated on both sides. Among the rarest and most interesting are the portrait tombstones with a bas-relief of the profile of the person buried there. The graveyard of Muddy Creek Church in Lancaster County has two such tombstones. There are curious old tombstones, too, in the old walled graveyard of Christ

Church, Tulpehocken, on the western border of Berks and at Swamp Church in Lancaster County. In this latter churchyard there is one of the quaintest epitaphs to be found on Dutch tombstones:

> Hier liegt ein Kleines Oechselein
> Dem alten Ochs sein soehnelein;
> Der liebe Gott hat nicht gewolt
> Dass er ein Ochsen werden sollt.

> (Here lies an ox—a baby one,
> Of the old Ochs his little son;
> The loving God did not decree
> That he an ox should ever be.)

Pennsylvania Dutch folk art was discovered by the rest of America only in the thirties of the twentieth century. Then almost overnight it caught the public fancy. Pennsylvania Dutch antiques soared in price and manufacturers began to turn out products decorated with what they supposed to be Pennsylvania Dutch motifs. Chests, china, pottery, toleware, fabrics, place mats, paper napkins, and even hats, most of them *aufgeputzed* [1] with tulips and hearts and peacocks, were offered for sale. Designers found it a source of inspiration, and quite properly so. Pennsylvania Dutch folk art is good largely because it is genuine. There is nothing trumped up, nothing affected about it. It is impregnated with the character of the people.

Despite the excellence of their folk art, the Pennsylvania Dutch produced almost no artists. Jacob Eichholtz was an early American painter, but hardly in a class with Stuart and Copley. Later on there were a fair number of painters, sculptors, and architects of Pennsylvania Dutch blood. In the eighteenth century, however, Pennsylvania Dutch art was on the folk level. Most of the creators of this art were anonymous; only a few are known by name. Christian Seltzer painted dower chests and never more than two flowers alike on the same chest. David Spinner bedecked his pie plates with spirited troopers. But the nun in the Ephrata Cloister who worked all winter through on the fraktur for a hymnbook, and the farmer who put in several rainy days carving a spoon rack to please his wife, and the young man who made a fancy valentine for a maiden who took his eye; these we do not know by name. They are only several of those who made up "the folk."

[1] Decorated.

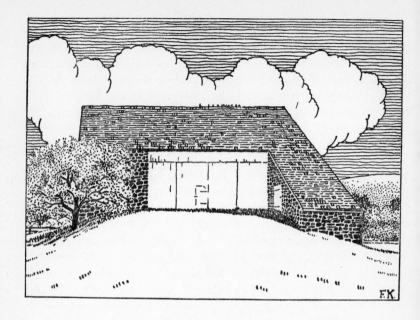

Church, House, Barn, and Garden

Aside from the great barns and the log cabins, the influence of Germanic architecture on Pennsylvania Dutch building has been slight. Good examples of other structures that are primarily Teutonic rather than English or American are so scarce that it is hardly an exaggeration to say that the specimens still extant number no more than a dozen. Among the most notable of these are the old Moravian buildings at Bethlehem, the Cloisters at Ephrata, the Moravian school in the Oley Valley, the old church at Trappe, the miller's house at Millbach, Zeller's Fort, and the tiny house on the De Turck farm near Oley.

Of these, the Moravian buildings at Bethlehem, especially the Bell House, and the Cloisters at Ephrata are the most ambitious. In both the buildings at Bethlehem and at Ephrata it is the steep pitch of the roof and the small flat-topped dormer windows that are largely responsible for their Germanic appearance. To an American the Ephrata Cloisters are strikingly foreign; and, what is even more surprising, they are medieval. To enter the Saal at Ephrata is to plunge into the Middle Ages. The austerity of its architectural detail, the simplicity of line, the tiny windows, and the crude winding stairs seem much closer to the fourteenth and fifteenth centuries than to the eighteenth, the century in which the building was erected. The Bell House at Bethlehem, a more sophisticated structure, seems much more recent than the Saal, even by some centuries, though both are of the same period. The Moravian school in the Oley Valley, now disfigured by a covering of tar paper, is the only half-timbered building in America that has come down from colonial times. It is a simple building, and when the half-timbered work could be seen it was a charming building; now it is a blot on the landscape. The Augustus Lutheran Church at Trappe is a little edifice that might belong to almost any Rhineland village. Its hipped roof, its high pulpit, and its steep gallery combine to give it a quaintness unusual in early American churches. The old Moselem church in Berks County was so like it that the two might have been peas out of the same pod, but like most of the eighteenth century churches in the Dutch country it was pulled down a long time ago. The house at Millbach is famous for its interior woodwork, particularly the staircase and the paneled doors. The kitchen, which was also the living room of the house, and one of the bedrooms are now set up in the Philadelphia Museum. Zeller's Fort is a little Rhenish house notable for the graceful detail of its doors and the overhanging eaves. The De Turck house near Oley is so small and so quaint that one instinctively feels that its proper place is a yard under a Christmas tree. The broken hood across the front gives the house its special character. Originally it had painted decorations on its shutters—roses on the upper panels and tulips on the lower ones. As far as I know, this is the only example of a building with decorated shutters in early America.

That there are so few Germanic structures in the Pennsylvania Dutch country is largely because there was neither money nor time in the first years of the settlement to build them. In the days before the Revolution the Pennsylvania Dutch were busy clearing the land. The simple houses in which the settlers lived for a generation or two were usually log cabins or small houses of stone. It was more important to them to have stout barns. The large houses came later. The early churches and schools were very like the first houses, often no more than log cabins. It was only where men joined together to form a communal society, as at Bethlehem and Ephrata, that large structures could be built. Only after the land was cleared and the barns were built did the ordinary settlers turn their attention to finer houses and churches; but by this time so many years had passed that the men who did the building were the sons or grandsons or even great-grandsons of the original settlers. There were no memories of buildings in the Rhineland to inspire them. Instead they copied the buildings put up by their English neighbors or those they had seen on their rare visits to Philadelphia. All through the Dutch country Georgian churches, usually known as colonial, began to arise. The "church people" looked at the Anglican churches and tried to do likewise. Christ Church in Philadelphia was obviously the model for Trinity Lutheran Church in Lancaster. The Mennonites and Amish and Dunkards, desiring something simpler, built their meetinghouses after the pattern of the Quaker ones.

Not many of the old churches in the Dutch country have graceful spires. The Pennsylvania Dutch seldom built a church steeple as beautiful and well proportioned as those that are the pride of New England. Yet a few are handsome. One of the highest and most ornate of the spires was that on Trinity Lutheran Church in Reading. This spire was destroyed by a minor tornado in the thirties of this century. The day before the spire was blown down there had been a bitter quarrel between two factions of the church, the one in favor of taking Communion in the pews and the other opposed. The next day a high wind of cyclonic fury lifted up the tall, needlelike spire from its base and sent it crashing through the roof of the very room in which the quarrel had taken place. More than one person looked upon this as an all too visible sign of God's displeasure.

By the middle of the nineteenth century there were many substantial churches in the Dutch country, simple in line and as a rule pleasing to the eye—far superior to most of the Pennsylvania churches built later. But occasionally the good taste so widespread in that day yielded to emotion. The Lutheran and Reformed church at Boonsboro, Maryland, was amusingly perverse—like its congregation. The Lutherans insisted on round-topped windows and the Reformed congregation held out for square tops. Failing to resolve their disagreement, they built the church with round-topped windows on one side and square-topped windows on the other. Furthermore, one group wanted a stove to heat the church, an idea that some of the older members denounced as "sacrilege and gross impiety." The stove was put up in the church, but on one side of the building instead of in the center. But little by little the flesh won out. On the cold Sundays of winter those who held the sterner view deserted the cold side of the church and moved over to the stove side.

During the latter half of the nineteenth century there was much re-building of churches. A desire for change, a passion for newness swept over the land. Most of the fine old stone churches were torn down and Victorian edifices of brick went up in their stead. None of the Victorian churches is an architectural masterpiece but a number of them are picturesque. Since many of them are built on hilltops, their spires rising above the maples and lindens can be seen for miles around.

The few public buildings of early days were all Georgian. The little courthouse in the square at Lancaster is a typical example. But most of them have long since been demolished. The Pennsylvania Dutch have little pride in their old buildings. York long ago tore down the courthouse in which the Continental Congress held its meetings. Reading has hardly any colonial buildings left. The old half-timbered Moravian schoolhouse in the Oley Valley is fast falling into decay; in another few years it will be gone. Clearly there is no ancestor worship here; there is not even a decent respect for ancestors.

The houses built by the earliest settlers were often log cabins, which had been introduced by the Swedes and the Finns, though it was the Germans and Swiss who first built them on a large scale. During the middle of the eighteenth century the log cabin was almost universal in the towns of the Dutch country. According to the French exile, Colbert-Maulevrier, Womelsdorf at that time was a village of log houses and Myerstown's hundred houses were all of logs. Seventy-five years later, in 1827, an anonymous traveler also mentioned the log houses of Womelsdorf, built of squared logs and two stories high: "They look to the eye like 'Wilmington stripes,' for the taste is to whitewash the smooth mortar between the logs but not the logs themselves, thus making the house *in* stripes of alternate white, and dusky wood color."

The log cabin was a type of house that had been known to many of the Dutch immigrants back in Europe, since it was common in the Black Forest and the Swiss Alps. Most of the Pennsylvania Dutch log cabins were well built, for in contrast to the Swedish log houses it was the German practice to square the logs and fit them together at the corners with exact notchings. A number of log cabins still stand in the hills of southeastern Pennsylvania, more than is commonly realized, for many of them have been disguised with a sheathing of boards.

After the French and Indian War stone houses began to replace the log cabins. As almost every farm in the Dutch country had good building stone, most of the early houses were built of stone instead of brick. Many of them were rather small, like Conrad Weiser's house in Womelsdorf. These stone cabins, for they were little more, were often built on the side of a hill over a spring. When later a larger house was erected, it was frequently built on to the small stone cabin. William Cobbett was much amused by this practice. He writes:

It is a curious thing to observe the *farm-houses* in this country. They consist, almost without exception, of a considerably large and a very neat house, with sash windows, and of a small house, which seems to have been *tacked on* to the large one: and, the proportion they bear to each other, in point of dimensions, is, as nearly as possible, the proportion of size between a *Cow* and *her Calf*, the latter a month old. But, as to the *cause,* the process has been the opposite of this instance of the works of nature, for, it is *the large house which has grown out of the small one*. The father, or grandfather, while he was toiling for his children, lived in the small house, constructed chiefly by himself, and consisting of rude materials. The means accumulated in the small house, enabled a son to rear the large one; and, though, when *pride* enters the door, the small house is sometimes demolished, few sons in America have the folly or want of feeling to commit such acts of filial ingratitude, and of real self-abasement.

On some of the most prosperous farms larger houses were erected at a relatively early date. Some of these earlier stone houses, especially those in the Oley Valley, show Teutonic influence: one chimney in the center of the house instead of two at the gable ends; a slightly steeper pitch to the roof; and arches, often of brick, over the windows. In much of their building, especially in the barns and in the cellars of the houses, the early Pennsylvania Dutch showed a fondness for arches. Very often, too, there was a solidity, a heaviness to the stone and timber construction that is reminiscent of medieval practice. A number of the old houses were covered with bright red tiles made in local potteries. Occasionally these tiles were used on a larger building, as the chapel of the Moravian buildings at Bethlehem. Held in place by lugs, the small projections on the under side, the tiles were hooked over horizontal laths. One tile was laid precisely above the other instead of the way shingles or slates are laid. Small grooves in the tiles led the water away from the joints, yet some water seeped through. Probably this is why these tiles are never seen on houses today, although the sight of them in the Oley Valley on springhouses, smokehouses, and other small outbuildings is not uncommon. In the gristmill at Bethlehem tiles were used to cover the floor as well as the roof.

Another feature of many old houses was the pent roof between the first and second stories. On some of the old log houses it was probably meant to protect the chinking between the logs. Because of its extensive use on the houses of Germantown, this penthouse was called a Germantown hood. It has been attributed—mistakenly, I think—to the south of England; it is more likely German in origin. After all, Germantown stayed German till the year of the yellow fever. And most of the Quakers who later settled there, though of English blood, were from the north of England rather than the south.

Another interesting architectural feature of many of the old eighteenth century stone houses is the house inscription carved on a stone, which was usually placed in the middle of the front of the house. As a rule this stone bore the name of the man who built the house and that of his wife, along with the year of its erection. Sometimes the inscription was far more ambitious, as the one on the Orth house in Lebanon County:

> Got segne dieses Haus.
> & Ales was da geh ein & aus.
> Got alein die Ehr
> & sonst keinen antern mer.
> Adam & Cathrina Orts
> 17   I.M.S.   62

Translated this is:

> God bless this house.
> & all who there go in and out.
> To God alone the glory
> & to no one else besides.
> Adam & Catharine Orth
> 17   I.M.S.   62

Among the house legends there are many variations on this verse. Sometimes the inscription is so lugubrious as to suggest the Graveyard School of poetry fashionable in the eighteenth century. Such is the one on the Spangler house near Myerstown: "God bless this house &

whoever goes in or out. Whether I go out or in, death stands and waits for me, 1782." Occasionally such a doleful thought is coupled with a more practical bit of wisdom. This inscription appears over the lintel of a house in East Petersburg, Lancaster County: "Whether I go out or in Death stands and waits for me. Better a dry morsel to enjoy than a house full of fresh meat with strife. 1740." John Baer Stoudt found an inscription with a touch of humor on a house between Lyons Station and Sally Ann Furnace:

> Der einen machts
> Der andere verachts
> Der nachts sagt was machts.

Rather freely translated, this is:

> One man builds,
> Another criticizes,
> The next asks, "What's up?"

Still another architectural feature, a kindly, homey one, often encountered in small stone houses built along village streets, were the benches or seats on either side of the stoop, an ideal place for leisurely conversations on a summer evening.

The largest and most elaborate of the Pennsylvania Dutch farmhouses were those built at the end of the eighteenth century and in the early years of the nineteenth. The year 1789 was one of disastrous crop failures in Europe, which sent up the price of grain on the world market. The boundless wheat fields of the Middle West were still unbroken prairie at that early date. Pennsylvania was then the principal wheat-growing section of America. With the price of wheat soaring to unheard-of heights, the Pennsylvania Dutch farmers made huge profits. Directly on the heels of the European crop failure came the French Revolution and after that the Napoleonic wars. Year after year war ravaged Europe and the price of grain remained high. These were fat years for the Pennsylvania farmers. Never before then and never again did they have so much money until the years following the Second World War, when once again widespread human misery in Europe enabled them—and this time the other farmers of America as well—to grow rich. It was during this earlier period of prosperity that the Pennsylvania farmers built their fine stone houses and enormous barns. Until that time it had been only the ironmasters who built large stone houses. Baron Stiegel's house near Brickersville, the Rutter house at Pine Forge, and the Maybury house near Huff's Church are but three specimens of the mansions the ironmasters built for themselves. But now the farmers, their chests filled with money, began to copy the ironmasters. None of these farmhouses matches the mansions of the greater ironmasters in size, but they did equal and even surpass the houses of the lesser ironmasters. The Fisher house in the Oley Valley is handsomer than the Spang house in Spangsville or the mansion at Sally Ann Furnace. The rough stone Georgian houses which the Pennsylvania farmers, both Dutch and Quaker, built for themselves at this time are the finest farmhouses ever erected in America.

Most of the early farmhouses were of rough fieldstone. The contrast of the undressed stone with the finely carved wooden doorways was startling but pleasing. This is one of the chief hallmarks of Pennsylvania Georgian. Characteristic, too, was the Doric doorway, of excellent proportions but heavier and more dignified than those of New England; the carving in the woodwork along the eaves; the beautifully proportioned dormer windows; and the solid shutters. The stone of which the houses were built varies from one section to another. The commonest and probably the most attractive is the soft gray limestone. Sometimes this stone is a solid gray, occasionally it is almost blue; but often there are traces of yellow—ranging from the palest fawn to coppery orange; or more rarely the stone is black, white, or green. Often several of these colors appear in the stone of one house; almost always it is a stone glowing with color. Nearly as common as the gray stone is the red sandstone, less beautiful than the gray, though warm and handsome in old houses and barns. The older stone houses, simple of line, solid and sturdy, fit into the landscape so well that they seem as much a part of the countryside as the fields and trees. They look as though they have grown out of the very soil—and so they have, for the stone of which they were built was usually quarried within a few miles of the houses. Sometimes the houses were built of undressed gray fieldstone, with corner quoinings of dressed red sandstone. Sometimes the stone was covered with plaster, although this practice was far commoner among the Quaker farmers of Chester County than among the Pennsylvania Dutch. The plaster was often a soft yellow, but sometimes white or light blue, mauve, or even raspberry. Needless to say, a raspberry house is quite a spectacle.

Southeastern Pennsylvania is the only part of the United States that commonly built houses of stone, yet in certain counties of Quaker and Dutch Pennsylvania there are more brick and frame houses than stone ones. Stone is particularly common in Berks County, while in Lancaster County farmhouses of wood and brick outnumber those of stone. As a rule the towns and cities are of red brick, the farmhouses and barns of stone. A further distinction may be made: the log cabin and the stone house were characteristic of the eighteenth century, brick and frame houses of the nineteenth. Brick was not much used for houses in the Dutch country until the second quarter of the nineteenth century.

Most of the best houses are out in the country and not in the towns. The villages were generally inhabited by workmen or small tradesmen, who were not nearly as prosperous as the farmers. Many of the cities once had fine houses; these, however, were often pulled down as the cities grew. A century ago the streets of the larger Dutch towns and cities were lined with red brick houses with white trim and green shutters. There was a stoop in front of the door and often a long, dark, narrow alley, scarcely three feet wide, leading to the back yard, sometimes little larger than the proverbial pocket handkerchief. All the houses had ells on the back, sometimes enormously long ells. Some of the larger houses were separated by narrow gardens, in which case the ell had a porch on the ground floor and often on the second floor as well. Often a grape arbor was built on the porch to shade it from the summer sun, with a brick pavement under the arbor. In the back yard, between the houses and the stables at the rear, there was a tree or two, often a pear or a cherry, and almost always some flowers—a couple of rose bushes, a few peonies, a bleeding heart, an August lily, and maybe a bed of lily of the valley. These side yards were pleasant, shady places on hot summer afternoons. Fortunately not all of these houses have been torn down. Lancaster is full of them, and there are a few left in all the other Dutch towns and cities.

Toward the end of the nineteenth century, when the population was increasing year by year and new mills and factories were being built in the Dutch country, the row house came into being. Twenty or forty houses, each alike, each tight against the other, were built in a row. Sometimes they extended for block after block. Beyond a doubt the row house is one of the worst ever devised by man. Outside it is deadly monotonous; inside it is dark, stuffy, and hot.

The other houses are better, but some of these have architectural oddities peculiarly Pennsylvania Dutch. Such a feature, occurring in a fair number of houses out in the country, is two front doors instead of one. Some, no doubt, indicate two dwellings under the same roof— the Grossdawdy house or the house in which a married son lives. But houses with two front doors are too common to be accounted for so easily. Was it for convenience at home funerals in the early days? Or did the Dutch suffer from claustrophobia? Were they uneasy unless there was a door to the outside world near at hand? Strange, too, is the practice of painting brick. This is rather a pity, for old brick that has weathered takes on lovely warm tones. In many houses the bricks painted are lined in white to simulate mortar. When the paint is fresh, the effect has a naïveté that is amusing. Sometimes only the wall forming the back of the porch is painted, a touch that gives the house a tidy air. Yet another oddity extremely common in Dutch towns and cities is the oversize plate-glass window in the front of the house, "picture windows" that long preceded the vogue of modern architecture. They are ugly, and few can be opened in summer to let in air. Then why are they so popular? Is it because from behind their lace curtains and barricade of ferns the sights of the street are in full view? Nothing is missed: there is Mrs. Schlegel hurrying to the corner grocery store before her husband gets home (You'd think she'd cook him a decent dinner once in a while!); there is Reverend Long all dressed up as though he has a funeral (Whose can that be?); and there goes Dr. Hartman on his rounds (I wonder how Mrs. Witman is getting along?).

Most of the houses, whether in town or country, are comfortable and warm, for the Dutch are a people who are stove-conscious. Earlier than the rest of America, they turned from fireplaces to stoves as a means of heating their houses. At first a few tile stoves like those of Germany were used. One made at the kiln of Ludwig Huebner in "the Swamp" was set up in the chapel at Bethlehem in October, 1742. But soon iron stoves were turned out in considerable quantity by the forges along the Manatawny and French Creek and rapidly came into common use among the Dutch. But money in the bank, as well as heat, is a comfort to the Dutch, and therefore many farmhouses to this day are heated only by a kitchen range. There is usually another stove in the sitting room or parlor, but if the family is a thrifty one there may be a fire in a room other than the kitchen only on Sunday.

The country kitchens, however, are pleasant places. They are large and often sunny in winter, for if possible there are windows facing south to catch the winter sunshine—windows crammed with pots of flowering plants. The furniture in the kitchen is simple: a stove, a table and chairs, a cupboard, and perhaps a rocking chair in one corner and a lounge along the wall. All is for use and not "for fancy." Braided rounds of rag carpet cover the linoleum on the floor. On the walls there may be a small mirror and most certainly calendars. On the ridge of the roof of the kitchen is the dinner bell, rung each working day to summon "the mister" from the fields. On one side of the kitchen is a porch and sometimes a grape arbor, a shady spot to sit of a summer morning to shell peas or pare apples.

Entirely separate from the house is the summer kitchen, although if the house is built on a hillside a room in the cellar may be made into a summer kitchen; but usually the summer kitchen is a little building by itself, convenient to the kitchen door. The purpose of the summer kitchen is to keep the heat of the kitchen stove out of the main house during the hot summer months. On the old farms where a large house had replaced the little stone house built by the first settlers, the old homestead is frequently used as a summer kitchen.

Sometimes attached to the house, sometimes in the summer kitchen, and sometimes in a separate building by itself was the bake oven. When it was built on to the main house, there was an opening into the fireplace on one side of the back. The old-time bake oven had a flat hearth and an arched roof, this last clearly shown by a bulge in the walls of a few old houses. Before the baker's truck was found on every road and byway, the bread and pies, the crumb cakes and shoofly pies for the week were baked in this oven; here, too, were dried the apple snitz and beans and corn for the winter.

Near-by was the smokehouse, where the hams and bacons, sausages and bolognas, tongue and dried beef were smoked over a smoldering fire—a hickory stump, if possible, though a stump of an apple or cherry tree would do. There were slits or tiny vents in the walls of the smokehouse. Here, too, the meats were kept after they were smoked. A few of the smokehouses were on two levels, a place for the fire below and for the meat above.

Some of the farms had washhouses, too, either adjoining the kitchen or near the spring. This was a small building with a fireplace in which hung a great iron kettle for heating the water for the Monday washing.

Very often, however, the washing was done outside, in which case there was an outdoor fireplace on which the water was heated. This fireplace was also used for frying out lard at butchering time and for cooking apple butter.

The springhouse was close to the main house, for it was often the spring that determined the site of the house. Though in most cases a separate building was built over the spring, some farmhouses had springs in their cellars. The springhouse had a paved shallow channel through which the water ran. Here in the cold spring water were set the stone crocks and pans of milk and the butter. On a hot August afternoon there was nothing more refreshing than a melon out of the springhouse, a melon sweet from the sun and cold as the first frost of October.

The root cellar or "the cave" was another important feature of the farm. Sometimes this was an arched room under the ramp leading to the threshing floor in the barn, sometimes it was a cave dug into a nearby hillside, but usually it was a large hole in the ground with ventilators. Occasionally this ground cellar would have a passage to the floor of the pump to let in the cool air from the well. Here in the ground cellar were stored winter apples, potatoes, cabbages, and root vegetables.

The chief glory of Pennsylvania Dutch architecture, however, is not the church or the house but the barn. This barn was copied by the Quakers and so many of the other English settlers that it became above all others the standard American barn. Sturdy and simple, with good proportions, the barn with its outbuildings often forms a composition that is all a painter could desire. Its texture—the combination of stone or brick with wood—and its color—the natural gray of limestone or the red of sandstone or stone whitewashed plus wood painted the usual barn red and gaudy with witch signs—are enough to make any painter's fingers itch for a brush.

Pennsylvania barns have long been noted as being bigger than the houses. Of course they are. This doesn't mean that the houses are small; it simply means that the barns are tremendous. As early as 1753, the geographer, Lewis Evans, spoke of Pennsylvania Dutch barns as being as "large as pallaces." One of the best descriptions of these barns was made by William Cobbett in an entry for February 16, 1818, in *A Year's Residence, in the United States of America*:

This is a fine part of America. *Big Barns,* and modest dwelling houses. Barns of *stone, a hundred feet* long and *forty wide,* with two floors, and raised roads up to them, so that the waggons go into the *first floor up-stairs.* Below are stables, stalls, pens, and all sorts of conveniences. Up-stairs are rooms for threshed corn and grain; for tackle, for meal, for all sorts of things. In the front (South) of the barn is the cattle yard. These are very fine buildings. And, then, all about them looks so comfortable, and gives such manifest proofs of ease, plenty, and happiness.

Although often known as Swiss barns, the Pennsylvania Dutch barns have no exact prototypes in Switzerland, where the house and barn were combined under one roof, a structure built against a hill with a driveway for wagons to the barn on the second floor. Apparently the Swiss Mennonites who settled in Montgomery and Lancaster counties had this building in mind when they built their barns in the late seventeenth and early eighteenth centuries, but from the beginning the barn and house were separate. Often both barn and house are built on the side of a hill, with one side of the basement wall right up against the hill. If there is any sort of knoll or hill on the farm—and in Pennsylvania not one farm in a thousand is without a slight rise of ground at the very least—such a site is invariably chosen for the barn. The driveway on the north side leading to the threshing floor on the second story of the barn is the most distinctive feature of the building, so important that these barns are commonly called "bank barns" to distinguish them from the English type. On land like the Lancaster Plain, which is absolutely flat, an artificial bank or ramp of earth is thrown up against the barn to form a driveway. The basement, walled up against the hill, is used as a stable for horses and cattle, with feeding passages opening by divided or Dutch doors in the front under the forebay.

On the floor above the stables is a spacious threshing floor with hay mows on either side. Heavy wagons loaded with hay or grain are driven up the bank on to the threshing floor. This threshing floor, with lofty mows rising on both sides and the shadowy rafters of the barn far above, is one of the pleasantest spots on the farm. With the great double doors on the north thrown open and the smaller doors of the forebay to the south, there is always air stirring—even on the hottest days of summer. Above in the half darkness pigeons coo and the barn swallows dart back and forth. No wonder that in the old days the housewives often spun their wool on the barn floor, and that even today the house Amish sometimes choose to hold their meetings for worship there and the Amish young folk their Sunday night "singings." And here in earlier days the grain was threshed with flails, hence the name "threshing floor."

To the south is the forebay, a projection of the upper story eight or ten feet over the lower. The forebay is often supported by the side walls and projecting ceiling beams, in which case the first floor or stable level is sunk into the front of the barn. But often the forebay extends beyond the side walls and is supported by round pillars of field stone.

The barns face south, with the barnyard on the sunny south side, where in the lee of winter winds cattle can be turned out on sunny January days and hens can scratch in the straw of the manure pile. To the east and west the barnyard is flanked by sheds, or at the very least by stone walls.

Most of the barns are large: 40 by 60 feet is the most usual size; 40 by 80 is common, as in Cobbett's time; and even 40 by 100 is found in some of the richest farming sections. The gable ends and the north side, except for the barn doors, are commonly of stone, as is the first floor on the south. The masonry, though often crude, is solid. There is no corbeling to carry the heavy beams of the forebay, but not infrequently the quoins are beautifully handled. Often there are louvred windows or narrow slits for ventilation in the masonry in the gable ends. Near the peak of each gable is a decorated swallow hole, commonly surrounded by brick. In Montgomery County the barns are usually of brick with apertures in elaborate X designs in the gable ends. In Frederick County, Maryland, where the whole barn is of wood, there is a delightful and innocent practice of painting louvred windows on the wood. Thus they have the semblance if not the fact. Ventilators on the roof of the barn, often three in a row or two ventilators with a cupola in the center, are not uncommon. Occasionally in the larger barns there are dormer windows. One of the more charming features of the barn is the small hooded doorways, much like those on Quaker meetinghouses.

In the eighteenth century and well into the nineteenth, barns were often thatched with rye straw. An anonymous traveler passing through Womelsdorf on August 3, 1829, speaks of the thatched roofs on the barns there: "The barns were large and well filled, generally constructed of squared logs or stone, but all the roofs were of *thatched straw*—a novelty to my eye—said to last fifteen years. Their houses were shingled with lapped shingles." Incidentally, this method of laying shingles, with one side lapped over the other, was characteristically German. It has since passed out of use in this country. Once thatch was discarded, cedar shingles were used to cover the barn roofs. Today, however, most of the roofs are of tin.

It is a minor miracle that so many of the old barns are still standing, for each summer lightning takes its toll of them. But many of the barns that appear to be old are old only in part. Quite a few have burned down at one time or another. Though the wooden part was destroyed, the stone walls stood firm. A floor, a roof, and a forebay, and the barn was as good as new.

Between the house and the barn—and on other sides of the house, too—is the garden; and relatively modest it is. Despite the Dutch passion for flowers, theirs is not a land of elaborate gardens. There is nothing to match the famous gardens around Charleston. It is the small dooryard garden, the tidy houseyard, rather than the box-lined parterre that is the typical Dutch garden. Only a very few of the ironmasters laid out formal gardens with beds lined with box. Such a box garden, now almost a maze, is still in existence at Robesonia. But the earliest Dutch gardens were the herb gardens, like the one planted in 1694 or 1695 on the ridge above the Wissahickon by the Society of the Woman of the Wilderness, or that later herb garden laid out in Bethlehem in March, 1747. Possibly the most ambitious of the early gardens in the Dutch country was the one at Nazareth with its low terraces on the slope of a hill. John Ogden described this garden in *An Excursion into Bethlehem and Nazareth in the Year 1799*:

> The strait and circular walks, the windings up the hill, the falling gardens ascended by steps, the banks, summer-houses, seats, trees, herbs, fruits, vegetables and flowers are seen in great variety.
>
> Most of the American forest trees and many exotic plants are here. It is an elegant garden in miniature.

At Bethlehem the garden in back of the Single Men's House supplied *die Apotheke* with medicinal herbs, especially snakeroot and sassafras, of which high hopes were entertained at that time. But an attempt was made to grow all the flora of the countryside as well as many European plants.

At Bethlehem, too, was a double row of black cherry trees lining the Single Sisters' Walk, a quarter of a mile long, which led down to the Monocacy. Probably the Moravians brought this idea with them from Germany. Wherever they got it, the cherry tree, along with the maple and the horse chestnut, is still the tree most planted on village streets in the Dutch country. During cherry time driving in a Pennsylvania Dutch village becomes hazardous because of the many ladders in the streets under the cherry trees. There is no doubt that there were many other gardens, largely of a small and unassuming nature. For a long time every farm has had its houseyard filled with flowers, while in the villages a house without flowers is conspicuous. Sometimes the garden is the woman's province, but just as often it is the man's. In every Dutch town there are men with a passion for gardening. Among them a man can declare his love of flowers without his masculinity being suspect, which may be an indication that the culture of the Pennsylvania Dutch has outgrown the pioneer stage.

There are but few records of the early gardens. We know that Pastorius had a garden in Germantown, because it was said to contain the century plant given to Penn by John Evelyn, the diarist. A number of the gardens of Germantown date back to colonial times. The Wister garden at Grumblethorpe is one of these. In Germantown, too, Christian Leman set out a nursery in pre-Revolutionary days. Though many of the early gardens had charm, they were not ambitious. Most of them were small, rather casual dooryard gardens. Among a few fruit trees bloomed the flowers sown from carefully treasured seeds or springing from bulbs and roots that survived the journey down the Rhine and the voyage across the Atlantic: pinks, sweet William, pansies, forget-me-nots, sweet rocket, "vanilla," rose campion, bachelor's-buttons, Canterbury bells, foxglove, hollyhocks, London pride, poppies, balsam, marigold, cockscomb, and honesty—these from seeds; crocus, daffodil, tulip, poet's narcissus, lily of the valley, "flags," peony, lemon lily, madonna lily, tiger lily, and chrysanthemum—these from root, bulb, or tuber. Eglantine or sweetbriar, flowering almond, snowball, lilac, mock orange, and box were grown from cuttings borrowed from their Quaker neighbors.

The old gardens were restful quiet places. The murmur of bees filled the air and hummingbirds hovered over the bergamot. The walks of brick or flag or fieldstone were half buried in an abundance of flowers. From the gold of crocus in the spring to the orange of tiger lily and magenta of phlox cheek by jowl in the summer to the copper of chrysanthemum in October these gardens were a riot of color a hundred years ago just as they are today. Then as now a Christmas cactus summered in a shady spot; and in the morning sunlight stood a tub of lilies, brought up from the cellar, and perhaps an oleander.

Not many Dutch gardens are permitted to grow at sixes and sevens. The Amish, at least, make their gardens toe the mark. Long rows of crimson cockscomb, blue lobelia, and dwarf orange marigold are as trim and as gay as the Amish themselves. These flowers know their place and keep it. But usually Dutch gardens are a little more casual. True, beds of geraniums and "colies" with an edging of dusty miller are tight and tidy, but many flowers grow at random.

Oddly enough, the Pennsylvania Dutch have a wild flower of their own unrecognized as wild by the rest of the country. This is the grape hyacinth, known locally as bluebottle, or to give it its Dutch name, *wei glessli* (little wine glass). Growing so prolifically in southeastern Pennsylvania as here and there to turn a field in mid-April into a sheet of the most intense blue, it is a great favorite of the children. It is a flower easy to pick and it keeps well in water. A little boy or girl with a tight bunch of bluebottles in his or her hand is a common springtime sight in the Dutch country.

Apparently botanists have given only the most casual consideration to the bluebottle. "An escape from gardens—*Muscari botryoides,*" they declare pontifically, without ever pausing to ask whether or not it was ever planted in Pennsylvania gardens. The Pennsylvania Dutch bluebottle, unlike *Muscari botryoides,* sends up no mat of leaves in the fall; instead fresh green spears, tinged orange-red, poke through the earth in early spring. Nor is the flower of the Dutch bluebottle as dark a blue or as large as that of *Muscari botryoides.* For this reason I am perverse enough to believe that the Pennsylvania grape hyacinth may be a native species and not an escape from gardens.

Herbs, of course, were usually confined to the kitchen garden along with the horseradish, the rhubarb, and the parsley. There grew the sage—blue and white flowered, two or three mints, chives, thyme, dill, summer savory, saffron, rue, and sometimes a rarer herb—sweet woodruff, hyssop, or perhaps Bible leaf. A few herbs were grown among the flowers, especially lamb's-ears and feverfew and bergamot, this last often known by its amusing Dutch name of *Chonni Hossesack* (Johnnie Pantspocket).

All through the winter the window sills of the kitchen or any other heated room were jammed with house plants: geraniums by the dozen, red, white, and pink as well as those grown for their fragrant leaves, whether the usual rose-scented geranium or the rarer lemon, nutmeg, or mint; "colies" with leaves as brave as Joseph's coat; begonias, both "angel wings" and the common kind with flowers of pink or coral; Chinese primroses; Christmas cactus; and fuchsia.

The kitchen garden was a model of neatness. A weed, while not exactly a disgrace, was something that needed to be explained away. Here the scallion—stubbornly called "scullion" by the Pennsylvania Dutch—stayed out all winter. Early in spring, before the last snow, the onions would be planted in straight exact rows next to the asparagus bed, along with lettuce, radishes, carrots, beets, and early peas. Often a few cabbage plants would be set out. Later, the main crop of peas were put in along with succulent sugar peas. When the apple trees came into blossom, corn was sown; still later, when all danger of frost was safely past, tomato and pepper plants were set out and beans and squash and cucumbers planted, and if the soil was right, perhaps some Jenny Lind cantaloupes. Celery and turnips were planted in the summer.

This is a typical Dutch vegetable garden, the sort one family after another would have. It might be slightly less ambitious, it might be more. If the garden was large enough to be dignified by the name of "truck patch," potatoes, sweet potatoes, eggplant, pumpkin, spinach, Swiss chard, watermelons, and even popcorn would be grown—and if the family's tastes were low ones, parsnips would be added to this list. Naturally there were several kinds of beans: string beans, pole beans, lima beans. Sometimes pole beans, or pumpkins or turnips, would be planted among the corn.

Usually there were a few berries grown too: frequently a row of currants and a bed of strawberries for jelly and jam or the last for shortcake or for "eating so." Sometimes there were a few gooseberry bushes, and very occasionally some red raspberries and blackberries. If the house had a springhouse, which was rarely the case in a village, there was probably watercress in the brook and mint along its edge.

Furniture and Other Household Gear

The day before yesterday Pennsylvania Dutch furniture suddenly became fashionable. New York and Philadelphia decorators and buyers for department stores began to scour the Dutch country in search of pieces they could sell to their customers, often at outlandish prices. This was the last of the colonial furniture to come into style. Compared to the fine furniture of eighteenth century Philadelphia or Boston or Providence or the tidewater South, it is lacking in elegance. Many Pennsylvania Dutch pieces are crude and clumsy. This is because some of the older Dutch furniture harks back to a still earlier period, the medieval, instead of the eighteenth century. There was, to be sure, much eighteenth century furniture in Pennsylvania Dutch homes; the prevalence of the Windsor chair proves that. There were even pieces in the styles of Chippendale and Hepplewhite and Sheraton, all of them clearly borrowings from Philadelphia and London, though the Pennsylvania Dutch craftsmen gave them a simplicity and sturdiness lacking in the originals. Although four-poster beds, drop-leaf tables, grandfather clocks, corner cupboards, bureaus and desks of mahogany and cherry—indeed, almost all the types of furniture that found favor in early Philadelphia—became popular with the Pennsylvania Dutch and were turned out in considerable quantity by local cabinetmakers, this is not what we mean by Pennsylvania Dutch furniture.

Pennsylvania Dutch furniture is chiefly of two sorts: the crude pieces preserving medieval traditions and the furniture of the beginning of the nineteenth century painted with folk designs. The furniture of the early period was inspired by that left behind in the Rhineland. With the exception of a few chests, the Pennsylvania Dutch brought very little furniture with them. Yet some of the furniture left in Europe remained clear in the minds of at least a few cabinetmakers and was copied by them in the native woods of Pennsylvania. Much of this furniture was medieval in character, some was Renaissance, and some had touches of the baroque.

The dower chests were not very different from chests elsewhere in Europe except that many of them were painted. The trestle tables were old in design; the fourteenth century had used tables of this sort. The benches, too, were medieval in pattern. The heavy rectangular tables, some of them with bulbous legs, were very like the Tudor tables in England. The tavern tables are later and so are the slat-back chairs with rush seats; both are seventeenth century in character. Hanging cupboards of one sort or another were made from the fifteenth century to the nineteenth. Crude hanging cupboards like those used in the Cloisters at Ephrata were probably made as early as the fifteenth century, while the more graceful and ambitious ones sometimes show the influence of the baroque. The capacious wardrobes or *schranks* are seventeenth century in design, and so are the open dressers. And it was probably in the seventeenth century, too, that the form of the dough tray became fixed. In Pennsylvania, of course, almost none of this furniture antedated the eighteenth century; but even so, much of it is so rare that a tavern table or hanging cupboard or slat-back chair in half-decent condition is considered a museum piece. Not the dough trays, however; they are still a glut on the market. And since chests still continue to be made, most antique dealers still have chests to sell.

The dower chests are the most famous of Pennsylvania Dutch furniture, not so much those of walnut and cherry, which were often left unpainted, as the painted ones of pine or tulipwood. In the spirited designs of many of the painted chests, Pennsylvania Dutch folk art reached its finest development. Though the chests vary in size, they are usually about four feet long and two high; they have four legs, a hinged top, and sometimes one or two or even three drawers. These chests were given by fathers to their daughters. In them a girl put the linens she wove, the towels she embroidered, and the quilts she stitched in preparation for marriage. The earliest chests doubtless came from the Rhineland filled with household linens and clothing, and these may have served as models for later chests.

The painters of the dower chests, like the painters of the witch signs on the barns, often traveled from farm to farm, but only within a small compass. Consequently, one general design is usually characteristic of a relatively small area. Although each end and even the top of the chest may be decorated, the most elaborate designs appear on the front, usually in the form of two or three panels. In Lancaster County the chests generally had three sunken panels with molded or fluted arches on the front; in the other counties the panels were painted on the chests. On most of the Lancaster County chests there are designs of birds and flowers, chiefly doves, parrots, peacocks, tulips, and pinks. The Lebanon County chests have an elaborate arrangement of tulips springing from a vase. Those painted by Christian Seltzer are the finest of all Pennsylvania Dutch chests. The Berks County chests have tulips rising from a vase or a heart, and with them unicorns and men on horseback, a star within a circle, and often at the corner a heart-shaped decoration half in front and half on the side. The Lehigh County and Montgomery County chests have formal geometric designs of interlacing circles, stars, flowers, and hearts, all of such accuracy that the painter must have used a compass.

Only the oval brideboxes can compare with the dower chests. If anything, the brideboxes are even gayer in color and sprightlier in design than the dower chests. Since they are small, probably most of them were brought from Europe; not many are of American origin. In the early period only the dower chests and the brideboxes were decorated. All other furniture was unpainted.

There is so little early furniture because most of the first settlers were too busy cutting down trees and building barns and houses to take time out for any but the simplest furniture. By the time they were able to turn their attention to furniture, two or even three generations had passed. The furniture admired in Heidelberg or Worms was pretty much forgotten. Only here and there in the Dutch country did European fashions prevail. At Lititz, for instance, the beds were built in the wall as they were in Central Europe. This was the sort of bed in which William Ellery, a member of Congress for Massachusetts, "lodged in Clover" on the night of November 14, 1777, on his way to York, where Congress was sitting.

We lodged in Cabins about 3 feet wide, a straw bed was at the bottom, a feather bed on that, sheets, a thin soft feather bed supplied the place of blankets, and a neat coverlid covered all; and our lodging room was kept warm during the night by a neat earthen stove [a tile stove] which in form resembled a case of Drawers.

The furniture the Dutch knew best was that of Philadelphia—in other words, furniture of English tradition. But not all the pieces were slavish copies of the work of London craftsmen. The cabinet-makers of Lancaster, Reading, and scores of other Dutch towns began to make Windsor chairs, which had originated in Philadelphia about 1725. They made rocking chairs, too; in fact, they may even have given birth to this characteristic American chair. Although the origin of the rocking chair is hidden in obscurity, the earliest specimens are from Pennsylvania; but whether it was Philadelphia or the Dutch country that has the proud honor of being the progenitor of this great American chair no one knows. More conventional furniture of all sorts, from highboys, secretaries, and grandfather clocks down to footstools, spice cupboards, and salt boxes, were likewise made in Pennsylvania Dutch workshops. Sometimes mahogany was used for the finest pieces, but much of the furniture was made of native woods, especially black walnut and cherry. Hickory was used in the Windsor chairs, pine for kitchen tables and dressers; maple, apple, gum, and tulipwood for other odds and ends of furniture. Certain designs became extremely popular—for instance, the rectangular drop-leaf table with one drawer. Some of the furniture was peculiarly Dutch: the water-bench with its low open shelves above and its cupboard below; the extremely low beds with footboards even lower than the low headboards; the dressers, first with open shelves above and drawers and a cupboard below and later with glass doors above and drawers below; and the metal pie safe, usually of pierced tin, the tiny holes forming intricate designs with characteristic Dutch motifs.

Grandfather clocks were much admired by the Pennsylvania Dutch. These and smaller clocks were made by master craftsmen in the Dutch towns and cities. The single town of Manheim had five makers of grandfather clocks. Yet there was never the mass production of clocks in Pennsylvania that there was in New England. A Pennsylvania clockmaker might turn out only four or five clocks a year. John Fitch as a young man was apprenticed to a clockmaker, and David Rittenhouse was a clockmaker in his youth. The grandfather clock made by Rittenhouse for Joseph Potts, the ironmaster, is the finest clock the American colonies ever produced. Standing over nine feet high, it records time in seconds, minutes, hours, and days; furthermore, it equates true and mean solar time. The position of the moon and stars is shown in a little planetarium placed on the face above the dial plate. Its many chimes also make it notable among clocks. Any one of ten tunes can be played every quarter-hour, every half-hour, on the hour, or every two hours. Potts found its price, $640.00, so exorbitant that he refused to accept the clock. Today it is one of the prized possessions of the Drexel Institute in Philadelphia.

In the early nineteenth century much of the furniture was painted, especially rocking chairs, side chairs, and settees. And once in a long time paint would be applied to a bureau, a cupboard, or even a grandfather clock. A Lancaster County corner cupboard of Amish blue has an interior of clear vermillion. In the Barnes Museum in Merion is a cupboard deep amber in color and decorated with baptismal angels and witch signs. Both cupboards show the robust use of color so typical of the Dutch. In a sense it is a childlike delight in bright color. Although there is nothing subtle about it, it bespeaks life and health and vigor. These gay splashes of color are innocent and naïve but enheartening too. It is completely un-Victorian, yet it was during the Victorian Age that painted furniture became popular with the Dutch. About 1840 stencils came into wide use. It was no longer necessary to employ a craftsman who was an artist as well to paint one's furniture. Any painter with a modicum of skill could decorate the backs of the rockers, side chairs, and settees. One house after another began to blossom forth with gayly painted furniture. There were formal scroll designs and flowers, but most popular of all were the distelfink and a piece or two of fruit: a peach, a plum, a pear, a bunch of grapes, and a bob of cherries.

Of prime importance among the household gear in any Dutch house is the stove. As I have pointed out before, the Pennsylvania Dutch were the first Americans to use stoves. This explains their practice of building the chimney in the middle of the roof instead of at both gable ends, as the Quakers did. A five-plate stove, with the back plate missing, was placed against a hole that led into the back of the fireplace so that the fire could heat two rooms instead of only one. Or at least it would take the chill off the second room. If more heat was desired, all one had to do was to shove some embers from the fireplace into the stove. Such five-plate stoves, which were commonly used until the Revolution, were made in Pennsylvania as early as 1726. Later a back plate, a door for wood, and a stovepipe were added, and the stove was moved out into the room. Still later an oven was built on and the cookstove had arrived. Legend has it that the first cookstoves were made by Stiegel, but there is no documentary evidence to support this story. As far as we know, the first ten-plate stove, which was the stove first used for cooking, was made at Mary Ann Furnace in Manheim Township, York County, in 1765. Two years later ten-plate stoves were also being made at Hereford Furnace in Berks County. But for a long time most of America clung to fireplaces. Even as late as the middle of the nineteenth century, many American families were still cooking over the open hearth.

Swan Song

The Pennsylvania Dutch culture was not a literary one. In the nineteenth century it produced no writers to match Thoreau and Melville nor even Lowell and Whittier. It may be that the language barrier turned whatever Pennsylvania Dutch genius there was to fields other than literature. The antiquated High German of church, the Sunday language of the Pennsylvania Dutch, was stiff and alien; the ordinary workaday dialect was lacking in dignity; and English was a language in which they were not quite at home. Now that English rather than the dialect has become the language of everyday speech, the Pennsylvania Dutch are beginning to find their tongues—and oddly enough, in Dutch as well as in English. With the dialect in danger of passing out of existence, zealous Pennsylvania Dutchmen have turned to it in a desperate attempt to create a literature before this speech becomes only a memory. As most of these poets have already died and the few left are growing old, and since almost none of the younger writers choose to express themselves in Dutch in preference to English, this burst of singing is almost certainly the swan song of the dialect. *Morituri salutamus!*

Before I go any further, let me warn the reader that in writing of literature in the dialect I am at a great disadvantage in being unable to read Dutch with any degree of ease. In my struggles with Pennsylvania Dutch I am the lame, the halt, and the blind all in one. Felicities that an ear attuned to the dialect would catch may have escaped me. My judgments, therefore, must be taken with at least several grains of salt.

And let me say here at the start that in my opinion there is not a great deal of Pennsylvania Dutch literature—some, yes, but not much that is really literature. In part this was due to the fact that the language the Dutch spoke was a dialect. In part it was because they were seduced by more material things—rich, fat barns and rich, fat factories.

The earliest literature was in German rather than the dialect. It was largely written by the leaders of the early immigrants, most of them of sound education and scholarly inclination. The first and best known of these leaders was Pastorius, whose *Kurtze Beschreibung,* published at Nuremberg in 1692, is the earliest of all Pennsylvania Dutch literature. To place him chronologically in early American literature, let me remind you that he was twelve years older than Cotton Mather. This was the man who placed over the lintel of his house in Germantown the Latin inscription, the English translation of which I append here: "A little house, but a friend of the good; remain at a distance, ye profane." His *Hive, Beestock Mellitrophium Alvear or Rusca Apium,* begun in 1696 and written in eight languages, was a commonplace book of encyclopedic proportions and scope. A thousand pages in length, little except the "garden poetry" of this manuscript has been published. But if one can judge by the poetry, which despite its pleasant archaic flavor has only slight literary merit, this vast work of Pastorius's is more a curiosity than literature. A good deal of the early writing was religious in character. The many hymns written at Germantown, Ephrata, and Bethlehem were a product of the religious fervor of the time. More mundane were the land-company advertisements such as Daniel Falckner's *Curieuse Nachricht in Norden-America* (1702) and the early travel literature such as Gottlieb Mittelberger's *Reise nach Pennsylvanien im Jahr 1750 und Rückreise nach Teutschland im Jahr 1754.* Christopher Dock's *Eine einfaltige und gründliche abgefasste Schul-Ordnung* is remembered because it was the first American treatise on education, while his *Hundred Rules for*

Children have an old-fashioned air that pleases. To these may be added Brothers Lamech and Agrippa's *Chronicon Ephratense* (1786).

With the death of the scholars educated in German universities, there was a distinct decline in literary activity; there was no one of equal education to take their place. Until well along in the nineteenth century there was almost no Pennsylvania Dutch literature. A knowledge of High German was disappearing except among the clergy of the Lutheran and Reformed churches, while the dialect was looked upon as a language to be spoken rather than written. If a man was learned, and few Pennsylvania Dutch at this period were, he wrote either in High German or English. With but few exceptions the years between the Revolution and the Civil War were devoid of poetry. The Moravian bishop, George Henry Loskiel, wrote a long poem in doggerel, "Ex tempore auf dem Wagen," about his journey west to the Ohio country in 1803. In 1849 another Moravian clergyman, Emanuel Rondthaler, wrote a lyric in the dialect, "Abenlied." Somewhere about this time Lewis Miller, better known for his drawings, tried his hand at poetry. One of his poems, a lively driver's song, was a favorite with the men who drove the Conestoga wagons. As for the prose, the dialect letters printed in some of the Pennsylvania Dutch newspapers such as the Reading *Adler* and the Easton *Unabhängige Demokrat* had some slight standing as literature. These letters reached their height— or possibly their depth—in the decade preceding the Civil War. In their attempt at satire and humor they made lavish use of the earthy and even the ribald. Like Kansas City they went about as far as they could go.

After the Civil War the dialect was rescued from the vulgarity of the letters by a group of educated Pennsylvania Dutchmen, mostly clergymen, teachers, lawyers, and doctors. These men set out to give the Pennsylvania Dutch a body of literature in their own dialect; and in a small measure, at least, they succeeded. The poetry they wrote is so similar in mood and subject matter that the writers may be said to form a school—the Nostalgic Poets or, if you prefer, the School of the Good Old Days. As a reaction to the earthiness of the newspaper letters, this later literature was overly moral and genteel, as was most of the writing in English in those Victorian days. A good deal of this dialect verse is remarkable for the pronounced enjoyment the Pennsylvania Dutch feel in being reminded of home. Naturally, with such emphasis on home the principal defect of the poetry is its sentimentality. The home scene is described in loving detail: the fire-place, the country store, the schoolhouse, the cider mill, the singing school, Christmas, the Fourth of July, the Allentown Fair, fishing, cooking apple butter, mowing, bringing in the harvest, a klook and her peeps [1]—whatever the subject, it is connected in one way or an-other with memories of home.

Though these men were filled with zeal and though they worked hard over their verses, not one is a major poet. Usually their verses scan and their rhymes are almost always true, but there is little magic with words or other signs of the poetic imagination at play that we look for in the work of the great poets. At best there is now and again a hint of Burns or Frost, for these are poets versed in country things.

The earliest and the best known, but by no means the best of the dialect poets, was Henry Harbaugh. He is remembered today largely for "Das alt Schulhaus an der Krick" and "Heemweh," both pub-lished in 1861. His tendency to moralize betrays his calling as a preacher, a quality that is somewhat offset by the tenderness of his verse. Many of these men wrote with grace of home and country ways—Eli Keller, Ezra Grumbine, Edward Hermany, Astor Wuchter, Lee Grumbine, and Charles Calvin Ziegler, to name but half a dozen. The tender note is particularly pronounced in the poetry of Ziegler, whose absence from the Dutch country for many years gave him a better right to homesickness than the poets who stayed at home. "Kitzel mich net" is merry enough, but many of his poems have an elegiac tone. To a certain degree the dialect determined the flavor of the literature. It is a dialect perfectly suited to the humorous and the homelike. This was pointed out by Lee Grumbine when he wrote, "The common range of everyday human experiences, human activities, human feelings, these are the domain, these are the materials and opportunities for the Pennsylvania German poet." For the most part the Pennsylvania Dutch poets followed this advice, yet every now and again there is a lyrical flight, often only a line or two, in which the poet tries to get above "the common range of everyday human experiences." The most successful attempt of this sort was made by Charles C. More in "Die Schatta uf der Krick," the finest serious poem in the dialect.

Though a few bolder spirits were able to stretch the dialect to encompass beauty, most of the writers recognized from the start that

[1] A hen and her chicks.

loftiness and even dignity were all but impossible. It was only natural that Edward H. Rauch should realize that the limitations of the dialect inevitably turned his translation of *Hamlet* into a parody. Take the opening speech of the ghost to Hamlet,

> "I am thy father's spirit,
> Doom'd for a certain term to walk the night,"

which in Rauch's Dutch version is transformed into,

> "Ich bin deim dawdy sei shpook;
> 'Bin g'sentenced for a g'wissy tseit rumma lawfa nachts."

Undoubtedly Rauch exaggerated the crudity of Dutch to underscore the humor, but in turning his translation of *Hamlet* into a burlesque he merely recognized his defeat and made the most of it. The beauty and grandeur of Shakespeare's lines are beyond the resources of the dialect.

Poetry is much the favorite form of the dialect writers. The prose is distinctly inferior. Thomas Hess Harter in his *Boonastiel* letters showed himself a belated descendant of Addison and Steele. Or to put it another way, *Boonastiel* is a country cousin of the *Spectator*. Charles C. More alone tried to write a novel in Pennsylvania Dutch. His short stories, "Der wiescht Mann vun der Flett," "En wieschter Draam," " 'S Wash Hellers ihra Chrischtagzug," "Der Hexedoktor," and "Die Kutztown Mail" are generally considered the finest the dialect has produced.

With the turn of the century writers using English became aware of the Dutch country. In 1902 appeared the first of Helen Reimensnyder Martin's stories, and for many years the market was flooded with her tales, each mediocre, each superficial, and each a slur on the Pennsylvania Dutch. Far superior to her is her contemporary, Elsie Singmaster, who writes with sympathy and insight of a people she knows well. A third woman to write about the Pennsylvania Dutch is Katharine Loose, who uses the pen name of Georg Schock. Her short stories and novels show an exact knowledge and understanding of this people. Cornelius Weygandt's essays devoted to Pennsylvania Dutch folkways and antiques date from the period between the two world wars. His description of the barn in *The Red Hills* is a masterpiece of modern American prose. In more recent years there have been several novels about the Pennsylvania Dutch. Mildred Jordan's *Apple in the Attic* (1942) is an earthy folk tale, and Conrad Richter's *The Free Man* (1943) is a short historical novel of the Revolution. In quite a different class is Joseph Yoder's *Rosanna of the Amish* (1940), which is biography cast in the form of a novel. Its artlessness gives the book much of the charm of a folk tale. Pearl Buck's *Portrait of a Marriage* (1945) has a sympathetic study of a Pennsylvania Dutch country-woman. Both James Boyd's *Roll River* (1935) and John O'Hara's *A Rage to Live* (1949) have a Dutch city, Harrisburg, as their setting. Poetry too, has made some slight use of the Pennsylvania Dutch scene. Stephen Vincent Benét's *John Brown's Body* has a Dutch farmer in Jake Diefer in addition to beautiful descriptions of the Pennsylvania Dutch countryside—red barns, springhouses, and long green meadows. In the last dozen years several writers have seized upon the more picturesque features of Dutch life for children's stories. These are pleasant but too unsubstantial to be really good. Mildred Jordan's *The Shoofly Pie* (1944) is the best; it has more body to it—indeed, it should prove a delicious morsel for any small girl.

Literature in the dialect, however, continues to be written. A number of newspapers in the Dutch country run columns written in Pennsylvania Dutch or at least columns that often print articles and poems in Dutch. Of these " 'S Pennsylfawnisch Deitsch Eck" in the Saturday issue of the Allentown *Morning Call,* a column that is largely the creation of Preston A. Barba, is the most notable. Possibly the most popular of all the writing in the dialect are the plays. Clarence Iobst's *En Quart Millich un en Halb-Beint Rahm* has had a tremendous success in Dutch towns and cities. Like most of the plays on Broadway, the plays written in Dutch have been frankly entertainment; their literary quality is more dubious.

Of the contemporary writers using Pennsylvania Dutch, the best is the poet John Birmelin. Compared to the nineteenth century poets, his fluency and facility in the use of the dialect make him appear a virtuoso. His knowledge and love of music have given his verse an unfaltering rhythm and a melody rare in Pennsylvania Dutch poetry. Most striking of all is his unusual range of mood. Grave or gay, familiar or lyrical, he strikes one note after another. The gravity of "Der Haerbschwind" and the humor of "Mei Model T" illustrate the extremes of the gamut. In "Buchschaaweschpielerei" he shows himself a juggler with words. "Der Braucher" makes effective use of folklore while "Regina Hartman" and "Der laaf Kaaf" turn history into ballad. Yet possibly some of the less ambitious poems are even finer. I am thinking of such beautifully unlabored poems as "Sprichwarde" and "Fimf Sarde Meis." This last group of poems has an unbuttoned ease that is particularly delightful. A cursory glance at his poetry is enough to show that Birmelin is a traditional poet. Not for him the experimentation of that other Berks County poet, Wallace Stevens. The very choice of Dutch as a language is a strong link to the past; a poet interested in modern trends would write in English. Birmelin in his age is even more archaic than Spenser was in the Elizabethan.

One word more: although written in Dutch this dialect literature is American in spirit and in spite of the short shrift it gets from scholars, a part of the literature of the United States. It has been slighted by American critics, not because it is devoid of literary merit, and not always because the critics have been unaware of its existence, but because it is written in dialect and the dialect is difficult to read. Possibly none of this is great literature, yet it does merit consideration by critics who profess to know all of American literature.

Food—and More Food

Cooking is an art with the Pennsylvania Dutch: this is the land
of shoofly pies, Moravian buns, smoked sausage, corn pie, chicken
corn soup, dandelion salad, and dozens of other tasty dishes. Here
quality is combined with quantity. To set a good table is a matter
of pride with nine out of every ten Pennsylvania Dutch families.
These people do not stint themselves; with them enough means more
than enough. The hell in which many of them live in fear is the one
of being caught short by unexpected guests. Though serving seven
sweets and seven sours with every meal may be more legend than fact,
the story has a base of solid truth. It set up the goal of the groaning
board loaded not only with meat and vegetables and possibly even
desserts but also with the accompanying sweets and sours: fox-grape
jelly, apple butter, strawberry jam, quince chips, honey in the comb,
spiced peaches, ginger pears, kimmel cherries, green-tomato pickle,
red beets, pepper cabbage, sour beans, Jerusalem artichokes, and
chowchow. Not all fourteen of the sweets and sours are likely to be
served at any one meal; but the conscientious housewife, who likes
to be on the safe side, feels that still another sweet or sour won't

do any harm. And somehow or other she finds room for another dish on the crowded table. At many meals there are two or three desserts, sometimes even more. Out on the farms there were four or five uncut pies to any of which—or to all of them—a man could help himself; but in general such prodigality went out with the nineteenth century.

Although an unexpected guest may not turn up more than once or twice a year, such a possibility the careful housewife never forgets. She pares two or three more potatoes than she needs and she buys an extra chop or two from the butcher. Even in the smallest families there is almost always enough food for one more person. Many of the leftovers, of course, go to the dog, the cat, or the chickens. A tramp begging for a meal is a godsend to most Dutch housewives, a fact that has made the Pennsylvania Dutch country the paradise of tramps and hobos. It is the easiest place in the world to get a handout. Yet the guest who surprises the hostess is seldom wholly welcome; the Dutch housewife likes to know when company is coming so that she can show what she can really do.

In recent years a few country hotels north of Philadelphia have loaded their tables with as much food as they can carry. Forty or fifty dishes are set out to stupefy a public that queues up for the privilege of gorging itself. There is no style; only food, and often indifferently cooked. The old country hotel set a more modest table, but sometimes the cooking was superlative. Earlier in this century the Black Horse Tavern at Reinhold's Station served meals that were good plain country cooking yet an epicure's delight. Today there is no restaurant or hotel anywhere in the Dutch country with cooking to match that of the Black Horse Tavern of the past. By and large Pennsylvania Dutch restaurants are almost as poor as those elsewhere in the United States. Many restaurants serve local dishes, but the cooking is seldom more than fair. There is better food served at church suppers than in hotels and restaurants.

As far as I know, there is today no hotel or restaurant in the Dutch country comparable to Bethlehem's old Sun Inn in its heyday. The anonymous "English gentleman" who translated the *Travels* of the Marquis de Chastellux wrote with relish of his stay at the Sun at the close of the Revolution:

The first time I was at Bethlehem, in company with my friends Major *Pierce Butler,* Mr. *Thomas Elliot,* and Mr. *Charles Pinkney,* Carolina gentlemen, we remained there two or three days, and were constantly supplied with venison, moor game, the most delicious red and yellow bellied Trout, the highest flavoured wild strawberries, the most luxuriant asparagus, and the best vegetables, in short, I ever saw; and notwithstanding the difficulty of procuring good wine and spirits at that period throughout the Continent, we were here regaled with rum and brandy of the best quality, and exquisite old Port and Madeira.

The worst feature of Pennsylvania Dutch cooking is its heaviness. Aside from that, it is the best in America with the exception of the French Creole cooking of the South. Most of the cooking of colonial America was English in origin, and all the world knows what English cooking is like. The surprising thing about the cooking of Virginia and New England is that it is as good as it is. One marvels at the happy effect of a sea change. Not that Pennsylvania Dutch cooking does not have its defects. There is too great a tendency to fry everything, there is too passionate a love of pork, and there are too many doughy dishes such as potpie, snitz un knep, and steamed apple dumplings. On the other hand, there are few things in this world as good as Berks County apple tart, gooseberry tart, lemon sponge pie, or even Pennsylvania Dutch pumpkin pie. I write as a Pennsylvania Dutchman and I realize the rashness of what I say, yet I dare to proclaim the Berks County apple tart the best pie between the Atlantic and the Pacific—and while I'm at it I'll include South America, Europe, Asia, Africa, and Australia as well.

To prove my willingness to defend this sweeping declaration I here present the recipe for Berks County apple tart. But one word of warning: good apples are necessary for a good tart. For the finest results choose the Yellow Transparent apple, which comes into the market in early July; but quite a good pie can be made with any good, tart, juicy cooking apple. Here is the recipe:

Line a pie dish with rich pastry. Cover the bottom generously with 2 tablespoonfuls flour and ¼ cup sugar. Place in the dish halves of apples peeled and cored—a half face down in the center and the other halves surrounding it. Fill in the crevices between the halves with smaller pieces of apple and sprinkle with ¼ cup sugar and with cinnamon. Fill in with rich top milk or light cream till the apples are half submerged, and dot each half with butter. Bake in a hot oven until the apples are soft. Cool and eat with thanksgiving. There is no top crust; this is what the Pennsylvania Dutch call a tart, whatever that word means elsewhere.

Another true masterpiece is the gooseberry tart. The contrast of the acid fruit and the sweet dough makes this one of the most delicious pies ever baked. For this top and tail a pint of green gooseberries. Beat an egg well and add nearly a cup of sugar, the amount of sugar depending on the ripeness of the berries. Mix the sugar, egg, and 1 tablespoonful of flour together and add to the berries. Stir and pour into a pie dish lined with rich pastry. Make a sweet dough of ½ cup sugar, 1 cup flour, 1 tablespoonful of butter, ½ teaspoonful of baking powder, milk enough to mix well, and 1 beaten egg. Make a lattice-work of this sweet dough over the tart and bake in a medium oven. Green currants or green fox grapes may be used instead of the goose-berries.

A third Dutch pie, the lemon sponge, though not the equal of the two already mentioned, is clearly one of the better pies of the coun-try. To bake it, beat the yolks of 2 eggs, add 1 cup of sugar, the juice and grated rind of 1 lemon, 2 heaping tablespoonfuls of flour, and a pinch of salt. Beat these thoroughly and add 1 cup of milk and the whites of the eggs well beaten. Line a pie dish with rich pastry, pour in the mixture, and bake in a slightly hotter than moderate oven for thirty minutes or more.

By this I do not mean to imply that the excellence of Pennsyl-vania Dutch cooking stops with its pies or even that all Pennsylvania Dutch pies are good. They are not. Milk pie I consider a pale make-shift of a pie. And there are those who think that the cheese pie of the Dutch country is curious rather than good, though I am not one of them. There are even some who sniff at snitz pie. Though this is not company pie, it is excellent when one brings a keen appetite to it; while that variation of the snitz pie, the Amish half-moon, is the perfect pie for "preachings" or the lunch boxes the youngsters carry to school. For this Amish dish soak sour apple snitz (the dried quarters or thick slices of apples) overnight and boil until soft. Take through a sieve and add sugar and cinnamon to taste and just a dash of cloves and nutmeg. (The juice and grated rind of an orange may also be added, in which case put the mixture back on the stove and simmer until the water is cooked away.) Roll out a small round pie crust and put 2 heaping tablespoonfuls of the snitz on half the crust. Fold over the pastry, forming into half-moons, and pinch the edges tightly to-gether. Prick the top with a fork. Bake in a moderate oven until a golden brown.

The ordinary pie with this filling with either a top crust or one of latticework is known as snitz pie, in the past one of the commonest of Dutch pies. The snitz pie glorified with rich crumbs on the top is the *snitzrivelkuche.*

Rhubarb pies, cherry pies, and raisin pies, while not confined to the Pennsylvania Dutch, are as good as it is possible for these pies to be, which is very good indeed. The name "funeral pie" is given to both raisin pie and prune pie, possibly because their dark color suggests mourning. These were the pies invariably served at the huge dinners that followed the funerals in the old days; but since raisin pie is so good it was not reserved for funerals. Every week, and almost every day, saw raisin pie on the table.

Pumpkin pies are better in the Dutch country than anywhere else. What usually goes under the name of pumpkin pie elsewhere is a spice pie or, to be precise, a ginger pie. As the Dutch bake it, it is possible to taste the pumpkin. For this pie separate the yolks of 2 eggs from the whites, adding the yolks to 1 cup of cooked strained pumpkin (a good crookneck or pie pumpkin is best), and mix thoroughly. Then add 3 tablespoonfuls of sugar, 1 tablespoonful of flour, ¼ teaspoon of cinnamon, ¼ teaspoon of nutmeg, 1 teaspoonful of brandy, and 1 tablespoonful of melted butter and mix well. To this add 2 cups of top milk and mix in, and last blend in the whites of the 2 eggs beaten to a stiff froth. Pour in a large pie plate lined with rich pastry and bake in a moderate oven.

A pie that belongs in a different category in that it is not a dessert but the *pièce de résistance* at a meal is the corn pie. This is one of the finest of all corn dishes, one of the masterpieces of Pennsylvania Dutch cooking. I would even go so far as to say that corn pie and corn on the cob are the two best ways of cooking corn that man has yet discovered. For this superb dish take corn fresh from the garden and cut off enough to fill a deep pie plate or a casserole. Add a hard-boiled egg sliced, 1 teaspoonful of flour for thickening, 1 tablespoonful of sugar, ½ teaspoon of salt, and a dash of pepper. Put in an unlined pie plate or casserole and fill up with milk to two-thirds of the depth; dot with butter and cover with a top crust of pastry. Bake in a medium-hot oven.

It is quite possible that pie is a Pennsylvania Dutch contribution to the American way of life. This is a moot question. The American pie as we know it seems to have been developed in this country about the middle of the eighteenth century. Though apple tart is mentioned by Shakespeare, the fruit pie is an American invention—a particularly happy one; there are no exact prototypes in European countries. Pies in England and on the Continent were mostly meat pies or at best mince pies. The evidence of the earthenware pie plates, common in Pennsylvania in the eighteenth century as well as later, points to a Pennsylvania Dutch origin for pie. Though the earliest dated pie plate is only 1773, it is likely that many pie plates are older inasmuch as it is a rare pie plate that is dated at all. It may be that the Pennsylvania Dutch genius gave birth to this ambrosial delight, the pie, and that during the Revolution men from other colonies came to know this dish in Pennsylvania and carried that knowledge back home to establish pie as the great American dessert. Why not? In much the same way the other colonies borrowed the log cabin and the Kentucky rifle and the covered wagon from the Pennsylvania Dutch.

The Dutch cookies are almost as good as the pies. Of these the Christmas cookies are the most famous and also the best. To most Pennsylvania Dutchmen a Christmas without cookies is not a Christmas at all. To have one you must have the other. Christmas cookies are baked only at Christmas. You may think them so good that you wish Christmas came several times a year, but it is a rare housewife who has the temerity to bake sandtarts or brown Moravian cookies in July.

Most popular of all is the animal cooky. While not a rich cooky nor as delectable as most of the others, it is the cooky the children love best. Each family has its own set of cooky cutters, which were usually made in times past by a local tinsmith from designs handed down for generations. As the name indicates, most of the designs are of animals. Rabbits, horses, fish, ducks, distelfinks, pigeons, roosters, and hens are among the commonest shapes. Equally popular are the heart, so beloved of the Pennsylvania Dutch, and the star and the doll, this last borrowed no doubt from the gingerbread man. Within the last decade or two avid collectors have been buying up all the old cooky cutters offered for sale at country auctions. If they are bought by people who use them, all is well; but to turn them into collectors' items and thus deprive children of untold delight is thoughtless and worse. May all such collectors have the itch, the palsy, and the gout! May their wives be Xantippes! May their husbands beat them!

The custom of baking animal cookies, it has been claimed, goes back to the days when the ancient Germans worshiped Thor and Wodin and Freya in the northern forests. To these gods game was sacrificed at a festival held at the time of the winter solstice. But as game became scarce, bread or cake was fashioned in the shape of animals. When the Teutonic tribes were converted to Christianity, the Church was wise enough to preserve many of the pagan customs, simply transferring them to the celebrations of the Church festivals— those of the winter solstice to Christmas. As time went on, the loaves or cakes baked in the shape of animals became smaller and smaller, until their diminutive size captured the fancy of the children. And because they so delighted the children, mothers went on baking them down through the centuries. Very often animal cookies are sprinkled with red sugar; this, some say, in token of the blood of the sacrificed animals. But more likely this is "for pretty" and for no other reason.

Much more elaborate and beautiful than the animal cookies are the springerles. These are a work of art, veritable cameos in pastry. They are relatively rare, too. The intricately carved springerle boards were the products of skilled workers in wood, of whom there could not have been many in colonial America. Few men had the art or the time to carve out the little designs of a deer, a rose, a castle, a thistle, a dog, a rabbit, a bird in flight, a bunch of grapes, or what not. Probably almost all of the early springerle boards were brought over from the Rhineland, and later ones filtered in with later immigrants. Though the springerle is a beautiful cooky to look upon and, with its delicate anise flavoring, a delicious cooky to eat, few families possess springerle boards and thus few families are able to bake this cooky.

One of the commonest of Christmas cookies is the sandtart. With many cooks it is a matter of pride to roll these out paper-thin—or at least just a trifle thinner than anybody else in the neighborhood. Sandtarts, brushed with egg and sprinkled with cinnamon and sugar and with half a hickory nut as a crowning touch, are almost as handsome as they are good. Today some cooks substitute a half a pecan for the hickory nut, which goes to show how morals have degenerated in this age. One of my sisters always begged to have the sandtarts made smaller—"because it took so long to come to the nut."

To make sandtarts beat 1 pound of sugar and ½ pound of butter; add the yolks of 3 eggs beaten to a cream, and then the whites well beaten. Mix well and add gradually enough flour to make a stiff batter—about 5½ cups. Chill thoroughly. It is best to mix the dough one day and bake the next. Roll on a floured board to a paper thinness, or as near it as it is possible to come. Cut with a round cutter 2½ inches in diameter, and place on greased tins. Before putting the tins in the oven, brush the cookies with a beaten egg, sprinkle lightly with sugar and cinnamon mixed, and place in the center of each cookie the perfect half of a hickory nut. Bake in a moderate oven until a very light brown.

The evening spent cracking nuts and picking out the kernels was one of the best features of the Christmas baking. On this evening the whole family gathered in the kitchen. My father, with an apron tied around his middle, cracked the nuts on a sadiron held between his knees. The rest of us tried to extract whole halves of hickory nuts from the shells. The hickory nut, though, is a most recalcitrant nut. Usually we did not succeed in getting out perfect halves. Fortunately, the small pieces could be used for hickory-nut macaroons or put aside for a loaf cake later in the winter. It is odd that a chore such as this could be so enjoyable, yet I look back upon those evenings as some of the pleasantest of my childhood. Was it the contrast of the warmth within—for there was always a good fire burning in the kitchen range— and the cold without? A December night with the winter stars brilliant in an indigo sky is usually a cold night with a steadily falling thermometer. Or was it that this task brought that most happy day of Christmas, if not really close, at least no longer so far away? Before this there had not been many signs of Christmas, only the first flower or two on the Christmas cactus and in school a calendar, a penwiper, or a fancy set of blotters made for a Christmas present. At home whenever we came into a room, a bit of knitting was hastily thrust under a cushion. Was it a stocking cap or a pair of mittens? Closets to which we formerly had access were now under lock and key. All of these were sure signs of Christmas, but none was so convincing as picking the nuts for the Christmas cookies.

The *Lebkuchen* is another great favorite. This is a satisfying tasty, chewy cooky to which citron gives a distinctive flavor. Though there are spices and almonds too, it is the citron that really counts. For these wonderful cookies sift 1½ cups of flour with 1 tablespoonful of cinnamon, 1 teaspoonful of ground cloves, ½ teaspoon of nutmeg, and ½ teaspoon of cream of tartar. Stir together 2 beaten eggs, ½ pound of brown sugar, ⅛ pound of chopped citron, and ⅛ pound of blanched almonds cut fine; add these to the flour and spices and mix thoroughly. Roll on a floured board and spread the batter ¼ inch thick on a buttered tin. Bake for 15 minutes in a slow oven. Cut in squares as soon as you take them out of the oven. When cold, ice with the thinnest possible coating of plain white frosting or lemon frosting and decorate with bits of maraschino cherry and citron. Store in a crock with an apple or two to keep them soft and chewy. They will keep for weeks if you can prevent people from eating them, but that you will not be able to do.

The macaroons, hickory-nut and chocolate, were the aristocrats among the cookies because of the prodigious work involved in the endless beating—no longer so weary a chore in this day of the electric mixer; yet the pleasure to the palate was so great that the drudgery of the prolonged beating seemed worth while. For these cookies beat the whites of 3 eggs until stiff, and then add ½ pound of pulverized sugar gradually, beating for half an hour. To this add ¼ pound of bitter chocolate, which has been grated, beating it into the white of egg and sugar mixture, and drop from the end of a teaspoon on a buttered tin. Bake in a slow oven. If desired, ½ pound of finely chopped hickory nuts may be used in place of the bitter chocolate. Both of these are very good, but the chocolate cooky, especially, is unbelievably delicious. Anything this good must be a sin to eat.

A little chocolate cooky no larger than half a dollar was from an old family recipe. My grandmother at Womelsdorf and my great-grandmother on the farm out Charming Forge way had baked these little black cookies sprinkled with granulated sugar. How much farther back they went no one knew. Though this is one of the most delicious of all Christmas cookies, I have never come upon it anywhere except in my own family. To keep so good a cooky a family secret seems selfish; I include the recipe here so that anyone who wishes may share in its delights. Mix ½ pound of sugar and 2 table-spoonfuls of melted butter and 2 tablespoonfuls of melted lard, then add the yolks of 2 eggs well beaten, next ¼ pound of bitter chocolate melted, and last the whites of the 2 eggs well beaten. To this add flour to make a dough stiff enough to roll, 1 teaspoonful of baking soda, and 1 teaspoonful of cinnamon. Mix thoroughly and chill slightly—but only slightly or it will be too hard to roll out. Roll as thin as possible on a floured board, cut the size of a half a dollar, sprinkle with granulated sugar, and bake on greased tins in a slow oven.

There are other cookies too; I have been singling out only the ones I knew in my boyhood. In-laws baked almond macaroons, and Lebanon County connections of the family baked thin spice wafers something like gingersnaps, only much better. Over Bethlehem and Nazareth way the Moravians baked white and brown Christmas cookies, which they served with wine to callers who came between Christmas and Twelfth Night to see the putz. For the white Moravian Christmas cookies cream ½ pound of butter and 1 pound of powdered sugar; add 4 well beaten eggs; then 1 scant teaspoon of cinnamon, ¼ nutmeg grated, and 2 tablespoonfuls of sherry. Stir well together and add 1 pound of flour gradually. Roll very thin on a floured board and cut out with cooky cutters in the shapes of animals (rabbit, duck, rooster, distelfink, and fish). Place on greased tins and bake in a moderate oven until a very light brown.

For the brown Moravian cookies cream ½ pound of butter with ½ pound of sugar; then add 1 tablespoonful of cream, 1 pint of dark molasses, 1 tablespoonful of cinnamon, ½ tablespoonful of ginger, and ½ teaspoon of ground cloves. Work in 2 pounds of flour gradually and roll out as thin as possible on a floured board; cut in various shapes and bake in a moderate oven. This is an excellent spicy cooky, and thinner than any but the finest glass. Both these Moravian cookies are justly famous.

Sometimes there was in the neighborhood a woman noted for her skill in baking cookies who would be willing to help out other families with their Christmas baking. Then all the baking could be crowded into three or four days; otherwise it would be drawn out for a fortnight. Each end of a day found the kitchen table covered with piles of cookies and the house filled with their tantalizing aroma. Hundreds upon hundreds of cookies were baked. The shelves of the larder would be jammed with this vast store of cookies. With all the friends and the *freindschaft* (relationship) too dropping in between Christmas and New Year, and with all the boxes sent to absent sons and daughters and sometimes to grandchildren and even great-grandchildren as well, the crocks and cake boxes brimming over with cookies were soon emptied. By Twelfth Night most of them were gone, and by Ground-hog Day not a cooky was left.

The Dutch counties inhabited by the "church people" are the stronghold of the Christmas cooky. The Mennonite and the Amish and the Dunkards were inclined to frown on the Christmas cooky as worldly. And when one sees all the butter and eggs and sugar and nuts and spices that go into these gargantuan bakings, it must be admitted that worldliness does enter in. But worldliness or no worldliness, I rejoice that the old recipes are still followed year after year in countless Pennsylvania Dutch homes just as I am glad that the "plain people" still wear their traditional bonnets. Pennsylvania is doubly fortunate in having saved both cooky and bonnet.

To leave the Christmas cookies and speak of any other food is pretty much of a comedown. Snitz un knep, steamed apple dumplings, *buwe schenkel,* and all other concoctions based on steamy dough I pass over. When it comes to them, write me down as *schnuppich.*[1] I do not like them. Let someone who does, praise them. But to show my tolerance I include one recipe for a dish of this sort, chicken potpie. I find this dish barely tolerable, but a brother of mine in London turned the city upside down in an attempt to find a cook who could make chicken potpie. Usually the bony pieces of chicken, left over from Sunday dinner, are the ones used. Boil the chicken in enough water to cover until it is tender. Add 1 tablespoonful chopped onion, 1 tablespoonful chopped parsley, and salt and pepper to taste. Then to make the dough for the dumplings sift together 2 cups of flour, 2 teaspoonfuls of baking powder, and ½ teaspoon of salt. Rub in 1 tablespoonful of butter with the tips of the fingers. Add ¾ cup of milk gradually, using a knife for mixing. Turn on a floured board and knead slightly. Then roll to a ¼-inch thickness and cut in 3-inch squares. Pare and cut potatoes in thick slices. Add a layer of potatoes and then a layer of dough to the chicken and liquid, alternating the potatoes and dough. Cover tightly and boil 25 minutes.

Fried noodles and noodle soup are another matter. Both are delicious, particularly the fried noodles with little crisp squares of bread that have been fried in butter. There are those who spend wakeful nights dreaming of fried noodles. Naturally the noodles are not "store" noodles but ones made at home with perhaps a pinch of saffron to give them color. To make home-made noodles beat 2 eggs until light and add 1 tablespoonful of melted butter, a pinch of salt, and enough flour to make a stiff dough. Work this for 15 minutes, adding more flour if necessary. Roll as thin as possible and hang up to dry for an hour. Then roll into a tight roll and cut the ends into 1/16-inch slices. To "fry" the noodles drop them into boiling water and boil for 20

[1] Fastidious—perhaps too much so.

minutes. Drain in a colander. Brown very small cubes of bread in butter and mix with noodles. These are particularly good with fried ham.

The fasnacht, too, I sing! Like Christmas cookies, these are made but once a year—on Fasnacht Day (Mardi gras in New Orleans and Shrove Tuesday to the rest of the country). The most delectable of the doughnut tribe, fasnachts are very like raised doughnuts; but they have no holes and instead of being round they are square, triangular, rectangular, or even quinquangular. At home they were eaten unsugared; with molasses on the second day and without on the first. Right after supper dissolve a cake of yeast in ½ cup of warm water and add to 2 cups of granulated sugar, 2 cups of mashed potatoes (unsalted), 2 cups of potato water, and 2 cups of flour sifted. Let raise for several hours. Then before going to bed add 1 cup of butter and lard, 3 eggs well beaten, 1 teaspoonful of salt, and flour enough to make a stiff dough. Cover and let rise in a warm place over night. In the morning knead lightly. If necessary, add more flour. Then roll out on a floured board to about ⅓ inch thickness, and with a pastry wheel cut in squares, triangles, rectangles, and quinquangles and slit each in the center. Put on a cloth on the table in a warm place, cover, and let rise once more for about an hour. Fry in deep hot fat.

Some years ago there would have been those who claimed that funnel cakes were even better than fasnachts, but today funnel cakes are rarely come upon. The days are past when a woman who masters the art of making funnel cakes is renowned throughout the township. It took a steady hand to make perfect cakes. A thin batter was run through a funnel on to deep fat. As the forefinger held under the spout of the funnel was removed, the batter was dropped upon the fat in ever enlarging spirals. When the cake was fried on one side, it had to be turned over. Small wonder that old men droning away on benches at the back of country stores still boast of the funnel cakes their mothers used to make.

Even the waffle is Dutch in origin, though this is a delicacy the Pennsylvania Dutch share with the Holland Dutch of New York. There was no such word as "waffle" in the English language until the Dutch of New York and Pennsylvania put it there. Some of the waffles of the Pennsylvania Dutch in pre-Revolutionary days were made in heart-shaped irons—and possibly all the sweeter for it. When maple syrup first came to be used on waffles I do not know, but since maple syrup was used in Pennsylvania from the very earliest days this blessed combination of waffles and maple syrup must be a heritage from colonial days.

The angel-foods and sponge cakes and the "high cakes," as the layer cakes are called, are as good as such cakes can be; yet they differ very little from these cakes elsewhere. Only a few, a spice cake and the hickory-nut loaf cake in particular, are distinctively Dutch. If you can come by some shellbarks, the hickory-nut loaf cake is well worth baking. Work ½ cup of butter and 1½ cups of sugar to a cream; add 2 cups of flour and ¾ cup of water, and stir until smooth. Then add half the whites of 4 eggs well beaten, then 1 cup of chopped hickory nuts, and then the rest of the whites. Bake 45 minutes in a moderate oven. This is a nut cake without any icing to impair the fine flavor of the shellbarks. Good as these cakes are, many Pennsylvania Dutch housewives have become so shiftless and lazy as to buy the inferior flavorless baker's cakes. The tremendous bakings of last century went out with the horse and buggy. In these sad streamlined times there are no bakings at all in many households.

Far more popular than the aristocratic "high cake" is the lowly coffeecake, and of these the shoofly pie is the best of all. The shoofly is not a pie but a wonderful molasses cake with a rich piecrust below and a top covered with crumbs. With a hot, steaming cup of black coffee it is heaven on earth, particularly after a long drive on a cold winter morning. Although counted as a breakfast cake, it is good at any hour of the day or night. The shoofly is a cake that the Pennsylvania Dutchman far from home longs for. Unfortunately, its delicious taste depends upon the right molasses—not one so light as table molasses nor yet so dark as New Orleans but halfway between the two, a molasses that today is unobtainable except in the old-fashioned country store, where a barrel of this dark, full-bodied molasses is usually kept down in the cellar. As for the shoofly itself, there are two schools of thought about the proper way to bake it: some prefer their shooflies gummy at the bottom and some do not. At home ours were moist but not gummy, and very high—the sort for which you had to open your mouth wide. I hesitate to boast, but there were never better shooflies baked anywhere than I have eaten this many a year at home. Nectar and ambrosia, *pâté de foie gras,* caviar, and terrapin have all at one time or another been fairly well thought of. None can compare with shoofly. Yet so low in the social scale is this plebeian food that to this day the proper way to eat it is not with a fork but to take a wedge of shoofly in your hand, open your mouth wide, bite, and then give your whole attention to savoring what is one of the most satisfying tastes on earth.

Here is the recipe for shoofly pie—enough to make three, which is probably what you will want. Line three deep pie tins with rich pastry. Mix crumbs of 3¾ cups of flour, 1 cup of brown sugar, and 1 scant cup of butter and lard. Then mix ¾ cup of dark shoofly molasses (the country-store kind), ¼ cup of dark New Orleans molasses, 1 cup of hot water, and 1 teaspoonful of baking soda. If you prefer a gummy bottom, pour the molasses mixture evenly into the three pie tins lined with pastry and then add the crumbs. If you like your shooflies drier—and since I am of the dry shoofly school this is the method I recommend—take out ¾ cup of the crumbs and mix the rest with the molasses mixture. Fill the pie tins with the batter and scatter the ¾ cup of crumbs over the tops of the pies. Bake in a moderate oven for a half an hour or a little longer.

There are other Pennsylvania Dutch coffeecakes and breakfast cakes deserving of praise. The cinnamon bun is a delicacy on which Philadelphia prides itself, but like such other Philadelphia foods as scrapple and pepperpot it is Pennsylvania Dutch in origin. I still remember with pleasure the cinnamon buns of my boyhood. This was in Souderton, a small town of upper Montgomery County. Just before supper I was sent to the bakery, where I went in the back way so as to see the baker fish the cinnamon buns out of the oven with his long shovel. The buns were piping hot when I left the bakery and almost piping hot when I got home. Spicy, light, and gooey and studded with raisins, they were as perfect as cinnamon buns can be. A misbegotten version of the cinnamon bun, one to be avoided, is that decorated with pecans; this is a gilding of the lily. The potato bun or crumb cake is fully as popular in the Dutch country as the cinnamon bun and in a quieter way fully as good. There is considerable variety in potato buns, especially in the sweetness of the dough. The Moravian bun is a Bethlehem form of potato cake. Another breakfast cake, and one of the best, is the Moravian sugar cake, which is sweeter than the potato buns. And the schwenkfelder, which takes its name from the people who brought it to these shores, is a wonderful cake yellow with saffron and rich in raisins. The Moravian butter semmels, prized for generations in Bethlehem, Nazareth, and Lititz, are fine cakes too; unluckily my knowledge of them is too limited to enable me to praise them as highly as they may deserve. I can only say that all who have eaten them speak of them with a light in their eyes. In much of what I write about food, I fear that I am grossly unfair to the Moravians. I lament that my acquaintance with their food is so slight.

It is odd that the Pennsylvania Dutch should have buns and breakfast cakes of such excellence and almost no bread that is worth eating. The bread sold everywhere is the usual tasteless, flavorless stuff sliced and wrapped in cellophane. There is little of the dark rye bread that was universally eaten by the Pennsylvania Dutch in colonial times, when white bread was served only on special occasions—weddings or funerals or high holiday. Except at Lancaster Market home-baked bread is hard to find. Today in most Pennsylvania Dutch cities one must turn to the Italians to get good bread. They have had the good sense to reject the vitamin-stuffed loaf of over-refined flour that most bakers sell as a substitute for bread. Italian bread is delicious to the mouth and a delight to man's whole being. It is a noble contribution of a great people. Frankly, I'd rank it ahead of Columbus's discovery of America.

This chapter is already overly long. Once a Pennsylvania Dutchman gets on the subject of food, he is hard to stop. To him the joys of the table are among the principal joys of life. In Berks and Lancaster and Lehigh a man who is not a good trencherman is suspect among his fellows. Second only to their pleasure in eating good food is their delight in talking about it. It is an inexhaustible topic of conversation.

To leave generalities and to return to the specific, fried mush too is good—in fact, for a cold winter day fried mush with maple syrup is absolutely right. And then there is scrapple. The name of this Pennsylvania Dutch food has long been linked with that of Philadelphia. One wonders how the Philadelphians got along for a whole year—that of 1682—until the Pennsylvania Dutch arrived and gave them scrapple. Scrapple is an excellent winter dish, although to my way of thinking better for lunch or supper than it is for breakfast. Of course, there is scrapple and scrapple; but when properly seasoned it deserves the popularity it possesses in Pennsylvania. Yet the secret of good scrapple is as much in the frying as in the seasoning. Scrapple should be sliced thin and fried over a slow fire until the outside is crisp and brown. Mildly toasted scrapple is anathema to any honest man.

Even better than scrapple is smoked sausage, a fine hearty dish when the frost is on the land. Smoked sausage is as different from ordinary sausage as ham is from pork. More highly seasoned than the run-of-the-mill sausage, it is a delight to the palate. Buy the very best smoked sausage obtainable, cut into pieces about 4 inches long, prick the skins with a sharp fork to prevent their bursting, and put into a frying pan. Add ½ cup of water, cover, and when the water has boiled down fry in their own fat until a nice brown. Serve with raw-fried potatoes, an admirable way of cooking potatoes that seems to be known only to the Pennsylvania Dutch. To make these pare 6 fair-sized potatoes and cut crosswise into thin slices. Put 2 tablespoonfuls of lard into an iron frying pan. When hot, put in potatoes and sprinkle with salt, and cover the pan with a lid. Fry and stir gently from time to time until the potatoes are a nice light brown here and there. With the sausage and potatoes something sour should be served—say, pepper cabbage. Apple butter, too, eaten of course on Italian bread or, if you are particularly blessed, home-baked bread, should be served with the sausage supper. Apple butter is a delicious Pennsylvania Dutch concoction that became widely known throughout the nation during the butter shortage after the last war. Unfortunately, most of the commercial apple butter is dull, insipid stuff utterly lacking in character. Only cinnamon, cloves, and the bark of sassafras root can give it the proper zest. Apple butter can be eaten on bread along with butter, though often smearkase [2] is spread on the "butterbread" and apple butter on the smearkase.

Apple butter to be really good should be made in one of the huge copper kettles now bid up at country auctions. Not that the people who buy the kettles have any idea of boiling apple butter; the kettles are usually put by fireplaces to serve as woodboxes. Cooking apple butter is a long, tedious process. The snitzing of the apples is quite a chore in itself, for every apple is pared, cored, and quartered. The apple butter is cooked all through the day on the outdoor fireplace on which water is heated for the Monday-morning washing. Furthermore, the apple butter has to be stirred so that it does not stick to the bottom of the kettle. In the old days women on the farm really worked. Once when my stepmother was cooking apple butter out of doors, a hard thunderstorm came up late in the afternoon. My poor stepmother was in a quandary: she was very much afraid of thunder-

[2] Cottage cheese thinned with cream and seasoned with pepper and salt.

storms, yet if she left the apple butter all her work would have gone for nothing. It is a mark of her courage that she stayed with the apple butter. Hastily putting out the fire, she borrowed an enormous umbrella from a farm wagon and stood guard all through the storm over the caldron of apple butter, protecting it from the pouring rain. I am glad to say that that particular batch of apple butter—all eighty quarts óf it—was as delicious as any that could be found that year between the Delaware and the Susquehanna. Even as late as the end of last century, people in as large a city as Reading used to cook apple butter in their back yards. This gave "life with Father" in Pennsylvania a twist that the New York play lacked. It makes the Victorian Age seem very distant and idyllic.

Another excellent Pennsylvania Dutch food is Lebanon bologna. This is a superior bologna, highly flavored and smoked rather hard. As its name indicates, it is a product of the city of Lebanon. Though usually served at supper, it is at its best in sandwiches. A full acquaintance with Lebanon bologna changes the meaning of the word *bologna;* it becomes a word of praise rather than one of derision. Lebanon bologna has no peer among its sister bolognas; it is easily the best in America.

Still another dish dear to the hearts of Pennsylvania Dutchmen is dandelion salad. This is the salad of springtime, as typical of that season as robins or pussy willows. Though confined to the limits of the Dutch country, it is one of the best salads man ever devised. We who are Pennsylvania Dutch further believe that it is as healthy as it is good. We are so convinced of this that we find it hard to understand how anyone can live through the spring without it. We know that people do manage to survive without eating dandelion salad, but somehow it doesn't seem sound. The taste of the salad is rather bitter; but since only the young, tender plants are used—the dandelion is picked before there is any sign of flower buds—it is not excessively so. The bitterness is modified by the hot dressing, and the final result is a most happy one. To make this dressing, cut two slices of bacon in tiny squares and fry until crisp. Mix in a bowl 1 egg beaten, ½ teaspoonful salt, 2 tablespoonfuls sugar, ½ cup of vinegar (if strong, use only ¼ cup), and ½ cup of milk. Mix thoroughly and pour into bacon pan and let come to a good boil. Cool slightly and pour over the greens, and garnish with slices of hard-boiled egg. This hot bacon dressing is one of the great achievements of Pennsylvania Dutch cooking. It is also good on endive and lettuce, especially young tender garden lettuce that has not yet reached adolescence. Come to think of it, dandelion salad may be such a prime favorite of the Pennsylvania Dutch because it gives them the satisfaction of killing two birds with one stone—gathering greens for salad and weeding the lawn at one and the same time.

It is almost unbelievable that there should be a vegetable common among the Pennsylvania Dutch but practically unknown elsewhere except to the Chinese; yet such a vegetable there is—the sugar pea. Though closely related to the ordinary garden pea, it is quite a different vegetable and one that is unusually good. Eaten for the pods and not for the peas inside the pods, sugar peas are picked just as the peas are forming. That a vegetable so easy to grow and so delicious to the taste should be ignored by the rest of the country strikes the Dutch as worse than obtuse; it is next door to idiocy. Sugar peas are very easy to prepare. Remove the ends and strings from the sugar peas and wash the pods. Toss into a small quantity of boiling water and cook until tender. Add butter, salt, and pepper to taste and serve. Or if desired, milk may be added: ½ cup to 3 cups of peas.

Dried corn is another characteristic Dutch food. This is a sweet corn that has been cooked and then dried in the oven. In recent years dried corn has been appearing in the commercial market. Admiral Byrd even carried some with him to the Antarctic. But that dried at home in small lots has a fine, nutty flavor that the factory product has not yet succeeded in capturing. Dried corn is always one of the vegetables served at a Pennsylvania Dutch Christmas dinner, the other being stewed onions. It is also served at Thanksgiving, a lesser mark of esteem in a land that honors the *Welcome* and the *Concord* rather than the *Mayflower*. Oddly enough, Thoreau speaks of "parched corn" as the traditional Thanksgiving dish in New England; and "parched corn" must be very like dried corn, if the two are not one and the same. When parched corn ceased to be traditional in New England I do not know, but the New Englanders to whom I have spoken of this dish had never heard of it. It is very simple to cook. Wash 1 cup of dried corn and soak for about 2 hours. Then boil until tender in the water in which it was soaked. By the end of the cooking most of the water will have boiled away. At this stage add about 1 teaspoonful of salt, 1 tablespoonful of sugar, a generous lump of butter, and about ½ cup of milk. Good reheated.

Even in so well known a food as baked beans the Pennsylvania Dutch have a version different from the familiar Boston dish. And not only different; Lebanon County baked beans are as good as any the country knows. To bake these, soak 1 pint of navy beans over night, cook slightly, and then drain. Mix 1 teaspoonful mustard, 1½ teaspoons salt, 1 tablespoonful molasses, and 1½ tablespoons dark brown sugar with ½ cup of boiling water and add to the beans. Cover the beans with broth from a ham that has been parboiled before baking. Bake slowly for 6 or 7 hours, removing the lid the last hour to brown the beans. Best rather dry. A pot of these beans should win any woman a husband.

Another fine dish that must be included in this chapter is the favorite Pennsylvania Dutch stuffing for turkey, chicken, goose, duck, and guinea hen, and mighty tasty it is. For this boil 6 large potatoes, mash and moisten with 2 well beaten eggs and enough hot milk to give them a fairly soft consistency. Melt 3 tablespoonfuls butter in a frying pan and add 1 onion chopped and 2 cups of bread cut in small cubes; fry until a light brown and add to the mashed potatoes along with ½ cup of celery cut in small pieces, 1 tablespoonful chopped parsley, and salt and pepper to taste. Mix thoroughly and stuff the fowl. There will be more stuffing than can be put in the fowl. Fill a casserole with this and bake in the oven.

Pennsylvania Dutch cooking covers such an extensive field that it is almost impossible to stop writing about it. There are even Pennsylvania Dutch candies—Easter eggs covered with bitter chocolate, *mojhey,* Moravian mints, and possibly the striped shepherd's crooks of the Christmas tree. I am not positive that the peppermint crooks or canes are Pennsylvania Dutch in origin, but they are produced in such quantity in the Dutch country that they have every appearance of being native to those parts. There are several flavors besides peppermint, and black, yellow, and green stripes add variety to the red ones; and there are candy baskets and even candy pretzels as well as the shepherd's crooks. The red and yellow toy candy of the Dutch country has the same origin as the animal cookies. These little red and yellow animals are all right "for pretty," but for eating they are singularly dull. Give me mojhey any day! Like snow ice cream mojhey is one of the sweets of childhood. Made in little patty pans and sold at a penny a piece by some woman living near the schoolhouse, this was the candy most beloved by Pennsylvania Dutch schoolchildren. It was better than sourballs or sweetwood and lasted just as long. As it is a simple candy and easy to make, perhaps some mother might like to make a batch for her children. Boil 1 cup of medium molasses, 1 cup of brown sugar, 1 cup of water, and 1 tablespoonful of vinegar until the candy hardens when dropped into cold water. When nearly done add 2 tablespoonfuls of butter. Pour into small patty pans in the bottom of which peanuts, walnuts, or shellbarks have been placed. Sometimes there was a chocolate flavoring, in which case the nuts were omitted. Far better than mojhey are the coconut Easter eggs. For these grate 1 good-sized coconut and add 1 teaspoonful vanilla. Work in about 2 pounds of XXXX sugar if the coconut is a good-sized one, but less if it is not. Shape into small eggs and place on a tin to dry for 24 hours. Then coat with melted bitter chocolate to which a little paraffin has been added. These, along with the hard-boiled eggs dyed with onion skins, are the eggs of Easter. The red-brown eggs are a pleasure to the eye, but the coconut eggs with their coating of bitter chocolate are as wonderful a kickshaw as a whole convocation of confectioners could create.

Of the other candies the Moravian mints are the most famous. The "mint cakes," as they are sometimes called, are a delicately flavored old-fashioned water mint that reached perfection in Moravian hands. There is an aura of the eighteenth century, even of lavender and old lace, about these mints. They fit in with polished old cherry and mahogany and Stiegel glass. One feels that they would have been the right mint for the ladies of Cranford. Fortunately, they are still made in twentieth century Bethlehem and sold at the Gemeinhaus.

I should stop, but first let me mention coleslaw, a wonderful dish when properly made. Slice a half of a small head of cabbage as fine as possible. Add 1 tablespoonful of salt and 2 tablespoonfuls of sugar; stir and mix well and let stand for a few hours. Then add ½ cup of cream— and it must be cream—and 2 tablespoonfuls of the very best cider vinegar. Pepper to suit the taste. Not bad; not bad at all. A dressing very like the one for coleslaw can be used for cucumbers and onions with equally happy results. Slice the cucumbers and onions; salt and let stand for 30 minutes. Then add a dressing of ½ pint of thick sour cream and 2 tablespoonfuls of the best cider vinegar. Season to taste with sugar and pepper. This is a real treat on a hot summer day.

Sauerkraut is too well known to stand in need of praise. With fresh pork, creamy mashed potatoes made with plenty of butter, good bread and apple butter, it makes one of the most completely satisfying dinners in the world. Fried ham is a favorite dish from Maine to California, but nowhere is there better ham than the country-cured ham smoked over hickory that a few right-minded farmers still bring to market in the Dutch country. Soup, too, deserves a word—brown flour soup, bean soup with rivels, and chicken noodle soup. I pass over pepperpot, for Philadelphia has made pepperpot known. This, too, is Pennsylvania Dutch in origin. No Englishman, no Quaker ever thought up a soup as highly seasoned as pepperpot. But at chicken corn soup I pause. Though unknown beyond the borders of the Dutch country, this is a soup worthy of wide popularity. Cut up and boil a small stewing chicken until tender, and then cut in small pieces. Add 1 cup of celery diced, 1 tablespoonful of chopped parsley, and a pinch of saffron. Then grate 6 ears of corn fresh from the garden and add to broth. Season with salt and pepper. Though this is a noble soup, one that deserves a blessing both before and after it, there are some who think that butter balls make it even better. Be careful in making these, for if there is too much butter the balls will crumble. Start in with about 2 tablespoonfuls of butter with a cup of flour and a pinch of salt. Mix these and add enough milk to moisten, but not too much, and add more butter if necessary. Roll into balls the size of small marbles. Place on a floured plate and put in the refrigerator until you wish to use them. Boil in the soup for a short time.

Much of this cooking was relatively simple; it was the cooking of people who lived on farms or who bought the food from farmers at market or from farmers with huckster routes in the small towns. There was always an ample supply of milk and cream and butter. Much of Pennsylvania Dutch cooking is rich, as the old rhyme indicates:

> Zucker un schmalz,
> Budder un salz,
> Oijer un mehl,
> Un saffran macht die kuche gehl.

> (Sugar and lard,
> Butter and salt,
> Eggs and flour,
> And saffron make the cake yellow.)

Certain foods were associated with particular seasons of the year. Hard-boiled eggs in red-beet juice were the very essence of summertime. Without them no picnic was complete. Others marked holidays, and some the day of the week. When the railroads began to bring oysters up from the Delaware Bay and the Chesapeake, oyster stew soon became the standard Saturday-night supper in winter. And in quite a few families the Sunday-morning breakfast was salt mackerel and raw-fried potatoes—and still is: even now two stands at Reading market are given over to the sale of salt mackerel. On weekday mornings in the old days buckwheat cakes were served for breakfast all winter through. Yeast was bought in the fall of the year, and each day a bit of the batter was saved and set in a warm place to form a sponge for the next morning's cakes. The buckwheat was grown in the neighborhood and ground in some near-by mill. Bethlehem for a long time was noted for the excellence of its buckwheat flour.

Although the temperance societies never won much favor with the Pennsylvania Dutch, the Dutch passion for food was not matched by a similar one for drink. Brissot de Warville, surveying the American scene in 1788, remarked of the Pennsylvania Dutch that they were "of all Americans, the least attached to the use of rum and other ardent spirits." Yet Cazenove, writing but six years later, said of the Dutch farmers, "When there is snow, they haunt the tavern." And elsewhere in his journal he had this to say of York: "As in every inland town of Pennsylvania, there is a quantity of taverns and inns, where the people come to talk and drink, morning and evening, as in the cafés of European cities." We must take into account, too, the great quantity of rum imported into Pennsylvania. As early as 1728 there was more than 200,000 gallons, all of which stayed in the colony except for 11,400 gallons. Surely the Quakers did not drink 188,600 gallons of rum all by themselves! They must have had some help from the Pennsylvania Dutch and the Scotch-Irish.

Beer has always been a popular drink with the Pennsylvania Dutch. From colonial days Reading has been noted for its breweries. Through the nineteenth century the corner saloon was as common in Pennsylvania Dutch cities as in Philadelphia and New York. Today every country hotel serves liquor. Farmers, though, are more likely to drink cider or home-made wine than anything else. These wines are good, bad, and indifferent. Grape, blackberry, wild cherry, currant, elderberry, plum, dandelion, elder flower: some are a boon to man, and some are first cousin to vinegar. Berks County produces the only commercial wine of the Dutch country, and very good wine it is. Such ancient beverages as mead and perry have all but disappeared; they are almost as obsolete as the Belsnickel.

A few of the Pennsylvania Dutch are heavy drinkers but not many. The Four Hundred are more likely to get drunk than the farmers. Out on the farm most families have a bottle of rum or a pint of Monongahela stuck away in the corner cupboard in case of the proverbial snake bite or a bad chill; but such a bottle may last five or six years. Probably the most excessive drinking takes place at the country club and in the small crossroad villages. Town drunkards are less frequent than they were last century. Today there is not much drinking on the scale of that at Conrad Weiser's funeral back in 1762, when 9 gallons of wine, 5½ of rum, and a great quantity of punch were downed by the mourners. Few Pennsylvania Dutchmen of the present generation are either teetotalers or souses.

EPILOGUE

Round the Year:
A Pennsylvania Dutch Calendar

In March the world is born again. Days of sunshine turn the snow into rivulets that freeze at night. Day by day the snow melts; winds rise and strip the last brown leaves from the oaks. The slender saplings sway in the high winds. Then comes stinging rain and the world outside turns into a world of mud. Along the creek bottoms skunk cabbages poke through the soggy ground. On the south side of the house snow-drops come into bloom early in the month. Maple buds begin to swell. The first klooks are given settings of eggs—an odd number, if you know what you're about. On a sunny morning in the middle of the month the cardinal whistles from a treetop, and from down in the meadow come the cheery notes of the song sparrow. The first crocus opens and bees appear from nowhere. The shy buds of the winter aconite spread golden petals in the warmth of the sun. Along the creek and in every bit of swampland the hylas start up their chorus.

But March is a month of many minds. Days of snow and sleet straight out of February follow days of balmy warmth borrowed from April. Snow falls, weighing down the branches of the hemlocks; yet in the pool by the springhouse the hylas sing on. On the morrow the snow is gone; once more the cardinals whistle and crocuses open golden cups. The plowman chucks to his horses as he drives a furrow in the spring earth. There may be another fall of snow, or two or three; but spring is here.

April is filled with fresh, budding green—the soft green of the willows, the bright yet tender green of the grass, and the shouting green of the winter wheat. The newly plowed fields are rich red-brown. Bloodroots, white and gold, star the floor of the woodland; along the brooks rise the honey-colored mists of the spicewood. April is color and bloom and birdsong: maples flaunt crimson buds against blue sky; the plum in the dooryard is white with blossoms; and far off the mourning dove sounds its plaintive notes over and over again. Robins are everywhere. In the kitchen garden rhubarb pushes forth crinkly leaves; onions, radishes, lettuce, and peas are straight green rows in red earth. Daffodils are a splash of gold along the fence. A hawk flies over, and in alarm the klook calls together her brood of peeps. In the schoolyard mumblety-peg and marbles are in full swing, and boys play catch. The thin shrill notes of the first willow whistles are heard in the land.

By the middle of the month the creamy buds of the pear have burst into bloom and peach trees shout aloud in pink. Bluebottles are blue waves in green fields. The phoebe is back, building its nest once more on the beams under the covered bridge. In the shallows, where the cat-o'-nine-tails grow, a red-winged blackbird flashes by. Suddenly showers, swift and sharp, set in. A robin sings in the rain.

By the end of the month the cherry trees have stolen the show. In every fence row, along every lane, on every hillside, even dotting plowed fields, there are cherries in blossom. At the edge of the woods their fleecy white melts into that of shadbush. Orchards are filled with banks of violets and meadows with whole yearly meetings of Quaker ladies. In the houseyard wrens inspect the birdhouses and the gourds hanging in the trees. In the pasture calves nuzzle the bags of the cows and woolly lambs play and bleat in the sun. Each day begins with a swelling symphony of birdsong.

Early May covers the hillsides with the soft pink haze of apple trees in blossom. Colonies of May apples unfold their umbrellas; pinxter comes into flower. Lilacs bloom in every dooryard. On the oak trees the tiny leaves are as big as squirrels' ears, a sign for the farmers to put in the first planting of corn. One flawless day follows another. The Baltimore oriole gathers strands of string and horsehair for its pocket nest. Warblers in the treetops sing a song as continuous as a waterfall. Under the new green leaves of the oaks and hickories and tulip trees the dogwoods are cool drifts of white. In the garden tulips, forget-me-nots, bleeding hearts, and lilies of the valley come into bloom. By the middle of the month tomatoes are set out in the kitchen garden, and poles are planted for lima beans. Baby rabbits sport in the morning mist and nibble the sugar peas and the tender young beets and carrots. House plants are brought out of doors to take the air. Locust trees, dripping blossoms, fill country lanes with fragrance; horse chestnuts, bright with flowery candelabra, light up village streets. In the pasture colts prance beside the mares. By the end of the month fields are gold and white with buttercups and daisies. In the woods gay, parrotlike petals flutter down from the tulip trees. Iris and peonies, lush and handsome, take over the garden; and on the mountains laurel is in flower. Before June the weather turns hot and muggy, a foretaste of July. Slatelike clouds bring rain and thunder and clear the air.

June is summer rather than spring, summer at its best with but little of the heat of July and August. In June the world is the young, innocent world of childhood and youth. Roses bloom in the garden and honeysuckle by the roadside; in the fields the farmers are making hay. Every breath of air is laden with perfume. On the trees the leaves are still fresh and green. White blossoms cover the catalpas, and on the topmost bough of the maiden-blush a rose-breasted grosbeak sings all the morning to his mate on the nest deep in the seckel pear tree. Wrens warble all day long. Bobwhites whistle from the fence posts, and in the woods the ring-necked pheasants crow the amateurish crow of the adolescent rooster. In the morning on the hearth are tiny eggshells, poked out of the nest by the chimney swifts once the young are hatched. Wild strawberries ripen and the first sowing of peas comes into bearing. Some Saturday night about the middle of the month the Ladies' Aid Society of the First Reformed Church will hold its annual strawberry festival. Stone walls along country lanes are festooned with wild roses. A streak of color across the garden is a scarlet tanager in flight. A sudden breeze, sprung from nowhere, brings the heady fragrance of wild grape in blossom. Barley ripens and wheat grows golden. From down in the meadow comes the tinkle of cowbells. Robins gorge themselves on cherries, and man rejoices in the first cherry pie of the season. "Sumer is icumen in." The long summer twilights are filled with the liquid fluting of the wood thrush, and in the dusk fireflies sprinkle the darkness with light. Days are warm, but the nights are cool enough for a blanket.

In early July the wheat turns the countryside to gold. For three or four wonderful days, as the wheat ripens, field after field is flaming copper and brass. Above is a blue sky with fleecy white clouds, and below the wheat; and till eleven in the morning there is the chickory, too, flowering by the roadside and matching the blue of the sky. Then as the wheat ripens the color fades. In a week or two, weather permitting—always weather permitting—the wheat is cut and sheaves fill the fields. Another week and clusters of conical ricks appear among the stubble.

By the garden path hollyhocks are spires of bloom. Bouncing Bet brightens the roadside, and in the garden the phlox comes into its own. Butterflies, copper, sulphur, and black, flutter above the flowers. Catbirds sing all day, and deep in the woods whippoorwills call at dusk. Apples ripen and blackcap raspberries. Oats turn from soft green to straw yellow. Corn grows tall. Down by the creek the deep bass "jug-of-rum" of the bullfrogs fills the summer night. Days grow hot and wet shirts stick to the back. In the old stone farmhouses under the lindens shutters are closed by ten in the morning to keep out the heat. Haze blots out the mountains. Not the faintest trace of the Pinnacle can be seen against the northern horizon. Boys trudge five miles on hot roads to the swimming hole at Black Rock deep in the hemlocks along the Branch. Days grow hotter and hotter; the thermometer shoots up and up. In the fat meadows the sooty Jerseys stand knee-deep in the creek. Hens spread their wings, and the dog digs himself a hole in the shade of the lilac. Water pitchers sweat, while man and beast pant for breath. Blankets have long since been packed away; even a single sheet is a sheet too many.

August, too, is hot. At the end of each day the sun sinks, a glowing red ball, in the western skies. Haze is ever present. Only once a fortnight do the Blue Mountains across the valley come into plain sight.

Hardly a breath of air stirs in the hot summer nights, nights filled with the incessant song of the cicadas. Early in the month oats are cut and stored in the barn. Peaches ripen, and in the garden fat red tomatoes hang from the vines. The shrill, high siren of the locust rises on the morning air, but no bird sings. On the elder bushes the parasol clusters of berries turn wine-red. Tobacco grows apace, and the first corn pie brings jubilation. By the edge of the wood-lot ruffed grouse feast on the rum cherries. In the brooks where the hylas sang, the giant lobelia is in flower and in country dooryards the rose of Sharon. Queen Anne's lace blooms in every untended field, and in the meadows boneset, iron-weed, and the tall joe-pye. Drought descends upon the land, and the very trees grow dusty. Wells go dry, and farmers haul water for their cattle from springs and creeks. Barn swallows swoop in the air, skimming the drying pond. Far above in the colorless sky a buzzard cuts lazy circles. Drought and more drought and finally rain. Black clouds sweep over the mountains. The farmer urges his horses with the last load of hay, and just in time they reach the shelter of the great bank barn. Rain lashes the earth, flattening the garden, bending over the corn. There is crash after crash of Wagnerian thunder as lightning stabs through the sky, striking here a church steeple, here a barn, and here a lone white oak and the cattle taking cover under it. The fury of summer storm, bringing melodrama and tragedy to the idyllic pastoral, gives the lie direct to the peacefulness of the landscape.

In September the countryside takes on a sharper beauty. The yellow of goldenrod and the soft blue of wild aster color the untilled fields. Leaves of blackberry vines and sumac and Virginia creeper turn purple-red, orange, and crimson. By country roads the high corn blots out all but the sky. This is the month of seckel pears and smokehouse apples. Ripe grapes, warm in the September sun, fill the air with heavy fragrance. Nights grow cooler, and even on warm evenings the song of the katydids promises frost. The garden is filled with the cymbal and brass of zinnia and marigold. On a bench by the kitchen door are rows of flowerpots with slips of geraniums for winter windows. Goldfinches feast on fat sunflowers packed with seeds, and great clouds of chattering blackbirds gather for the journey south. Milkweed pods swell and burst, sending their parachutes abroad. In the orchard the red globes of winesaps hang from the boughs, while under the trees cows munch the windfalls in the grass. By the end of the month apple picking gets under way. Trucks and wagons loaded with apples make the trip to the cider press. The big copper apple-butter kettle is brought forth and the day is filled with the spicy aroma of cooking snitz and cider, cloves, cinnamon, and sassafras. Walnut clusters hang fat and heavy on strong dark branches from which the leaves are already beginning to fall. Mounds of potatoes fill the fields. And before the first signs of frost the rowen, the tenderest hay of all, is cut and stowed away in the barn.

Then comes October when the woods burn with color—the tulip tree pure gold and the hickory a richer ocher, the sour gum crimson and the sassafras flame, the maples pale honey or lemon or orange or scarlet, the oaks wine-red or deep purple. Against a backdrop of such splendor the hemlocks and junipers are dark black-green. October is the gaudiest month in the year. A whole palette of color has been splashed drunkenly across the landscape. No hue is too striking, no tone is too bold. The halfpenny beauty of the blossoming witch hazel goes unnoticed; even the fire-orange of the bittersweet strikes a minor note.

The air has a winelike crispness that makes the blood sing. In the fields the long straight lines of corn have given way to rows of wigwam corn shocks. Here and there between the shocks are small mounds of golden corn or orange pumpkins. In the distance the long, level ranges of the mountains to the north are smoky blue. Overhead V-formations of wild geese honk their way, while down below a flock of robins pays a last call. On Hawk Mountain a lone golden eagle circles down into the woods. Along village streets boys and girls hunt for the russet nuggets the horse chestnuts spill to the ground. The nights with a hunter's moon of punkin' yellow hanging low in the sky are almost as fine as the days; they are cold enough to make the house seem snug and warm, and for frost to blacken the dahlias. In the morning there is a pane of ice on the rain barrel. Toward the end of the month there comes a day or two of driving wind and rain to bring the hickory nuts rattling down from the trees. After such a storm the children are up at the crack of dawn and off to the woods to gather the fallen nuts before the squirrels and chipmunks can carry them all away.

November, like March, is a Janus month, sometimes cold, raw, and dreary but more often a prolonged Indian summer—soft, golden days with the sun comfortably warm on man's back and the whole world enveloped in peace and amethyst haze. These are lazy, unruffled days.

Russet and golden chrysanthemums bloom on in the garden. Fox sparrows scratch busily among the fallen leaves. In the fields the violet tops of turnips dot the red earth. A few persimmons, tiny suns of flame, still cling to the boughs. Except for the oaks the trees are bare. In the sunshine the Oley Hills are a warm pinkish brown, the color the Victorian painters loved so well. Shadows are deep violet. Banks of honeysuckle along the road are rosy crimson. Then suddenly the sun is gone; the day grows sullen and gray, and gathering juncoes foretell the coming snow. "The people along the Blue Mountains are plucking their geese," say the country folk at the sight of the snow. In the woods the falling flakes hiss on the dry leaves blanketing the ground. Lamps are lighted at four in the afternoon; chickens are fed early so that they can find the grain scattered in the deep straw. From the kitchen comes the heavy aroma of smoked sausage frying for supper. Life is still worth living.

December brings cheerless weather. The sickly sun sets in a pale green sky. By morning the grass, the winter wheat, roofs of houses and barns, and even the bare earth is covered with frost. By ten the frost is gone except on the north side of house and barn. Later in the month leaden skies bring snow. Against the whiteness of the snow brick houses are bright rose, their shutters vivid green; barns are vehemently red. The twigs on the willows are saffron yellow or orange-red. White snow and gray sky bring out every suggestion of color in the landscape. Long hanks of grass poking through the snow are soft gold; the black alder studded with scarlet berries is a brilliant accent in a white world. In a few days the snow is gone and winter wheat is green again. The delicate tracery of wineglass elm, the strength of oak, even the witches' brooms on the hackberry stand out against the sky. Days are crisp and cold, but a sturdy sun shines in the heavens. In a sheltered corner under a lilac the Christmas rose is in flower. In the barnyard, where the stone walls keep off the winter winds, hens scratch in the straw; under the forebay the barn cats come out to take the sun. By night Orion and Sirius are magnificently bright in a blue-black sky studded with stars. Other days bring rain—furious driving rain that makes man give thanks for a tight roof over his head. After the rain come gray, lowering clouds and wild squalls of snow. Indoors the rose buds of the Christmas cactus swell and burst into bloom. The winter pears, laid out on the attic floor in early October, are amber yellow and ripe, filling the whole upper part of the house with their fruity fragrance. Downstairs the kitchen is the busiest spot in the house. The smell of baking is in the air: fruit cake, lebkuchen, springerles, sandtarts, shellbark macaroons, and animal cookies—down to the mince pies of Christmas morning. Outside the fields and woods are naked and cold; within doors all is Christmas cheer.

After Christmas real winter sets in. January roads are drifted shut. In the morning windowpanes bear delicate, fernlike patterns left by the frost. Steaming teakettles of hot water are needed to prime the pump by the kitchen door. There are paths to be shoveled to the barn and to the mailbox out by the road in case the mailman gets through the drifts. By ten the day is one of shattering brilliance, the bright sun catching the diamonds in the snow till all the world is powdered sun-dust. Overhead the sky is chickory blue; below are blue shadows on white snow. Boots screech on the surface of the snow, man's breath hangs a tiny mist before his face; yet the blood courses through the body and these are good days to be alive. The dog, let out the house, goes somersaulting through the snow. The sociable titmice, clinging to the lower branches of the beech, bespeak their pleasure in a snowbound planet. And let it warm up only a little, the January jasmine on the south side of the house will put forth half a dozen cheerful blossoms. Yet the nights are cold; stars are yellow and red in an indigo sky. The chickens get an extra handful or two of whole corn to keep them warm, the house plants are moved away from the frigid windowpanes, and in the oven there goes a brick—or two or three—to comfort man, woman, and child through the January night. But these nights when the wind howls down the chimney and snow piles up in drifts can be snug and comforting—to a man indoors by a hearth. For this is the time to draw a chair up to the fire, to fill a pipe, and with a bowl of winesaps close at hand to settle down with a good book—to reread *Tristram Shandy* for the fifth time, to explore *Arabia Deserta,* or to dig into *The Anatomy of Melancholy.*

February, too, is cold. Again the roads are drifted shut. Juncoes, tufted titmice, chickadees, and cardinals visit the feed tray daily. Tracks in the snow show that the rabbits are out searching for food. Inside all is snug and warm. The geraniums in the south windows of country kitchens are blooming with immodest abandon. Outside a fall of snow in the night has turned the fine twigs of the dogwood into lace. A fringe of Brobdingnagian icicles hangs from the eaves of the kitchen ell. But the days are growing longer, and toward the end of the month there is a day or two of thaw with a promise of spring in the air. Daring snowdrops poke their way through the snow, and pussy willows show glimmerings of silver. On the summer side of the hills crows are cawing. Against the intense blue of the sky the chalky patches on the gnarled limbs of the buttonwoods are as white as any snow. Then skies grow leaden again, more snow falls, and winter is back. This is the moment to pick up the seed catalogues that the mailman has been bringing for the past month and as you hug the stove dream of the riot of bloom and the bushels of perfect vegetables the summer will bring. Peppers can be planted in a pot, and the hyacinths put in last fall can be brought up from the cold-cellar. Despite the snow and the cold the back of winter is broken. Spring is on its way.

Acknowledgments and Selected Bibliography

This book is largely built upon the labor of the many scholars of Pennsylvania Dutch culture. To the painstaking research and unflagging devotion of these men and women I owe much. The many detailed articles in the *Proceedings of the Pennsylvania German Society* have been invaluable. Extremely helpful, too, have been the volumes of the Pennsylvania German Folklore Society and the publications of the historical societies of the several Dutch counties, especially Berks, Lancaster, Lehigh, Montgomery, and Lebanon, as well as the transactions of the Moravian Historical Society. I have drawn also on articles in the *Pennsylvania Magazine of History and Biography,* the *American-German Review,* and the *Pennsylvania Dutchman.* The columns in local newspapers devoted to things Pennsylvania Dutch, particularly " 'S Pennsylfawnisch Deitsch Eck" in the Allentown *Morning Call,* and to a lesser degree "Scholla" in the Reading *Times,* and Dr. Alfred L. Shoemaker's articles in the Reading *Eagle* have been a stimulus to me as well as providing me with odds and ends of information.

Of the more general books I found the chapters on the Pennsylvania Dutch in Thomas J. Wertenbaker's *The Founding of American Civilization: The Middle Colonies,* New York, 1938, of particular aid. That fine collection of articles grouped under the title of *The Pennsylvania Germans,* Princeton, 1942, edited by Ralph Wood, was likewise very helpful. I also wish to acknowledge my debt to Russell W. Gilbert's *A Picture of the Pennsylvania Germans,* Gettysburg, 1947, and to the Pennsylvania and Maryland guides compiled by the WPA. Yet of all the books I read, I found Sydney George Fisher's *The Making of Pennsylvania,* Philadelphia, 1932, the most provocative, largely because I disagreed so violently with what he said about the Pennsylvania Dutch. Walter E. Baum's *Two Hundred Years of Germans in Pennsylvania,* Sellersville, Pa., 1938, I found both pleasant and stimulating, and this was also true of Cornelius Weygandt's books on Pennsylvania Dutch ways and antiques, *The Red Hills, The Blue Hills, The Dutch Country,* and *The Plenty of Pennsylvania.*

For firsthand material I consulted principally the collections of the Pennsylvania Historical Society and the Berks County Historical Society. May I express my gratitude for the kindness shown me at both places? I also wish to thank Miss Virginia Walker and Miss Dorothy G. Harris of the Friends' Historical Library, Swarthmore College, for their help, and Mrs. Catharine J. Pierce of the reference department of the Swarthmore College Library for her assistance in running down obscure references and in procuring rare books for me through interlibrary loan. In addition, I wish to say Thank you to the many librarians at the Reading Public Library, the Ridgeway and Logan Square branches of the Philadelphia Free Library, the Library of the University of Pennsylvania, and the Swarthmore College Library whom I have pestered over a period of years; from all of them I have met with unfailing courtesy. And for help in translation and suggestions of felicity of phrase I thank Miss Lydia Baer of the German Department of Swarthmore College.

To Townsend Scudder of Woodbury, Connecticut, I am indebted for the good example he set me but even more for his advice, encouragement, and friendly offices. To Martin and John Eshelman of Oley Furnace, Pennsylvania, I owe much for the many good hours of sprightly conversation I have enjoyed in their home. A number of the stories I heard at their fireside appear in the pages of this book.

PART ONE: RELIGION

As I had the good fortune to spend much of my boyhood in a Mennonite town, Souderton, in upper Montgomery County, I was able to bring much personal observation to bear on this people. Yet I lean heavily on Charles Henry Smith's fine book, *The Story of the Mennonites,* Berne, Ind., 1941. Much of the account of the early Anabaptists is drawn from Thomas H. Lindsay's *A History of the Reformation,* New York, 1907. For information of the great work done by Mennonites in feeding and clothing a war-torn world I am indebted to workers of the Mennonite Central Committee at Akron, Pennsylvania. I am happy to express my gratitude for their kindness to me and for the frankness with which they answered my many questions.

As the Amish have interested and delighted me for many years, much in this chapter is based on firsthand observation, which I have supplemented with three fine books on the Amish: Walter M. Kollmorgen's *Culture of a Contemporary Rural Community: The Old Order Amish of Lancaster County, Pa.,* Washington, D.C., 1943; Calvin G. Bachman's *The Old Order Amish of Lancaster County,* published as Vol. 49 in the *Proceedings of the Pennsylvania German Society;* and Joseph Yoder's novel, *Rosanna of the Amish.* In addition, I have drawn once more on *The Story of the Mennonites* by Charles Henry Smith. My knowledge of the Sunday night "singings" was increased by a chapter on this subject in Ann Hark's *Hex Marks the Spot,* Philadelphia, 1938, though in general what I have to say of the music of the Amish has been gathered from that scholarly study published anonymously in three volumes under the aegis of the National Society of Colonial Dames of America, *Church Music and Musical Life in Pennsylvania in the Eight-*

eenth Century, Philadelphia, 1926–1947, and from an article by George P. Jackson, "The Strange Music of the Old Order Amish," in the July, 1945, issue of the *Musical Quarterly.*

For the chapters on the other early religions of Pennsylvania, I have consulted William Warren Sweet's two books, *The Story of Religions in America,* New York and London, 1930, and *Religion in Colonial America,* New York, 1942, and also Willard L. Sperry's *Religion in America,* New York, 1946. In addition I have found the following specialized books of much value: for the Brethren, Martin G. Brumbaugh's *History of the German Baptist Brethren in Europe and America,* Mount Morris, Ill., 1899, and Frederick Denton Dove's *Cultural Changes in the Church of the Brethren,* Philadelphia, 1932; for the Reformed Church the several books by Joseph H. Dubbs, and also H. M. J. Klein's *The History of the Eastern Synod of the Reformed Church in the United States,* Lancaster, 1943; for the Lutherans, Henry E. Jacobs's *A History of the Evangelical Lutheran Church in the United States,* New York, 1893, and *Martin Luther,* New York, 1907; for the United Brethren and the Evangelical Association the histories of those two churches in Vol. XII of the American Church History Series, New York, 1900; and for the Moravians, Joseph Mortimer Levering's extraordinarily thorough and invaluable book, *A History of Bethlehem, Pennsylvania,* Bethlehem, 1903, as well as Grace Stuart Reid's *The Barony of the Rose,* New York, 1906. Yet since I have known the Reformed and Lutheran churches all my life and members of these churches by the hundred, what I write of them has been inevitably influenced by this intimate contact. For the very early religious history I have relied once more on Thomas H. Lindsay's *A History of the Reformation.* For the Jews in early Pennsylvania I have found Anita L. Lebeson's *Jewish Pioneers in America, 1492–1848,* New York, 1931, of help and also Charles P. Keith's *Chronicles of Pennsylvania,* Philadelphia, 1917. My story of the Dunkards' heifer project is based on information I received from the Brethren Service Committee at New Windsor, Maryland.

The standard authority on Ephrata is the *Chronicon Ephratense* of 1786 by Brothers Lamech and Agrippa, which was translated by J. Max Hark and published at Lancaster in 1889. Two good secondary sources are Julius F. Sachse's *The German Sectarians of Pennsylvania,* Philadelphia, 1900, and Walter C. Klein's *Johann Conrad Beissel,* Philadelphia, 1942. Julius F. Sachse's *The German Pietists of Provincial Pennsylvania,* Philadelphia, 1895, was of help for its treatment of the Order of the Woman in the Wilderness. Charles Coleman Sellers's *Theophilus, the Battle-Axe,* Philadelphia, 1930, was consulted for that particular religious vagary.

PART TWO: THE PAST

William J. Hinke and Walter A. Knittle are the two authorities who most influenced me in my account of the Palatine emigration. For redemptioners and indentured servants my chief sources are Karl Frederick Geiser, Cheesman A. Herrick, and Abbott Emerson Smith, as well as the pages of the *Pennsylvania Gazette*. And in one or two other chapters of this part I have drawn on Mühlenberg's *Journals*.

Paul A. W. Wallace's painstaking biography, *Conrad Weiser*, Philadelphia, 1945, and Chester H. Sipe's *The Indian Wars of Pennsylvania*, Harrisburg, 1929, have been of great help in writing the early part of this section. Also extremely useful was *Pennsylvania Colonial and Federal, A History*, edited by Howard M. Jenkins and published in Philadelphia in 1903. Such standard works as Parkman and Trevelyan have also been consulted. I also wish to acknowledge my debt to Harry E. Wildes's excellent volume on the Delaware in the Rivers of America series and to Archer B. Hulbert's *Historic Highways of America*.

For an understanding of the period between the French and Indian War and the Revolution, I found C. H. Lincoln's *The Revolutionary Movement in Pennsylvania, 1770–1776*, Philadelphia, 1901, especially enlightening. For the Revolution itself I have drawn on a great variety of sources, chief of which is Sir George O. Trevelyan's *The American Revolution*, in four volumes. Morison and Commager's *The Growth of the American Republic* helped me to see the picture as a whole. Useful, too, though in part out of date, was Bancroft's history. Among the more specialized articles two particularly helpful ones were Horace Kephart's "The Birth of the American Army" in *Harper's* for May, 1899, and Roger Burlingame's "The Rifle That Won the Revolution" in *Scribner's* for February, 1938. Wilbur H. Siebert and the *Colonial Records of Pennsylvania* are my sources for the Pennsylvania Dutch loyalists; J. G. Rosengarten and the memoirs of Major General Riedesel for the Hessians. For the medical history I drew on James E. Gibson's *Dr. Bodo Otto and the Medical Background of the American Revolution*, Springfield, Ill., 1937. Victor Leroy Johnson's *The Administration of the American Commissariat During the Revolutionary War*, Philadelphia, 1941, supplied me with much vital information on that subject. On the more popular side but extremely stimulating was Harry E. Wildes's *Valley Forge*, New York, 1938. I am thankful, too, to Arthur D. Graeff for emphasizing the connection between the Conestoga wagon and the mobility of Washington's army. I am indebted also to Richard H. Shryock for articles that opened my eyes to the treatment of the Pennsylvania Dutch in American history.

Douglas Southall Freeman's fine book, *Lee's Lieutenants*, New York, 1942–1944, is my chief source for the Civil War.

PART THREE: BY THE SWEAT OF THEIR BROW

Among older works on Dutch farms and farmers, Benjamin Rush's *An Account of the Manners of the German Inhabitants of Pennsylvania*,

1789, is the classic in the field. On a pedestrian level but useful in spots are P. W. Bidwell and J. W. Falconer's *History of Agriculture in the Northern United States, 1620–1860,* Washington, D.C., 1925; H. F. James's *The Agricultural Industry of Southeastern Pennsylvania,* Philadelphia, 1928; and *Climate and Man, Yearbook of Agriculture, 1941,* Washington, D.C. Far more suggestive than these were Kollmorgen's book on the Amish and his chapter on agriculture in *The Pennsylvania Germans;* Wertenbaker's *The Middle Colonies;* and Richard H. Shryock's article, "British Versus German Traditions in Colonial Agriculture," published in the *Mississippi Historical Review,* June, 1939.

A. C. Bining's *Iron Plantations of Early Pennsylvania,* Philadelphia, 1933, and *Pennsylvania Iron Manufacture in the Eighteenth Century,* Harrisburg, 1938, are my principal sources for what I have written on the early forges of the Dutch country. Victor S. Clark's *History of Manufactures in the United States, 1607–1860,* Washington, D.C., 1916, and Rolla M. Tryon's *Household Manufactures in the United States, 1640–1860,* Chicago, 1917, both proved useful for their more general treatment of early American industry. For the later period I relied largely on Edward C. Kirkland's *A History of American Economic Life,* New York, 1941, and J. Russell Smith's excellent geography, *North America.* The legend of the ironmaster and the hounds is taken from an account in the *Publications of the Lebanon County Historical Society,* Vol. III, No. 1.

In writing of wagon roads Hulbert's *Historic Highways* has once more been of help, but the book to which I owe much the greatest debt is John Omwake's *The Conestoga Six-Horse Bell Teams of Eastern Pennsylvania,* Cincinnati, 1930, which first brought to light the part played by the Conestoga wagons in deciding that America should drive on the right-hand side of the road. I am also indebted to Frank E. Lichtenthaeler for his articles in the *Berks County Historical Review* on the trek of the Schoharie pioneers to the Tulpehocken country. Other important sources for this chapter were Alexander K. McClure's *Old Time Notes of Pennsylvania,* Philadelphia, 1905; Caroline MacGill's *History of Transportation in the United States Before 1860,* Washington, D.C., 1917; Carl Bridenbaugh's *Rebels and Gentlemen,* New York, 1942; and Charles I. Landis's article, "The Lancaster Stage Dispatch," in the publications of the Lancaster County Historical Society for 1915.

PART FOUR: THE COUNTRY AND THE PEOPLE

In these chapters I owe relatively little to other sources, yet I have made some use of Thomas J. Wertenbaker's volumes, *The Middle Colonies* and *The Old South,* and J. Russell Smith's *North America.* In the chapter on place names I was inevitably influenced by George R. Stewart's *Names on the Land,* New York, 1945, and I must also acknowledge my debt in this same chapter to George MacReynold's *Place Names in Bucks County, Pennsylvania,*

The Pennsylvania Dutch

450

Doylestown, Pa., 1942. For the chapter, "Town and City," I found some of the older books of travel particularly useful, especially William Cobbett's *A Year's Residence in the United States of America,* 3rd ed., London, 1822; William Faux's *Memorable Days in America,* London, 1823; and Priscilla Wakefield's *Excursions in North America, Described in Letters from a Gentleman and His Young Companion to their Friends in England,* London, 1806.

The *Dictionary of American Biography,* edited by Allen Johnson, proved an invaluable source in its brief lives of notable Pennsylvania Dutch men and women of the past. In addition I am indebted for a part of my material on Christopher Ludwick to the life by Benjamin Rush, first published in Philadelphia in 1801, and for most of my information on Lorenzo da Ponte to the memoirs edited by Arthur Livingston, Philadelphia and London, 1929.

PART FIVE: FOLKWAYS

Though most of what I have written of dialect and the three R's is my own, I must mention H. L. Mencken's *American Language,* especially the second supplement, and James P. Wickersham's *A History of Education in Pennsylvania,* Lancaster, 1886.

In the chapter on superstition and folklore I am most indebted to Thomas Brendle and William Troxell for their extraordinary collection of folk tales in Vol. 50 of the *Proceedings of the Pennsylvania German Society.* Other articles from the same publication were also useful in the preparation of this chapter, as well as Vol. 6 of the Pennsylvania German Folklore Society and an article by Frank Trexler in Vol. 36 of the publications of the Lehigh County Historical Society. But the literature on this subject is so rich and I have read so widely and borrowed so much that I can do little more in listing my sources than suggest that the reader consult Emil Meynen's admirable *Bibliography on German Settlements in Colonial North America,* Leipzig, 1937.

Though the chapters of this section are based mainly on my own observation, I have found at least several books very helpful, among them Cazenove's *Journal,* 1794, edited by Rayner W. Kelsey, Haverford, Pa., 1922. For the highfalutin toasts on Battalion Day I am indebted to an article in the *Berks County Historical Review.* Black Dan, the chimneysweep, I borrowed from an article by Alliene De Chant in the *Kutztown Patriot.* My authority for the origin of the Christmas tree is William S. Walsh's *Curiosities of Popular Customs and of Rites, Ceremonies, Observances, and Miscellaneous Antiquities,* Philadelphia and London, 1897.

PART SIX: THE ARTS

The most important authority for Pennsylvania Dutch music is *Church Music and Musical Life in Pennsylvania in the 18th Century,* the three volumes published anonymously by the National Society of Colonial Dames of America. Among other books I found of use are Raymond Walters's

The Bethlehem Bach Choir, Boston, 1923, and Ludwig Lewisohn's *Expression in America,* New York, 1932.

Most of "For Fancy" is my own, for the folk art is a phase of Pennsylvania Dutch life that has long interested me. But there are a number of good books in this field, most of which I have read. Frances Lichten's *Folk Art of Rural Pennsylvania,* New York, 1946, is one of the best popular treatments. Henry Kauffman's *Pennsylvania Dutch American Folk Art,* New York, 1946, is also good. The numerous Home Craft pamphlets under the editorship of Mrs. C. Naaman Keyser of Plymouth Meeting treat of everything from pottery to pewter to quilts. Of the more learned books Henry S. Borneman's *Pennsylvania German Illuminated Manuscripts,* Norristown, Pa., 1937, and Henry C. Mercer's *The Bible in Iron,* Doylestown, Pa., 1914, are among the best. Wrought iron is treated extensively by Albert H. Sonn in his very beautiful book, *Early American Wrought Iron,* New York, 1928.

The sections on church and house are largely my own, but in what I write on the barn I owe much to two fine articles, "The German Barn in America" by Marion D. Learned, published in *University Lectures,* University of Pennsylvania, 1913–1914, and "The Origin and Significance of the Pennsylvania Dutch Barn Symbols" by August S. Mahr in Vol. LIV of *The Ohio State Archeological and Historical Quarterly.* The description of the garden at Nazareth is from John C. Ogden's *An Excursion into Bethlehem and Nazareth in the Year 1799,* Philadelphia, 1800.

For the greater part of the chapter on furniture I must take the responsibility, though in an indirect way I may owe something to Earl F. Robacker's *Pennsylvania Dutch Stuff: A Guide to Country Antiques,* Philadelphia, 1944. For the description of David Rittenhouse's extraordinary clock I have relied on Edward Ford's life of Rittenhouse and for clocks in general on George H. Eckhardt's *Early Pennsylvania Clocks,* Lancaster, 1938.

In the chapter on literature the scholarly judgments are apt to be borrowed; the erratic and prejudiced pronouncements are my own. I have leaned most heavily on Earl F. Robacker's *Pennsylvania German Literature: Changing Trends from 1683 to 1942,* Philadelphia, 1943, and Harry Hess Reichard's chapter in *The Pennsylvania Germans,* Princeton, 1942.

For the recipes I am most indebted to my stepmother, Mayme Siegfried Klees, and my sister, Eleanor Klees Seltzer. For the Lebanon County recipes I wish to thank Mrs. Laura Seltzer Light and Miss Helen Seltzer, both of Lebanon; for the fasnacht recipe my good neighbor, Mrs. Irene Rothermel of Richmond Township, Berks.

EPILOGUE: This is my own, though I was inspired by Hal Borland's fine editorials in the New York *Times* to go and do likewise—in so far as it was in my power to do likewise.